AF352235

Understanding Economic Reforms in Africa

Also by the editor:

BLACK CANADIANS: HISTORY, EXPERIENCE, SOCIAL CONDITIONS

GLOBALIZATION AND THE HUMAN FACTOR: CRITICAL INSIGHTS (*co-edited with E. O. K. Prempah and S. Adjibolosoo*)

Understanding Economic Reforms in Africa

A Tale of Seven Nations

Edited by

Joseph Mensah

First published 2006 by
PALGRAVE MACMILLAN
Houndmills, Basingstoke, Hampshire RG21 6XS and
175 Fifth Avenue, New York, N.Y. 10010
Companies and representatives throughout the world

PALGRAVE MACMILLAN is the global academic imprint of the Palgrave
Macmillan division of St. Martin's Press, LLC and of Palgrave Macmillan Ltd.
Macmillan® is a registered trademark in the United States, United Kingdom
and other countries. Palgrave is a registered trademark in the European
Union and other countries.

ISBN-13: 978-1-4039-8756-3   hardback
ISBN-10: 1-4039-8756-4   hardback

This book is printed on paper suitable for recycling and made from fully
managed and sustained forest sources.

A catalogue record for this book is available from the British Library.

Library of Congress Cataloging-in-Publication Data

Understanding economic reforms in Africa: a tale of seven nations / edited
by Joseph Mensah.
      p. cm.
   Includes bibliographical references and index.
   ISBN 1-4039-8756-4 (cloth)
   1. Africa–Economic policy–Case studies. 2. Africa–Economic
conditions–Case studies. I. Mensah, Joseph, 1960–

HC800.U515 2006
338.96–dc22   2006043158

Transferred to Digital Printing 2007

*This book is dedicated to the Global Development Network (GDN)
for its concerted efforts to make the world a better place by
improving the human condition in Africa and the rest of the
developing world through the sharing of knowledge.*

Contents

List of Tables

List of Figures

List of Abbreviations and Acronyms

BOP	Balance of Payments
BWIs	Bretton Woods Institutions
EAC	East African Community
ERP	Economic Recovery Programme
ESAF	Enhanced Structural Adjustment Facility
GDN	Global Development Network
GDP	Gross Domestic Product
IFIs	International Financial Institutions
IMF	International Monetary Fund
SAL	Structural Adjustment Loan
SAPs	Structural Adjustment Programmes
SOE	State Owned Enterprise

Acknowledgements

From its inception as Country Reports for the Global Development Network's (GDN) worldwide research project on Understanding Reforms (UR) to its present form, this book has benefited from the support of several individuals and organisations, to whom I am deeply indebted. In particular, I would like to thank the GDN whose generous financial and logistical support to all the country research teams facilitated the writing of the chapters in this book. To Gary McMahon (Principal Economist, GDN) and José María Fanelli (Senior Professor of Macroeconomics at the University of Buenos Aires and Senior Researcher at the Center for the Study of State and Society [CEDES]) who not only spearheaded the UR project and provided meticulous comments on the Country Reports, but, more importantly, supported my efforts to bring all the African case studies together in this book, I am immensely grateful. I would also like to thank Lyn Squire (Director of GDN), Klaus Schmids-Hebbel (Chief of Economic Research at the Central Bank of Chile) and many others who worked at, or with, the GDN in various capacities (e.g. reviewers, conference planners and travel coordinators) to assist the UR project and its corresponding Workshops at the 4th and 5th Global Development Conferences at Cairo (2003) and New Delhi (2004), respectively. Similarly, I would like to offer my customary African salutation to all the contributors for their willingness to transform their voluminous Country Reports into abridged book chapters in a timely fashion, thereby reducing my editorial workload.

All the chapters in this book have benefited from several thematic papers, commissioned by the GDN for the UR project, and I would like to extend special thanks to each of the authors of those insightful papers. And to all those who offered research assistantship, constructive suggestions, and critical commentaries to any of the country research teams, I say thank you. I am also indebted to Amanda Hamilton, Katie Button, Jo North and many others at Palgrave Macmillan who provided editorial assistance, encouragement, and timely reminders on important deadlines for this book. Lastly, but certainly not the least, I would like to acknowledge the support of my wife, Janet Mensah, and our two daughters, Nicole and Cassandra, whose patience and indulgence were severely tested by my 'mental absence' (albeit physical presence) from their conversations during the Christmas season of 2005 when I was frantically working to complete this manuscript.

Contributors

Rose Aiko is a Research Economist with the Bank of Tanzania; before that she worked with the Economic and Social Research Foundation – a non-profit development research organisation in Tanzania. Her research interest is in economic development issues, including social security, policy reforms, institutional economics and financial stability. She has authored and co-authored a number of research papers.

Haidari K. R. Amani is Professor of Economics and the Executive Director of the Economic and Social Research Foundation (ESRF). He has extensive experience in policy research, particularly in the areas of agriculture and rural development, and has co-authored several books and published many papers.

Godfrey Asiimwe teaches History and Development Studies at Makerere University. He obtained his BA and MA degrees in History from Makerere University and a PhD in Development Studies from the Institute of Social Research, The Hague. He has implemented research projects funded by the Council for Development and Social Science Research in Africa (COSESRIA) among other agencies.

Brahim Elmorchid is Professor of Economics at the Faculty of Law and Economics of Cadi Ayyad University, Marrakesh, Morocco.

Kwame Frempah-Yeboah holds an MSc in Development Planning and Management from the University of Dortmund in Germany and the Kwame Nkrumah University of Science and Technology in Ghana. He is a development practitioner who joined the development circle as a Participatory Trainer and Community Development Manager in 1994. He is currently working with the Ministry of Works and Housing in Ghana.

David Kibikyo is a Fellow of the Center for Basic Research (CBR) in Kampala. He obtained his first degree in Economics and his Masters in Economic Planning and Policy from Makerere University. He is now a PhD candidate at Roskilde University in Denmark.

Julius Kiiza teaches Political Economy of Development and Policy Analysis at the Department of Political Science and Public Administration at Makerere University. He holds a First Class Master of Public Policy from the University of Sydney, and a PhD in Economics from the same university. He has published widely in the areas of economic governance, institutional reform, and the political economy of development.

Phyllis Makau is a Senior Economist at the Kenyan Ministry of Finance in Nairobi. She has long experience in the government and civil service of

Kenya, particularly in planning, budgeting and public expenditure management. She has participated in a number of research projects.

Dr Brahim Mansouri is Professor of Economics and the Director of the Group on Research in Economics and Finance (GREF) at the Faculty of Law and Economics of Cadi Ayyad University, Marrakesh, Morocco.

Joseph Mensah is Associate Professor of Geography at the Atkinson School of Social Sciences, York University, Toronto. He is the author of *Black Canadians: History, Experience and Social Conditions* (Fernwood Publishing, 2002) and the co-editor of *Globalization and the Human Factor: Critical Insights* (Ashgate, 2004).

Bernard Mufute is the Manager for Economic Research and Policy Intervention at the Confederation of Zimbabwe Industries. He holds a BSc degree in Economics from the University of Zimbabwe. He worked in the Ministry of Finance from 1990 to 1998, specialising in tax policy and tax administration. He is currently studying for a Masters in Business Administration at the University of Zimbabwe.

Charles Mujajati is a Director responsible for Economic Affairs in the Ministry of Economic Development, Zimbabwe. He holds an MSc in Economics from the University of Zimbabwe. His speciality is in microeconomics and macroeconomic modelling.

Takawira Mumvuma holds a PhD in Development Studies from the Institute of Social Studies (ISS) in the Netherlands. He currently teaches Development Economics, Social Economic, and Industrial Economics at the University of Zimbabwe. His research interest is in the areas of small enterprise development, local economic development, social accountability, and trade and policy reforms.

Floribert Ngaruko currently works at the African Capacity Building Foundation (ACBF) in Harare, Zimbabwe. He holds a PhD in Economics, and is affiliated with the Centre d'Etudes en Macroéconomie et Finance Internationale (CEMAFI), Nice, France. He has worked at the World Bank, Washington, DC, from 1999 to 2004. His research deals with the political economy of reform, conflicts, civil wars in Africa, and gender and development.

Rose Ngugi is a Lecturer in the Department of Economics at the University of Nairobi as well as a Policy Analyst and Head of Private Sector Development Division at KIPPRA. She holds a PhD in Finance, and is a member of the Monetary Policy Advisory Committee. Her research interests are in finance and issues related to private sector development.

Janvier D. Nkurunziza works for the United Nations Economic Commission for Africa (ECA) in Addis Ababa, Ethiopia. He earned his doctorate in Economics from the University of Oxford and was a Postdoctoral Fellow at Harvard University where he coordinated a Discussion Group on African Politics.

Dr Nkurunziza's research areas include Africa's political economy, conflict, growth, development macroeconomics and applied industrial organisation.

Roger Oppong-Koranteng is a Senior Consultant at the Ghana Institute of Management and Public Administration (GIMPA). He was the Coordinator and Acting Director of the World Bank Distance Learning Centre located at GIMPA. He has undertaken a number of research and management consultancies. He holds an MA in Public Policy and Administration from ISS, The Hague. His major specialisations are in policy-making and analysis, public administration, and decentralised governance and management.

S. Mohamed Rigar is Professor of Management at the faculty of Law and Economics at Cadi Ayyad University in Marrakesh, Morocco.

Dennis Rweyemamu is a research economist currently working with the Economic and Social Research Foundation (ESRF). His research interests cover a range of economic development issues, including economic reforms, poverty and rural development, and institutional economics. He has co-authored a number of journal articles and other scholarly papers.

Godwill G. Wanga is a Research Economist working with Daima Associates Limited as Senior Research Associate; before that he worked with the ESRF for eleven years. His research interests include a range of economic, social, political and development issues and policy analysis. He has co-authored several research papers, books, journal articles and other scholarly works.

Samuel M. Wangwe is Professor of Development Economics and a Principal Research Associate at the Economic and Social Research Foundation (ESRF). He has over 25 years of experience in research in development and economic issues, and has authored and co-authored several books and scientific papers.

Maureen Were is an Assistant Policy Analyst at the Kenya Institute for Public Policy Research and Analysis (KIPPRA) in Nairobi. She has in the past taught Economics at Egerton University; she has published a number of research papers on macroeconomics and health issues.

Mustapha Ziky is a Professor of Economics at the Faculty of Law and Economics of Cadi Ayyad University, Marrakesh, Morocco.

Introduction: Understanding Economic Reforms in Africa

Joseph Mensah

During the immediate post-independence era, many African governments embarked on inward-looking, statist development ideologies that entailed an extensive use of public enterprise and import substitution industries, within the framework of long-term Development Plans (D-Plans). It was generally envisaged that given the rudimentary level of development at the time and the continent's loathsome experience with colonialism, African governments had to be directly involved in productive activities – in addition to providing public and social services, such as education, health care, railways and electricity – to help increase the size and scope of the emerging modern sector. Several notable African leaders, including Kwame Nkrumah of Ghana, Julius Nyerere of Tanzania, Sékou Touré of Guinea and Leopold Sénghor of Senegal, were, understandably, of the view that only an active government participation, couched in protectionism, could solidify their hard-won independence by obviating the need for imports; reducing the dominance of foreigners; and freeing them from dependence on ex-colonial masters, in particular, and the so-called First World, in general (Ajakaiye, 2004; Kline, 2006).

Unsurprisingly, given the proliferation of both orthodox and home-grown socialist ideologies across the continent (e.g. Julius Nyerere's *ujamaa* in Tanzania, Muammar Qadhafi's *jamariya* in Libya, Kenneth Kaunda's *humanism* in Zambia and Didier Ratsiraka's *fokonolona* in Malagasy), the direct involvement and intervention of African governments in the economy knew no limits. The work of Ajakaiye (2004: 54), for instance, shows that 'between the late 1950s and the early 1980s, virtually all African governments drew up comprehensive development plans', usually in consultation with local and foreign experts, to help coordinate their decision-making and involvement in the emerging economy.

It is not uncommon now to find analysts blaming the statist model of development for the continent's protracted economic woes. For instance, Devarajan et al. (2001: 7) note that '[n]ot only did these [statist] policies fail to improve living standards in Africa – despite substantial amounts of foreign aid – but they seemed to exacerbate the effects of the external shocks of the 1970s'.

Similarly, Hope and Kayira (1997: 4) assert that 'the primary factor precipitating the economic crisis in Africa was the implementation of development policy through a statist ideological framework. In this framework, state planning became paramount and markets and choices were deliberately undermined.' At the same time, other scholars, including influential African economists and development scholars, such as Babu (2002), Onimode (2004), Ajakaiye (2004) and Adedeji (1990, 1993), insist the inward-looking, D-Plan-based policies of the past were among the best things that ever happened in Africa. Using data from Dani Rodrik's work (1999: 106), Olu Ajakaiye, the Director-General of the Nigeria Institute for Social and Economic Research, noted that:

> between 1960 and 1973 the average *per capita* GDP of sub-Saharan African countries grew at 1.88 per cent, implying that during the decade of independence, when the planning approach to development was dominant, appreciable progress was made in improving the warfare of the people. During the second decade of independence, however, the average *per capita* GDP growth rate had decelerated to 0.31 per cent.
>
> (Ajakaiye, 2004: 55)

As with several academic debates about Africa, the truth of the matter perhaps lies somewhere in the middle. For one thing, the use of average GDP figures in the above quotation obviously glosses over inter- and intra-national variations, and provides no insight into what actually transpired in individual countries – even assuming that we accept, for the sake of argument, that GDP per capita is the main indicator of development. And who can reasonably downplay the mass corruption, favouritism, tribalism and elitism, and their attendant inefficacies, wrought by Africa's statist policies during the early post-independence era in any candid analysis of the continent's development problems? Add to this the millions of people who were marginalised, especially in rural Africa, as a result of the neglect of agriculture in the zeal towards mass industrialisation in major cities, and it becomes clear that the statist model has not been as pristine as we are made to believe by its proponents. Conversely, as we shall soon see, the neo-liberal, free-market economy, with limited government involvement, has not worked that well in Africa, either.

Set in the broader context of development theorisation, the preceding scholarly clash is almost coterminous with the modernisation-dependency debate that raged among development analysts for decades. Following the publication of Rostow's *The Stages of Economic Growth: a Non-Communist Manifesto* (1960), in which he extolled capitalism and equated development not only with modernisation but also with industrialisation and Westernisation, some development thinkers (notably, Lipset, Almond and, of course, Rostow) have proffered the view that developing countries would eventually develop if, and perhaps only if, they follow the Western-style industrial model. This development, according to Rostow, will come in five stages: moving from an initial stage of a 'traditional society', through a second stage which establishes the 'preconditions for takeoff', to a third stage of actual 'takeoff', before proceeding through a penultimate phase in which there is a 'drive to maturity', to the final destination of 'high mass consumption'. Arguably no single country would be poor by now if the paths to progress and development were as linear, as orderly, as smooth, as evolutionary, and as predictable as Rostow and his supporters seem to suggest. More substantively, as the work of the renowned Harvard political scientist Samuel Huntington shows, modernisation and Westernisation are indeed different phenomena. This explains why such countries as Japan, Singapore, Saudi Arabia, Libya and Egypt are prepared to accept modernisation, by adopting its key tenets (e.g. industrialisation, literacy, urbanisation), and yet exhibit discernible indifference, if not open opposition, to Westernisation and its main canons: the rule of law, individualism, Christianity and the separation of religious and secular authorities (Huntington, 2002).

Dependency theorists (e.g. Amin, Wallerstein, Frank, Santos, Friedmann, Baran and Sweezy), for their part, draw on Marxist theorisation of imperialism to contrapuntally link underdevelopment to the exploitations of the world's peripheral and semi-peripheral regions (i.e. Africa, Asia and Latin America) by the core (i.e. US, Europe and, more recently, Japan). In their view, only an interventionist, protectionist and socialist-minded government in the periphery could implement development policies in the interest of the masses to ward off the exploitation and neo-colonial proclivities of the metropolitan core (Kline, 2006).

Regardless of which theoretical perspective, or point of departure, one adopts, there is no denying that by the early 1980s, most African economies were 'teetering towards complete collapse', to borrow the phrase of the Ghanaian geographer Konadu-Agyemang (2002: 1) for a moment. A wide range of internal and external factors – including Africa's statist ideologies, ethnic conflicts, political instability, economic mismanagement, corruption, unfair terms of trade, Western exploitation and imperialism, and the OPEC oil shocks of the 1970s – have been cited in the available literature for the deplorable socioeconomic circumstances Africans found themselves in during the 1980s – dubbed 'Africa's lost decade' by some scholars, such as Ngagwa and Green (1994) and Chazan et al. (1992).

The persistent biting poverty across the continent prompted calls from Africans, in particular, and the international development community, in general, for a lasting solution to the 'African condition' (Adedeji and Shaw, 1985), culminating in the publication (in 1981) of a World Bank report, *Accelerated Development in Sub-Saharan Africa: an Agenda for Action*, under the leadership of Elliot Berg, a development economist. The now famous Berg Report placed much of the blame for the African crisis on domestic policy inadequacies and some external factors. In particular, the report saw the inward-looking, protectionist policies across Africa, and their attendant restrictions on trade and foreign exchange, as the main culprits. Unsurprisingly, to rectify the situation, many African governments have been advised, if not coerced over the years, to make a Copernican change from their endocentric, statist economic policies towards IMF/World Bank-sponsored economic reforms, commonly dubbed Structural Adjustment Programmes (SAPs).

Structural Adjustment Programmes and Africa

SAPs are programmes by which the World Bank and the IMF lend in support of economic and institutional reforms rather than for specific investments. These reforms aim at enhancing economic growth through economic efficiency in the use and allocation of economic resources. Thus, SAPs provide loans to countries on the condition(ality) that they embark on a number of economic policy reforms to foster long-term economic growth (Lodewijks, 2006; Rupananda and Mensah, 2002). Even though SAPs are almost always negotiated in the context of economic crisis and in an effort to resolve balance of payment problems, they are increasingly used to purportedly boost the international competitiveness of borrowing nations (Lodewijks, 2006).

The World Bank and the IMF work closely together in pursuance of SAPs; the latter, generally deemed the senior partner in this regard, takes the lead by providing short-term stabilisation loans aimed at restoring macroeconomic stability, before the Bank comes in with its long-term adjustment programmes, dealing with such matters as taxation, privatisation, financial liberalisation, international trade and civil service reforms. Over the years, with the proliferation of neo-liberal globalisation and the Washington Consensus,[1] loan conditionality has become an important instrument by which the Bretton Woods institutions control and regulate the economic policies of Africa (and, indeed, the developing world as a whole). Indeed, until the early 1980s, loan conditionality had focused mainly on macroeconomic policies, but since then it has become far more comprehensive, more austere and more ideological, demanding anything from privatisation, financial deregulation and trade liberalisation to the removal of subsidies, currency devaluation, cutbacks in wages and social spending, civil service retrenchment and democratic and institutional reforms (Lodewijks, 2006; Stiglitz, 2003). It is not clear where SAPs were first applied. Whereas Konadu-Agyemang (2001: 2), for instance, writes that they 'were first introduced in Turkey in 1980', Joe Stiglitz in his 2003 opus, *Globalization and its Discontent*, puts their very first application in Latin America (2003: 16). Also, there are indications that the World Bank and the IMF derived much of their theoretical grounding and support for Structural Adjustment Programmes from the neo-liberal agenda of the US and British governments under Ronald Reagan and Margaret Thatcher, respectively (Stiglitz, 2003; Harvey, 2003; Chang and Grabel, 2004; Kline, 2006).

This is how David Harvey, the pre-eminent geographer and social theoretician, puts it in his well-received *The New Imperialism*:

> Together with Reagan, she (Thatcher) transformed the whole orientation of state activity away from the welfare state and towards active support for the 'supply-side' conditions of capital accumulation. The IMF and the World Bank changed their policy framework almost overnight, and within a few years neo-liberal doctrine had made a very short and victorious march through the institutions to dominate policy, first in the Anglo-American world but subsequently throughout much of the rest of Europe and the world.
>
> (Harvey, 2003: 157–8)

Regardless of its origins and impetus, one thing is virtually indubitable: that, by the mid-1990s, SAPs have been applied in one form or another to most African countries – from Morocco, Algeria and Egypt in the north to Zimbabwe, Namibia and Mozambique in the south, and from Nigeria, Côte d'Ivoire and Ghana in the west to Kenya, Tanzania and Uganda in the east (Noorbakhsh and Paloni, 2001; Devarajan et al., 2001). A common supposition by the advocates of SAPs, notably the World Bank and the IMF, has been that in the case of Africa, *there is no alternative* to SAPs – the infamous TINA syndrome/dictum first used by Margaret Thatcher in her advocacy for neo-liberal reforms in Britain in the 1980s (Chang and Grabel, 2004: 1).

As SAPs became widespread across Africa by the end of the mid-1990s, the old fetishism of protectionism yielded to an even stronger faith in free-market enterprise, albeit with considerable coercion from the Bretton Woods institutions, with terms such as privatisation, divestiture, deregulation and liberalisation dominating the continent's development discourse. Notwithstanding the dramatic shift towards SAPs, African economies continue to perform very poorly: economic growth in many of them has been slow, or virtually non-existent, and poverty, malnutrition, infant mortality, the scourge of AIDS/HIV and many other socioeconomic challenges persist across the continent.

Unsurprisingly, criticisms against SAPs have been mounting, not only from African intellectuals, policy-makers and social resistance movements, but also from a wide range of international organisations (e.g. Oxfam, UNDP, UNICEF); renowned economics professors such as Robert Rowthorn of Cambridge, Paul Krugman of Stanford and Pual Streeten of Boston University; Nobel prize-winners in economics, such as John Tobi, Maurice Allais and Joseph Stiglitz; public intellectuals such as David Harvey, Noam Chomsky and Susan George; powerful Wall Street investment bankers such as Felix Rohatyn, George Soros and Warren Buffet; and even from religious organisations including the Ecumenical Council of Churches and the Latin American Episcopate (De Rivero, 2001; Dunkley, 2004; Onimode, 2004).

In the specific case of Africa, the chronology of a continent-wide organised resistance to SAPs goes back to 1986, when the Organisation of African Trade Union Unity (OATUU) initiated its campaign against SAPs, under the leadership of Hassan Sunmonu, the then Secretary General of the OATUU (Sunmonu, 2004). But by far the highest-profile anti-SAPs campaign came in 1989 through the United Nations Economic Commission for Africa (ECA) – under the leadership of the renowned Nigerian economists, and the then Executive Secretary of the ECA, Professor Adebayo Adedeji – with the publication of the African Alternative Framework to SAPs (AAF-SAPs). In this publication, Adebayo Adedeji, the progenitor of the famous Lagos Plan of Action, called for an alternative, holistic approach to adjustment in Africa, based on self-reliance, food self-sufficiency, and a diversified productive capacity, together with a simultaneous democratisation of the entire development process. Even though the AAF-SAPs won the approval of the heads of states and governments of the Organisation for African Unity (now Africa Union) in their July 1989 summit, and was also endorsed by the General Assembly of the UN in December of the same year, it did not gain the support of the IMF and the World Bank and, consequently, could not procure the necessary financial backing for its implementation (Kankwenda, 2004). Of course, prior to these continental anti-SAPs campaigns, there were numerous national 'IMF riots' and upheavals across Africa, notable among which included those of Egypt in January 1977, Morocco in June–July 1981 and Sudan in early 1982. And since then many other African countries (e.g. Côte d'Ivoire, Ghana, Niger, Nigeria, Uganda and Zambia) have all come under the unfortunate spell of IMF riots. That is not all: a number of anti-SAPs and anti-globalisation social resistance movements have since taken root across the continent – well-known examples are the African chapter of Jubilee South; the Anti-Privatisation Forum in South Africa; the Press for Change Movement in Kenya; the Third World Network-Africa, based in Accra, Ghana; and the African Women's Economic Policy Network, based in Kampala, Uganda.

Over the years, the debate surrounding SAPs and their impact has become so emotional, so vitriolic and, indeed, so ideological that the usual distinctions between statements of fact, opinion and mere conjectures have virtually dissolved. For the most part opponents, such as Biel (2000), George (2001: 207) and Harvey (2003), contend that SAPs are nothing but an imperialist, neo-colonial ploy to siphon off financial and natural resources from Africa (and the rest of the developing world) to the so-called first world, and thereby perpetuate the dependence, through debt, of the former on the latter. There is also the concern that SAPs have been used by the Bretton Woods institutions to interfere with the domestic affairs of many African and southern countries. Even allegations that the Bank and the Fund undermine the basic sovereignty of poor countries, especially in Africa, abound in the available critical literature (Hoogvelt, 2001; De Rivero, 2001; Chomsky, 2001; Stiglitz, 2003; Barber, 1996). Additionally, some critics (e.g. Konadu-Agyemang, 2001; UNICEF,

1986; Cornia et al., 1987) contend that the very poor in the developing world tend to bear a disproportionate share of the negative consequences of SAPs by way of increased poverty and unemployment, and the lack of access to social services such as education and health care.

Conversely, supporters of SAPs, especially IMF and World Bank officials and their sympathisers, continue to praise African countries such as Ghana and Uganda as good examples of SAPs-induced success stories. For instance, in their well-disseminated book, *Aid and Reform in Africa*, Devarajan et al. (2001: 1) emphatically noted that 'Ghana and Uganda were successful reformers that grew rapidly and reduced poverty'. The snag, though, is that anyone reading Konadu-Agyemeng's edited collection on Ghana's SAPs, also published in 2001, for instance, could hardly be oblivious to the bitter-sweet socio-economic outcome of Ghana's SAPs skilfully documented in that volume. Following their comprehensive analysis of SAPs in ten African countries – Cameroon, the Gambia, Ghana, Guinea, Madagascar, Malawi, Mozambique, Niger, Tanzania and Zaire – Sahn et al. (1997: Preface) observed that contrary to popular opinion, SAPs 'do not hurt the poor in Africa. Reforms in fact actually benefit the poor slightly, but alone are insufficient to reduce poverty significantly.'

Understanding economic reforms in Africa

It is against the background of this contentious, and often emotional, debate on SAPs that the Global Development Network (GDN) – an international development organisation (formerly based in Washington, DC, but now in New Delhi, India) – launched its research project, *Understanding Reform*, in 2002 to help broaden our knowledge on the true nature and impacts of economic reforms around the world. This ambitious, internationally coordinated research project dealt with thirty countries worldwide. This book brings together all the African case studies in this project – i.e. those of Burundi, Ghana, Kenya, Morocco, Tanzania, Uganda and Zimbabwe (with the exception of Nigeria, which could not be included due to circumstances beyond the control of the editor). Guided by the project's terms of reference, all the country studies in this book seek, at a general level, to address three main issues: (a) *Why* did African countries embark on economic reforms? (b) *What* were the characteristic features of the economic reforms undertaken in the selected countries; put differently, what kinds of reforms have been implemented? And (c) *How* well did the reforms perform?

Following Hope and Kayira (1997: 3–4) and Ruis and van de Walle (2003: 2), we define 'reforms' as changes in government policy, institutional structures and administrative procedures aimed at fostering market-oriented economic activities to sustain economic development, with such changes often occurring within the context of more open political systems. Even though we frequently – and, quite justifiably, based on the preceding definition – qualify 'reform' with the adjective 'economic' (as in the book's title), we do not draw a hard-and-fast line between what is *social, political, cultural* or *economic*, given our strong belief in the intricately interwoven and mutually reinforcing nexus between these spheres of human endeavour. Also, instead of using the simplistic 'before' and 'after' comparative approach commonly deployed in many of the previous assessments of economic reforms, all the contributors adopt a historically informed, country-specific institutional and political economic approach which highlights the link between states and markets; between government actors, on the one hand, and private, civil society and individuals, on the other; and identify the 'losers' and 'winners' of the various reform programmes – our general approach is akin to what Robert Bates et al. (1998) call *analytic narrative*. Moreover, many of the contributors combine both qualitative data (mostly from focus group discussions and in-depth interviews) with secondary and quantitative data in their analysis. What we consciously avoid throughout the book is high-level econometrics or quantitative analysis, which would be of limited value to the general audience we seek to address.

It bears noting here that all the research team leaders met twice at special workshops organised in conjunction with the Fourth and Fifth Annual Global Development Conferences at Cairo (in 2003) and New Delhi (in 2004), to discuss and firm-up the project's research methods and preliminary findings, respectively. Furthermore, cognizant of the acute dearth of empirical data and up-to-date library resources in many African countries, the GDN commissioned several thematic papers for the project. These papers – written by renowned scholars in the field – were made available to all the country research teams, together with a comprehensive virtual library resource created specifically for the *Understanding Reform* project. This virtual library was accessible to country research teams via a secret website hosted by the GDN. Additionally, all the country research teams were provided with some funding to facilitate the procurement of data and publications in pursuance of the project's objectives. Thus, the papers in this monograph have benefited from funding, international coordination, deliberation and brainstorming, under the auspices of the GDN.

In the light of the openly caustic and ideological debate surrounding SAPs, it is important to note that, unlike many of the existing publications on Africa's economic reforms that are written by either outsiders or by World Bank and IMF officials, the case studies here are all authored by researchers drawn from the respective African countries. This is certainly not a simple feat, considering Kwadwo Konadu-Agyemang's observation in the preface to his *IMF and World Bank Sponsored Structural Adjustment Programs in Africa* (2001) that 'Although the original intention was to use case studies from several African countries undertaking economic restructuring under the auspices of the Bretton Woods Institutions, no researchers with expertise on those countries responded to our call for papers.' This basic difficulty compelled Konadu-Agyemang to refocus his book on the sub-title – *Ghana's Experience, 1983–1999*. Evidently, the present book fills an important gap, by examining Africa's experience with SAPs from the perspectives of Africans themselves, using the case studies of seven different African countries.

A tale of seven nations

> 'It was the best of times, it was the worst of times, it was the age of wisdom, it was the age of foolishness, it was the epoch of belief, it was the epoch of incredulity, it was the season of Light, it was the season of Darkness, it was the spring of home, it was the winter of despair, we had everything before us, we had nothing before us, we were all going direct to Heaven, we were all going direct the other way – in short the period was so far like the present period.'
>
> (Charles Dickens)

With these opening words, Charles Dickens vividly describes the ambivalence, insecurity, uncertainty and, indeed, contradictions at the time of the French Revolution, which serves as the setting for one of his only two historical fictions, *A Tale of Two Cities*, first published in 1859. The two cities involved are London and Paris, and Dickens seamlessly switches his narrative between these two cities throughout the book. He characteristically uses this novel to highlight the problems of the poor in both England and France, to rail against oppression and socio-economic inequality in society, and to describe the dynamics of class struggles and mob action in a highly charged revolutionary period. While Dickens uses characters – such as the Englishman Sydney Carton, the heroic French nobleman by birth, Charles Darnay, who renounces his status to show his resentment towards his aristocratic uncle and the Marquis de St Evrémonde, and the evil of oppression he represents – to tell the tale of London and Paris, the main focus of the narrative is on class rather than on specific individuals, as noted by Ruth Glancy in her 1991 commentary.

'The tale of the seven nations' presented in this book is certainly not a fiction; yet, like Dickens's *Tale*, it is historical, set in the context of modern African history – from the post-independence era to the early twenty-first century – focusing on the economic reforms of the recent past, rather than of the future. Like Dickens's book, we document the tensions between the social classes in the various nations covered; we relate the story of mass action vis-à-vis 'IMF riots'; identify the 'gainers' and 'losers' of the different reform policies; and reveal the tactics, strategies and manoeuvres deployed by the key reform players to simultaneously foster their own interest and to undermine that of the groups, institutions and individuals they perceive as threats or opponents in the reform game. In all this, in true Dickensian spirit, we pay attention to the plight of the poor, shedding a sympathetic light – or *verstehen*, to use the term of the German phenomenologist Edmund Husserl – on how the economic reform programmes have either helped or destabilised the poor over the years. More than anything else, like Dickens's *Tale*, most of the chapters in the volume highlight the ambivalence, uncertainties and, indeed, the contradictions surrounding economic reforms in Africa.

While some analysts are quick to label the reform programmes of some African nations as 'successful' and others as 'failures', the findings in nearly all the chapters in this volume seem to suggest that any such binary oppositional branding is unsustainable. Contrary to the entrenched dogmatism commonly exhibited by both supporters and opponents of SAPs, we contend that reform outcomes are, indeed, too complicated and dialectical to be amenable to any simplistic binarism – e.g. between success and failure. For one thing, no less a vocal critic of SAPs than Susan George of the Transnational Institute in Amsterdam – the author of the thought-provoking *How the Other Half Dies: the Real Reason for World Hunger* and *The Debt Boomerang: How Third World Debt Harms Us All* – aptly notes in her analysis of 'Third World' debt that: 'Rarely in human affairs can one show a linear, one-to-one causal link between events; the consequences of the debt crisis are no exception . . . Thus we stress feedbacks more than linear connections and tend to see debt and its multiple consequences as mutually reinforcing' (George, 2001: 212). Like Susan George, we find it problematic to draw a direct, cause-and-effect link between SAPs and their perceived outcomes.

Before moving to the next section to shed light on how the book is organised, it bears stressing that despite the analogy drawn between this book and Dickens's *Tale of Two Cities*, we by no means seek to imply that the conditions in Africa are akin to those of England and France at the time of the French Revolution in the eighteenth century. For sure, there are some, more specifically from the *Economist* (London), who would have us believe as recently as May 2000 that Africa is a 'Hopeless Continent', and others who assert, quite emphatically, that Africa's SAPs have been 'a catastrophic failure' (Onimode, 2004: 23), or have 'actually worsened the (African) situation' (Ajakaiye, 2004: 55). But, as the case studies in this book show, the conditions in Africa in general, and the impacts of SAPs in particular, are not homogeneous. At the risk of sounding politically incorrect, the case studies in this book suggest that there are, perhaps, as many positive outcomes of SAPs as there are negative, most of which vary both within and between nations. In the final analysis we need to remember that SAPs embody a wide diversity of policies, implemented in a variety of national contexts, in response to equally heterogeneous prior conditions, the final outcomes of which are invariably filtered through a host of confounding socio-economic institutions before finally reaching any household (Sahn et al., 1997). Rather than feeding into the common, broad and, indeed, facile generalisations about SAPs, we hope to use our case studies to show how relevant variables played out in the specific context of each of the seven nations covered here.

Organisation of the book

With the preceding discussion in mind, the seven case studies that constitute this book are presented in two major parts, not on the basis of their presumed 'success' or 'failure', but on their respective SAPs implementation dates or chronology. Part I, 'Early Reformers', deals with the structural adjustment experiences of Kenya, Uganda, Ghana and Morocco, respectively; these four nations are those in the sample whose major IMF/World Bank-sponsored economic reforms were initiated by the first half of the 1980s. Kenya's economic reform, which started under President Daniel Arap Moi in 1980, is, indeed, the first in sub-Saharan Africa. Following Kenya is the case of Uganda (Chapter 2), whose reform is among the few acclaimed cases on the continent. Uganda's adjustment programme was first initiated in 1981/2, under President Milton Obote, but, as we shall soon see, this initial encounter backslid drastically until 1986, when it was resuscitated under the government of President Yoweri Museveni. Chapter 3 deals with the case of Ghana, another structural adjustment 'star' in the African context. Ghana's SAPs, which started in 1983 under Jerry Rawlings, have also been extolled in the available literature. Ghana's SAPs underwent some stalling between 1992 and 1996 – albeit in a less dramatic fashion compared to Uganda's – mostly as a result of undisciplined election-related spending on the part of Rawlings's government. It is important to note at this juncture that many of the countries profiled in this book (and, in fact, elsewhere in the available literature) exhibit similar spells of stalling and backsliding; consequently, the chronology used here is not beyond criticism. For one thing, Ghana's case could be placed ahead of Uganda's given the dramatic backsliding endured by the latter and the fact that some of Uganda's technocrats received their SAPs-implementation training in Ghana. Chapter 4, the last of Part I, deals with Morocco, whose adjustment programme started, in earnest, in 1983, but had several skirmishes and false starts with adjustment programmes before then. For instance, in 1978 the Moroccan government embarked on a stabilisation programme to help resolve its balance of payment difficulties, but its war in the Western Sahara and the protracted mass demonstrations resulting from the adjustment austerities compelled the government to abandon it by 1981, until in 1983 when the IMF approved another stabilisation loan and other international creditors agreed to reschedule its external debt.

Part II of the book, made up of Chapters 5 to 7, deals with the Late Reformers, or the three countries in our sample which embarked on their major economic reforms since the second half of the 1980s: Burundi, Tanzania and Zimbabwe, respectively. As their stories will show, their late encounter with SAPs stems mainly from unusual circumstances, such as protracted civil wars in the case of Burundi, long-standing socialist experimentation (i.e. *ujamaa*) in the case of Tanzania, and late political independence and a prolonged adherence to communism in the case of Zimbabwe. Burundi's case (Chapter 5), in particular, shows the devastating impact of ethnic-laced civil wars on economic development. Since its independence in 1962, the country has experienced no less than five civil wars, mostly caused by tensions and power struggles between its Tutsi and the Hutu populations, resulting in the death of more than half a million people to date. Burundi's SAPs, instituted in 1986, were preceded by inward-looking, protectionist ideology amidst neo-patrimonialism, coups and counter-coups. The tale of Tanzania (in Chapter 6), on the other hand, is one of political stability, ascertained by way of a one-party system imposed and headed by the nation's founding leader, President Julius Nyerere, who led the nation from 1964–85 and put Tanzania through one of the longest spells of home-made socialist experimentation with his infamous Arusha Declaration of 1967. It was not until 1986 that the new President Ali Hassan Mwinyi, who succeeded Nyerere in 1985, accepted IMF/World Bank-sponsored SAPs, in the face of a rapidly deteriorating economy and an acute lack of external funding from Tanzania's northern and eastern bloc friends. The case of Zimbabwe, the youngest nation among our sample, is presented in Chapter 7. Following its independence from Britain in 1980, Robert Mugabe, the nation's leader since independence, adhered quite doggedly to communism until early 1991, when the need to change course dawned on him as a result of mounting foreign debt and balance of payment difficulties.

Until the mid-1980s, most African leaders cared little about multiparty democracy. To facilitate their stranglehold on power, many of them – including Tanzania's Nyerere, Kenya's Jomo Kenyatta, Togo's Gnassingbe Eyadema, Côte d'Ivoire's Félix Houphouët-Boigny, and Uganda's Idi Amin – deployed all the plausible and not-so-plausible arguments they could possibly garner in support of a one-party state. The economic crisis of the 1980s, however, sparked intense calls not only from Africans, but also from the international development community, especially the IMF and the World Bank, for democracy in Africa. It is worth noting that the Bretton Woods institutions had generally ignored the need for democratisation in Africa, until the late 1980s, when they started imposing conditionality for institutional reforms and good governance vis-à-vis SAPs, following the publication of the World Bank's *Sub-Saharan Africa: From Crisis to Sustainable Growth* in 1989. What the careful reader of the present book will, consequently, detect is a situation where most of the early reformers discussed in Part I, including Ghana, Uganda and Kenya, enjoyed much longer spells of what has been called the 'authoritarian advantage' in the implementation of their SAPs. In contrast, the late reformers had little choice but to move rather quickly to incorporate institutional and democratic reform into their SAPs. Thus, in addition to facilitating the orderly presentation of the seven case studies and helping to reduce the level of monotony in the book, the two-part approach deployed here is informed, albeit mildly, by the continent's tenuous move towards democratic reforms. Synopses of the case studies in both Part I and Part II are provided in their respective introductions.

Note

1. This term was coined in 1990 by John Williamson of the Institute of International Economics to stress the near religious adherence to free-market principles by the

IMF, the World Bank, the US State Department and other Washington, DC-based institutions in their dealings with the developing world (De Rivero, 2001: 56; Khor, 2001, 73; Kline, 2006, 462).

References

Adedeji, Adebayo (1990) *Preparing Africa for the 21st Century: Agenda for the 1990s* (Addis Ababa: Economic Commission for Africa).

Adedeji, Adebayo (1993) *Africa and the World: Beyond Dispossession and Dependence* (London: Zed Books).

Adedeji, Adebayo and Shaw, T. M. (eds) (1985) *Economic Crisis in Africa: African Perspectives on Development Problems and Potentials* (Boulder: Lynne Rienner).

Ajakaiye, Olu (2004) 'The Centrality of Planning to Alternative Development Paradigms in Africa', in Bade Onimode et al. (eds), *African Development and Governance Strategies* (London and New York: Zed Books; Ijebu-Ode, Nigeria: African Centre for Development and Strategic Studies), pp. 54–62.

Babu, Abdulrahman Mohamed (2002) *The Future that Works: Selected Writings of A. M. Babu* (Trenton, NJ: Africa World Press, Inc.).

Barber, Benjamin R. (1996) *Jihad vs. McWorld: How Globalism and Tribalism are Reshaping the World* (New York: Ballantine Books).

Bates, Robert H., Levi, Margaret, Rosenthal, Jean-Laurent and Weingast, Barry R. (1998) *Analytic Narratives* (Princeton, NJ: Princeton University Press).

Biel, Robert (2000) *The New Imperialism: Crisis and Contradictions in North/South Relations* (London and New York: Zed Books).

Chang, Ha-Joon and Grabel, Ilene (2004) *Reclaiming Development: an Alternative Economic Policy Manual* (London and New York: Zed Books).

Chazan, Naomi et al. (1992) *Politics and Society in Contemporary Africa* (Boulder: Lynne Rienner).

Chomsky, Noam (2001) 'Free Trade and Free Market: Pretense and Practice', in Fredric Jameson and Masao Miyoshi (eds), *The Culture of Globalization* (Durham and London: Duke University Press), pp. 356–70.

Cornia, G. A. et al. (1987) *Adjustment with a Human Face*, Vol. 1 (New York: Oxford University Press and UN Children's Fund (UNICEF)).

De Rivero, Oswaldo (2001) *The Myths of Development* (Dhaka: University Press Ltd.).

Devarajan, Shantayannan, Dollar, David R. and Holmgren, Torgny (2001) 'Overview', in S. Devarajan, D. R. Dollar and T. Holmgren (eds), *Aid and Reform in Africa* (Washington, DC: World Bank), pp. 1–41.

Dickens, Charles [1859/undated edition] *A Tale of Two Cities* (London: Odhams Press Ltd.).

Dunkley, Graham (2004) *Free Trade: Myth, Reality and Alternatives* (Dhaka: University Press Ltd.).

Economist (2000) 'Africa, the Hopeless Continent', 13–19 May, p. 15.

George, Susan (1986) *How the Other Half Dies: the Real Reason for World Hunger* (Harmondworth, Middlesex: Penguin Books).

George, Susan (1992) *The Debt Boomerang: How Third World Debt Harms Us All* (London: Pluto Press).

George, Susan (2001) 'How the Poor Develop the Rich', in Majid Rahnema and Victoria Bawtree (eds), *The Post-Development Reader* (London and New Jersey: Zed Books), pp. 207–13.

Glancy, Ruth (1991) *A Tale of Two Cities: Dickens's Revolutionary Novel* (Boston: Twayne Publishers).

Harvey, David (2003) *The New Imperialism* (Oxford and New York: Oxford University Press).

Hoogvelt, Ankie (2001) *Globalization and the Postcolonial World: the New Political Economy of Development* (Baltimore: Johns Hopkins University Press).

Hope, Kempe R. Sr. and Kayira, Gladson (1997) 'The Economic Crisis in Africa: an Analytical Perspective on its Origins and Nature', in K. R. Hope, Sr. (ed.), *Structural Adjustment, Reconstruction and Development in Africa* (Aldershot: Ashgate), pp. 3–12.

Huntington, Samuel (2002) 'A Universal Civilization? Modernization and Westernization', in Susanne Schech and Jane Haggis (eds), *Development: a Cultural Studies Reader* (Oxford: Blackwell), pp. 19–31.

Kankwenda, Mbaya (2004) 'The AAF-SAP: First Step on the African Path to Sustainable Human Development', in Bade Onimode et al. (eds), *African Development and Governance Strategies in the 21st Century* (London and New York: Zed Books; Ijebu-Ode, Nigeria: African Centre for Development and Strategic Studies), pp. 49–53.

Khor, Martin (2001) *Rethinking Globalization: Critical Issues and Policy Choices* (London and New York: Zed Books).

Kline, Gary W. (2006) 'Development History and Theory', in Thomas M. Leonard (ed.), *Encyclopedia of the Developing World*, Vol. 1 (New York and London: Routledge), pp. 457–64.

Konadu-Agyemang, Kwadwo (2001) 'An Overview of Structural Adjustment Programs in Africa', in Kwadwo Konadu-Agyemang (ed.), *IMF and World Bank Sponsored Structural Adjustment Programs in Africa: Ghana's Experience, 1983–1999* (Aldershot: Ashgate), pp. 1–15.

Lodewijks, John (2006) 'Structural Adjustment Programs (SAPs)', in Thomas M. Leonard (ed.), *Encyclopedia of the Developing World*, Vol. 3 (New York and London: Routledge), pp. 1498–1500.

Ngagwa, P. and Green, R. H. (1994) *Africa to 2000 and Beyond: Imperative Political and Economic Agenda* (Nairobi, Kenya: East African Educational Publishers).

Noorbakhsh, Farhad and Paloni, Alberto (2001) 'Structural Adjustment and Growth in Sub-Saharan Africa: the Importance of Complying with Conditionality', *Economic Development and Cultural Change*, 49, 3: 479–500.

Onimode, Bade (2004) 'Mobilisation for the Implementation of Alternative Development Paradigms in 21st-century Africa', in Bade Onimode et al. (eds), *African Development and Governance Strategies* (London and New York: Zed Books; Ijebu-Ode, Nigeria: African Centre for Development and Strategic Studies), pp. 20–9.

Rodrik, D. (1999) *The New Global Economy and Developing Countries: Making Openness Work*, Policy Essay No. 24 (Washington, DC: Overseas Development Council).

Rostow, W. W. (1960) *The Stages of Economic Growth: a Non-Communist Manifesto* (Cambridge: Cambridge University Press).

Ruis, Andres and van de Walle, Nicolas (2003) 'Political and Cultural Institutions and Economic Polity Reform', paper presented to the GDN Workshop on Understanding Reform, Cairo, Egypt, 16–17 January.

Rupananda, W. and Mensah, J. (2002) 'Structural Adjustment and the Rural Agricultural Economy: the Case Study of the Monaragala District of Sri Lanka', *Regional Development Studies*, pp. 119–37.

Sahn, David E., Dorosh, Paul A. and Younger, Stephen D. (1997) *Structural Adjustment Reconsidered: Economic Policy and Poverty in Africa* (Cambridge: Cambridge University Press).

Stiglitz, Joseph E. (2003) *Globalization and its Discontents* (New York and London: W. W. Norton & Co.).

Sunmonu, Hassan (2004) 'Implementation of Africa's Development Paradigms: Solutions to Africa's Socio-economic Problems', in Bade Onimode et al. (eds), *African Development and Governance Strategies* (London and New York: Zed Books; Ijebu-Ode, Nigeria: African Centre for Development and Strategic Studies), pp. 63–71.
UNICEF (1986) *Ghana: Adjustment Policies and Programs to Protect Children and Other Vulnerable Groups* (Accra: UNICEF).

Part I
Early Reformers

Introduction

Joseph Mensah

Part I of this book has four chapters, the first of which, 'Understanding the Economic Reform Process in Kenya', is written by the Kenyan policy analysts Maureen Were and her colleagues Rose Ngugi and Phyllis Makau. The chapter focuses primarily on Kenya's reform process since the early 1980s and discusses the Kenyan government's reluctance to embark on SAPs, despite long-standing macroeconomic instability in the country. The chapter sheds light on the various resistance mechanisms deployed by those opposed to SAPs, and discusses how the government used various forms of political patronage to facilitate the implementation of some of its reform policies. It is clear from the chapter that while the government made bold moves in implementing certain reforms (e.g. trade liberalisation), it engaged in discernible foot-dragging, for reasons of vested political interest, in other areas such as good governance and public sector reforms. With regards to impact, the authors note that Kenya's SAPs, like many of the cases in this book, disproportionately affected the poor and worsened the asymmetries in income distribution in the country.

The Ugandan political scientist Julius Kiiza and his colleagues Godfrey Asiimwe and David Kibikyo begin their analysis of Uganda in Chapter 2 with a brief overview of the historical and macroeconomic context of the nation's SAPs. Following this, they explore the veracity of three main hypotheses (or what they called propositions), not by way of statistical testing, but via a qualitative approach which relies mostly on institutional and political economic analysis. These propositions are: (a) that Uganda's reforms reflected the preference of those who controlled the state at the time of their implementation; (b) that vested interest in developing nations, such as Uganda, tends to be inactive, or even apathetic, at the stage of reform design, but active at the point of implementation; and (c) that reform ownership tends to change with the changing phases of reform. After providing an empirically grounded theoretical narrative in support of these three propositions, Kiiza and his colleagues then lament the fact that Uganda's economic reforms, like nearly all others discussed in this book, have relied too much on donor funds to be sustainable in the long run. Unsurprisingly, the authors conclude by calling for the use of domestic resources to effect the structural transformation of Uganda's economy from its long-standing dependence on primary exports to higher, value-added and technologically enhanced industrial and information activities.

Chapter 3, on Ghana, is written by Joseph Mensah, a human geographer, together with his colleagues Roger Oppong Koranteng and Kwame Frempah-Yeboah. As with the chapters on Kenya and Uganda, Mensah and his co-authors rely on both quantitative and qualitative data to profile the historical, socio-economic and political contexts of Ghana's economic reform. They examine a number of key issues and ask the questions: Why did Ghana embark on reforms? To what extent did the major stakeholders and institutions participate in the design and implementation of Ghana's reform? What institutional and regulatory instruments were initiated to facilitate the implementation of the reform? And how well did the reform perform? The authors note that while many factors instigated Ghana's shift towards SAPs, the leading trigger was the economic crisis that prevailed in the country from the early 1970s to the early 1980s, an observation that is reiterated in nearly all the chapters in Part I. The analysis in Chapter 3 lends some credence to the common finding, by previous World Bank and other supporters of SAPs, that Ghana witnessed noteworthy growth in her real GDP, industrial capacity, domestic investment and infrastructural development as a result of the economic reforms. At the same time, there are indications from this chapter to suggest that Ghana's SAPs, like those of Uganda, severely aggravated the nation's debt situation, and increased income polarisation among Ghanaians, similar to the discovery made by Were et al. in Chapter 1 on Kenya.

The final chapter of Part I, on Morocco, is written by the economist Brahim Mansouri, with the assistance of Brahim Elmorchid, Mustapha Ziky and Mohamed Rigar. Starting with the premise that many of the previous studies on Morocco's reform have been ideologically driven, Mansouri and his colleagues set out to give an objective account of why Morocco embarked on economic reforms, what types of reform were implemented over the years, and how well the reforms fared. The chapter divides the Moroccan reform into three main episodes: the first, from 1983 to 1993, dealing with macroeconomic stabilisation of the initial structural reforms; the second, from 1993 to 1998, on the reinforcements that were made to the earlier reform period; and the third, from 1998 to the present, characterised by a number of political and institutional reforms. The recurrent theme of this chapter is its call for the incorporation of cultural factors into the planning and implementation of economic reforms. This call is certainly warranted, given the long-standing resistance to reforms posed by pre-capitalist cultural traditions in Morocco.

Part I of the book, therefore, brings together four countries from different parts of Africa – Morocco from the north, Ghana from the west, and Uganda and Kenya from the east – with a wide diversity of history, economic policies, and relationship with, and resistance to, the Bretton Woods institutions. At the same time, a careful reading would show that they share some common characteristics. For one thing, like most African countries, their economies are overwhelmingly dominated by agriculture, in particular, and primary production in general. Also, their level of urbanisation is relatively low, and – with the notable exception of Morocco, whose GNP per capita is $1180, according to the World Bank's *World Development Report (2000)* – they all have fairly similar GNP per capita: ranging from $300 for Uganda to $350 for Kenya, with Ghana in between with $340. More importantly, one should notice from reading Part I that nearly all the four countries relied on the so-called *authoritarian advantage* for the implementation of their SAPs for a longer period of time than the countries in Part II.

1
Understanding the Reform Process in Kenya[1]

Maureen Were, Rose Ngugi and Phyllis Makau

1 Introduction

Kenya gained independence from Britain in 1963. Since then, the country has gone through a number of political and economic changes. Like most African countries, Kenya's economy in the 1960s and 1970s was characterised by state controls and a protective, inward-looking trade regime. The economy was able to achieve outstanding economic growth in the first decade after independence – with an average real Gross Domestic Product (GDP) growth rate of 6.6 per cent during the period 1964–73. However, in the 1970s, the nation witnessed a series of economic crises: trade shocks, fiscal indiscipline and several structural distortions. The oil crises of the 1970s compounded the problems by exposing the country's vulnerability to external shocks. This was a major blow to the nation's import-substitution industrialisation programme. The government responded to these crises by tightening the trade regime and by seeking financial assistance from donors. By the late 1970s, the economy had deteriorated even further, but the government resisted dismantling the control regime for market-oriented reforms.[2]

However, as the economic crisis deepened, the easiest option of borrowing from abroad demanded the liberalisation of the Kenyan economy. Thus, the government, reluctantly, embraced economic reforms under Structural Adjustment Programmes (SAPs) in 1980, making Kenya the very first Black African country to embark on a major adjustment programme. However, little was achieved in the 1980s; it was not until the 1990s that the nation's SAPs were revamped.

This chapter offers an in-depth analysis of the reforms in Kenya. More specifically, it investigates the reform process, with the aim of exploring the impetus for reform; the role of key stakeholders, especially the state and the donor community; the political constraints faced in the implementation process; matters concerning the reform's ownership and outcomes; and the successes and failures of the various aspects of reform. Our analysis is guided by three key questions: Why reform? What kind of reform? How well did the reform perform? In seeking to answer these questions, we rely on analytical narrative[3] to help us understand some of the subtle issues and to gauge causal and logical relationships in the reform process in Kenya. Undoubtedly, any attempt to understand reforms engenders questions that give rise to difficult methodological issues. Economic reform is a complex, dynamic and multi-faceted process that calls for a multidisciplinary approach that pays due attention to political, historical, economic, cultural and geographical matters simultaneously (Fanelli, 2003). Consequently, rather than using the traditional time series or panel data econometric models, we deploy a historically grounded, institutional and political economic approach to the study of Kenya's reforms.[4]

The chapter proceeds as follows: section 2 profiles the political economy of Kenya since its independence in 1963. This is followed by an in-depth analysis of the economic reforms that were implemented during the 1980s and 1990s in sections 3 and 4, respectively. Section 5 examines the outcomes of the reform, while section 6 focuses on the 'winners' and 'losers' of the nation's reform, before drawing the chapter to a conclusion in section 7.

2   Kenya: political economy prior to economic reform

Throughout the colonial period, the country was run as a unitary entity in which the colonial centre in Nairobi exercised overwhelming authority over the peripheries. The decision by the outgoing colonial authorities to replace such a system with a loosely organised federal structure was bound to fail, as it did, largely because the country had no meaningful experience with power sharing between the centre and peripheral localities in the governance process (Oyugi, 1994).

Upon winning the first post-independence elections, the Kenya African National Union (KANU), which favoured a unitary system, embarked on a deliberate effort to destroy the opposition and the federal constitution (Tamarin, 1978). In the face of mounting frustration from the ruling party, politicians from the opposition party, the then Kenya African Democratic Union, found it difficult to operate, and ultimately defected to the ruling party. The demise of the opposition was quickly followed by the dismantling of the federal constitution, which had ceased to function by the end of 1964 (Oyugi, 1994). By 1969 Kenya had become a *de facto* single-party state (Throup and Hornsby, 1998). The Kenyatta government quickly 'Africanised' the civil service and other public sector appointments in order to consolidate national sovereignty (O'Brien and Ryan, 2001).

Having assumed power at a very advanced age, President Kenyatta surrounded himself with a group of trusted ministers and personalities, drawn largely from his ethnic community, the Kikuyu, who constituted the 'kitchen cabinet'. The group had a vested interest in maintaining the presidency in the central province (the president's home province) to protect and perpetuate their political and economic interests. The foundation of a deep-seated politico-economic client system was slowly being laid. The stakes were very high, and the group orchestrated a series of manoeuvres to dilute the independence constitution (Okoth-Ogendo, 1972). By the end of the first decade of independence, the constitution had been amended ten times to strengthen the position of the presidency over parliament. The powers and authority of the executive were also enhanced. These powers were used discriminately on the basis of patronage, as senior civil servants understood that they served at the pleasure of the president (Anyang' Nyong'o, 1989). The civil service, however, enjoyed more powers over routine and technical policy issues during the Kenyatta era relative to the subsequent regime. By the mid-1970s, Kenyatta had grown old and feeble. Without any opposition party, the inner cabinet became dictatorial and resorted to assassinations and detentions of government critics, mainly backbenchers in parliament. Corruption, nepotism, favouritism and inequity grew dramatically over every aspect of the Kenyatta administration's sunset years.

It is against this background that Daniel Arap Moi assumed power in August 1978 following the demise of Mzee Jomo Kenyatta. He moved fast to assure the mourning nation that he would follow in the footsteps of his predecessor. True to his word, the new president embarked on the business of leading the country using the same state apparatus. Thus parliament remained subdued. In no time, Moi resorted to issuing populist policy statements and directing civil servants to implement them (Odhiambo-Mbai, 1998). By the early 1980s, the constitutional amendments had created an overarching executive with immense interventionist powers in the economy (Gacheru and Shaw, 1998).

As with many developing countries at the time, Kenya's post-independence economy was influenced by the prevailing development paradigm, namely, import substitution industrialisation, with a significant role accorded to the state in the economy. At the time of independence, Kenya's colonial heritage provided a variety of rent-seeking opportunities to the country's newly elected government (Ryan, 2004). The new government elites maintained and endorsed colonial institutions so as to capture the consequent privilege when expatriates were replaced by Kenyans. The colonial government had already established marketing boards for the sale of commodities such as coffee, and in the quest for economic sovereignty, the new government expanded its involvement in productive activities through the creation of more state-owned enterprises (O'Brien and Ryan, 2001). The impetus for this move came mainly from the recommendations of the infamous *Sessional Paper No. 10 on African Socialism and its Application to Planning in Kenya*, which sought to 'Africanise' the economy and jump-start industrialisation.

The government managed to expand economic output and employment, fuelled mainly by expansionary fiscal policy and increasing exports to Tanzania and Uganda under the newly established common market – the East African

Community (EAC) (Wagacha, 2000). However, after the remarkable economic growth in the first decade, Kenya started experiencing macroeconomic instability in the 1970s. For instance, in 1971, deterioration in terms of trade led to the first balance of payments (BOP) crisis. Following the first oil shock of 1973, the economy experienced escalating BOP and current account problems, to which the government responded by introducing import controls. Then came a positive shock in the form of a commodity (coffee) boom in 1977, which sparked of a spending spree on the part of both the government and the private sector, leading to a fiscal deficit of 9.5 per cent of GDP in 1975/6 (O'Brien and Ryan, 2001). The economy was also set back by the collapse of the EAC in August 1977. The second oil crisis of 1978/9 compounded the problems and exposed the country's vulnerability to external factors (Were et al., 2002). But the government was not ready to dismantle the controlled policy regime. Instead, it reacted to these crises by tightening the trade regime and seeking external financing assistance. Despite the shocks, the economy performed fairly well in the 1970s, and was able to achieve a real GDP growth rate of 5.6 per cent for the period 1974–9. However, the country had serious problems of unemployment and underemployment, income distribution and land ownership. It is clear from the turn of events that there was a need for reform from as early as the beginning of the 1970s.

3   Economic reforms in the 1980s

By the early 1980s, it was clear that the macroeconomic policies pursued before had glaring loopholes. At the same time, the economic management had begun to weaken and fiscal indiscipline was rising. The public sector was overextended. By the end of the 1970s, the government had shares in about 250 commercial firms (Ikiara, 2000). The state-owned enterprises were not only lagging behind in economic performance, but were also draining the national budget. The inability to control expenditure was partly the result of a general lack of discipline in expenditure allocation and execution. Most state corporations were highly inefficient, despite enjoying economic privileges such as direct subsidies. In the social sector, the overstretched public sector and increased inefficiency became a major challenge to the ambitious programme of free university education and health.

Table 1.1 shows some of the macroeconomic indicators during the reform process. As can be seen, in the early 1980s, when the reform process was getting started, the BOP and current account were both in huge deficits. For example, in 1980, the BOP and current account deficits amounted to US$317 million and US$878 million, respectively. There was also a scarcity of foreign exchange reserves as exemplified by the huge negative net foreign reserves. In addition, the ratio of budget deficit to GDP in 1981 and 1982 was over 7 per cent and inflation was relatively high. The economy was in crisis. Some action had to be taken. This happened to be the time when the

Table 1.1: Kenya: selected macroeconomic indicators, 1971–1999

PERIOD	GDP	INVEST	NETRES	RES	BOP	CAB	DEF	LEND	TBILL	EXR	INF
1971	5.23	25.3	1200	1230			−2.6	9	1.42	7.143	
1972	4.62	23.2	1331	1416			−5.7	9	3.45	7.143	
1973	4.01	21.2	1546	1603			−4.4	9	1.92	6.9	8.89
1974	3.06	30.8	962	1347			−3.0	9.5	4.63	7.143	17.33
1975	2.89	20.5	534	1427	(43)	(220)	−6.0	10	6.08	8.26	16.06
1976	4.40	23.0	1446	2301	84	(120)	−6.1	10	5.54	8.31	10.47
1977	8.13	27.0	3610	4259	269	35	−3.1	10	2.13	7.947	13.53
1978	7.66	34.3	1954	2732	(220)	(661)	−2.4	10	4.29	7.404	14.77
1979	4.92	26.1	3275	4780	72	(495)	−6.1	10	6.01	7.328	7.80
1980	3.99	35.4	1830	3784	(317)	(878)	−2.5	10.58	5.26	7.569	13.16
1981	5.97	33.3	128	2577	(306)	(563)	−7.5	12.42	7.61	10.286	12.23
1982	3.40	26.4	(2167)	2957	(160)	(308)	−7.7	14.5	12.58	12.725	22.30
1983	3.04	25.0	(1027)	5459	98	(50)	−2.4	15.83	14.15	13.796	12.83
1984	0.35	25.5	(374)	6444	62	(130)	−3.7	14.42	13.24	15.781	9.75
1985	5.13	25.5	(1975)	6807	(52)	(118)	−3.7	14	13.9	16.284	12.25
1986	5.54	21.8	(411)	7115	137	(47)	−4.8	14	13.23	16.042	5.16
1987	4.87	24.3	(2159)	4753	(25)	(503)	−7.5	14	12.86	16.515	6.25
1988	5.14	25.0	(3651)	5558	(44)	(472)	−3.7	15	13.48	18.599	9.91
1989	5.09	24.7	(2370)	7310	122	(590)	−3.8	17.25	13.86	21.601	11.09
1990	4.21	24.3	(5450)	6630	(93)	(527)	−4.3	18.75	14.78	24.084	13.31
1991	2.08	21.3	(7945)	5339	(44)	(213)	−5.0	19	16.59	28.074	17.55
1992	0.48	16.9	(5975)	6315	(257)	(180)	−1.3	21.07	16.53	36.216	25.01
1993	0.24	17.6	30 146	34 527	412	71	−4.5	29.99	49.8	68.163	43.46
1994	3.03	19.3	15 903	28 227	62	98	−5.8	36.24	23.32	44.839	29.80
1995	4.82	21.8	23 546	25 683	(142)	(400)	−1.3	28.8	18.29	55.939	0.50
1996	4.64	20.4	47 434	47 266	39	(74)	1.2	33.79	22.25	55.021	7.87
1997	2.36	18.5	55 669	44 499	120	(377)	−2.2	30.25	22.87	62.678	10.91
1998	1.77	17.3	53 787	47 103	74	(363)	−0.8	29.49	22.83	61.906	5.44
1999	1.42	16.1	55 121	57 816	87	(90)	−0.7	22.38	13.87	72.931	4.48

Key: GDP is real gross domestic product growth rate; INVEST is investment rate defined as the ratio of gross investment to GDP; NETRES is net foreign reserves; RES is foreign reserves; BOP is balance of payment (US$m); CAB is current account balance (US$m); DEF is the ratio of budget deficit to GDP; LEND is nominal lending rate; TBILL is the nominal treasury bill rate; EXR is the exchange rate (Kshs/US$); INF is the inflation rate.
Source: IFS and KIPPRA.

international financial institutions (IFIs)[5] were ready with a reform recipe in the form of SAPs.

While the government at first resisted dismantling the control regime, the easiest option of borrowing from abroad then (and even now) invariably demanded liberalisation. Consequently, with the rising pressure from the IFIs, the government started, reluctantly, to liberalise the economy – a major component of which was the removal of import controls and a shift from import-substitution to an export-promotion strategy (Were et al., 2002). Indeed, as hinted earlier, Kenya was the first sub-Saharan African country to receive structural adjustment lending from the World Bank and later on among the first to receive an Enhanced Structural Adjustment Facility (ESAF) loan from the IMF[6] (O'Brien and Ryan, 2001).

The reform programme was therefore driven by both domestic and external factors. Besides the imbalances in external accounts, there was immense pressure from outside – notably from the IFIs – to implement reforms as part of the preconditions for donor funding. The policy-based structural transformation programmes included several conditions within their policy matrices (Ryan, 1998). The domestic factor was mainly the economic crisis propagated by such factors as budgetary problems, inefficiency problems, deteriorating economic performance, and increasing demand for services in the face of declining per capita real public expenditures. The external pressure from the IFIs acted as a catalyst, hence facilitating the process.

Stallings (1992) argues that international influences can affect domestic policies. However, as cited by Liew et al. (2003), Kahler (1992) writes that the prominence of IFIs and the lack of alternative sources of finance in the 1980s did not increase the leverage of IFIs as expected because the proposed programmes were in conflict with the political interests in developing countries. Despite the pressure from IFIs and the economic crisis that had deepened by the early 1980s, the government only managed to implement piecemeal reforms. Among other factors, the control regime was still attractive for maintaining the status quo, and for providing rent-seeking opportunities and political patronage. Following Swamy (1994), we divide Kenya's SAPs period into two major phases: 1980–4, which forms the first phase of reform, and the 1985–91 period, which forms the second phase, during which a sectoral approach was adopted.

3.1   Economic reforms: 1980–4

The first phase of reforms mainly targeted the BOP, with the removal of import controls. The government presented its structural adjustment programme in *Sessional Paper No. 4 of 1980 on Economic Prospects and Policies*. Among other policy changes, the programme suggested the need to eliminate quantitative restrictions on imports and replace them with equivalent tariffs; to relax industrial protection; and to institute a relatively high interest rate regime.

With the escalating economic crisis, the government urgently needed quick disbursement, which happened to coincide with the World Bank's decision on medium-term BOP support (programme lending). A planned industrial sector loan was thus converted into a Structural Adjustment Loan (SAL) by adding conditionalities, which included the replacement of quantitative restrictions with tariffs and their rationalisation by 1983 (Mwega, 1999). This was done with the hope of effecting a quick response in exports, but the response did not materialise as expected. However, in the 1980/1 budget, some of the proposals were implemented. For example, import controls were relaxed and interest rates were adjusted upwards. Also, a new system of licensing was put in place in November 1981. At the same time, it was proving difficult to contain government spending and to achieve the income policy.

In 1982, faced with a worsening economic situation, the government approached the IMF again and also requested another SAL from the World Bank. However, by mid-1982, the Kenyan Central Bank's credit to the government had exceeded the agreed ceiling and the agreement was thus suspended. The second SAL was even more ambitious, taking on trade reforms, grain marketing, interest rates, energy and family planning (Swamy, 1994). However, the trade reforms were largely not implemented and grain marketing was not liberalised. The *Sessional Paper No. 4 of 1982* spelt out further attempts to reform import controls, by which items could be moved from the quota-based schedules to quota-free ones, at a rate to be determined by the availability of foreign exchange. But because of the growing foreign exchange crisis, this shift was never implemented. The individual scrutiny of import licences was also reintroduced in mid-1982.

In terms of export promotion, the idea was to reduce anti-export bias and increase industrial efficiency. The proposals included simplifying the administration of the incentive system, and introducing an export insurance and finance system. These were in addition to the Export Compensation Scheme (ECS), established in 1974 primarily to compensate exporters of eligible products for the additional input costs due to the imposition of duties on imported inputs whose burdens were considered excessive. In 1984, the compensation was revised upwards from 10 per cent to 15 per cent for general ECS and downwards from 15 per cent to 10 per cent for new and additional exports.

By the end of 1983, when the exercise was expected to be completed, minimal achievements and policy reversals had been witnessed. Moreover, to the extent that quantitative restrictions were removed, tariffs were raised on restricted items even to over 100 per cent. In addition, with the foreign exchange crises of 1982–4, tariffs were increased by 10 per cent across the board. The programme was implemented without a consistent framework so that the imposition of high tariffs on some goods and the reduction of tariffs on others were done in an ad hoc manner. Efforts to improve BOP position, therefore, had very minimal results. The fixed exchange rate regime was not conducive for export promotion; and the ECS did not function well. The design of ECS was flawed, as it left loopholes that could easily be exploited, thus defeating the purpose of the reform. For example, given that new exporters were eligible for the additional compensation, all they needed to do was to change the company's name and, thus, requalify for it. There was also mounting pressure from the urban elite group (i.e. urban salary and wage earners, especially employees of state corporations) who were thought to be a political threat if drastic changes were implemented.

Swamy (1994) argues that this episode of import liberalisation was not successful because it coincided with a period of macroeconomic crisis, which was followed by rapid stabilisation, hence making trade policy become hostage to the needs of stabilisation. He describes the first adjustment attempt as one marked by the lack of compliance, partly due to design and timing problems, and lack of government commitment to the reform process. The pervasiveness of the import licensing and regulatory system created enormous opportunities for rent-seeking and for executive discretion. Commitment to the stated policy changes was limited to a small coterie of top civil servants. The group seemed to underestimate the strength of the vested interests or overestimate the World Bank's willingness and ability to enforce the conditionalities. Due to the unsatisfactory implementation, there was a pause in adjustment lending for nearly four years.

Vested interests aside, the reform agenda was overambitious and at the same time underestimated state capacity constraints in undertaking a myriad of reforms within the stipulated time.[7] This confirms the observation made by Rius and van de Walle (2003) that the first generation of reform programmes typically did not view implementation issues as paramount. However, as they rightly argue, state capacity is generally posited to be positively correlated with the level of development, but it would be a mistake to treat state capacity as entirely exogenous to the political system. The government's capacity to implement reforms was compromised by a weakening economic management brought about by the policy drift of the late Kenyatta years and a corresponding loss of influence of the cabinet and civil service technocrats (O'Brien and Ryan, 2001). The constitutional powers bestowed upon the president to appoint and dismiss top civil servants at will interfered with professionalism of the civil service as other factors such as ethnicity, tribalism and patronage became central in appointment and promotion within the service.

Unlike Kenyatta, Moi lacked adequate room for manoeuvre and the personal authority that Kenyatta enjoyed. He also lacked a broader ethnic political base comparable to Kenyatta's (Hyden, 1995). He thus resorted to concentrating power and authority in the presidency in order to maintain control of the state. In 1982, the president made a major constitutional amendment, which made Kenya a *de jure* one-party state. During this period, the presidency increasingly dominated the public policy-making process, especially through presidential decrees (Odhiambo-Mbai, 1998). The civil service was relegated to the position of mere policy implementers. Even in situations where technocrats had been empowered to come up with coherent policies, the policies could be contradicted by 'presidential decrees' at the implementation stage.

In terms of economic outcomes, the first half of the 1980s performed poorly, with real GDP growth rate declining to about 3.4 per cent. Although the economy showed some stability between 1982 and 1984, virtually no progress was made towards structural adjustment. As in many African countries (e.g. Uganda and Ghana, see Chapters 2 and 3), SAPs paid off rapidly in terms of macroeconomic stabilisation such as lowering of inflation and fiscal deficits at the expense of investment and growth (Table 1.1).

3.2   Economic reforms: 1985–1991

Due to the lack of adequate commitment to the reform process and limited implementation in the first phase, the international funding agencies had to slow down the pace of an otherwise ambitious reform programme. On its part, the government prepared a long-term policy document – *Sessional Paper No. 1 of 1986 on Economic Management for Renewed Growth* – to demonstrate that it had a clear reform strategy. In the policy document, the government committed itself to adopt an outward-looking development strategy and proposed several measures to liberalise the economy. The government also acknowledged the need to limit its primary role in the development process to facilitating the growth of the private sector. In terms of comprehensiveness, the document marked a major policy shift towards liberalising the economy, and was later used as the basis for sectoral reforms.

With minimal success in the implementation process, there was a shift in the implementation strategy from a broad to a sectoral basis. The World Bank moved into sectoral adjustment lending as a way of focusing structural transformation into narrower areas, while the IMF was to continue monitoring the macroeconomic balances. This was justified on the basis of the limited implementation capacity of the government, and the need to build greater consensus in support of the reform process (Swamy, 1994). Hence, adjustment programmes were developed in agriculture (supported by two sector loans in 1986 and 1990), industry (in 1988), the financial sector (in 1989), export development (in 1990) and education (in 1991) (O'Brien and Ryan, 2001; Swamy, 1994).

During the reform period, some attempts were made to liberalise the economy, but the level of progress was still limited. With regards to import liberalisation, the reform programme first reclassified imports into five categories: Schedules I (unrestricted licensing), II, IIIA, IIIB and IIIC, with progressively stricter licensing requirements (Swamy, 1994). Over time, automatic or unrestricted licensing was extended to Schedules II, IIIA, and IIIB. Trade liberalisation had started with conversion of quantitative restrictions to tariffs

Table 1.2:   Economy-wide average tariffs, fiscal years 1985–1991 (in percentages)

All schedules	1985	1988	1989	1990	1991
Unweighted	40	39.6	41.3	41.0	38.8
Import-weighted		29.6	27.3	24.5	22.0

Source: Swamy, 1994.

equivalent in the early 1980s, though less successfully. The tariff reform made some progress as shown by a declining trend in the economy-wide average tariffs in Table 1.2. In 1990, the government embarked on phased tariff reductions and rationalisation of the tariff bands. The highest tariff rate was reduced from 135 per cent to 60 per cent, while tariff rates on non-competing imports were lowered.

That notwithstanding, the liberalisation process was far from complete. The tariff rates were still on the high side (hence high effective protection), the import licensing system was still in place with considerable executive discretion, and foreign exchange restrictions were still in operation.

Under the export promotion strategy, a host of export incentive and promotion programmes were initiated. These included Manufacturing under Bond, Export Processing Zones and the Export Promotion Council, among others. In addition, the general rate under the ECS was increased from 15 per cent to 20 per cent while additional compensation was abolished following concerns over its sustainability.

Other reform efforts included decontrolling domestic prices, which was linked to the liberalisation of trade. To implement this politically unpopular policy, a strategy to break it up incrementally into the smallest possible pieces was agreed upon, in order to avoid substantive shock to the system (Ryan, 2004). This appears to have worked well. In 1988, the Kenya Association of Manufacturers (KAM), a well-organised lobby group, commissioned a study on the experiences of price controls, which revealed deleterious effects such as time-consuming procedures for presenting requests for price changes, bureaucratic hassles and administrative delays (KAM, 1988). They used the survey results to lobby the government for price decontrols. KAM managed to conquer resistance from the monopolies created under the import substitution strategy. However, according to Ryan (2004), the study results had no effect on the adoption of the policy. There is still no denying that KAM has been vocal in advocating for policies in their favour. It bears noting that in Kenya, most stakeholders are often unorganised and inarticulate (Ryan, 2004). Thus, potential winners (or losers) in a reform of a sector may be unaware and may lack an effective organisation to present their case. In several instances, farmers calling for reform of a controlling parastatal monopoly, as in the case of milk, maize, coffee, tea or sugar, would usually be bought off by releasing money to enhance crop payments rather than by major institutional changes.

In the financial sector, very little was achieved, as actions were limited to amendments to the Banking Act and adjustment of interest rates. The shift to indirect monetary policy instruments was initiated in 1988, while the treasury bill rate was liberalised in November 1990. The government was also under pressure to implement cuts in expenditure on social sectors, particularly health and education. In the health sector, for instance, this meant a shift from a 'free' healthcare policy to user-charges in public health facilities. However, despite repeated announcements of policy intentions in several policy documents, the government was still reluctant to implement the reform, and kept deferring actual implementation. This can be explained in the context of looming uncertainty over the outcome of reform implementation – especially political uncertainty regarding the reaction of the masses after having been used to the consumption of 'free' healthcare services.

It took a lot of effort, through a series of donor-funded studies and the use of carefully chosen 'friendly' terminologies such as 'cost-sharing' and 'participant support', before the government could finally levy user-charges,[8] albeit hesitantly, in December 1989. As a compensatory mechanism to the losers – basically, the poor and the vulnerable – preventive services and treatment for catastrophic illnesses were exempted from the fees, while the poor were exempted from paying, upon producing evidence of their inability to pay. Meanwhile, the government dispensaries continued to provide outpatient services free of charge. However, the policy was reversed in September 1990 by suspending the outpatient fee, only nine months after its inception. After implementation, there was a public outcry through the press that the poor were being denied access to services and there was no improvement in quality (Collins et al., 1996). This shows how sensitive the government was about the public response, and was not fully confident, despite having implemented the reform. The media played a key role in highlighting and exacerbating the unpopularity of the reform.

In general, the extent of the reform and the pace of its implementation were unsatisfactory, as most of the conditionalities were not met. For instance, by 1991, the last year of the ESAF, three out of the four quantitative performance criteria were not satisfied, including the ceilings on net domestic assets of the domestic banking sector, government borrowing from the banking system, and net official international reserves. Swamy (1994) observes that though an effort was made to build a broader consensus in the second phase and the pace was incremental, commitment was patchy and intermittent throughout. There was concern that macroeconomic management was deteriorating as a result of the lack of budgetary control on the expenditure front and a slow progress in other areas of economic reform. Little was achieved as the reform effort was characterised by policy reversals and delays, as well as failures in implementation of planned activities. This led to donor dissatisfaction, occasionally resulting in a halt in adjustment lending, as the relationship with development partners began to sour.

The actual implementation of the reform strategy can be described as sporadic and limited to selected issues. In fact, reforms were undertaken just on the periphery. The most sensitive ones, especially those with a direct impact on the electorate, such as retrenchment in the civil service, removal of maize marketing controls and user-fees in the social sector, were deferred or reversed during implementation. Despite recommendations of earlier commissions, the *Sessional Paper No. 1 of 1986* remained silent on the issue of parastatal reforms. The intricacies of implementation capacity notwithstanding, major reforms were basically deferred or avoided because of the looming political uncertainty of the effects of reforms and the fear of losing patronage. Fidrmuc and Noury (2003) note that if individuals are highly risk-averse, they may resist changes because of the inherent uncertainty. The government was highly risk-averse as the controlled policy regime was lucrative for economic rents and political patronage. External pressure thus coincided with strong domestic patronage and rent-seeking interests, especially by top state elites, thereby ensuring that the government was still able to keep enough elements of control. This situation confirms Rius and van de Walle's (2003) observation that when governments oppose the reform but feel compelled to undertake partial implementation, they are likely to undertake the least onerous, the most easily reversible component of the reform, or the one that has the least impact on the status quo.

To understand the reform process, one also needs to appreciate the context in which the reforms were being undertaken. For one thing, the policy-making process was highly centralised, in that public decision-making was exclusive to a small cadre of public elites. Most policies were a secret of top government officials, even though they would be well known in the circles of development partners who, after all, were the main driving force and initiators of policy reforms. Ministries would just be shown a paragraph or sentence to implement, without a clear understanding of the broader picture. The cabinet ministers, on the other hand, were not given copies of the agreements, but a synthesised version by top civil servants. The closed decision-making process also meant that the reform process was subject to manipulation by vested interest groups, such as political elites, often to their own advantage.

Clearly, secrecy and limited consultation were common techniques employed by the government in the development and implementation of its policies. This limited the scope of consensus building about the design and implementation of reforms with relevant stakeholders. It is thus not surprising that the reform effort was prone to resistance and reversals. Societal groups for which the policy outcomes had a direct impact were rarely able to have their preferences or concerns taken into account before policies were implemented. Such groups have been noted to assert their social power and influence during the implementation phase, well after policies have been decided upon (Rius and van de Walle, 2003). This was manifested in the case of user-fees reform in the health sector, and later on witnessed under the civil service reform.

Additionally, political interference of the civil service undermined the government's capacity to implement reform. Senior civil servants often understood that they served at the pleasure of the president and hence owned their loyalty to him. The situation was further aggravated by a constitutional amendment in 1988 that gave the president power to fire members of the Public Service Commission, the Judicial Service Commission and the judiciary. President Moi used the powers to reduce the preponderance of Kikuyu civil servants, especially in the higher ranks of the civil service. He replaced them with candidates largely from his own ethnic community under the pretext of promoting social cohesion. The parastatal jobs became an opportune avenue for this venture. This policy had the effect of undermining efficiency in the public sector, and to a certain degree, replacing one group of rent-seekers with another, many of whom lacked the experience to run the organisations they inherited (Throup and Hornsby, 1998). Public institutions, especially parastatals, were transformed into conduits of patronage. It is no wonder the government was not in a hurry to undertake parastatal reforms.

Although economic performance in the second half of the 1980s was better than in the first half, economic growth started deteriorating continuously from the early 1990s. The average real GDP increased from 3.4 per cent for 1980–4 to 5.2 per cent during 1985–9, but dropped to 2.3 per cent in 1991. There was also a notable improvement in BOP and the current account deficit (see Table 1.1). The improvement in 1986 was occasioned by a mini-coffee boom, resulting in a BOP surplus. However, in spite of export promotion measures, export orientation in the 1980s remained weak, largely due to very high effective rates of protection, exchange rate bias against exports, high cost of imported inputs, and foreign exchange controls, among other factors (Were et al., 2002).

One of the remarkable aspects of the first generation of reform in the 1980s is the dramatic build-up in nominal aid flows (both gross and net) during the 1980s. The government's pro-Western stance during the Cold War period also ensured a continuous inflow of bilateral aid from the West. Perhaps that is why the government could afford to get away with piecemeal reforms. It was not until the 1990s that a comprehensive reform programme was implemented.

4   Reform in the 1990s

The 1990s saw a greater degree of economic liberalisation and reform implementation, mainly on a sectoral basis. Reforms were initiated in virtually all the key sectors. Even then, the development partners exerted a lot more pressure on the government to demonstrate commitment and to implement reforms. Tight conditionalities and technical assistance became the major factors defining the flow of funds to support the reform process. Hence, the government–donor relationship became more critical than ever before, but that did not entirely prevent vested political interests from influencing government policy.

Kenya's reform at this period, like many profiled in this book (e.g. the cases of Ghana, Uganda and Morocco), was shaped by the supremacy of the Washington Consensus ideology, deeply rooted in the belief in markets and limited government intervention; the rapid wave of globalisation; and the more stringent conditionalities of the so-called 'second generation reform'. The latter incorporated good governance, democratisation and the need for building institutional infrastructure alongside market liberalisation policies. Hence, unlike the prior periods, economic reforms had to be undertaken simultaneously with political reforms. Unlike the 1980s, there was increased democratic space and freedom of expression, leading to a more active role for civil society and the media. Whether such a move accounted for more comprehensive economic reforms is debatable, but it certainly played a role, particularly in exposing corruption and some of the economic scandals in Kenya.

Domestically, this economic reform period coincided with a growing discontent about the monopoly powers created by the one-party political establishment (the then ruling party KANU). The political establishment had become dictatorial. Kenya's image in international circles was tarnished by rising corruption and human rights abuses, as exemplified by the detention and oppression of political activists agitating for multipartyism. Besides the civil society, pressure for more democracy and good governance became a key agenda for donor communities – multilateral and bilateral funding institutions alike. It was the donor pressure culminating in the suspension of BOP support in 1991 and domestic agitation for multipartyism that forced the government to relent and repeal Section 2A of the constitution in December 1991, allowing for a multiparty political system. However, the repeal left intact all other amendments that had concentrated power in the executive at the expense of the other branches of government. As a result, the civil society and the opposition parties made the constitutional reform their main agenda in the post-1992 elections.[9]

The curtailment of aid flows was one of the greatest challenges the country faced. While in the 1970s and 1980s the government responded to external shocks by increased borrowing and aid inflows, expansionary fiscal policy and instituting controls, in the 1990s, it no longer had the luxury of using these options. Unlike in the earlier periods, there was slackened donor support, resulting in a sharp decline in flow of aid since the peak in 1990. With the disintegration of the Soviet Union and the end of the Cold War,

Kenya fell from favour, coming to be viewed as just another African state mired in a familiar pattern of economic decay. The collapse of international communism basically eliminated the geopolitical motivation for aid. Kenya's strategic role was no longer needed. With the declining aid flows, the external debt arrears problem emerged for the first time. Net resource flow remained negative for the better part of the 1990s. The debt burden became so acute that Kenya had to reschedule its debt in 1994 for the first time. Net foreign exchange reserves were negative in the early 1990s, and the GDP growth rate was quite low, falling from 5 per cent in 1989 to 2.1 per cent and 0.5 per cent for both 1991 and 1992 (see Table 1.1).

As economic performance deteriorated, the budgetary crisis deepened and access to financial resources was curtailed, the IFIs had a considerable leverage and thus used the opportunity to push for reform implementation. Citing Grindle and Thomas (1990), Rius and van de Walle (2003) noted that policy reform has typically occurred during periods of intense economic crisis, as states delay difficult economic policy reform decisions until the old economic policy regime has brought about a non-sustainable economic disequilibrium. Liew et al. (2003) make similar observations by arguing that economic crises can tighten economic constraints to the extent that some countries are forced to reform, notwithstanding the political interest of the ruling party. This description fits the Kenyan case, especially in the 1990s, when the financial constraints became binding due to suspension of funding. The implementation of reforms not only intensified, but the reform agenda was also broadened. Funds were only disbursed when there were signs that the government was back on track with the reforms. Donors (IFIs and bilateral funding institutions) thus became key stakeholders in spearheading the reform process. However, domestic actors, mainly the media, the opposition party and the civil society, also played a critical role in pushing for political reforms.

4.1   Economic reforms: 1991–6

Most of the economic reforms were implemented in the first half of the 1990s, which forms the third phase of reforms. The period saw bold reforms in trade, civil service, agriculture and social sectors.

4.1.1   Trade reforms

Trade liberalisation started with the conversion of quantitative restrictions on tariffs equivalent to those in the 1980s. By 1991, quantitative restrictions affected only 5 per cent of imports compared with 12 per cent in 1987 (Swamy, 1994). The average unweighted tariff rate declined from 41.3 per cent in 1989/90 to 34 per cent in 1992/3. In June 1995, the maximum tariff rate was reduced to 40 per cent (Mwega, 1999).

Speedy progress was made in liberalising the foreign exchange market. In October 1991, Foreign Exchange Bearer Certificates (Forex-Cs) were introduced, marking the first step towards liberalisation of the foreign exchange market (Were et al., 2001). The Forex-Cs could be used for automatic import licensing. During the same year, currency declaration forms were abolished; a series of other measures followed. In August 1992, for instance, retention schemes were introduced, allowing 100 per cent retention of foreign exchange earnings from non-traditional exports. In February 1993, foreign exchange allocation by the Central Bank of Kenya (CBK) was abolished. However, in March of the same year, the retention accounts were suspended and import licensing and exchange controls reinstated. Apparently, this led to unsuccessful negotiations between the government and the IMF for the resumption of quick-disbursing loans. Consequently, in May 1993, import licensing was again abolished and retention accounts reintroduced for all exporters of goods and services at the rate of 50 per cent.

Despite the efforts made in liberalising international trade, the export incentive schemes that had been put in place to promote exports were not being utilised effectively. In particular, the ECS and pre-shipment export financing scheme[10] were highly abused as other issues such as vested interests and patronage crept in. For instance, both schemes were linked to what became known as the 'Goldenberg scandal', in which the government was swindled of billions of shillings in one of the country's biggest financial scams.[11]

In so far as the liberalisation reform effort is concerned, the manner in which the incentive schemes, such as the ECS, were executed left a lot to be desired. For one thing, what was the purpose of retaining the ECS when trade liberalisation measures were in place, if not for rent-seeking purposes? This was a policy measure instituted under the controlled trade regime, and had failed to serve the purpose for which it was instituted. Above all, the Goldenberg scandal took effect despite the stringent donor conditionalities, illustrating how powerful vested interests, clientelism and access to political power can be.[12] With a freeze on donor funding, the extra compensation and the other monies involved must have largely been sourced domestically. It is likely that this partly explains the observed surge in domestic stock of debt, particularly around 1993 (Table 1.3). From this turn of events, it is clear that rent seeking, clientelism, and patronage informed resistance to further trade liberalisation. It was not until September 1993 that a decision was made to end the much abused ECS.

It was upon realising the extent of the resultant economic crisis that the government responded by hurriedly implementing some of the donor demands, such as liberalising the foreign exchange market. But unfortunately, with a looming financial crisis and the sky-rocketing inflation, that was poor timing. The shilling depreciated to unprecedented levels against the dollar (see Figure 1.1). As one commentator puts it, 'it was like lifting the lid off a pressure cooker without first opening the steam valve'.[13] Scarcity of foreign exchange following the aid freeze aggravated the problem. It was

Table 1.3:   Kenya: analysis of domestic debt (in millions of Kenyan shillings)

Fiscal years	Total domestic debt	Domestic interest	Growth in domestic debt (%)	Domestic debt/GDP
1989/90	52 521	6786.60		28.6
1990/1	63 597	10 462.40	21.09	30.5
1991/2	70 809	10 920.20	11.34	29.7
1992/3	112 295	23 775.80	58.59	38.1
1993/4	162 843	44 448.80	45.01	44.4
1994/5	119 446	25 897.00	−26.65	27.6
1995/6	120 356	29 320.80	0.76	24.2
1996/7	159 077	25 544.20	32.17	27.6
1997/8	171 730	32 037.14	7.95	26.1
1998/9	174 305	27 903.20	1.50	24.4
1999/00	206 127	21 409.40	18.26	27.0
2000/01	213 772	20 576.91	3.71	24.6

Note: Generally, the domestic debt figures tend to vary depending on the source.
Sources: Treasury and CBK publications.

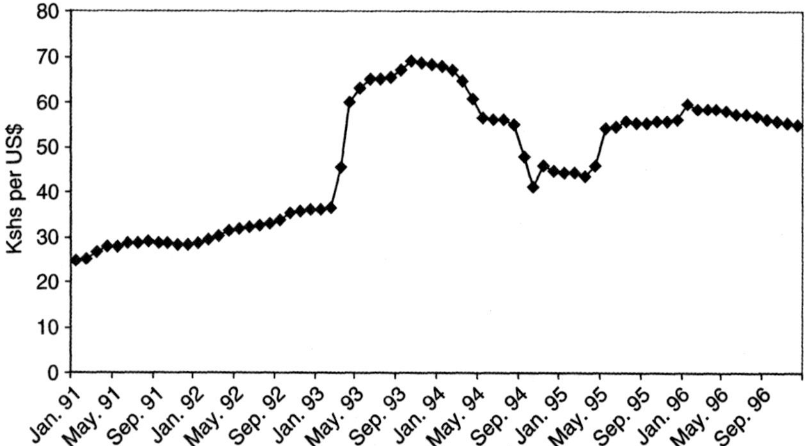

Figure 1.1   Nominal exchange rate (Ksh/US$), Jan. 1991–Dec. 1996

largely the alarm caused by these developments that prompted the president to reinstate the foreign exchange controls and import licensing in March 1993, in a bid to minimise the resultant short-run cost of the reform. A hasty implementation without the necessary preconditions such as macro-economic stability had worsened the situation, leading to policy reversal. However, the temporary backtracking seems to have averted further adverse effects of the reform.

Further liberalisation of the foreign exchange market proceeded. In October 1993, the official exchange rate was abolished, paving the way for a freely floating exchange rate. With the trade liberalisation having moved a substantial step forwards, capital controls were relaxed for offshore borrowing in February 1994, subject to quantitative limits. Over 1993–4, all current account and virtually all capital account restrictions were lifted. By 1995, all the foreign exchange restrictions had been eliminated – foreign exchange bureaux were permitted and the Exchange Control Act was repealed. Overall – although some backtracking or policy reversal was witnessed – foreign trade liberalisation and liberalisation of the foreign exchange market was undertaken, thereby placing Kenya among the pioneer countries in Africa to comprehensively open up the economy.

Domestically, the petroleum market was liberalised in October 1994. However, price liberalisation of basic commodities like cereals (especially maize and maize flour) was a highly sensitive issue given that these were commodities consumed by the majority of the population. Politicians wanted to act cautiously given the high political uncertainty of such a reform. Hence, some policy reversals were again witnessed.

4.1.2   Financial sector reforms

Several achievements were made during the period, including liberalisation of interest rates, removal of credit controls, and streamlining the money market trading system. Interest rates were liberalised in July 1991, a month after the introduction of open market operations. However, the reform efforts were thwarted by political patronage and interference, whereby the politically connected were allowed to get unsecured loans from some banks, especially state-owned and politically connected banks, just before the first multiparty elections. Following the run up to the general election in December 1992, there was a heightened activity of financial transactions, as money changed hands to finance the then ruling party's election campaign. Part of the finances was used as a means of buying political loyalty or rewarding those who were able to deliver votes, especially with the emergence of a multiparty system which was posing a threat to the ruling party KANU.[14] All of a sudden, a number of banks that were politically connected flourished. In short, KANU devised several schemes to finance its election bid, which also translated into printing lots of money. As would be expected, inflation rose drastically to over 50 per cent (Figure 1.2), with immediate repercussions in the exchange rate market. By April 1993, a financial crisis was imminent. This was a major drawback to the reform effort that IFIs were struggling to push through.

The donor community, particularly the IMF, expressed dissatisfaction, pointing to the need to restore financial prudence, adequate enforcement, and monitoring of the banking regulations. In particular, the situation created by the Exchange Bank and other political banks that were basically instrumental in financing the elections was of great concern.[15] This, together

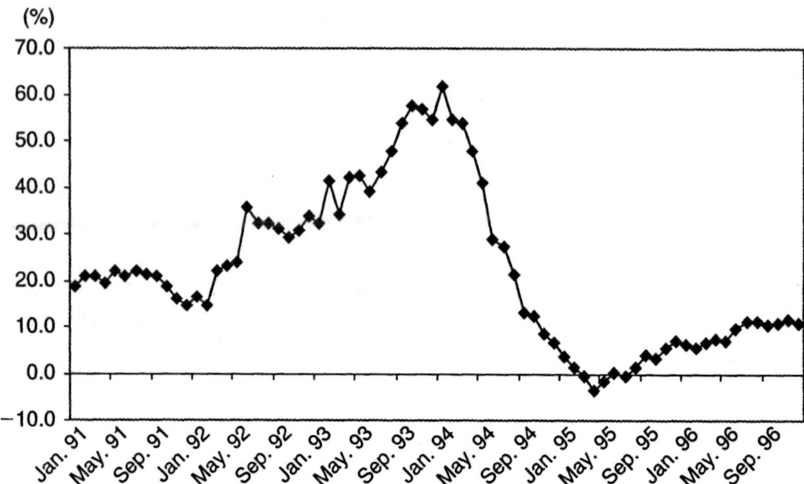

Figure 1.2   Inflation rate (monthly), Jan. 1991–Dec. 1996

with the huge unsecured loans amounting to billions of Kenyan shillings, triggered a financial crisis and eventual collapse of most of the political banks. Most of the troubled banks had to be put into liquidation, culminating in the closure of several banks and non-bank financial institutions in December 1993. It appears that the turbulence in Kenya's monetary situation in 1993 was part of its political business cycle. The literature on the political business cycle postulates that parties in power will manipulate policy in the short run in order to maximise their electoral chances (Haggard and Webb, 1993). KANU used the financial sector for such manipulation in a bid to finance its election.

To deal with the resultant monetary overhang, the government, under pressure from the IMF, decided to aggressively mop up the excess liquidity by issuing treasury bills. But this move only created another problem – a soaring treasury bill rate, which acts as an anchor for other forms of interest rates. At one point, the treasury bill rate was over 70 per cent. This was one of the bases of the high interest rate structure that became almost a permanent feature of the Kenyan economy. The lending interest rate has been overly high, reaching over 30 per cent in some years (Table 1.1). Critics of the IMF argue that they could have done a better job in advising the government to deal effectively with the crisis. In any case, it was wrong for the IMF to have insisted on financial liberalisation at a time when the banking legislation and bank supervision were inadequate (Stiglitz, 2002). Furthermore, until the amendment of the Central Bank Act in 1996, the independence of the CBK, and therefore monetary policy, had been grossly compromised. For example, before the amendment, there was no maximum limit on CBK advances to the government. This encouraged fiscal indiscipline as well as high budget deficits.

Rolling over the treasury bills and selling more of them kept interest rates high and the Kenyan shilling strong. The situation evolved into what economists refer to as a 'ponzi' game, with the government issuing attractive debt instruments to repay old ones. The beneficiaries of the game became financial institutions, especially commercial banks, which held over 50 per cent of total stocks of treasury bills. The dramatic increase in domestic debt (Table 1.2) and high domestic interest rates were also precipitated by resort to domestic financing, following the curtailment in donor funding. Overall, sequencing problems and political interference affected the successful implementation of reforms in the financial sector.

4.1.3   *Public sector reforms*[16]

Public sector reforms were perhaps the most difficult and, understandably, the government kept on employing delaying tactics in this area. Other than mere job creation, public service employment was also a means for political patronage and ethnic- or tribe-based favouritism. Due to a bloated public sector, the wage bill became unmanageable, accounting for about 10 per cent of GDP and about 70 per cent of the recurrent budget by the late 1980s. This left very little for operations and maintenance, as well as for development expenditure. Part of the reform was to reduce the number of ministries in order to contain cost.

Having postponed the civil service reform for quite some time, the government had to finally launch the reform programme in 1992 after much pressure from the development partners. The reform was to be implemented in three phases and was to cover only those civil servants paid directly by the exchequer, excluding teachers. A high-level steering committee, chaired by the head of the civil service, was set up and mandated to report to the cabinet. Its role was to set the overall direction; review and approve reform work plans; and inform the cabinet on reform progress. Like most reform initiatives, there was not much consultation on the reform with the stakeholders, though parliament as well as the general public had been informed through the various budget speeches. The civil servants were not formally consulted. Moreover, the sequencing of the civil service reform was not done properly. Ideally, the government should have first defined its core business and key job description, and in this way, identify areas to get rid of and, consequently, the officers and the percentage of staff to lay off. This was not done. The introductory phase of the retrenchment programme was on a voluntary basis. This was, however, highly contested especially by the development partners who argued that the best employees would leave the civil service. But to the government, this was the easiest way of implementing such an unpopular reform. The first phase was, therefore, less controversial.

In his budget speech of 1993/4, the Minister for Finance pledged to prune 16 000 civil servants in a three-year period. In five months, 3959 employees had been pruned through natural attrition (retirement), while 13 954 job vacancies that had been budgeted for were cancelled. The retrenchment programme was restricted to the civil servants, who, for lack of a formal labour union, were relatively easier to deal with. Although teachers were a major contributor to the huge wage bill, they were untouched, largely because of their strong union (Kenya National Union of Teachers) and the fact that they formed a strong political base in terms of votes. It is also important to note that the retrenchment programme was not extended to parastatals. In fact, some of the retrenches in the civil service could find their way to parastatals with even higher salaries, thus defeating the purpose of the reform.

With regard to parastatal reforms, nothing much was achieved, although some institutional structure was put in place. Parastatals had become avenues for perpetuating predatory behaviour by public officials, and for a long time the government was reluctant to divest from some of the enterprises. The stakes were high, as that would also jeopardise political support and power. The reforms basically entailed restructuring and privatisation of public enterprises, with the aim of enhancing the role of the private sector, reducing the claims on the budget, rationalising the public enterprise operations, improving regulatory environment and broadening the base of ownership (Republic of Kenya, 1998). In 1990, the Department of Government Investment and Public Enterprises was created and charged with the responsibility of overseeing the parastatal reform programme. Also, a Parastatal Reform Programme Committee, a high-level policy-making body, was set up under the chairmanship of the vice-president and Minister for Finance. A further arm, the Executive Secretariat and Technical Unit, was created to manage, coordinate and implement the programme while approvals were to be made by the committee. After internal consultations at cabinet level, the government drew up a privatisation programme whose strategies and objectives were spelt out in the *Policy Paper on Public Enterprises Reform and Privatisation*. However, the privatisation framework was inadequate as it lacked legislative principles to be followed – basically in the form of privatisation law. The procedures and institutional framework in the policy paper were not grounded in law.

The government categorised public enterprises into strategic enterprises (totalling some thirty-three) and non-strategic enterprises (numbering some 207). The former were to be restructured to improve efficiency and profitability, while the latter were to be privatised. The implementation encountered resistance and, more often than not, laid-down procedures were not followed by the implementing institutions. As Stiglitz (1999) rightly points out, if privatisation is conducted in ways that are largely viewed as illegitimate and in an environment that lacks the necessary institutional infrastructure, the longer-run prospects of a market economy may be undermined. The privatisation process lacked both functional and legal autonomy from the executive, and as such, privatisation did not weaken patronage, as one would expect (Gacheru and Shaw, 1998).

4.1.4   Social sector reforms

The major component of Kenya's social sector reforms in health and education was the implementation of cost sharing, also known as user-charges in the case of health.[17] Cost sharing in public universities was introduced in 1991. Following public discussions and workshops on the merits and demerits of user-charges, and the lessons learned from the initial attempt, the government announced a phased reintroduction of user-fees in April 1992. This time, the outpatient fee was reintroduced as a fee to be paid only after receiving treatment. To enhance institutional capacity in the health sector, the Health Financing Secretariat was expanded; new management systems were developed; a cost sharing operations manual was produced; new accounting and reporting systems put in place; and revenue collection targets were also set. The revised policy was introduced in phases and on a pilot basis (Collins et al., 1996). The reintroduction was sequenced, starting with the national referral hospital, provincial hospitals, district hospitals, and the community health centres, respectively. As before, no fee was charged for services offered at the dispensaries. In addition, the segment of the population exempted from the fees had been expanded to include civil servants, the military and the unemployed (Owino and Were, 1998). The new (revised) reform was accompanied by other changes, notably the decentralisation of management.

The successful implementation of the revised policy, compared to the initial attempt, can be attributed to consultation and consensus-building among stakeholders (e.g. senior medical and administrative staff); gradual and sequential implementation, which quickly became successful at the higher level, facilitating implementation at lower levels and enhancing acceptance; and the relatively stronger institutional framework put in place. The broad range of automatic exemptions to compensate the real and perceived 'losers' were also helpful in gaining political and public acceptance of the user-fees, although the revenue forgone was high. Hence after achieving acceptance, the exemptions for civil servants and children aged between 6 and 15 years were removed, since there was no clear public health benefit (Collins et al., 1996).

We can, thus, infer from the cost-sharing experience that successful implementation is achieved when there is consensus-building, when the process is gradual and sequential and the necessary institutional capacity is developed. However, the nature of the reform in question and how widely it affects the economy should also be taken into consideration.

4.1.5   Government–donor community relationship, 1991–6

The 1990s were characterised by a stop-go relationship with donors,[18] leading to aid embargoes and intense pressure from donor agencies to undertake reforms. For instance, quick disbursements were suspended in 1991 due to what was described as rising levels of corruption, failure to correct macroeconomic imbalances caused by fiscal indiscipline, slow reforms in the civil service, lapses in the privatisation of public enterprises, and a slow pace of political reforms. After the IMF suspended quick-disbursing funds, other donor agencies, such as the World Bank and the IDA, followed suit.

By then the instability in the macroeconomic framework was becoming apparent. To help restore economic stability, a shadow programme was agreed upon between the government and the IMF in April 1992. However, the government quickly veered off course – the IMF/IDA mission in 1992 and 1993 found evidence of significant violation of monetary targets due to abuse of the pre-shipment export financing scheme[19] and access of certain commercial banks to CBK overdraft and rediscount facilities, part of which had some links with the Goldenberg scandal. This created a strained relationship between the government and the donors.

Several expediency measures were undertaken after the aid was withheld. In an attempt to regain lost confidence, the president made changes, by replacing key government officers who were in office when the Goldenberg scandal started. In January 1993, Musalia Mudavadi replaced Professor George Saitoti as the Minister for Finance, while Micah Cheserem replaced Eric Kotut who resigned as governor of the CBK. The new officers gained goodwill from donors as reformists, and influenced a decision by the World Bank to call for a consultative group meeting to discuss Kenya's case in Paris in November 1993. They pushed through various reforms that were being sought by the IFIs, leading to the IMF's approval of some US$63 million credit under ESAF in December 1993, half of which was to be disbursed immediately.

After the IMF opened its doors, there was some goodwill from other donors, including bilateral ones, which often use the IMF and the World Bank as a benchmark for their own funding decisions. In February 1995, an IMF team arrived in Nairobi to open talks on new three-year ESAF worth US$200 million. But in September 1995, the IMF announced that talks with the government on the ESAF had effectively stalled because the IMF needed to convince itself that the government was vigorously prosecuting public officials and others implicated in the Goldenberg scam. It was proving difficult for the government to deal with the issue objectively, given the involvement of some members of the cabinet and the inner cabinet in the scandal.

In April 1996, the long-awaited ESAF was finally approved after the government reiterated its commitment to reform in the *Policy Framework Paper 1996–1998*. The broad objective was to bring in fiscal and public sector transparency. However, the bilateral donors were more concerned with the then forthcoming general elections, including the role of the electoral commission, the funding of parties, creating a level playing field for all parties and access to the media. Four months after the approval of ESAF, nothing seemed to move as scheduled. The IFIs expressed concern about the level of government borrowing from the CBK and noted that certain strategic targets set out in the *Policy Framework Paper* had not been achieved on schedule. Hence, the IMF decided to withhold the release of the second tranche of the approved ESAF until these conditions were satisfied.

Although the IFIs ensured a greater degree of reform implementation, they were overambitious in their reform agenda, given the prevailing conditions and institutional framework. At times they pushed the reform agenda too far and too fast, and the fact that the government yielded to their demands did not necessarily mean they were ready and willing to fulfil the conditionalities. They took for granted the institutional capacity and political will to implement reforms. Strict targets and schedules, including dictating what laws the parliament should pass and when, undermined consensus-building and local ownership of the reform process. If conditionalities are expected to overcome time inconsistency problems, in the Kenyan case, they did not. This is exemplified by the policy reversals and stop-go pattern in reform implementation.

4.2   Economic reforms: 1997–2001

Failure to make significant moves in fulfilling donor conditionality of good governance led to the suspension of ESAF in August 1997. By this time, emphasis in conditionalities was not merely on economic targets but also on implementation flaws and poor governance. There were concerns about widespread corruption and a poor human rights record as well as the politically instigated tribal and ethnic clashes witnessed in the run-up to the general elections in December 1997.

Consequently, much of the reform effort during this period was geared towards fulfilling conditionalities that led to the suspension of funding, particularly the lack of good governance (read corruption) issues. For instance, the president put together a team in July 1999, with technocrats mainly drawn from the private sector, to occupy key public office positions, including the head of civil service. Dubbed the 'dream team', the team was expected to spearhead reforms that would put the country back on the path to economic recovery and eliminate the rampant corruption in government. Although there were renewed efforts to stamp out corruption, these efforts were thwarted by senior political hardliners with entrenched power bases. Further efforts to stamp out corruption were hindered when the parliament rejected two bills in the fight against corruption – the Civil Service Code of Conduct Bill and the Anti-Corruption and Economic Crimes Bill. It was argued that the bills were purely donor-initiated and that the government was simply attempting to fulfil donor conditionalities. These developments cast doubt on the government's commitment to fighting corruption. It was apparent that either the 'kitchen cabinet' was reasserting itself or the hiring of technocrats was a mere smokescreen to hoodwink donors into releasing withheld funds. That notwithstanding, the period saw progress in the implementation of some economic reforms, particularly the public sector reforms that had lagged behind.

4.2.1   Public sector reforms

The second phase of the civil service reform was relaunched in 1998, largely driven by the government's needs for new funding from donors, and the

IFIs' pressure for a leaner and efficient government. The target was to reduce the civil service by 30 per cent and a target of 32 000 staff was agreed upon. Within a short while, committees were set up in ministries to decide who was to leave, especially at the lower levels. Although there were criteria to be followed, these were never circulated to the civil servants. This left civil servants guessing who was to leave next, thus creating anxiety and suspicion among officers. However, the right-sizing was halted by parliament before the target was achieved. As expected, it was argued that there was not enough consultation about the policy, which was seen as having been implemented as a directive from donors. The parliament argued that a Sessional Paper should have been prepared before implementing the policy and lobbied to stop the process. Again, rushed implementation without adequate consultation in the designing of the reform and consensus-building among key stakeholders affected its successful implementation. Compared with the first phase, it was far more difficult to implement reforms in the second phase, due primarily to diminishing authoritarian advantage and increasing demands for public consultation and consensus.

In September 1999, the president announced ministerial changes, which saw the number of ministries reduced from twenty-seven to fifteen. This was viewed as phase two of the much touted recovery strategy after the appointment of the technocrats into senior civil service positions. But this was just a change in portfolio as none of the ministers or assistant ministers was dismissed. Instead, they ended up sharing a ministry, thus defeating the purpose of the reform. That was not surprising given that the power base of the president was vested in offering posts to regional power brokers who could deliver him the support of their ethnic constituencies.

With the newly appointed head of the civil service, it was expected that the process of cutting back the civil service would resume. However, the reform suffered another setback when the sacking of 25 783 civil servants was halted, after they sued the government, accusing it of contravening the Employment Act by terminating employment contracts without adequate notice. The matter was complicated by the fact that many civil servants had still not received their redundancy packages which, it was felt, were not even adequate. At least 19 000 civil servants had received retirement letters after the programme was resumed in September 2000.

Fiscal reforms continued in early 2000 with the rationalisation of the budget process. A major component of the reform was the adoption of the Medium Term Expenditure Framework to budgeting, which replaced the previous forward-rolling budgeting system. The aim was to move revenue and expenditure more closely into balance and achieve fiscal discipline. The stock of pending bills, which stood at Kshs. 2227 million as of 30 June 1991, had significantly increased to Kshs. 10 976 million by the end of June 1999 – an increase of about 392 per cent (Kirira, 2002). Pending bills were one of the loopholes for fiscal indiscipline. Projects and programmes were initiated without taking into consideration their financial implications and at times without seeking parliamentary approval, which is constitutionally illegal (Kirira, 2002). The new budgeting approach was to be directly linked to the priorities contained in the *Poverty Reduction Strategy Paper*. However, with no specific targets and sanctions and incentives where necessary, fiscal discipline remained elusive. This was exacerbated by weak institutional structures. For example, although budget execution is a prerogative of parliament, mechanisms to control discretionary spending within the executive remain weak. Only the office of the president can discipline the permanent secretaries, who also act as accounting officers in their respective ministries (Kirira, 2002). Moreover, the high turnover of permanent secretaries to the treasury intimidated holders of this office, who were also delegated with financial control and management, thus undermining their authority and firmness on financial matters and expenditure management. Additionally, the high turnover of ministers, particularly in the Ministry of Finance, at times disrupted the reform process.

More importantly, the government kept on dragging its feet in regard to parastatal reforms. By the end of 1998, the government had sold shares in only twenty-five enterprises in which it had direct ownership out of the total of 165 (Anyang' Nyong'o 2000: 131). Privatisation proceeded without a privatisation law, thus leaving gaping holes for manipulation.[20] Moreover, the government avoided privatising some of the parastatals that caused a major drain on the budget, thus bringing to the fore the question of whether the objectives of parastatal reforms have all been met. During the 1999/2000 fiscal year, a number of state-owned corporations that were to be restructured and privatised were not privatised as planned. Strategic reasons aside, there was the fear that privatising some of the parastatals would jeopardise the business interests of politically connected individuals and close avenues for rent-seeking and patronage.

4.2.2 Financial sector reforms

In the financial sector, the aftermath of unsecured loans and 'political banks' continued to be felt. Further instability was experienced when five banks were put under statutory management by the CBK in 1998, after failing to meet their financial obligations. The bank failures were attributed to high non-performing loans due to poor lending practices, conflict of interest, loans to non-viable projects, insider lending to directors, and undercapitalisation. Some banks, such as the state-owned National Bank of Kenya, had a huge amount of non-performing loans. To arrest the waning confidence in the banking sector, the CBK was given increased power to censure commercial banks that failed to comply. Penalties for non-compliance were also raised. There was an increased capital base requirement together with strict enforcement of capital/lending ratios. Financial institutions were expected to publicly display or publish their audited accounts promptly.

Some financial stability was witnessed in 1999. Three out of the five banks under statutory management were restructured and reopened. During the 2000/1 period, measures that were undertaken included amendment of the Banking Act to restrict insider lending and enforcement of banking laws, especially with regard to lending and provisioning for non-performing loans. That notwithstanding, the experience with the banking crises and high interest rates attest to the fact that something was not right in the reform process. Financial market liberalisation is based on the belief that competition among banks will lead to lower interest rates. But that has not been the case. Pill and Pradhan (1997) observe that the success of financial liberalisation depends on the appropriateness of macroeconomic policy, institutional development and structural reforms. Leite (1993) adds that strong banking regulatory and supervisory policies ensure the viability and health of the industry and enhance effectiveness of interest rate liberalisation. The hurried financial market liberalisation saw a situation where the amendments to the banking legislation and the tight regulatory and supervision policies were being put in place long after the implementation of the reform. Moreover, successful interest rate liberalisation also calls for fiscal discipline, which was not apparent in Kenya.

4.2.3   Government–donor community relationships, 1997–2001

Donor dissatisfaction with the reform particularly vis-à-vis corruption persisted. The IMF team visiting the country in March and July 1999 was still dissatisfied with governance reforms and, therefore, deferred any decision about re-establishing the ESAF. This came as a bitter blow to the government, which had already factored donor support into the budget. It was then that President Moi, in his usual tactful style, made a swift move and appointed the 'dream team'. By this time, poverty had become widespread while the economy was in the doldrums. In fact, it was in the year 2000 when the economy recorded a record negative real GDP growth rate of −0.3 per cent in Kenya's economic history.

The IMF set tough conditions when it finally agreed to lend to Kenya some US$198 million credit under the Poverty Reduction and Growth Facility, which had replaced the EASF. As often happens, the agreement with the IMF opened up the door for funds from other donors such as the World Bank, the African Development Bank, the European Union, the United Kingdom and Japan. But the relationship between the government and the IFIs went sour again at the beginning of 2001. The IMF's major areas of concern included the stalled privatisation bill and the failure of parliament to enact the pending Civil Service Code of Ethics and Economic Crimes Bill. Consequently, in March 2001, the IMF decided to withhold lending to Kenya again, citing insufficient progress in the proposed reforms; and as before, there was a heightened activity on the part of the Kenyan government in terms of reform implementation.

In general, the donor–government relationship depicts a carrot-and-stick approach to the reform process. It is this that largely ensured that major reforms were implemented. That notwithstanding, this approach raises issues of ownership of reforms, since reforms became a donor agenda and could be hurriedly implemented in a bid to appease donors to release funding. As it turned out, this often left little or no room for consultation with the relevant stakeholders in the design and implementation of reforms. Although donors eventually managed to push their agenda through, there are cases when such a move led to unexpected outcomes or was met with stiff domestic resistance especially on sensitive reform issues like civil service reform or where the proposed reforms threatened rent-seeking and other political interests of the ruling elite. Ryan (2004) points out that conditionalities or reforms agreed upon with an external funding body may not necessarily be seen as policies, and sometimes continuing with the status quo is in itself a policy decision.

The fact that implementation of reforms was reactive rather than proactive not only undermined local ownership but also affected sustainability of reforms. There has been a lack of a clear long-term vision as IFIs have preoccupied themselves with setting and resetting short-term targets, which the government strives to achieve if only to access funding. The problem is that, as Stiglitz (2002) contends, many of the reform policies became ends in themselves rather than means towards a more equitable and sustainable growth.

5   Economic outcomes of Kenya's reform

Economic reforms are often undertaken with the aim of promoting high growth and improved welfare in the long run. For instance, trade liberalisation measures are undertaken on the assumption that they will eventually improve exports and economic growth (Mwega, 1999). Following liberalisation of the foreign exchange in 1993, there was an immediate positive response in terms of imports and exports. In particular, the export response seems to have been combined with a price effect due to a steep devaluation of the Kenyan shilling in 1993. In total, the effect was a rise in export earnings, from about 13 per cent of GDP in 1992 to over 20 per cent between 1993 and 1996.

However, in general, export growth has been highly erratic, based on fluctuations in earnings from a few traditional primary commodity exports and the tourism sector. While certain non-traditional exports such as horticultural products have experienced rapid growth in the last few decades, manufactured goods account for only a small proportion of total exports. Kenya's trade share (value of imports plus exports in GDP), which is commonly used as a measure of openness, shows no clear trend but has been over 50 per cent since the 1970s, reaching a peak in the first half of the 1990s, following liberalisation of the foreign exchange market. The value of exports of goods and services as a percentage of GDP has been below 30 per cent except for a few years, particularly in 1993 following the steep depreciation of the shilling.

In general, the real GDP growth rate has been highly erratic, but it depicts a declining trend over time (Figure 1.3 and Table 1.1). Growth performance

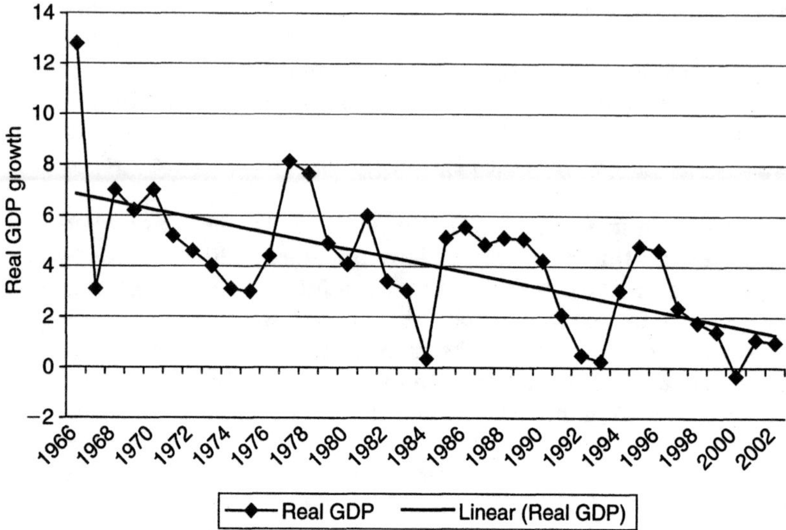

Figure 1.3   Trend in real GDP growth, 1966–2002

has remained depressive in the 1990s and into the new millennium, with a declining growth in volume of investments (both private and public) and exports. The value of total investment to GDP ratio has remained below 25 per cent while total savings as a proportion of GDP has been about 11 per cent. Given the population growth rates of about 2 per cent per annum in recent decades, it is evident that real per capita income has been on the decline since the mid-1990s. This partly accounts for the declining wage employment in the formal sector, leading to a surge in informal employment. Poverty remains widespread; by 2000, an estimated 56 per cent of the Kenyan population lived below the poverty line (Mwabu et al., 2002). Although Kenya has the potential to spearhead economic development in the region, the challenges that lie ahead cannot be overemphasised.

6   'Winners' and 'losers' of Kenya's SAPs

Although its ultimate goal is a better-off society, reform has distributive consequences, resulting in 'winners' and 'losers' in the process (Fidrmuc and Noury, 2003). However, given the multiplicity and dynamism of reform, it is not that easy to identify winners and losers precisely. Moreover, reform might benefit one sector while hurting another. One of the most affected sectors following trade liberalisation was the local textile industry, which collapsed due to cheap imports. The resultant unemployment affected a wide range of people given the backward and forward linkages in the textile industry. But this created an opportunity for small-scale traders who proliferated in the industry with the sale of imported second-hand clothes. The net employment benefits are hard to discern, but arguably the poor and low-income earners benefited to the extent that they could easily access cheaper imported second-hand clothes and other domestic products. In general, as with the case of many of the countries profiled in this book (notably in the cases of Uganda and Ghana), the beneficiaries of economic liberalisation were largely the capitalists, traders, firms and exporters that were able to compete domestically and internationally. Others, like manufacturing firms, benefited to the extent that they could easily and cheaply access imported capital and intermediate goods, but they had to contend with competition from cheap imports. Trade liberalisation also opened avenues for non-traditional agricultural exports such as horticulture. On the losing front were small-scale farmers who lacked credit, particularly after the removal of subsidies, and those who lacked the technological skills to access world markets. To the extent that the protective trade regime provided avenues for rent-seeking, losers also included individuals who benefited from the system by rent-seeking.

In the financial sector, there has been a concentration of banks in the urban areas, which target upper and middle-income earners, thus shutting out the majority of the rural population as well as low-income earners and the working poor in urban areas. Additionally, the lending rates have been overly high, thereby denying potential borrowers access to credit facilities. Reforms in other sectors such as health, education and the civil service disproportionately affected the poor and the vulnerable groups – again, this finding seems to surface in nearly all the other case studies in this book. With the introduction of user-fees in public institutions, most poor families have also been unable to give their children better healthcare and basic education. Thanks to the programme of free primary education under President Kibaki's new government, there has been a surge in primary school enrolment. The victims of retrenchment programmes were mainly employees in the lower cadres in the civil service, who, given the small compensation package and massive unemployment exacerbated by poor economic performance, often joined the pool of the poor. Overall, it can be argued that distributional consequences of reforms deepened the asymmetries in incomes and access to resources.

7   Conclusion

Kenya's path to reforms was largely driven by both external pressure from donors, particularly the IFIs, and domestic economic factors. However, the IFIs set the pace and the agenda for most of the reform programmes that sought to rectify the situation. Initially, the government was not willing to dismantle the protective economic regime, which was also attractive for rent-seeking opportunities and political patronage. However, continued borrowing from abroad was predicated on undertaking certain reforms in the form of conditionalities within the framework of the Washington Consensus.

That notwithstanding, it was not until the 1990s that comprehensive reforms were implemented. Even then, the nation's development partners had to exert a lot of pressure, adopting a carrot-and-stick approach to ensure reform implementation. Stringent conditions leading to suspension of funding kept the government on its toes. Reforms were sometimes undertaken simply to hoodwink donors. Donor conditionalities were broadened to include political democracy and good governance besides the traditional economic policies. Thus, the reform period also coincided with political reforms, major components of which were a change to multipartyism and agitation for constitutional reform. Besides the donors, civil society and religious groups played a critical role, particularly in pushing for political reforms.

Weak commitment to the reform process strained the relationship between the donors and the government, leading to a stop-go pattern in lending and reform implementation. Although the government often outlined policy reforms in various policy documents, the implementation process was often characterised by delays, lack of commitment and policy reversals or backtracking. Weak commitment was rooted in the political structure that was not supportive of either political or economic reforms, especially because of the vested interest groups, which feared losing their political patronage and power bases. For example, it was difficult to reduce the size of the public sector since public institutions had become conduits of patronage.

Evidently, the reform process in Kenya was reactive rather than proactive. As a result, there was weak ownership of reforms. Moreover, there was no specific attempt to coordinate and prioritise reform programmes. Thus, the reform agenda failed to spell out a clear long-term path. The IFIs themselves also lacked a clear focus, as they preoccupied themselves with short-term targets and failed to view the reform in a holistic manner. They also took institutional capacity and political constraints for granted.

Policy reversals and uncertainty about the reform can be attributed to lack of a clear analysis of the reform impact, poor preparation, and limited consultation in the design and implementation, as reforms were often hastily implemented due to donor pressure. It is thus not surprising that issues of timing and sequencing were often not taken into consideration. This was made worse by the closed decision-making system. In some cases, the reversals were made as a way of minimising the short-run cost of the reforms or inherent political uncertainty. That notwithstanding, the government managed to implement several reforms such as trade liberalisation. Some reforms, however, were more sensitive and difficult to implement, especially those with immediate welfare implications on the wider population, such as cost-sharing in the health sector, liberalisation of basic commodities like cereals, and downsizing of the civil service. These were associated with high political uncertainty given that the majority of the losers were bound to be ordinary citizens, who also form the majority of voters. Thus, even though they were eventually implemented, there were delays and reversals. In the financial sector, sequencing problems and political interference affected the successful implementation of the reforms, with the aftermath being a high interest rate structure.

Despite undertaking the market-oriented reforms, results show marginal gains in terms of economic growth and investment. Economic growth has been dismal, especially in the 1990s. Poverty worsened, having been estimated to be 56 per cent by 2000. Overall, the reforms disproportionately affected the poor and other vulnerable groups – e.g. employees in lower cadres in the civil service and mothers and children in the case of the health sector.

Notes

1. We are indebted to Linet Oyugi and Joseph Wambua for their excellent research assistantship. We would also like to thank Christopher Wambua, Professor Terry Ryan, Njeru Kirira, Solomon Kitunga and Dr Kang'ethe Gitu for their critical comments on earlier drafts. We acknowledge the Global Development Network for their financial support. Errors and omissions are all ours.
2. We focus on the market-oriented reforms. For details on definition and measurement of market-oriented reforms, see Loayza and Soto, 2003.
3. For more on the analytical narrative approach, see Bates et al., 1998, 2000.
4. For more on political institutions and reforms, see Rius and van de Walle, 2003; Liew et al., 2003; Haggard and Webb, 1993.
5. In this chapter, IFIs refer to the IMF and World Bank.
6. ESAF replaced the Structural Adjustment Facility.
7. There were over ninety monitorable conditions in the second SAL.
8. Despite the fact that the policy of user-charges had been agreed upon in the Sessional Paper No. 1 of 1986, its implementation was avoided until it was incorporated in the World Bank policy matrices so that the World Bank could be seen as the 'culprit'.
9. To date, the constitutional debate still rages on.
10. The pre-shipment export finance scheme was a soft loan that was extended by the CBK in the early 1990s to exporters through their commercial banks.
11. The famous Goldenberg scandal arose when the government acceded to a request to pay additional export compensation to a company that claimed that it would buy and export gold and ostensibly assist with the foreign exchange and BOP problems that the country was experiencing due to donor aid freeze. Interestingly, the company was granted monopoly rights on 35 per cent export compensation, which was over and above the regular 20 per cent that was in operation by then. When the National Rainbow Coalition party took over from KANU in December 2002, a Judicial Commission of Inquiry was set up by President Mwai Kibaki to investigate irregular payment of billions of Kenyan shillings to Goldenberg International Limited and associated companies in the early 1990s, and whether any gold and diamond jewellery was actually exported and export remittances made to the CBK.
12. Those who have access to the president have power and thus those who have access to those have access to the president have indirect power.
13. *Sunday Nation*, 29 March 1998.
14. Part of the money was linked to the Goldenberg scam, perhaps in exchange for favours that the company enjoyed.

15. In early April 1993, Exchange Bank, which was linked to Goldenberg International, received Kshs 23.9 billion from CBK and four other political banks in a four-day period. These included Kshs 13.5 billion (US$210 million) from CBK.
16. For the purpose of this chapter, public sector reforms include civil service and parastatal reforms.
17. This section focuses on the health sector reform.
18. It is worth noting that the term 'donors' as a generalisation is misleading since the bulk of the money is on a loan basis, even if on concessionary terms.
19. After much abuse, commercial banks were advised not to enter into new commitments under the facility in March 1993.
20. There has been a privatisation bill which is yet to be turned into law.

References

Anyang' Nyong'o, P. (1989) 'State and Society in Kenya: the Disintegration of the National Coalitions and the Rise of Presidential Authoritarianism', *African Affairs*, 88, 351.

Anyang' Nyong'o, P. (ed.) (2000) *The Context of Privatization in Kenya* (Nairobi: African Academy of Sciences).

Bates, R., Greif, A., Levi, M. and Rosenthal, J. L. (1998) *Analytical Narratives* (Princeton, N. J: Princeton University Press).

Bates, R., Greif, A., Levi, M., Rosenthal, J.-L. and Weingast, B. (2000) 'Analytical Narratives Revisited', *Social Science History*, 24, 4: 685–96.

Collins, D., Quick, J. D., Musau, S. N., Kraushaar, D. and Hussein, I. M. (1996) 'The Fall and Rise of Cost Sharing in Kenya: Impact of Phased Implementation', *Health Policy and Planning*, 11, 1: 52–63.

Fanelli, J. M. (2003) 'Understanding Reform: a Global GDN Research Project', a paper prepared for the GDN Workshop on Understanding Reform, Cairo, 16–17 January.

Fidrmuc, J. and Noury, A. G. (2003) 'Interest Groups, Stakeholders, and the Distribution of Benefits and Costs of Reform', a paper presented at the GDN Workshop on Understanding Reform, Cairo, 16–17 January.

Gacheru, W. and Shaw, R. (1998) *Our Problems, Our Solutions: an Economic and Public Policy Agenda for Kenya* (Nairobi: Institute of Economic Affairs).

Grindle, M. and Thomas, J. W. (1990) 'After the Decision: Implementing Policy Reform in Developing Countries', *World Development*, 18, 8: 1163–81.

Haggard, S. and Webb, S. B. (1993) 'What Do We Know about the Political Economy of Economic Policy Reform?' *World Bank Research Observer*, 8, 2: 143–68.

Hyden, G. (1995) 'Party, State and Civil Society: Control versus Openness', in J. D. Barkan (ed.), *Beyond Capitalism vs. Socialism in Kenya and Tanzania* (Nairobi: East African Educational Publishers Limited).

Ikiara, G. K. (2000) 'A Review of Kenya's Public Sector', in P. A. Nyong'o (ed.), *The Context of Privatization in Kenya* (Nairobi: African Academy of Sciences).

Kahler, M. (1992) 'External Influence, Conditionality, and the Politics of Adjustment', in S. Haggard and R. R. Kaufman (eds), *The Politics of Economic Adjustment: International Constraints, Distributive Politics and the State* (Princeton: Princeton University Press).

Kenya Association of Manufacturers (KAM) (1988) *Price Controls: Experiences and Opportunities in Kenya's Manufacturing* (Nairobi: English Press).

Kirira, N. (2002) 'Report on Domestic Debt Study 1990–2000', a report prepared for the World Bank, Nairobi.

Leite, S. P. (1993) 'Coordinating Public Debt and Monetary Management', *Finance and Development*, March: 30–3.

Liew, L. H., Bruszt, L. and He, L. (2003) 'Causes, National Costs and Timing of Reforms', a revised version of the paper prepared for the Global Development Network Workshop on Understanding Reform, Cairo, 16–17 January.

Loayza, N. V. and Soto, R. (2003) 'On the Measurement of Market-Oriented Reforms', a paper presented at the GDN Workshop on Understanding Reform, Cairo, 16–17 January.

Mwabu, G. (1995) 'Health Care Reform in Kenya: a Review of the Process', in P. Berman (ed.), *Health Sector Reform in Developing Countries: Making Health Development Sustainable*, Department of Population and International Health: Harvard School of Public Health (Boston: Harvard University Press).

Mwabu, G., Kimenyi, M. S., Kimalu, P., Nafula, N. and Manda, D. K. (2002) 'Predicting Household Poverty: a Methodological Note with a Kenyan Example', KIPPRA Discussion Paper Series (Nairobi: KIPPRA).

Mwega, F. (1999) 'Trade Liberalization, Credibility and Impacts: a Case Study of Kenya, 1972–94', in A. Oyejide, B. Ndulu and J. W. Gunning (eds), *Regional Integration and Trade Liberalization in Sub-Saharan Africa*, Vol. 2: *Country Case Studies* (London: Macmillan Press).

O'Brien, F. S. and Ryan, T. C. I. (2001) 'Mixed Reformers: Kenya', in S. Devarajan, D. R. Dollar and T. Holmgren (eds), *Aid and Reform in Africa: Lessons from Ten Case Studies* (Washington D.C: World Bank).

Odhiambo-Mbai, C. (1998) 'The Nature of Public Policy-Making in Kenya: 1963–1996', in N. Ng'ethe and W. Owino (eds), *From Sessional Paper No. 10 to Structural Adjustments: Towards Indigenizing the Policy Debate* (Nairobi: Institute of Policy Analysis and Research).

Okoth-Ogendo, H. W. O. (1972) 'The Politics of Constitutional Change in Kenya since Independence 1963–1969', *African Affairs*, 71, 282.

Owino, W. and Were, M. (1998) 'Enhancing Health Care among the Vulnerable Groups: the Question of Waivers and Exemptions', IPAR Discussion Paper Series. DP No. 014/98 (Nairobi: Institute of Policy Analysis and Research).

Oyugi, W. O. (1994) 'The Uneasy Alliance: Party–State Relations in Kenya', in W. O. Oyugi (ed.), *Politics and Administration in East Africa* (Nairobi: East African Educational Publishers).

Pill, H. and Pradhan, M. (1997) 'Financial Liberalization in Africa and Asia', *Finance and Development*, 34, 2: 7–10.

Republic of Kenya (1965) *Sessional Paper No. 10 of 1965 on African Socialism and its Application to Planning in Kenya* (Nairobi: Government Printer).

Republic of Kenya (1980) *Sessional Paper No. 4 of 1980: Economic Prospects and Policies* (Nairobi: Government Printer).

Republic of Kenya (1986) *Sessional Paper No. 1 of 1986 on Economic Management for Renewed Growth* (Nairobi: Government Printer).

Republic of Kenya (1996) 'Economic Reforms for 1996–1998: the Policy Framework Paper', prepared by the government of Kenya in collaboration with the IMF and the World Bank.

Republic of Kenya (1998) 'Policy Paper on Public Enterprise Reform and Privatization' (Nairobi: Ministry of Finance).

Republic of Kenya (2001) *Poverty Reduction Strategy Paper for the Period 2001–2004* (Nairobi: Government Printer).

Ruis, A. and van de Walle, N. (2003) 'Political Institutions and Economic Policy Reform', a paper presented at the GDN Workshop on Understanding Reform, Cairo, 16–17 January.

Ryan, T. C. I. (1998) 'The Experiences of the Kenya Government Working with the World Bank and the IMF since Independence', a paper presented to KAAD Association of Scholars in East Africa, Nairobi.

Ryan, T. C. I. (2004) 'Kenya: Policy Research and Policy Reform', in P. C. Lucie and D. Seck (eds), *Fixing African Economies* (Colorado: Lynne Rienner).

Stallings, B. (1992) 'International Influence on Economic Policy: Debt, Stabilization and Structural Reform', in S. Haggard and R. R. Kaufman (eds), *The Politics of Economic Adjustment: International Constraints, Distributive Politics and the State* (Princeton: Princeton University Press).

Stiglitz, J. (1999) 'Whither Reforms? Ten Years of the Transition', a paper prepared for the Annual Bank Conference on Development Economics, Washington, D.C., 28–30 April.

Stiglitz, J. (2002) *Globalization and its Discontents* (Harmondsworth: Penguin Books).

Swamy, G. (1994) 'Kenya: Patchy, Intermittent Commitment', in I. Husain and R. Faruqee (eds), *Adjustment in Africa: Lessons from Country Case Studies* (Washington, D.C.: World Bank).

Tamarin, M. (1978) 'The Roots of Political Stability in Kenya', *African Affairs*, 78, 308.

Throup, D. and Hornsby, C. (1998) *Multi-Party Politics in Kenya* (Oxford: James Currey).

Wagacha, M. (2000) 'Analysis of Liberalization of the Trade and Exchange Regime in Kenya since 1980', IPAR Discussion Paper Series: DP No. 023/2000 (Nairobi: Institute of Policy Analysis and Research).

Were, M., Geda, A., Karingi, S. N. and Ndung'u, N. S. (2001) 'Kenya's Exchange Rate Movement in a Liberalized Environment: an Empirical Analysis', KIPPRA Discussion Paper No. 10 (Nairobi: KIPPRA).

Were, M., Alemayehu, G., Ndung'u, N. S. and Karingi, S. N. (2002) 'Analysis of Kenya's Export Performance: an Empirical Evaluation', KIPPRA Discussion Paper Series, DP No. 22 (Nairobi: KIPPRA).

2
Understanding Economic and Institutional Reforms in Uganda[1]

Julius Kiiza, Godfrey Asiimwe and David Kibikyo

1 Introduction

Over the last two decades, several countries in Africa have implemented pro-market reforms, ranging from the Structural Adjustment Programmes (SAPs) of the 1980s to the institutional and pro-poor reforms of the 1990s and beyond. The dominant view in the literature is that extensive reformers (such as Ghana and Uganda) have reaped more growth and poverty reduction dividends than reluctant reformers (e.g. Zambia) and non-reformers such as Ethiopia (Devarajan et al., 2001). Critics have, however, urged caution. Mkandawire and Soludo (1999: xi), for example, argue that 'SAPs have not worked and . . . as designed, they are grossly defective as a policy package for addressing the endemic poverty and pervasive underdevelopment of the [African] region'. Stein and Nissanke (1999) concur. According to them, 'accumulated evidence generally points to the weak link between adjustment and performance in Africa' (1999: 399). Even the Bretton Woods institutions have shifted from the 'get-the-prices-right' dictum of the era of structural adjustment to a new regime of 'good' institutions (World Bank, 2001).

The problem, critics contend, is that 'good' institutions are defined narrowly to mean liberal democracy, private property rights and other Western institutions (read 'best-practices' institutions). According to Chang (forthcoming, 2007), ' "orthodox economists" do not use available evidence to concede that "orthodox" policies are flawed. Rather, they use institutions to "explain" why "good" policies based on "correct" economic theories have consistently failed'. Thus, '[b]y talking about deficient institutions, [mainstream economists] argue that their policies and theories were never wrong, and did not work *only because* the countries that implemented them did not have the right institutions for the "right" policies to work' (Chang, forthcoming, 2007).

It is the purpose of this chapter to examine the economic reform in Uganda, a former British 'protectorate' with a current population of about 26 million people. A substantial proportion of Ugandans (85 per cent) live in rural areas, primarily as peasant farmers using poor production technologies. The economy is predominantly agricultural, which constitutes 43 per cent of GDP, compared to only about 38 per cent and 19 per cent for the services sector and industry respectively (Uganda, 2005). This chapter seeks to explain why Uganda (which is a largely agrarian economy with a substantial non-market sector) embarked on reform; what reforms have been implemented; and how well they performed. It will be noted that Uganda has implemented extensive and intensive macro-stabilisation policies, backed by institutional and pro-poor reforms, not all of which can be accorded detailed analytical space here. What this chapter does is to focus on the SAPs, which represent the first-generation reforms, public sector reforms (representing governance-related reforms), and the Poverty Eradication Action Plan (PEAP), which attempts to operationalise what Cornia et al. (1987) call *adjustment with a human face*.

2   Analytical framework and methodology

This study adopts an institutional political economy approach. The problem with this approach is the absence of a clear definition of institutions, notwithstanding the burgeoning literature on the subject. In his Nobel Prize lecture, Douglas North (1994: 360) defined institutions as 'the rules of the game: the humanly devised constraints that structure human interaction'. According to him, institutions 'are made up of formal constraints (such as rules, laws, constitutions), informal constraints (such as norms of behaviour, conventions, self imposed codes of conduct), and their enforcement characteristics' (North, 1994: 360). For Chang and Evans (2005): 'Institutions are systematic patterns of shared expectations, taken-for-granted assumptions, accepted norms and routines of interaction that have robust and durable effects on shaping the motivations and behaviour of sets of interconnected social actors.'

Neither of the two definitions is sufficiently specific to guide research. For the purposes of this study, the term 'institutions' refers to international financial institutions (IFIs), particularly the IMF and the World Bank, offices of political and bureaucratic elites in Uganda, local NGOs and other interest groups, that have played an important role in the design, implementation and/or review of reforms. We uphold the major conclusion of institutional political economy analyses that institutions affect economic performance in several important ways. The 'political economy' element in our approach seeks to rethink the link between states and markets; between governmental actors on the one hand and private firms, civil society and individuals on the other. We contend that IFIs, domestic political and bureaucratic elites, and organised interests (such as NGOs) have been important in shaping the content, breadth and depth of reform. They are, therefore, crucial for understanding why Uganda embarked on reform, what types of reform have been implemented and how well. The methodology of this study is predominantly qualitative. This is because we focus on unique political, institutional and economic events in Uganda. We also examine the role of different institutional and individual stakeholders in the reform's success or failure. These are complex context-specific issues calling for qualitative rather than quantitative research methods. Moreover, we gathered from the 'Understanding Reform' workshops in Cairo (2003) and Delhi (2004) that understanding reform calls for clear appreciation of the philosophy underpinning reform design, reform implementation, and the issue of winners and losers. Qualitative approaches are more suitable than quantitative methods in this case.

The study participants (representing the major institutional and individual stakeholders in the reform process) were purposively selected. They included: representatives of donor agencies based in Kampala (e.g. the World Bank); political and bureaucratic heads of key government departments; government bureaucrats in charge of government–donor relations; knowledgeable people from academia; and selected NGOs such as the Anti-Corruption Coalition, Uganda (ACCU) and the Uganda Debt Network, which 'monitors' government performance in the use of the Heavily Indebted Poor Countries (HIPCs) relief funds.

Different data collection techniques were used. Literature review (using the literature search guide as a tool) was an important source of information for this study. Additionally, we carried out critical documentary analysis, focusing on raw and semi-processed information from official reports and databases. We also carried out 'elite interviews' with officials of the institutions outlined above. Our 'elite' interviews used unstructured interview guides, which allowed for flexibility in the research process.

We tested three propositions, *not* hypotheses. Strictly speaking, hypotheses are tested empirically in quantitative studies while propositions are used in qualitative studies and are tested using argument and evidence. This study did the latter and tested the following propositions:

1. The reform package that was implemented in Uganda reflects the *preferences* of those who controlled the state at the time (elite politicians and bureaucrats).
2. Vested interests in developing countries tend to be inactive (or even apathetic) at the stage of reform design, but active at the point of reform implementation. This hypothesis explores the role of organised interests in resisting or supporting reform.
3. Reform ownership tends to change with the changing phases of reform. We sought to test whether or not 'scaling' of ownership is possible from the donor-driven SAPs through institutional reforms (moderate ownership) to PEAP reforms (full ownership).

For clarification, our research methodology, the type of data that was collected and our data sources are summarised in Table 2.1.

The information collected has been classified thematically as follows. First, a brief outline of the macroeconomic context and the chronology of reform

Table 2.1:   Methodological matrix

Research issue	Data types/indicators	Data sources	Data collection methods	Data analysis technique
Timing and content of first-generation reforms	Macroeconomic challenges of the time Political situation Constraints/ preferences of state officials	Libraries Databases of donor agencies MoFPED; MoTIT Elite bureaucrats Political elites	Literature search Documentary review Elite interviews In-depth interviews	Thematic analysis Content analysis
Timing of 'inputs' from organised interests	Modus operandi of reform: top-down or bottom-up? Degree of Inclusion? Strength of CSOs	Libraries Databases of donor agencies, govt depts, and CSOs e.g. ACCU	Literature search Documentary review In-depth interviews	Content analysis
Reform ownership	Role of conditionality vs. technical assistance Spaces for dialogue or consultation/ inclusion?	Libraries Databases of donor agencies MoFPED, etc.	Literature search Documentary review Elite interviews	Thematic analysis Content analysis

Notes:
ACCU: Anti-Corruption Coalition, Uganda
CSOs: Civil Society Organisations
MoFPED: Ministry of Finance, Planning and Economic Development[2]
MoTIT: Ministry of Trade, Industry and Tourism
UMA: Uganda Manufacturers' Association

is given. Particular attention is given to the initial conditions and the extent to which Uganda's point of departure shaped macroeconomic stabilisation, growth and poverty reduction initiatives. Next, we document the major economic and institutional reforms that have been implemented. An outline of the institutional political economy of reform follows, paying attention to the key individual and institutional players (e.g. political elites, bureaucratic elites and IFIs) who shaped the trend and pace of reform. The chapter attempts a more controversial task of assessing 'how well' Uganda implemented both economic and institutional reforms. A brief comment on the national capacity to design and implement reform follows. The chapter ends with a summary and conclusion section.

3 Context of reform

When Uganda obtained political independence from Britain in 1962, it was the 'pearl of Africa' with one of the most promising economies in the region.[3] Between 1963 and 1970, GDP (at 1966 prices) grew by 4.8 per cent a year, while population increased at an estimated rate of 2.6 per cent, implying an annual increase in per capita income of about 2 per cent. Uganda's domestic savings averaged 13 per cent, a level that 'permitted implementation of an ambitious investment program without undue pressure on domestic prices and the balance of payments' (World Bank, 1982: 3). In the 1960s, the terms of trade for Uganda's exports were favourable and export earnings were, by and large, sufficient to finance the country's imports. In the latter half of the 1960s, government revenue increased faster than recurrent expenditure, leading to a relatively healthy state of public finances. Revenue from taxation, together with non-bank domestic borrowing, helped finance a significant proportion of development outlays (World Bank, 1982: 3–4; Uganda, 1999). With the rise of Idi Amin to power in 1971, Uganda's rosy economic (and institutional) development indicators were reversed (Mensah, 2006). By the late 1970s, Uganda was experiencing a huge economic crisis, thanks to the bad policies, the economic mismanagement and institutional decay of the Amin dictatorship[4] (Mensah, 2006). According to Collier and Reinekka (2001), the country's GDP shrunk by 40 per cent between 1971 and 1985. It is in response to the development crisis that Uganda implemented macro-stabilisation, structural adjustment and institutional reforms.

3.1 Chronology of reforms

Uganda embarked on the first-generation reforms (economic stabilisation, economic openness, exchange rate liberalisation) in the early 1980s under the second regime of President Milton Obote II (1981–6) who had been previously overthrown by Idi Amin in 1971. The country graduated from the first-generation reforms in the early 1990s and embarked on massive institutional or governance-related reforms (privatisation, civil service reforms, decentralisation) under the regime of President Yoweri Museveni (1986–present). In the mid-1990s, Uganda pioneered the Poverty Eradication Action Plan (PEAP). This endeared the country, and Museveni's regime in particular, to the World Bank and the IMF – the key architects of similar initiatives called the Poverty Reduction Strategy Papers (PRSPs) (Rawden and Nyamugasira, 2002).

3.2 Breadth and speed of reform

Uganda has implemented broad, far-reaching reforms, ranging from macroeconomic stabilisation and adjustment measures to public institutional and pro-poor reforms. The macroeconomic reforms were implemented rapidly and without much consultation, thanks to the 'shock therapy' approach that was used. The institutional reforms were also broad, ranging from constitutional reforms and public institutional restructuring to 'right-sizing', retooling and computerisation in the public sector. Public sector reforms have also been deep – the deepest two being decentralisation of governmental authority to local units and privatisation. However, unlike the first-generation reforms, public management reforms had some degree of consultation (as will be elaborated later). The PEAP reforms have had the largest degree of local participation and country ownership. PEAP reforms have also covered broad areas – agricultural modernisation, universal primary education, primary healthcare, gender mainstreaming, and rural water and sanitation. All of these were designed to promote poverty reduction. Ironically, Uganda has implemented broad and deep economic, institutional, and pro-poor reforms *without* political liberalisation. This raises important questions about the quality of governance.[5]

3.3 Why reform, and from what to what?

Economists generally agree that 'path dependence' is a crucial feature of the growth process – that is, what eventually happens to an economy is largely associated with the concrete socioeconomic and institutional dynamics pertaining at the 'point of departure' (e.g. Mkandawire and Soludo, 1999: 1–20). It is also common wisdom that the reform rationale, the economics of implementation and the key stakeholders (the winners/supporters versus the losers/resisters of reform) cannot be clearly understood unless one understands the initial conditions of reform.

3.4 It takes a crisis

In Africa, the first stabilisation measures of the IMF and the adjustment programmes of the World Bank (which are collectively termed structural adjustment programmes – SAPs) started in the late 1970s and the early 1980s in the wake of the African economic crisis (for details, see Callaghy and Ravenhill, 1993: 1–2; World Bank, 1989). The crisis of Uganda was perhaps the prototype of the African crisis. The country's real GDP declined at an average rate of 3.8 per cent a year during 1973–9, in contrast with the positive growth rate of

4.8 per cent per year between 1963 and 1970. Between 1973 and 1979, inflation skyrocketed to over 40 per cent a year, compared with an average rate of 8.2 per cent during 1967–70 (Collier and Reinekka, 2001). Gross domestic investment declined from 12.7 per cent in 1963–70 to 8.6 per cent in 1971–8 and the national savings rate fell from 13.4 per cent to 7.7 per cent over the same period. Recurrent government revenues declined from 14.6 per cent of GDP in the 1960s to 9.9 per cent by 1978, while government expenditure changed marginally from 17.5 per cent to 15.5 per cent of GDP (Uganda, 1998: 3–4). The 'liberation' war of 1979 (which led to the overthrow of Amin) worsened matters. GDP declined by 9.7 per cent, with gross domestic investment falling to 6 per cent of GDP. In 1980, the manufacturing sector was producing at 60 per cent below its 1971 peak (Uganda, 1988).

The question of *why* Uganda embarked on reform should, therefore, be clear. The massive economic crises of the early 1980s left the country with no option but to reform. It has been argued elsewhere (Kiiza, 2002: ch. 5) that traditional debates on the merits or demerits of reform miss the most crucial point. In today's dynamic political economy, the choice between reform and 'non-reform' is out of the question. The issue is not *whether or not* countries need to adjust their economies. The real question is *how* and whose interests the reforms ultimately serve.

3.5   Goals of reform

The purpose of the first stabilisation and adjustment programmes was to bring about 'structural' changes to Uganda's economy, stimulate production in all sectors and ameliorate the impact of economic stagnation. The programmes also sought to substantially reduce hyperinflation and fight *magendo* – the parallel market transactions (Uganda, 1998: 5). With funding from the IMF/World Bank fraternity (who provided aid to Uganda to the tune of SDR 373.2 million for the fiscal year 1981/2–3/4), Uganda embarked on the first-generation reforms. These reforms had the following goals:

- realignment of the Uganda currency (the shilling) to its 'realistic' level (in the early 1980s, the term that was used was 'flotation' of the shilling);
- abolition of state controls on product and factor prices;
- Equalisation of sales tax on imported and locally produced goods;
- Payment of producer incentives. This involved payment of incrementally higher prices to export-crop producers (Mwenda, 2004).

The ultimate goal was to stimulate production in the export crop sector; reduce government deficits; overcome the balance of payments disequilibria; and restore growth. It is worth noting that while the Obote II government embraced pro-market reforms, there was little progress in deepening revenue collection. State capacity to generate revenue had shrunk to 5 per cent of

GDP (Chen et al., 2001). Budgetary discipline also deteriorated in 1984–5, leading to expansionary fiscal policy. The government accumulated expenditure arrears equivalent to 21 per cent of total expenditure commitments and then 'stepped up the issue of long-term bonds to finance the arrears' (Devarajan et al., 2001: 117). The monetary policy instruments of the time were ineffective in mopping up excess liquidity and this triggered inflationary pressures and rapid depreciation in the value of the shilling. The government imposed restrictions on the hitherto floating exchange system (Kasekende and Ssemwogere, 1994). This meant violation of the monetary benchmarks agreed with the IMF. The programme with the IMF 'died' in 1984, thereby opening the way for the second SAPs.

The dominant view in the MoFPED is that Obote's government had implementation failures arising from the limited number of 'right economists' (interviews, 2004). Some interviewees, however, suggested that the austerity measures of the first SAPs were imposed via a top-down approach with no consultation. They were, therefore, 'doomed to fail' (interviews, 2004). We tried to probe whether organised interests – parliament, NGOs or workers' unions – tried to block the reform. An official of the Uganda Debt Network (a local NGO) stated that while the reforms were autocratic, and while local ownership was initially not factored into the reform agenda, 'no organised interests are known to have resisted reform until the students and workers protests of 1989–1992'. This suggests that the economic crisis had stifled resistance to reform. Things had become so bad that reform (any reform) was seen to offer new hope of recovery from the prevailing crisis.[6]

4   Second phase of adjustment

The second phase of adjustment was operationalised under the Movement government of Yoweri Museveni (1986–present) who captured power after a guerrilla war (1981–6). When the Movement government came to power, the politics, the economy and all state institutions had virtually collapsed (Mwenda, 2004). Civil and political upheavals were the order of the day. The bureaucracy or civil service, which is the engine of modern governments, had not yet recovered from the decay, underpayment and demoralisation of Amin's time. More importantly, the economy was in bad shape. As Table 2.2 indicates, GDP growth rate declined from 11.7 per cent in 1982 to −1.5 per cent in 1986. Inflation averaged 135.6 per cent in 1986 and rose to 232.6 per cent by 1987. Virtually all other economic indicators (e.g. the balance of payments) had worsened. The crisis of the mid-1980s appears to have been the *raison d'être* for the second phase of reform. Yet the new government of Museveni could not embrace pro-market reforms, largely because Marxism was the official ideology of the Movement. To the ideologues of the Movement regime, pro-market reforms were instruments of Western 'imperialism' (NRM, 1987). Several 'bad' policies, such as foreign exchange controls, state

Table 2.2:   Uganda: selected economic indicators, 1980–2004 (with a projection for 2025)

Year	Pop. (million)	Pop. growth rate	GDP (million US$)	Per capita (US$)	GDP growth rate	Exports (million US$)	External debt (million US$)	Debt/ export ratio (%)
1980	12.30	2.3	2195	136	−5.2	415	568	212.3
1981	12.64	2.1	1724	146	7.5	331	733	262.4
1982	12.64	2.0	1596	144	11.7	274	794	232.2
1983	13.00	1.9	1746	147	9.6	347	938	265.3
1984	13.38	1.9	2194	161	−8.5	368	1020	269.3
1985	13.79	2.0	2628	187	−1.9	424	1031	305.3
1986	14.22	2.9	3507	226	−1.5	372	1171	367.1
1987	14.68	2.9	3893	261	3.8	410	1286	479.2
1988	15.16	2.9	4354	276	5.7	334	1659	610.0
1989	15.67	2.9	4899	280	6.1	266	1799	744.8
1990	16.21	2.9	4213	200	6.4	246	2663	1084.6
1991	16.77	3.1	3250	210	5.8	199	2857	1436.5
1992	16.60	3.3	2830	240	3.1	195	3023	1549.3
1993	16.90	2.9	3165	265	8.4	242	3131	1294.4
1994	17.10	2.8	3950	260	5.3	463	3370	1008.5
1995	18.20	2.6	4365	270	10.5	560	3573	638.0
1996	19.10	2.7	4719	285	8.1	639	3674	575.0
1997	19.60	2.8	4967	290	5.2	619	3712	599.7
1998	20.20	2.8	5240	296	5.5	496	3640	733.9
1999	22.00	2.5	6000	300	7.0	663	3613	520.0
2000	22.20	2.5	7770	350	6.2	677	3575	N/A
2001	23.00	2.5	8234	358	5.3	701	3786	N/A
2002	23.50	2.5	7520	320	6.3	774	4284	N/A
2003	25.00	3.4	6125	245	4.9	928	4310	N/A
2004	26.00	3.4	6500	250	5.8	1071	N/A	N/A
2025	37.00	1.7	33 300	900	7.0	N/A	N/A	<200

Sources: Adapted from: Uganda, 1999; Ministry of Finance Statistics, various issues; World Bank, various reports; Economist Intelligent Unit.
* The 2000 estimates are from the *Statistical Abstract*, 1998.
* The 1999 figures and the 2025 projections are computed from Uganda (1998/9); MoFPED, 2004.
N/A means data were not available at the time of research.

ownership of enterprises and price controls (on sugar and other essential products), were implemented. This state-guided development strategy alienated the new regime from IFIs (interviews, MoFPED, 2004). Government missions to 'friendly' socialist countries (such as Cuba) did not yield the funds needed for reconstruction and development. Yet Western authorities refused to extend credit to the new government unless it made 'friends' with the IMF.[7] This meant abolishing state controls, liberalising the economy, privatising state-owned enterprises, abolishing subsidies on education and health and, in a word, adopting SAPs.

Interviews with state officials suggest that the late 1980s were moments of crisis and inter-agency rivalry, particularly between the Ministry of Finance and that of Planning and Economic Development.[8] Most state officials covertly resisted reform (some for nationalistic reasons, others because they were beneficiaries of the status quo – e.g. SOEs). A small team of Western-trained economists, led by Tumusiime-Mutebile, advocated for reforms. Donors allied with these reformers to 'convince' President Museveni to accept reform using carrots (donor funds) and sticks (conditionality). In May 1987, the government embraced the IMF/World Bank reforms, and announced several policy measures, such as tight budgetary and monetary policies (aimed at controlling inflation and achieving macroeconomic stability) and the adoption of an Open General Licence for private sector imports (Sharer et al., 1995). That was the beginning of the Economic Recovery Programme (ERP) in Uganda.

The political economy realities under which conditionality was accepted call for modification of our first proposition. Acceptance of SAPs by government officials appears to have reflected less of their preferences and more of their constraints. Tumusiime-Mutebile, a long time Permanent Secretary of the Ministry of Finance, Planning and Economic Development, conceded that the reforms were initially driven by IMF/World Bank conditionality (Tumusiime-Mutebile, 1995). But he contends that once government resolved intra-agency contestations over the decision to adopt or reject adjustment, 'the government's reform programme swiftly overtook the reform agenda of the IFIs – e.g. the decisions to tackle the overvaluation of the exchange rate and the legislation of the forex bureau markets were internal government decisions and far exceeded the requirements of IFIs conditionality' (interview, 2004). His conclusion is informative: 'There is no reason why sound economic management should be driven, or even constrained, by the conditionalities attached to donor assistance' (Tumusiime-Mutebile, 1995).

This 'official' view is upheld by Tim Lamont, former member of a UNDP/IDA-funded advisory team. According to Lamont:

> Obviously the donors, particularly the IMF and the World Bank, had a large part to play in formulating the structural adjustment programme, and their credits do not come without conditionalities. The interesting point is whether such conditionalities were imposed against the will of the government, whether it was a cooperative process.
>
> (Lamont, 1995: 4)

In short, key state officials and (former) employees of donor agencies interpreted 'acceptance' of conditionality as 'borrower ownership' of reforms, a position that is questioned by civil society organisations.

4.1 Goals of the Economic Recovery Programme (ERP)

The ERP, which was supported by the Economic Recovery Credits (ERC), Structural Adjustment Credits (SAC) and the Enhanced Structural Adjustment Facility (ESAF), had the following goals:

- to achieve and maintain an economic growth rate of around 5 per cent per annum;
- reduce inflation by restoring fiscal and monetary discipline;
- reduce the balance of payments deficit;
- generate surplus foreign reserves in excess of at least four months of import expenditure;
- rehabilitate the major sectors of the economy (see Uganda, 1999: 6).

An assessment of how successful Uganda was in realising the goals of first-generation reforms will be given below.

5 Governance-related reforms

Alongside the SAP II reforms, Uganda embarked on governance-related reforms. It was realised in the late 1980s that however successful the macroeconomic reforms might be, they would not create big impacts unless complementary institutional reforms were carried out. Institutional reforms were deemed to be crucial for other reforms to take hold. This conclusion is associated with the World Bank Implementation Completion Report on Uganda's SAC I and II. The report concluded that 'the program's focus and internal coherence had improved government performance and the private sector environment' (cited in Holmgren et al., 2001: 146). However, there was unfinished business, calling for continued macro-stabilisation and BOP support, backed by micro-level sectoral and institutional reforms. Institutional reform and capacity building were seen to be particularly crucial for the success of other reforms. (This was corroborated with international research on the importance of 'good' institutions for development.) A key outcome of the institutional turn was a new era of *adjustment* plus *governance-related reforms*. Uganda implemented four types of governance-related reforms: denationalisation/privatisation; constitutional reform; reform of grassroots institutions; and public management reforms.

5.1 Reform of economic institutions

Denationalisation and privatisation were key elements of reforming economic institutions in Uganda. The denationalisation programme started in the early 1980s under the regime of Milton Obote II (1981–5). Obote's denationalisation policy took the form of returning to Indian entrepreneurs properties that had been confiscated by Amin's regime in 1972. When President Museveni came to power in 1986, he continued with denationalisation (after some foot-dragging).

By October 1993, some 3327 applications had been received and 2647 properties were returned to their previous owners (*New Vision*, 27 November 1993).

Two major political economy factors underpinned the decision to return properties to their previous owners. First, there had been no proper nationalisation in the first place. What happened under Amin's regime was *ethnisation* of confiscated properties. Amin simply allocated productive enterprises to his fellow Muslims and ethnic Nubians who lacked the business acumen to run the businesses. By the late 1970s, virtually all the enterprises had collapsed, thanks to poor management worsened by the economic embargo that was imposed on Amin's government. Secondly, donors put pressure on post-Amin governments to resolve the Asian properties issue. Arguably this would persuade the international community that Uganda was creating a conducive environment for private sector-led growth (which hopefully would attract foreign capital to Uganda). USAID (1991), for example, insisted that increased aid to Uganda was conditional on the 'equitable resolution of the Asian property question'.

In addition to resolving the Asian question, Museveni embarked on an ambitious privatisation programme. With donor funding and covert pressure, Uganda set up a Public Enterprise Reform and Divestiture Secretariat (PERDS) under the PERDS Statute of 1991. PERDS was essentially charged with the duty of implementing the privatisation programme. The claim was that the state was a bad business manager and that state involvement in the economy had stifled economic activity. The solution was to be found in kicking the state out of the economy and limiting government's economic role to the creation of an 'enabling' macro, legislative, and institutional environment for private sector-led growth.

5.2   Constitutional reform

One of the most important politico-institutional reforms of the NRM government was the review of the independence constitution of 1962. The constitutional review exercise started in 1989 with the appointment of the Constitutional Review Commission headed by Justice Benjamin Odoki. The rationale for constitutional reform was simple: Uganda's independence constitution was 'Made in England' along a foreign Westminster model. It was imposed upon Ugandans who had neither debated nor accepted it (Mugaju, 2000; Kabwegyere, 2000). The Odoki Commission was charged with making wide-ranging consultations and initiating a document that would be the basis for a home-grown national constitution. The Commission completed its work in July 1993. The election of Constituent Assembly members to discuss the Odoki Report and write a new constitution for the country took place in March 1993. The Assembly members were no ordinary parliamentarians. Unlike the MPs of Western liberal democracies, the Constituent Assembly members were elected via a bottom-up approach premised on Museveni's philosophy of popular participatory democracy. Second, the Assembly members were not political 'representatives'; they were delegates who were directly answerable to the grassroots voters, or so it was argued (Makara et al., 2003).[9] In reality, however, the 'delegates' to the Constituent Assembly danced to the tune of several caucuses: the pro-monarchy caucus, the pro-multiparty caucus, and the pro-Movement caucus (which was the most dominant, thanks to the power of incumbency of the Movement government). Indeed Article 269 of the new constitution legislated against all political parties, except the ruling NRM, which, as already hinted, claimed that it was not a political party but an all-inclusive movement supposedly embracing all shades of opinions.[10]

5.3   Grassroots institutions

The third major reform of the National Resistance Movement government was the overthrow of the village chief. The institution of the village chief (*Omutongole*) was created by British colonialism. Its major aim, according to Mamdani (1996), was to mediate colonial despotism through local rulers, who would serve as shock absorbers of the wrath of oppressed natives. But that is not the point. The point is that village chiefs were highly unaccountable. When Uganda obtained independence in 1962, the *Omutongole* institution remained intact. It continued to unleash terror onto the rural population. With the advent of the Movement regime in 1986, Local Councils (LCs) were established to replace the *Omutongole* institution. The Local Councils started in the countryside as institutions for the mobilisation and recruitment of members into the then guerrilla fighting forces of the National Resistance Movement, led by Yoweri Museveni. When Museveni came to power, the Councils were expanded to cover all parts of the country. The Councils were, by design, organs of popular participatory democracy – the very antithesis of the 'representative' model of Western liberal democracy, or so it was argued (NRM, 1987). Organisationally, the Local Councils run from the local village level through the parish and sub-county levels to the county and district levels. Each of Uganda's fifty-six districts is subsequently represented in the national legislature.[11]

What is important for this study is that the first- and second-generation reforms (which negatively impacted the rural and urban poor) were never debated by Local Councils. Notwithstanding the rhetoric that the people had been 'liberated' by the NRM and that they now had the right to determine public policies that impacted their private rights, SAP policies simply passed them by (Kabwegyere, 2000). This appears to have arisen from (a) the top-down approach that was adopted, thanks to the strong role of donor conditionality; and (b) the high level of illiteracy (58 per cent for males; 73 per cent for females). Matters were compounded by the fact that over 80 per cent of Ugandans live in rural areas (primarily as peasant farmers) and that civil society organisations are weak and incapable of shaping reform design and implementation. Civil society organisations in Uganda are weak largely because they have a narrow urban base and represent poorly paid teachers, doctors and other urban workers, most of whom do not even pay their membership fees. Societal weaknesses, by default, increased the scope of state elites and IFIs to determine the content, breadth and depth of reform.

5.4   Public management reforms

Public management reforms in Uganda started in the late 1980s. They took place against the backdrop of maladministration under Amin's regime. Aminism led to substantial erosion of public sector ethics. This had a two-pronged consequence: first, patrimonialism became the basis for recruitment and promotion in the public service; second, corruption became a huge problem (and appears to have become worse today). By the end of Amin's regime in 1979, Uganda's civil service which had been hailed as the best in sub-Saharan Africa had become inefficient, corrupt and unresponsive to societal needs (Uganda, 1994, 1999). Uganda's public management reforms signified a shift from Weberian public administration to market-oriented public management. The marketisation of public administration is consistent with the mainstream neo-liberal agenda, which claims that public service delivery must be driven by the market mechanism. In line with the World Bank's (1990) *Public Choices for Private Initiatives* and the broader managerial model of the OECD countries (OECD, 1997; Hughes, 1998), the Uganda government has, since 1989, been implementing radical public sector reforms.

Uganda's public management reforms had four major goals, including organisational restructuring, reviewing the management of employees, improving the conditions of service, and enhancing accountability in public financial management (Table 2.3).

Table 2.3:   Major goals of market-oriented public management in Uganda

---

1. Organisational restructuring
Rationalisation of ministries
Restructuring of government departments
Creation of 'steamlined' policy-focused 'core' departments
Decentralisation of local governments
Privatisation of state-owned enterprises

2. Review of public personnel management
Down-sizing of the workforce through:
Expulsion of 'overdue' leavers (ghost-employees and those aged 55 years and over)
Expulsion of habitual drunkards, absentees, unskilled employees and the corrupt
Retrenchment of bona fide employees rendered 'redundant' by reforms

3. The conditions of service
'Motivate' employees by:
Computerisation of information management
Improving salaries and wages
Minimum 'living wage' by July 1996

4. Public financial management and accountability

Sources: Computed from World Bank (1990, 1999); Uganda (1994).

The ultimate objective of these public management reforms was to create a leaner, thinner and fitter government, with a view to reducing the cost of public service delivery.

Unlike the first-generation reforms, which affected Ugandans broadly, the public management reforms *directly* affected organised interests and urban elites. Restructuring of government departments led to loss of jobs for civil servants. Privatisation led to the erosion of rental havens for corrupt officials. And the introduction of 'user-pays' policies in universities and colleges directly affected students and their parents. Thus, unlike SAP reforms, the implementation of public sector reform was resisted. Between 1989 and 1992, for example, students, doctors and urban workers staged massive protests (Mwenda, 2004).

It is worth noting that the opposition to reform came at the point of reform implementation, rather than reform design. While this upholds our third proposition, it begs the question: 'Why?' Why were organised groups inactive during policy formation and dynamic at the time of implementation? Interviews with the Uganda Debt Network (a local NGO) suggested that IFIs and their local allies designed reform packages without consultation. From this perspective, most victims of change knew about the reforms at the time of implementation. Even in the face of substantial resistance to change, the government never backed down, thanks to the commitment to reform of President Museveni, the elite bureaucrats and IFIs. However, in some cases, the big-bang approach was abandoned in favour of a gradualist approach to implementation. For example, cost-sharing in institutions of higher learning was initially designed to begin abruptly in 1989. Although students who had not been involved at all in the policy reform process staged massive strikes, no policy reversals happened: government and its donor-partners stuck to the policy. According to one official of the Uganda Debt Network, 'The NRM government crushed the students and urban workers who were protesting reforms and labelled them "disgruntled minorities".' However, while government did stick to the reform policies, the implementation was eventually phased out in response to the protests. The first- and second-generation reforms led to substantial social exclusion, according to our interviewees, some of whom indicated that the programmes not only had no input from the rural majority (for whom the Movement government allegedly stood) but they deepened poverty in several ways. It is this realisation that appears to have informed the design and implementation of Uganda's Poverty Eradication Action Plan.

6   The Poverty Eradication Action Plan (PEAP)

From the perspective of 'pro-poor' growth, Uganda's most important reforms fall under the Poverty Eradication Action Plan (PEAP). The PEAP, which started in 1997, is a local chapter of the PRSPs of the World Bank and the Poverty Reduction and Growth Facility (PRGF) of the IMF (Piron and Evans, 2004). Both PRSPs and the PRGF are associated with the decision of the IFIs to link aid to the development by recipient countries of a comprehensive poverty reduction strategy. Uganda's PEAP came in the wake of the realisation by IFIs of the need to reform SAPs, to shift from top-down approaches and create space for local participation in programme design, implementation and review (interviews, 2004). However, critics doubt the degree to which this ideal is adhered to in practice. As already hinted, the rationale of PEAP was that the first and second phases of adjustment, together with privatisation and public management reforms (such as retrenchment) had not worked as well as expected. For example, the austerity measures of SAPs pushed a large number of vulnerable groups (such as the rural poor, women and youths) into poverty and/or prevented those living on less than a dollar a day escaping from poverty. The voices of these poor people had to be heard if resistance to reform was to be minimised. In 1995, two years before the launch of PEAP, 60 per cent of Ugandans were living below the poverty line (Uganda Poverty Status Report, 1997, 2002). This was a point of concern.

The stated purpose of the PEAP was to ensure that poor people benefit from economic growth through increased incomes from self-employment, wage employment, and improved access to public services (MoFPED, 2003). The PEAP had four specific goals or pillars, namely to attain:

- sustainable economic growth and structural transformation;
- good governance and security;
- increasing the ability of the poor to raise their incomes;
- increasing the quality of the life of the poor (Uganda, 2003).

The Action Plan identified several priority poverty areas, including primary healthcare, rural feeder roads, education, water and modernisation of agriculture. The government embarked on the implementation of PEAP through sector policies and sector-wide investment programmes.[12]

7   Political economy of reform

Researchers such as Burnside and Dollar (2000) have argued that reforms are spurred or hampered by underlying political economy variables – for example, regime stability or the lack thereof, the severity of the crisis, and whether or not leaders were democratically elected (Devarajan et al., 2001: 4). It has also been established that the presence or absence of politico-institutional variables such as strong political leadership, the expertise of bureaucrats and participatory approaches to reform are all key determinants of winners (who *ipso facto* support reform) and losers (who tend to resist reform).

In the case of Uganda, reform has been implemented by a regime of ex-Marxists who shot their way to power. In 1986, however, the new regime was highly unstable. Insecurity was not just a problem in the north (where rebels led by Alice Lakwena organised a popular uprising against Museveni's government). The whole country was mired in political and civil strife.

While the Movement had won the battle over Kampala, the struggle to 'sell' the new government's agenda was not over, particularly in northern Uganda where former President Obote had substantial support. Regime instability was worsened by the fact that most political and bureaucratic cadres of the Movement party were inexperienced in public affairs and economic management. State incapacity was, therefore, a major obstacle to the design and implementation of reform. Yet, within the Movement government, the dominant leftist ideology was antithetical to pro-market reforms, which were, therefore, resisted, albeit covertly – covertly because the Movement followed a military code of conduct under which state officers had to obey directives without question (Mwenda, 2004).

It must be conceded that the first austerity measures were harsh. Currency reform involved a 30 per cent conversion tax, which was charged on everyone. Sharp devaluation, increase in interest rates, and tight budgetary and monetary policies negatively affected fixed income earners. The withdrawal of government subsidies and allowances from urban constituencies made matters difficult for this section of society. As already hinted, medical professionals, university lecturers and students went on strike protesting the 'belt-tightening' economic reforms of the late 1980s and early 1990s (Mwenda, 2004). With its support-base in the rural areas, the NRM dismissed these protests as 'elitist'. President Museveni mobilised the military muscle of the state to suppress the protesters (Kiiza, 1997). Live bullets were used to terrorise protesters into submission: for example, two students at Makerere University, Tom Okema and Tom Onyango were shot dead.[13]

Two issues must be emphasised. First, the macroeconomic reforms (which were hardly discriminatory in their impacts) were less resisted than second-generation reforms such as privatisation and civil service reform that directly threatened vested interests (Tsikata, 2003: 33). Second, while state officials resisted reform between 1987 and 1992, their resistance amounted to procrastination and delayed implementation rather than outright rejection of reform.

By 1992, resistance to reform had waned. The question worth posing is: what political economy variables account for the 'acceptance' of reform? First, the crisis was so severe in 1986/7 that it stifled resistance to reform – as the African proverb goes: a drowning person will cling to a straw! This appears to uphold the hypothesis that crises weaken social forces opposed to reform, thereby creating a window of opportunity for reformers *à la* Cardoso and Galal (2003: 20).

Second, Uganda had a nucleus of pro-reformers within key government departments, particularly the Ministry of Economic Planning and Development and that of Finance. Around this nucleus, strong pro-reform bureaucratic cadres (grounded in economic liberalism) have been groomed. Technocrats such as Tumusiime-Mutebile (Oxford University economics graduate, Fellow of the World Bank Institute, long-time Permanent Secretary of MoFPED, and now Governor of the Bank of Uganda) understand the vocabulary of donors and they have become key ideologues of reform. They have also been pivotal in translating the reform philosophy of IFIs into concrete plans for implementation.

Third is the Museveni factor. President Museveni has not just been an avowed pro-market reformer since 1992, he has also exercised strong leadership in the politics and economy of Uganda (Mwenda, 2004). This has been possible because, as Mwenda (2004) observes, Museveni enjoys unrivalled military, political and ideological power within the establishment.[14] His government has also been in power for nearly two decades. Regime stability has created an opportunity for both political and bureaucratic elites to learn from mistakes. It has also ensured policy consistency for a substantial period of time. Moreover, Museveni's regime has not been constrained by the checks and balances that prevent democracies from implementing unpopular policies. Although several presidential, parliamentary and local council elections have been conducted since 1986, the democratic credentials of Museveni's regime are suspect (Makara et al., 2003). As Moncrieffe (2004) points out, Uganda's procedural democracy has not been translated into genuine democratic governance. The Movement regime combines both democratic and despotic tendencies (Kjare, 1999; Hauser, 1999; Barya et al., 2003). The absence of democratic checks appears to have created an opportunity for Museveni to implement tough reforms without fear. Added to this is the fact that Museveni is a pragmatic politician. In the face of resistance to reforms, he sided with the pro-reformers within the civil service. He also merged the Ministries of Finance and Economic Planning into a mega Ministry of Finance, Planning and Economic Development (MoFPED) and appointed Tumusiime-Mutebile (an avowed free-marketeer) Permanent Secretary of the new MoFPED and Secretary to the Treasury. Tumusiime-Mutebile and the elite bureaucrats from the Ministry of Planning who had contributed immensely to the reform efforts took over the leadership of the new ministry (Devarajan et al., 2001: 122). They formed, among other units, the Aid Liaison Department whose goal was to improve government–donor relations.

Additonally, Uganda's reforms have been successful because of massive donor support. In other words, donors have been a key force behind reform. Donor support has taken different forms. In the pre-reform period, donors supplied technical assistance and 'good' policies (macroeconomic stability, functioning markets, the rule of law, etc.). Once the reform philosophy had been adopted and institutionalised, policy dialogue, capacity-building and finance assumed greater significance (Holmgren et al., 2001 for details).

Finally, according to some, reform ownership has been factored into the reform agenda. Devarajan et al. (2001:11) contend that the reform process has been consultative:

President Museveni established the Presidential National Forum to debate reform issues in 1987. The Uganda Manufacturers' Association sponsored seminars and discussion papers during the 1987–9 period. The

Presidential Economic Council had open debates on reform and sponsored a December 1989 conference on trade liberalisation that has been described as a turning point in public opinion.

'Domestic ownership' of reforms appears to have increased with the shift from first- and second-generation reforms to the pro-poor reforms, although the quality of this 'ownership' is found wanting by critics (e.g. Hauser, 1999). Quarterly meetings between MoFPED, donors, NGOs, like-minded researchers and the media have been encouraged. The PEAP, for example, has adopted a philosophy of popular consultation and country ownership of development initiatives. These initiatives appear to have turned former anti-reformers into sympathisers, thereby galvanising support for economic and institutional change.

8   Assessing the success of reform

This section attempts to assess the success of reform in Uganda. This is a difficult task because several commentators on reform success or failure tend to invoke ideological considerations, rather than objective analysis. As such they would rather be told what they want to hear. What this section does is to give credit where credit is due and criticise where criticism is unavoidable.

8.1   On the stabilisation and adjustment programmes

A major component of the first SAPs was flotation of the shilling. Flotation in effect led to *devaluation* of the national currency. The shilling depreciated by 90 per cent from the 1981 rate of UShs 7.80 to the US dollar to about UShs 80.0 to the dollar by early 1982. Devaluation, backed by the liberalisation of Uganda's export crop sector, led to an increase in the volume of exports (Table 2.2). On the face of it, exporters were beneficiaries and therefore potential supporters of reform. Unfortunately, while the volume of exports increased, the value *declined* from US$415 million in 1980 to US$274 million in 1982 (Uganda, 1999; Kiiza, 2002: Table 5.1). Thereafter, it increased gradually to US$368 million in 1984. The pre-flotation level of US$415 million was only surpassed in 1985, but it subsequently declined in the late 1980s and early 1990s. By the end of the 1990s, the value of Uganda's exports was *not* substantially higher than its 1980 level (Uganda, 1999, 2000). This suggests that exporters were not really beneficiaries of reform. Urban workers and other formal sector employees also lost out, given that their incomes were not adjusted fast enough to cope with the erosion of the purchasing power of the shilling. In short, devaluation produced two distinctive groups of losers – exporters and fixed income earners.

The abolition of state subsidies and the strengthening of the price mechanism more generally produced mixed results. The 'death' of the ancient regime of subsidised services made economic sense. Government made some savings. However, vulnerable social groups (e.g. the rural poor) lost out. User-fees or cost-sharing in institutions of learning and hospitals led to the exclusion of both the rural and the urban poor, the widows and orphans, many of whom were victims of the devastating scourge of HIV/AIDS in the country.

It is worth noting that the country's GDP growth recovered from the pre-adjustment (1980) level of –5.2 per cent to 7.5 per cent in 1981, reaching a peak of 11.7 per cent in 1982 (Table 2.2). However, this positive development was not sustainable. GDP growth declined after 1982 until the overthrow of Obote II in January 1986. Additionally, between 1981 and 1985, the country's external debts increased from US$733 million to US$1031 million, signifying an increase in the debt/export ratio from 262.4 per cent to 305.3 per cent over this period. By 1998, Uganda's external debt amounted to US$3640 million, signifying a debt/export ratio of nearly 734 per cent. The verdict on the performance of the first SAPs is best captured in the Uganda *Vision 2025* (which was written with donor support):

> although the first structural adjustment package of 1981–84 may have achieved some success, it generally failed to fulfil its intended objectives . . . Industrial production initially reacted positively but later stagnated due to problems associated with foreign exchange allocations. Agricultural production did not respond as anticipated largely because Government price incentives failed to trickle down to producers.
>
> (Uganda, 1998: 5)

8.2   Assessment of reforms under the Museveni regime

After some foot-dragging, the regime of President Museveni implemented reform. The reforms of 1987–92 again had mixed results. Financial assistance to government increased substantially, thanks to the role of conditionality in driving reform. Between 1987 and 1992, donor support averaged US$500 million annually, reaching a peak of US$786 million in 1992 or 24.4 per cent of GDP (BoU, 1998). Foreign aid played a critical role in the rehabilitation of infrastructure, the delivery of social services and BoP support. Aid was, therefore, a key driver of growth.[15] Economic recovery was, in turn, used by government elites to claim legitimacy and consolidate regime stability. The benefits of reform strengthened the political clout of reformers and helped silence dissenting voices. This helped to deepen reform. GDP growth averaged 6 per cent per year between 1987 and 1992 (Henstridge and Kasekende, 2001). But this growth primarily came from low value-added activities dominated by construction and rain-fed agriculture. Nevertheless, Uganda's recovery from negative growth in the 1970s to positive rates in the 1990s and beyond was important.[16]

It is also important to note that a non-democratic regime was able to acquire legitimacy locally and popularity internationally on the basis of its ability to deliver positive growth. This suggests that democracy is *not* a necessary prerequisite for growth, desirable as it may be. This contradicts the UNDP (2002) study entitled *Deepening Democracy in a Fragmented World*, which claims that there is no trade-off between democracy (one of the goals of reform) and growth, and that democracies contribute to equitable development (2002: 52).[17]

After 1992, the Ugandan government fully embraced reforms, thanks to the consistency of donor funding, increased coordination (particularly in the MoFPED), greater bureaucratic capacity to implement reform, plus the early positive outcomes of macro-stability and growth; thus, since 1992, Uganda has implemented more far-reaching economic reforms. The economy has been fully liberalised: the capital account and foreign exchange markets have been deregulated; a liberalised regime of trade and industrial policy has also been institutionalised; and, as already hinted, several state-owned enterprises (like the Uganda Commercial Bank) have been privatised. The following outcomes are associated with the current reforms:

- Uganda registered growth rates of 7.4 per cent a year between 1987 and 2000 and is now (2004) growing at 5.5 per cent (MoFPED, 2004).
- Inflation rates have been brought down from 232.6 per cent in 1987 to about 6.0 per cent in 2004.
- Foreign reserves are now in excess of five months of import expenditure.
- A specialised agency – the Uganda Revenue Authority (URA) – was set up (in 1992) to deepen revenue collection. Domestic revenue as a share of GDP increased substantially between 1992 and 2004.

Unfortunately, the exchange rate is weak and unstable (US$1 = UShs 1750). More importantly, Uganda's capacity to continue growing *without* continued donor support is suspect. This is because the country is still a primary commodity economy whose domestic revenue base is narrow. Yet a number of reforms appear to have constrained Uganda's ability to build domestic industrial capability, or what Amsden (2001) calls effective 'late' industrialisation. According to Yash Tandon:

> Liberalised trade and industrial policies have exposed Uganda's embryonic firms to stiff competition with more advanced industries in the global marketplace. Liberalisation of the foreign exchange market in the early-to-mid-1990s also tilted the balance of power in favour of trade rather than productive industrial and agricultural activities. Thus, import-export business (which delivers short-term profits) has taken precedence over industry, agriculture and other sectors, which are more important for long-term development.
>
> (Interview, 2004; also see Kiiza, 2001)

Another problem of reform in Uganda is that the equalisation of sales tax on imported and locally produced goods is driven by the goal of extending to foreign investors what the WTO rules call 'national treatment'. In the WTO lexicon, 'national treatment' refers to the legal requirement that foreign companies investing in a given (developing) country shall not be 'discriminated' against in the name of economic nationalism. This implies that foreign MNCs are entitled to the benefits host governments normally give to local investors such as tax holidays or concessional loans. National treatment, unfortunately, signifies the death of country-specific trade and industrial policies, which may hurt late industrialisers like Uganda.

8.3   Assessment of privatisation

In line with the welfare economics of the post-World War Two period, Uganda's independence government created state-owned enterprises in virtually all sectors of the economy – notably in agriculture, trade and commerce, industry and banking. A consensus has now emerged that this was a mistake (MoFPED, 2003). The state should have limited its interventionism to strategic sectors where private sector capacity was still weak. In the case of Uganda, infrastructural development, industrial promotion and development banking would have been eligible candidates. Some interviewees argued that the state has no role in the economy at all. The only exception, it was suggested, is state involvement in creating a conducive environment for market-led development.[18] Accordingly, it was asserted that privatisation was the right thing to do. Public enterprises were a chronic burden to the taxpayer. Moreover, government is 'good' if it is small. It is 'horrible' if it 'strays' into the economic sphere, which is not the domain of government. Good government plays a limited regulatory role – that is, defining contractual law, institutionalising property rights, and formulating business-friendly legislation. Finally, globalisation, it was argued, has led to the erosion of the economic role of the state.

A small but crucial number of interviewees (consisting mainly of political economists and some members of parliament) disagreed with the mainstream economists. The problem with privatisation, it was argued, is not necessarily the sale of *public* enterprises to 'private' individuals. The problem is that Uganda's privatisation defies economic logic. According to Ddumba-Ssentamu, the divestitures completed so far have achieved less than their asset value (interview, 2004). This is arguably because the parastatals (e.g. Uganda Commercial Bank) were grossly undervalued, thanks to the high degree of domestic and cross-border corruption. Second, government is injecting *more* money into the enterprises (prior to divestiture) than it is realising from the sales. By 30 June 1997, 'the net accumulated sales proceeds from privatisation amounted to Shs 90 billion, leaving a net deficit of Shs 5.6bn'.[19] Third, by the beginning of the year 2000, only twenty-eight of the fifty-five privatised enterprises had been fully paid for. Yet, the monies from divestiture have been reportedly 'borrowed' by politically connected 'predators' who have been major beneficiaries of reform (diplomacy forbids mentioning names).[20] These and other internal flaws of privatisation question its 'efficiency' benefits.

8.4 Assessment of constitutional and political reforms

Donors have recently shifted their focus from 'getting the prices right' to a new regime that underscores the political and institutional foundations of capitalist development. The accent is now placed on 'getting the (political) institutions right' (World Bank, 2002; Chang, 2002).[21] Uganda's constitutional and political reforms are, in principle, consistent with these key changes within the donor community. With or without donor support, the writing of a home-grown constitution as a basis for a new democratic dispensation was a great development. Constitutionalism will hopefully become the basis for the rule of law, democratic pluralism, and regular, free and fair elections. Unfortunately, the new constitution (1995) largely entrenched the wishes of the incumbent NRM government. Article 269, as already noted, restricts the activities of all political parties – save for the ruling NRM. During the presidential elections of 12 March 2001, the NRM also demonstrated clearly that it is not ready to tolerate rival claimants to state power. According to Nabudere (2001) the incumbent President, Museveni, mobilised 'the security agencies . . . to intimidate the supporters of the main opposing candidate, Dr [Kiiza] Besigye'; this intimidation took the form of the Presidential Protection Unit, commanded by Museveni's own son, to create an atmosphere of terror in areas where Besigye had substantial support. The outcome of the election was pre-determined: 'Museveni was re-elected with 69.3 per cent of the total votes cast, while Besigye was declared to have obtained only 27.8 per cent' (Nabudere, 2001: 1–2). This suggests that constitutional reform has not resulted in a new culture of tolerance and democratic governance. In the run-up to the 2006 presidential and parliamentary elections, President Museveni worked hard to amend Article 105 (2) of the Constitution to allow himself another term in office. Members of parliament were bribed with UShs 5 million to delete term limits from the Constitution. They complied. And the outcome of the February 2006 presidential elections favoured the incumbent who supposedly obtained 59 per cent of the votes, compared to his closest rival, Dr Kiiza Besigye of the Forum for Democratic Change (FDC) party, who was declared to have obtained 37 per cent of the votes. Besigye petitioned the Supreme Court to nullify the elections and order a re-run on the grounds that the elections were marred with intimidation, shooting of FDC supporters, vote buying and failure by the Electoral Commission to impartially observe the electoral laws. The seven justices of the Supreme Court concurred that the run-up to the election was neither free nor fair, but by a 4:3 decision, ruled that the electoral outcome was fair (*Monitor*, 7 April 2006). The unfair electoral processes had resulted in a fair electoral outcome, according to the Justices of the Supreme Court. President Museveni was accordingly declared a legitimately elected president.

The decentralisation of decision-making authority to the local governments and Local Councils was clearly a positive aspect of political and institutional reform. A detailed analysis of decentralisation in Uganda falls outside the scope of this chapter (see Villadsen and Lubanga, 1996; Langseth et al., 1997; Sonko, 2002). What is worth stating here is that decentralisation first took the form of de-concentration under which decision-making authority and control over financial resources were left under the parent ministries. Today a qualitative shift has taken place involving substantial devolution of powers and resources to the districts and Local Councils. The nuts and bolts of decentralisation have been error-prone. For example, some of the local governments still lack the very basic infrastructure to run public business (Sonko, 2002). But the principle of furthering democratic governance through popular participation is a great idea. In the late 1990s, the World Bank crafted a new Local Government Development Programme (LGDP) that significantly departs from the top-down approach to change management.[22] A major problem for Uganda's decentralised governance today is that it has substantially increased the cost of public administration. Government is already considering the idea of recentralising the powers of local government, a development that would reverse the current decentralisation trend.

8.5   Assessment of public management reforms

No scholar or practitioner worth the title would question the necessity of public sector reform in Uganda. The massive deterioration in the recruitment, deployment and remuneration systems during Amin's dictatorship translated into poor public service delivery. As already indicated, Amin's Machiavellianism and the misgovernance of the post-Amin period were characterised by massive erosion of civil service ethics, underpinned by full-scale violation of public service laws.[23] Political mismanagement triggered massive breakdown of disciplinary and other control measures; the performance appraisal systems collapsed; the terms and conditions of service deteriorated; and a mismatch arose between the quality of the people being recruited and the requirements of the established jobs (Kiiza, 2000). Many employees entered the public service through patrimonial ties with well-placed public officials. A structural surgery was, therefore, necessary.

A major component of the reform programme was the rationalisation of ministries and government departments. Ministries were (in July 1991) reduced to twenty-one through a presidential directive. However, the number of ministers has today swollen again to sixty-five, thanks to the patrimonial role of ministerial appointments in mobilising political capital for the incumbent President. Uganda has also implemented public personnel management reforms. A critical aspect of this exercise was down-sizing. In pursuit of this goal, public servants were grouped into two. The first category comprised the 'overdue' leavers, defined as the individuals who did not 'legally' enter the public service, and who were therefore ordered to leave before retrenchment proper could begin.[24] The second category is that of the true 'retrenchees' – i.e. those seen as the bona fide public servants who had the requisite skills and satisfactory performance records, but had been rendered redundant by the reforms, and therefore had to quit the public service, in the interest of 'good' government. By February 1994, 45 000 employees had been lost from Uganda's public service total of 320 000 people. An additional 18 000 were removed from the payroll by July 1994. Today, the public sector employs only 150 000 people (Uganda, 1998). However, the reforms have not taken hold, as 'ghost' workers have again cropped up on the government's payroll. Was there (in)sufficient ownership of the change management process?[25]

Civil service reform in Uganda also sought to improve working conditions, including the salaries and wages and the office equipment. With donor support, basic computerisation has been carried out. However, a lot remains to be done with regard to the pay of civil servants. According to the Minister of Finance, the country's 'mean salary levels for public servants are only 40 per cent of the private sector salaries for equivalent jobs, while for some professionals, such as accountants, economists and engineers, public sector salary levels are only a third of market levels' (Ssendaula, 2000: 37–8). This constrains government's capacity to attract, retain and utilise the most capable people resources. Thus, the dream of recreating the motivated, well-remunerated public service of the 1960s remains exactly that – a dream.

8.6   Assessment of pro-poor growth under the PEAP

The most important and comprehensive social reform that has been implemented in Uganda falls under the Poverty Eradication Action Plan (PEAP). The PEAP emphasises local ownership of development programmes and a participatory approach to development management. This seems to have been a response to the persistent demands by both local civil society organisations (such as the Uganda Debt Network) and international NGOs (e.g. the Jubilee 2000 Coalition) that the IMF, the World Bank and other IFIs change their 'technocratic' (read undemocratic) approaches. The World Bank, in particular, seems to have acquired a new identity in the 1990s. Rather than stick to its 'aloof', 'Washington' identity, it is now marketing itself as a 'pro-South', 'pro-poor' and 'pro-sustainable growth' institution – an identity that has been recently reinforced by the notion of a 'knowledge bank' which recognises the importance of institutions in the pursuit of poverty-reducing growth (World Bank, 2002); even the IMF has factored poverty reduction into its programmes.

In line with this 'new spirit' among donors, all countries receiving IDA funding and the Enhanced Structural Adjustment Fund (ESAF) are required to do two crucial things: first, to prioritise poverty reduction (under the PRSPs); secondly, eligible countries are required to show clearly how savings from debt relief (e.g. under the Highly Indebted Poor Countries Initiative – HIPC) would be spent on poverty-reducing activities. Under the new philosophy, poverty reduction strategies have to be 'homegrown', 'country-owned' and 'poverty-focused', with substantial participation of civil society organisations in the design, implementation and evaluation processes (Piron and Evans, 2004). This denotes a positive change in the World Bank/IMF operations in the LDCs. Unfortunately, the effectiveness of poverty alleviation programmes is compromised by patrimonialism and corruption. According to ACCU (2004), funds that are spent on the construction of classrooms and health centres (under the Universal Primary Education and Primary Health Care programmes respectively) have been thrown down the drain, thanks to high levels of official corruption. The classroom blocks collapsed two to three years after completion. The problem, it was noted, was not because of a lack of qualified masons, but that a contractor would spend up to 30 per cent of the monies budgeted for construction work bribing state officials responsible for awarding tenders (interviews, 2005).

Notwithstanding the above constraints, the evidence on the ground suggests that stakeholder involvement in the design, implementation and review of public policies has increased. In November 1995 for example, a Consultative Group meeting was held in Kampala to review the poverty situation in Uganda. This two-day national conference was organised by government, facilitated by the World Bank and attended by a wide range of stakeholders – the President, other high-level government officials, parliamentarians, donors, civil society organisations, private sector groups, social researchers, academics, the press and members of the general public. Three months' notice given to the stakeholders enabled civil society organisations and other interest groups to prepare and present critical and/or constructive papers (Holmgren et al., 2001; Tsikata, 2003: 32).

In addition to fostering a new participatory approach, PEAP has been effective in mobilising poverty-specific resources. In 1998, for example, the Poverty Action Fund (PAF) was set up using funds from the HIPC's debt relief funds, donor contributions and the Uganda government's own resources. The aim of PAF was and still is to finance the Priority Poverty Areas, defined as sectors that are *directly* linked to the goals of increasing the ability of the poor to raise incomes, improving their quality of life and, in so doing, ensuring a substantial and measurable contribution to poverty reduction. On the basis of these criteria, the priority areas for funding are universal primary education; primary healthcare; water and sanitation; rural feeder roads; agricultural extension services; micro-finances; livestock restocking programmes; and control of HIV/AIDS.[26]

The third strong point of PEAP is that it is integrated with two other institutional initiatives – the Medium Term Expenditure Framework (MTEF) and the Sector Wide Approach (SWAP). The MTEF is a rolling three-year expenditure plan, setting out the medium-term expenditure priorities against which sector plans are refined. The SWAP, on the other hand, is (as the name suggests), a government-wide approach that seeks to integrate policy-making with expenditure plans based on priority poverty areas. Under the MTEF and SWAP, line ministries and local governments are required to practise 'prospective' planning and demonstrate a link between their budgets (i.e. valued inputs) and desirable outcomes, which must be linked to poverty reduction as defined under the PEAP (MoFPED, 2004).

The evidence on the ground shows that the PEAP is delivering some positive outcomes. As a result of PEAP and other pro-poor reforms, national poverty declined from 56 per cent in 1992 to 35 per cent in 2000 (although it rose again to 38 per cent in 2003). In the education sector, total primary school enrolment increased from less than 3 million in 1992 to 6.8 million in 2001 and 7.3 million in 2002 (MoFPED, 2004). In the health sector, the percentage of the budget allocated to the Poverty Action Fund has grown tremendously in the MTEF framework from 17 per cent in 1997/8 to 29 per cent in 2000/1 and to 33 per cent in 2001/2 (MoFPED, 2003). Uganda continues to register progress in the fight against HIV/AIDS. Prevalence rates have fallen considerably throughout the 1990s and are currently at 6.1 per cent, although critics estimate the figure to be 17 per cent.

However, several important challenges remain. First, while the impressive decline in national poverty is true overall, the reality on the ground is that 51.7 per cent of the people in rural areas (where over 80 per cent of Ugandans live) are below the poverty line, compared to 19.5 per cent of the urban population (MoFPED, 2004). Secondly, northern Uganda has been left behind, thanks to seventeen years of civil war. The proportion of people in the north below the poverty line fell from 72 per cent in 1992 to 60 per cent in 1997, but rose again to 66 per cent in 2000. In the face of these unpalatable trends, 'donors and their local allies prefer to focus on the impressive national averages between 1992 and 2000' (UDN interviews, 2004). Third, according to the latest estimates, the *actual* number of Ugandans that have been lifted out of poverty changed only marginally, from 6.3 million in 1992 to 6.0 million in 2000 (MoFPED, 2004). All these figures suggest that national averages need to be handled with care. Moreover, many critical voices have suggested that PEAP, the most participatory reform programme in Uganda, is a contract between donors, technocrats and political elites. For one thing, more discussions on economic policy take place between state elites and donors than between officials and fellow Ugandans (Hauser, 1999: 636). Moreover, the technical language used in PEAP workshops is inaccessible to the majority of Ugandans, most of whom cannot even read and/or understand basic English. Notwithstanding these shortcomings, it is only fair to acknowledge that the PEAP has adopted the right philosophy of participatory policy design, implementation and review.

8.7   On national capacity to design and implement reforms

As already hinted, the SAPs of 1980–5 and 1987–92 were designed and heavily influenced by donors with minimal local input, in part because of limited domestic capacity to design and implement reform. In 1980, the European Commission (now European Union) sent a mission to Uganda to write a status report and advise the donor community on the 'corrective' intervention strategies. The EC mission was followed by an IMF team that specifically sought to identify short-term economic stabilisation measures for Uganda. Neither the EC mission nor the IMF team had substantial local participation.

The public sector reforms, however, had a substantial degree of local input. While donors supplied the funds and the ideas, government owned the reform process. By Legal Notice No. 2 of 1989 the government set up the Public Service Review and Reorganisation Commission in 1989. The Commission worked within the terms of reference designed by IFIs; however, the handsomely paid commissioners (and therefore, the Uganda government) wholly owned the country's public management reforms. This shows clearly in the vocabulary that was used to castigate state 'interference' in the economy. According to the Commission:

> Government [in Uganda] has, over the years, *over-extended* itself, *competing* with its own citizens by *straying* into areas of economic, industrial and commercial activity [which are] otherwise not the domain of government. This over-extension has affected the machinery of government . . . thereby fostering proliferation of activities, overlaps in jurisdictions, duplication of functions and poor coordination.
>
> (Uganda, 1990, emphasis added)

It is important to note that the Commission exercised some degree of consultation. It organised seminars and workshops with public sector employees, with the aim of preparing them for impending public sector reforms, which would involve 'tough' decisions such as retrenchment.

The PEAP, as already indicated, has gone further than earlier reforms. It has encouraged national ownership, community participation, and increased government–donor–NGO consultations in the design, implementation and review of poverty-reducing growth initiatives (MoFPED, 2003). This, together with the emphasis by IFIs on technical assistance, financing and the 're-tooling' of local officials, appears to have resulted in improved capacity for reform implementation.

The lesson to be drawn from the reform paths of Uganda is simple. For reform to succeed, donors and state elites need to adopt a multi-pronged strategy. In the pre-reform period, ideas, conditionality and technical assistance play a critical role. When bureaucratic and political elites begin to accept reform, dialogue, capacity building and finance become crucial. Once reforms have been institutionalised and bureaucratic capacity developed to implement reform, more participatory and consultative approaches need to be encouraged.

9   Conclusion

All in all, Uganda has been one of the most committed reformers in the world. Macroeconomic stability has been achieved. Inflation was reduced from 232 per cent in 1987 to 6 per cent by 2004. Over the same period, GDP growth averaged 6.5 per cent per year. Poverty was also reduced from 56 per cent in 1992 to 35 per cent in 2000 (although the figure rose again to 38 per cent in 2003). More recently, the positive economic and social outcomes have been reinforced by governance-related reforms that encourage wide participation in the design and implementation of reform programmes.

The challenge for Uganda and its development partners is multi-pronged. First is the inequitable distribution of the benefits of reform between rural and urban areas and between the north and other parts of the country. The unimpressive poverty situation in northern Uganda (in the context of declining national levels) is disturbing. The durability of reform in Uganda also needs to be addressed. Resistance to reform has undoubtedly waned, thanks to strong political leadership, the long tenure of the Movement government and the positive macroeconomic indicators. Bureaucratic capacity to implement reform has also improved, particularly in the Ministry of Finance. Unfortunately, Uganda's reforms have largely relied on donor funds, not domestic savings. About 50 per cent of the national budget has been donor-funded – in the 2004/5 budget, the figure was reduced to 48 per cent, which is still high. The country needs to deepen domestic savings as a basis for Uganda's future growth and poverty reduction. To make this happen, the country has to transcend macro-stabilisation, adjustment and institutional change and engage a higher developmental gear. The solution for Uganda appears to be the use of both borrowed and domestic resources to effect a structural transformation of the economy from primary commodity production to higher value-added industrial and information activities, issues that are hardly addressed by the types of reforms that have been implemented so far.[27] But that is not all. Monies from increased domestic revenue (and foreign savings) will not be put to good use unless the rampant corruption in Uganda's public institutions is uprooted. This calls for tough leadership from the President, backed by strong participation of NGOs, donors and the citizenry. If there is anything donors can urgently do for Uganda, it is to peg further assistance to zero-tolerance for official corruption.

Notes

1. This paper benefited from the Global Development Network's workshops on Understanding Reform (Cairo, 2003; New Delhi, 2004). We also acknowledge, with thanks, the helpful comments we got from Gary McMahon, Jose Maria Fanelli and Peter Warr. Unfortunately, but perhaps inevitably, we were unable to include all the suggestions in the final version. Errors and omissions, if any, are ours.
2. The Ministry of Finance, Planning and Economic Development was a result of a merger between the Ministry of Finance and Ministry of Planning and Economic Development.
3. It was Sir Winston Churchill who dubbed Uganda the 'Pearl of Africa'. Having travelled across Africa and elsewhere in the world, Churchill was amazed by the immense potential of this evergreen country: 'Uganda . . . is alive by itself. It . . . ought in the course of time to become the most prosperous of all our East and

Central African possessions, and perhaps the financial driving wheel of all this part of the world . . . My counsel plainly is: "Concentrate upon Uganda." Nowhere else will the results be more brilliant, more substantial, more rapidly realised' (1904, quoted in Worthington, 1946: i).

4. The rise to power of Idi, son of Amin, was occasioned by several factors. Amin ethnically belongs to the Nubian community of north-western Uganda. This is the area, which, together with northern Uganda was gazetted as recruitment ground for the British colonial army. The Nubians in Uganda migrated from Sudan. By the time of British colonisation in the late twentieth century, an important Nubian legacy in West Nile was that of pillaging, looting and terrorising neighbouring communities. It is to these people that the British imperial officer, Captain Lugard, gave the epithet 'the best material for soldiery in Africa' – the criminals. Amin was this type of material. He was unschooled and was recruited into the 4th (Uganda) Battalion of the Kings African Rifles as a private. Under the promotion guidelines of the KARs (followed since 1946), Amin was not supposed to rise beyond corporal (for lack of education). This was, however, waived because he excelled in sports. He also became the darling of colonial officers because he ruthlessly suppressed African nationalist movements opposed to imperialism. By 1962, Amin had been promoted to the rank of captain. It is this Amin, grounded in the legacy of suppressing nationalism, who overthrew the first post-independence government of Obote in 1971. (Obote's socialist rhetoric of the late 1960s was read as a sign of 'dangerous nationalism'.) For details, see Mamdani (1976) and Mensah (2006).

5. The country has been under the tight political control of the National Resistance Movement (NRM) of President Museveni since 1986. Until recently, when the NRM was named the National Resistance Movement Organisation (NRM-O), its leaders have been claiming that it is an all-inclusive *movement*, not a political party. Its critics have insisted that NRM is a one-party dictatorship, dominating political space under the guise of an all-inclusive political dispensation. Recently, Museveni announced his readiness to restore multiparty politics. But Opposition politicians are still harassed whenever they try to hold political rallies (*The Monitor*, 2 July 2004). However, while the major Opposition parties disagree with the NRM on political and constitutional issues, none is fundamentally opposed to NRM's neo-liberal ideology. Reform reversals are, therefore, unlikely even if the Opposition captures power.

6. The collapse of the first SAPs in 1984 was partly due to insecurity. The civil war led by Museveni (1981–6) against Obote's regime appears to have a disorganised government. This echoes the claim (e.g. Addison, 2003: 3) that security and economic progress are interlinked, and that however good economic policies might be, growth and development are unlikely to be realised unless basic security exists.

7. For a more detailed analysis, see Sarwar (1991).

8. Prior to the institutional reforms of the 1990s, the Ministry of Finance and that of Planning and Economic Development were separate. This created problems of coordination of government economic policies. The Ministry of Planning and Economic Development (headed by pro-reformist Tumusiime-Mutebile as Permanent Secretary) favoured the pro-market reforms championed by the IMF and the World Bank. The Ministry of Finance doubted the merits of market-driven reforms in the Ugandan context. This created rivalries and procrastination in the adoption of reform. The donor institutions threatened to withhold balance of payments support unless government embraced reforms. In 1992, President Museveni merged the two Ministries and appointed Tumusiime-Mutebile Permanent Secretary of the

mega-Ministry of Finance, Planning and Economic Development. Since then, the Ministry has played a pivotal role in pro-market economic and institutional reforms in Uganda.

9. Museveni's populist ideology had little to do with Latin American populism. It was apparently acquired from Tanzania while he and other individuals (such as Edward Sekandi, Speaker of Parliament) who have become top NRM elites, were doing their tertiary education at Dar es Salaam University. President Julius Nyerere and socialist scholar-activists like Walter Rodney (who taught at Dar University) apparently influenced today's NRM elites.

10. Two issues are worth noting: (a) the first two presidential elections under the new constitution were held in March 1996 and March 2001 respectively. The incumbent President (Museveni) won both elections, although the multipartyists cried foul; (b) Article 105(2) provides that a President of Uganda shall have a maximum of two five-year terms of office. Museveni, whose term of office expires in 2006, has already initiated processes to lift the constitutional limits on the tenure of the President (suggesting that he wants to be Uganda's second 'life president' after Idi Amin).

11. The Local Councils promote women's participation in politics. Of the total of nine councillors at each of the local government levels, one seat is by law reserved for a woman. Additionally, while each electoral college sends one representative to the national Parliament, each district-level Council sends one female representative to the National Assembly. This institutional innovation has resulted in increased female participation in both local and national politics in Uganda. Today, women constitute roughly 20 per cent of the National Assembly. For details, see Goetz (1998).

12. The revised (2004) PEAP document has five pillars. First is economic management (macroeconomic stability, fiscal consolidation). Second is export promotion and private sector investment. Third is boosting production, competitiveness and incomes (via agricultural modernisation, preservation of natural resources, and infrastructural development). Fourth is conflict resolution/disaster management. Fifth is governance (human rights, democratisation, accountability and elimination of corruption) (MoFPED, 2004).

13. The peasants/rural poor in Uganda (whose access to subsidised health, education and other public services was negatively affected by the reform) did not go on strike. The reason is because unlike Zambia where the losers from reform protested the abolition of subsidised maize (a staple food), Uganda's peasants are self-sufficient in food production.

14. Indeed, the Movement system has, from the days of its guerrilla struggle (early 1980s), had a substantial fusion of military and political powers (along the socialist model of Nyerere's party – Chama Cha Mapinduzi (CCM) and the Tanzania People's Defence Forces). Museveni stands in the commanding heights of the Movement's power structures.

15. For a recent analysis of the role of foreign aid in shaping public policy and economic growth in Uganda, see Collier and Reinekka (2001).

16. However, inflation rates were erratic (reflecting government's inconsistency in monetary and fiscal discipline). Inflation declined from 296 per cent in 1986/7 to 29 per cent in 1989/90 before increasing to 32 per cent in 1990/1 and 62.9 per cent in 1991/2 (Sharer et al., 1995). (Today, inflation is down to 6 per cent.)

17. Yingyi Qian (2001), who grapples with 'the puzzle' of partial reform and rapid growth in China, also argues that China's story defies conventional wisdom. While

it has adopted many policies recommended by economists (such as openness to trade and investment), China's reform has succeeded without complete liberalisation, without privatisation and without democratisation.

18. The views stated in the rest of this paragraph were gathered from officials of the Ministry of Finance, Planning and Economic Development, Ministry of Trade, Tourism and Industry, the Uganda Investment Authority (UIA), Private Sector Foundation Uganda (PSFU), and the Economic Policy Research Centre.

19. Ddumba-Ssentamu, 'The Privatisation Process and Its Impact on Society', cited in *The Monitor*, 14 March 2001 at http://www.monitor.co.ug/news.

20. At least seven enterprises – Uganda Grain Milling Co. Ltd., Entebbe Handling Services (ENHAS), Printpak Uganda Limited, Soroti Meat Parkers Limited, Lira Hotel, Kabale White Horse Inn and Soroti Hotel – went to NRM cronies at give-away prices. Most beneficiaries have not even paid the small amounts they were charged. This suggests that several supporters of reform are beneficiaries of crony capitalism.

21. For a critique of 'governance-related conditionalities' see Kapur and Webber (2000).

22. The new LGDP is action research-based, flexible, participatory and capacity building. For once, the World Bank has conceded that no one coat fits all; that 'local level priorities will differ from one local government to another'. The new programme still has provisions that are inconsistent with the concrete realities on the ground (e.g. the call for '*user*-fees' requiring the poor peasants to pay for local government services). But the World Bank (1999) appears to be learning to be realistic.

23. The laws of the Uganda Civil Service are found in (a) the Public Service Regulations of 1964, which lay down the rules of operation, and the matters related to recruitment, control, discipline and dismissal; (b) the Public Service Act 1969, which defines the procedure, composition and method of work of the Public Service Commission (the recruiting organ of Uganda's public service); (c) the Public Service Standing Orders 1964, which *inter alia* lay down the civil service ethics, dos and don'ts; (d) the Constitution of the Republic of Uganda 1995, Ch. 10; plus various memoranda, minutes and circulars.

24. The 'overdue leavers' included (i) the 'ghost' employees, i.e. people who appeared on the government's payroll but were not actually in service. They were either deceased, or had been added to the payroll by corrupt senior officers who would actually receive the salaries and wages. The teaching service alone had an estimated 15 000 ghost employees (Uganda, 1994); (ii) those who had reached the mandatory retirement age of 55 years; (iii) the poor performers, namely the habitual drunkards and absentees; and (iv) those who lacked the necessary skills and/or had bribed their way into the public service outside the civil service legal provisions.

25. Most of our interviewees answer this in the affirmative. It was also pointed out that today's ghost employees are smuggled onto the payroll by senior officials who *probably* share the salaries of ghost workers with top politicians.

26. It is important to note that the Poverty Action Funds (PAF) are used exclusively for conditional grants to districts (which are the main units of decentralisation in Uganda). A committee consisting of government and civil society representatives oversees allocations and monitors the use of PAF resources.

27. Sadly, nowhere in Africa has 'structural' adjustment delivered *structural* changes from the colonial commodity economy to a qualitatively better industrial or information economy. Nowhere is the source of GDP growth, the composition of exports and imports, or the sectoral distribution of employment *fundamentally* different from the structure left behind by colonialism forty years ago. In Uganda, for example, coffee fetches 55 per cent of total export receipts. Tea, tobacco and cotton account for

another 11 per cent, bringing the total share of commodity exports to 66 per cent (UBS, 1999: 86).

References

ACCU (Anti-Corruption Coalition, Uganda) (2004) *Nature, Impact and Extent of Political Corruption at National and Local Government Level, a* study carried out by the Centre for Basic Research and Dr Julius Kiiza for ACCU (Kampala: Vimers Limited).

Addison, T. (2003) 'Introduction', in T. Addison (ed.), *From Conflict to Recovery in Africa* (Oxford: Oxford University Press).

Amsden, A. (2001) *The Rise of 'The Rest': Challenges to the West from Late-Industrialising Economies* (Oxford: Oxford University Press).

Barya, J. et al., (2003) 'Democratic Transition in Post-Conflict Societies: a Case Study of Uganda', a paper prepared on behalf of the Centre for Basic Research, for the Netherlands Institute of International Relations.

Bates, R. H. (1989) *Beyond the Miracle of the Market: the Political Economy of Agrarian Development in Kenya* (Cambridge: Cambridge University Press).

BoU [Bank of Uganda] (1998) *Balance of Payments Statement: Analytical Presentation,* Vol. 24, August (Kampala, Uganda).

Brautigam, D. (1997) 'Institutions, Economic Reform, and Democratic Consolidation in Mauritius', *Comparative Politics*, 30, 1: 45–62.

Burnside, C. and Dollar, D. (2000) 'Aid, Policies and Growth', *American Economic Review*, 90, 4: 847–68.

Callaghy, T. M. and Ravenhill, J. (eds) (1993) *Hemmed In: Response to Africa's Economic Decline* (New York: Columbia University Press).

Cardoso, E. and Galal, A. (2003) 'External Environment, Globalization and Reform', *Working Paper*, 80, April (Cairo: Egyptian Centre for Economic Studies).

Chang, H.-J. (2002) *Kicking Away the Ladder: Development Strategies in Historical Perspective* (London: Anthem Press).

Chang, H.-J. (forthcoming, 2007) 'Understanding the Relations between Institutions and Economic Development: Some Key Theoretical Issues', in Ha-Joon Chang (ed.), *Institutional Change and Economic Development*, Tokyo: United Nations University and London: Anthem Press, Chapter 2.

Chang, H.-J. and Evans, P. (2005) 'The Role of Institutions in Economic Change', in G. Dymski and S. Da Paula (eds), *Reimagining Growth* (London: Zed Press).

Chen, D., Matovu, J. and Reinikka, R. (2001) 'A Quest for Revenue and Tax Incidence', in P. Collier and R. Reinekka (eds), *Uganda's Recovery: the Role of Farms, Firms and Government* (Washington, DC: World Bank).

Collier, P. and Dollar D. (1998) *Aid Allocation and Poverty Reduction* (Washington, DC: World Bank).

Collier, P. and Reinekka, R. (eds) (2001) *Uganda's Recovery: the Role of Farms, Firms and Government* (Washington, DC: World Bank).

Common, R. (1998) 'The New Public Management and Policy Transfer: the Role of International Organizations', in M. Minogue, C. Polidano and D. Hulme (eds), *Beyond the New Public Management: Changing Ideas and Practices in Governance* (Cheltenham: Edward Elgar), 59–75.

Cornia, G. A. (1991) *Is Adjustment Conducive to Long-Term Development? The Case of Africa in the 1980s*, Development Studies Working Papers (University of Oxford: Queen Elizabeth House), No. 42, November.

Cornia, G. A., Jolly, R. and Stewart, F. (eds) (1987) *Adjustment with a Human Face*, vol. 1 (New York: Oxford University Press).

Devarajan, S., Dollar, D. and Holmgren, T. (eds) (2001) *Aid and Reform in Africa: Lessons from Ten Case Studies* (Washington, DC: World Bank).

Dollar, D. (1998) *Assessing Aid: What Works, What Doesn't and Why,* a World Bank Research Report (New York: Oxford University Press).

Easterly, W. (2001) 'The Lost Decades: Developing Countries' Stagnation in Spite of Policy Reform 1980–1998' (Washington, DC: World Bank), mimeo.

Edmonds, K. (1998) 'Crisis Management: Lessons for Africa from Obote's Second Coming', in H. Hansen and M. Twaddle (eds), *Uganda Now: Between Decay and Development* (London: James Currey).

Fanelli, J. M. and Popov, V. (2003) 'On the Philosophical, Political and Methodological Underpinnings of Reform', paper presented at the 4th Annual Global Conference on 'Globalization and Equity', workshop on Understanding Reform, organised by the Global Development Network, Cairo, Egypt, 15–21 January.

Fidrmuc, J. and Noury A. G. (2003) 'Interest Groups, Stakeholders, and the Distribution of Benefits and Costs of Reform', paper presented at the Global Development Network Workshop on Understanding Reform, Cairo, Egypt, 15–21 January.

Foster, M. and Mijumbi, P. (2001) *How, When and Why Does Poverty Get Budget Priority: Uganda Case Study* (Kampala: Economic Policy Research Centre).

Gibbon, P. and Olukoshi, A. O. (1996) *Structural Adjustment and Socio-Economic Change in Sub-Saharan Africa: Some Conceptual, Methodological and Research Issues,* Research Report No. 102 (Uppsala: Nordiska Afrikainstitutet).

Goetz, A. M. (1998) 'Fiddling with Democracy: Translating Women's Participation in Politics in Uganda and South Africa into Gender Equality in Development Practice', in M. Robinson and G. White (eds), *The Democratic Developmental State: Politics and Institutional Design* (Oxford: Oxford University Press), 245–79.

Green, R. H. (1993) 'The IMF and the World Bank in Africa: How Much Learning?' in T. M. Callaghy and J. Ravenhill (eds), *Hemmed In: Response to Africa's Economic Decline* (New York: Columbia University Press), 54–89.

Hansen, H. B. and Twaddle, M. (1988) *Uganda Now: Between Decay and Development* (London: James Currey).

Harris, J. (2003) *Reconstruction and Poverty Alleviation in Uganda, 1987–2001* (Washington, DC: World Bank).

Hauser, E. (1999) 'Ugandan Relations with Western Donors in the 1990s: What Impact on Democratization?' *Journal of Modern African Studies,* 37, 4: 621–41.

Helgesen, G. and Xing, L. (1996) 'Democracy or *Minzhu:* the Challenge of Western versus East Asian Notions of Good Government', *Asian Perspective,* 20, 1 (Spring–Summer): 95–124.

Henstridge, M. and Kasekende, L. (2001) 'Exchange Reforms, Stabilization and Fiscal Management', in P. Collier and R. Reinekka (eds), *Uganda's Recovery: the Role of Farms, Firms and Government* (Washington, DC: World Bank).

Holmgren, T., Kasekende, L., Atingi-Ego, M. and Ddamulira, D. (2001) 'Uganda', in S. Devarajan, D. Dollar and T. Holmgren (eds), *Aid and Reform in Africa: Lessons from Ten Case Studies* (Washington, DC: World Bank), 101–63.

Hood, C. (1997) 'Contemporary Public Management: a New Global Paradigm?', in M. Hill (ed.), *The Policy Process: a Reader* (London: Prentice Hall/Harvester Wheatsheaf), 404–17, http://www.foreignpolicy.com/issue_marapr_2001/rodrick.html, accessed 2 January 2002.

Hughes, O. E. (1998) *Public Management and Administration: an Introduction,* 2nd edn (Melbourne: Macmillan).

Kabwegyere, T. B. (2000) *People's Choice, People's Power: Challenges and Prospects of Democracy in Uganda* (Kampala: Fountain Publishers).

Kapur, D. and Webber, R. (2000) 'Governance-Related Conditionalities of the IFIs', *Discussion Paper Series*, G. 24, No. 6 (Geneva: UNCTAD).

Kasekende, L. and Ssemwogere, G. (1994) 'Exchange Rate Unification and Economic Development: the Case of Uganda 1987–1992', *World Development*, 22: 1183–98.

Khadiagala, G. M. (1995) 'State Collapse and Reconstruction in Uganda', in I. W. Zartman (ed.), *Collapsed States: the Disintegration and Restoration of Legitimate Authority* (Boulder & London: Lynne Rienner Publishers), 33–48.

Kiiza, J. (1997) 'Liberalisation Policies and University Education in Uganda: an Assessment of the Cost-Sharing Policy', *Makerere Political Science Review*, 1, 1, available at http://www.afrst.uiuc.edu/makerere/vol_1/chapter3.htm.

Kiiza, J. (2000) 'Market-Oriented Public Management in Uganda: Benchmarking International Best-Practice?' *UFAHAMU: a UCLA Journal of the African Activist Association*, 28, 1 (Fall): 94–124.

Kiiza, J. (2001) 'Neo-liberal Globalisation and Economic Governance in Africa: Uncomfortable Bedfellows?' in E. Maloka and E. Le Roux (eds), *Africa in the New Millennium* (Pretoria: Africa Institute of South Africa), 37–59.

Kiiza, J. (2002) 'Does Economic Nationalism Make Sense in an Era of Globalisation? A Comparative Analysis of Taiwan and Uganda' (Sydney: University of Sydney, Dept. of Government, PhD Thesis).

Kiyonga, C. (1989) 'The State of the Economy as Inherited by the NRM Government in 1986: the Economic Challenges and Policy Direction Taken', speech given at the government seminar on the economy, Kampala, 12–16 December.

Kjare, M. (1999) 'Fundamental Change or No Change? The Politics of Constitutionalizing Uganda', *Democratization*, 6, 4: 93–113.

Lamont, T. (1995) 'The Process of Economic Policy Formulation in Uganda', *Research Bulletin* (Kampala: Economic Policy Research Centre).

Langseth, P., Katorobo, J., Brett, E. and Munene, J. (eds) (1997) *Uganda: Landmarks in Rebuilding a Nation* (Kampala: Fountain Publishers).

Liew, L. H., Bruszt, L. and He, L. (2003) 'Causes, National Costs, and Timing of Reform', revised version of a paper presented at the Global Development Network Conference on Understanding Reform, Cairo, 15–21 January.

Makara, S., Tukahebwa, G. B. and Byarugaba, F. (eds) (2003) *Voting for Democracy in Uganda: Issues in Recent Elections* (Kampala: LDC).

Mamdani, M. (n.d) 'A Response to the Mutebile/IMF Logic', mimeo.

Mamdani, M. (1976) *Politics and Class Formation in Uganda* (London and Nairobi: Heinemann).

Mamdani, M. (1996) *Citizen and Subject: Contemporary Africa and the Legacy of Late Colonialism* (Princeton, NJ: Princeton University Press).

McKevitt, D. and Lawton, A. (eds) (1994) *Public Sector Management: Theory, Critique and Practice* (London: Sage).

Mensah, Joseph (2006) 'Amin, Idi', in Thomas M. Leonard (ed.), *Encyclopaedia of the Developing World*, vol. 1 (New York and London: Routledge), 36–7.

Mkandawire, T. and Soludo, C. (1999) *Our Continent, Our Future: African Perspectives on Structural Adjustment* (Dakar: CODESSRIA).

MoFPED (Ministry of Finance, Planning and Economic Development) (2000) *Background to the Budget, 2000/01: Increasing Efficiency in Poverty Reduction Service Delivery Through Output Oriented Budgeting* (Kampala: Uganda), June.

MoFPED, (2003) 'Uganda's Progress in Attaining PEAP Targets in the Context of the Millennium Development Goal', paper presented at the Expenditure Review Meeting, Kampala, 21 May.

MoFPED, (2004) *Poverty Eradication Action Plan* (Kampala: Uganda), draft revised edition.

Moncrieffe, Joy (2004) *Uganda's Political Economy: a Synthesis of Major Thought*, Report Prepared for DFID Uganda (London: Overseas Development Institute), January.

Moore, M. (1995) *Creating Public Value: Strategic Management in Government* (Cambridge, MA: Harvard University Press).

MoPS (Ministry of Public Service) (1998) *Public Service Reform Program: Report of the Year* (Kampala: Uganda).

Mugaju, J. (2000) 'An Historical Background to Uganda's No-Party Democracy', in J. Mugaju and J. Oloka-Onyango (eds), *No-Party Democracy in Uganda: Myths and Realities* (Kampala: Fountain Publishers).

Mwenda, A. (2004) 'Global Learning Process on Scaling Up Poverty Reduction: Uganda Case Study', paper prepared for the World Bank/Government of China Conference in Shanghai, 22–26 March.

Nabudere, D. W. (2001) 'Flawed Elections! The Case of the Ugandan Elections of 2001', *Working Paper*, 1, 2 (Mbale, Uganda: Africa Study Centre).

North, D. C. (1994) 'Economic Performance Through Time', a Nobel Prize lecture given on 19 December 1993, published in *American Economic Review*, 83, 3: 359–68.

North, D. C. (1997) 'The Contribution of the New Institutional Economics to an Understanding of the Transition Problem', WIDER Annual Lectures 1, Helsinki, March.

NRM [National Resistance Movement] (1987) *Ten Point Programme* (Kampala: NRM Secretariat).

OECD (Organisation for Economic Cooperation and Development) (1997) *Governance in Transition: Public Management Reform in OECD Countries* (Paris: OECD).

OECD (2000) *Reform and Growth in Africa* (Paris: OECD).

Onimode, B. (1988) *A Political Economy of the African Crisis* (London & Atlantic Highlands, NJ: Zed Books).

Piron, L. H. and Evans, A. (2004) 'Politics and the PRSP Approach: Synthesis Paper', *Working Paper 237* (London: ODI).

Piron, L. H. and Norton, A. (2004) 'Politics and the PRSP Approach: Uganda Case Study', *Working Paper 240* (London: ODI).

Rodrik, D. (1999) *The New Global Economy and Developing Countries: Making Openness Work* (Washington, DC: Overseas Development Council).

Rodrik, D. (2001) 'The Developing Countries' Hazardous Obsession with Global Integration, published as "Trading in Illusions" ', *Foreign Policy*, March-April.

Rawden, R. and Nyamugasira, W. (2002) *Poverty Reduction Strategies and Coherence of Loan Conditions: Do the New World Bank and IMF Loans Support Countries' Poverty Reduction Goals? The Case of Uganda* (Action Aid), April.

Sahin, D. E., Dorosh, P. A. and Younger, S. D. (1997) *Structural Adjustment Reconsidered: Economic Policy and Poverty in Africa* (Cambridge: Cambridge University Press).

Sarwar, L. K. (1991) 'Structural Adjustment in Uganda: the Initial Experience', in H. Hansen and M. Twaddle (eds), *Changing Uganda* (London: James Currey).

Schick, A. (1998) 'Why Most Developing Countries Should Not Try New Zealand's Reforms', *World Bank Research Observer*, 13, 1 (February): 123–31.

Semwogerere, Kyazze (2004) 'Funny that Museveni Feels Betrayed by Donor Friends', *The Monitor*, 4 February.

Sharer, R., De Zoysa, H. and McDonald, C. (1995) 'Uganda: Adjustment with Growth', *Occasional Paper*, No. 121 (Washington, DC: IMF).

Sonko, J. (2002) *Conflict in Decentralized Local Governments* (Kampala: Fountain Publishers).

Ssendaula, G. M. (2000) 'The Ugandan Reform Experience', in OECD, *Reform and Growth in Africa* (Paris: OECD), 33–8.

Stallings, B. (1992) 'International Influence on Economic Policy: Debt, Stabilisation, and Structural Reform', in S. Haggard and R. R. Kaufman (eds), *The Politics of Economic Adjustment: International Constraints, Distributive Conflicts, and the State* (Princeton, NJ: Princeton University Press).

Stein, H. and Nissanke, M. (1999) 'Structural Adjustment and the African Crisis: a Theoretical Appraisal', *Eastern Economic Journal*, 25, 4: 399–420.

Stiglitz, J. E. (1998) 'More Instruments and Broader Goals: Moving toward the Post-Washington Consensus', WIDER Annual Lectures 2, Helsinki, January.

Stiglitz, J. E. (1999) 'Whither Reform? Ten Years of the Transition', paper presented at the Annual Bank Conference on Development Economics, Washington, DC, 28–30 April.

Thandika, M. and Soludo, C. (1999) *Our Continent, Our Future: African Perspectives on Structural Adjustment* (Dakar: Council for the Development of Social Science Research in Africa).

Tsikata, Y. M. (2003) 'Owning Economic Reforms: a Comparative Study of Ghana and Tanzania', in S. Kayizzi-Mugerwa (ed.), *Reforming Africa's Institutions* (Tokyo: United Nations University Press), 30–53.

Tumusiime-Mutebile, E. (1995) 'Management of the Reform Programme', in P. Langseth, J. Katorobo, E. Brett and J. Munene (eds), *Uganda: Landmarks in Rebuilding a Nation* (Kampala: Fountain Publishers).

UBS (Uganda Bureau of Statistics) (1999) *Statistical Abstract* (Entebbe: Government Printers).

Uganda (1988) *Uganda: Background to the Budget* (Kampala: Government Printers).

Uganda (1990) *Public Service Review and Reorganisation Commission Report, 1989/90*, 2 vols (Kampala).

Uganda (1994) *Managing Change* (Entebbe: Government Printers).

Uganda (1998) *Vision 2025: a Strategic Framework for National Development*, Background Papers, vol. 2, December, Kampala.

Uganda (1999) *Uganda Vision 2025: a Strategic Framework for National Development*, vol. 1 (Kampala: Ministry of Finance, Planning and Economic Development), February.

Uganda (2000) *Learning From the Poor: Uganda Participatory Poverty Assessment Report* (Kampala).

Uganda (2001) *Poverty Eradication Action Plan* (Kampala), February.

Uganda (2002) *Deepening the Understanding of Poverty: Uganda Participatory Poverty Assessment Process* (Kampala), Second Report.

Uganda (2003) *Background to the Budget* (Kampala).

Uganda (2005) *Background to the Budget* (Kampala).

UNDP (United Nations Development Programme) (2002) *Human Development Report 2002: Deepening Democracy in a Fragmented World* (New York: Oxford University Press).

USAID (1991) *Country Program Strategic Plan, Uganda 1992–96*, vol. 1, *Main Report* (Kampala).

Villadsen, S. and Lubanga, F. (1996) *Democratic Decentralization in Uganda: a New Approach to Local Governance* (Kampala: Fountain Publishers).

Weiss, L. (1999) 'Globalization and National Governance: Antimony or Interdependence?' *Review of International Studies*, 25, 5, December.

World Bank (1982) *Uganda: Country Economic Memorandum* (Washington, DC: World Bank).

World Bank (1989) *Sub-Saharan Africa: From Crisis to Sustainable Growth: a Long-Term Perspective Study* (Washington, DC: World Bank).

World Bank (1990) *Public Choices for Private Initiatives: Prioritizing Public Expenditure for Sustainable and Equitable Growth in Uganda*, 9203 – UG, December.

World Bank (1993) *Uganda: Growing Out of Poverty* (Washington, DC: World Bank).

World Bank (1994) *Adjustment in Africa: Reforms, Results, and the Road Ahead* (New York: Oxford University Press).

World Bank (1995) *Uganda Institutional Capacity Building Project*, UGPA2976, Washington, DC Internet Edition.

World Bank (1997) *World Development Report 1997: the State in a Changing World* (Washington, DC: World Bank).

World Bank (1998) *The World Bank Experience in Post-Conflict Reconstruction: Uganda Case Study* (Washington, DC: World Bank).

World Bank (1999) *Uganda Local Government Development Program* UGPE2992, Washington DC Online Live Data.

World Bank (2000) *World Development Report, 2000/2001: Attacking Poverty: Opportunity, Empowerment, and Security*, available at http://www.worldbank.org/poverty/wdrpoverty/report/index.htm, accessed 26 May 2001.

World Bank (2002) *World Development Report 2001/2002: Building Institutions for Markets* (New York: Oxford University Press).

Worthington, E. B. (1946) *A Development Plan for Uganda* (Entebbe: Uganda Protectorate Government Press).

Yeatman, A. (1994) The Reform of Public Management: an Overview', *Australian Journal of Public Administration*, 53, 3, September.

Yingyi Qian (2001) *How Reform Worked in China* (Berkeley: University of California, Berkeley), mimeo.

3

Understanding Economic Reforms: the Case of Ghana[1]

Joseph Mensah, Roger Oppong-Koranteng and Kwame Frempah-Yeboah

1 Introduction

This chapter has three broad objectives:[2] (a) to examine why the Ghana government embarked on economic reform, i.e. Structural Adjustment Programmes (SAPs); (b) to identify the features of Ghana's reform, including its design, scope and implementation strategies; and (c) to assess the results of the reform, highlighting its major successes and failures. There are significant impetuses and justifications for the inclusion of Ghana's case in a monograph of this nature. In addition to being the first Black African nation to gain independence, Ghana was among the first African nations to embark on a comprehensive economic reform under the auspices of the IMF and the World Bank (commonly dubbed SAPs), and also one of the few nations in the developing world to institute a compensatory initiative, such as the Programme of Action to Mitigate the Social Cost of Adjustment (PAMSCAD), to help reduce the burdens of SAPs on disadvantaged groups (e.g. the rural and urban poor, women and children). The chapter is organised under five major sections. In section 2 we outline our research hypotheses and approach, following which we profile Ghana's political economy and explore the main triggers of its reform. We then move on to identify the characteristic features and components of the reform, before exploring its accomplishments in the penultimate section. The paper concludes with a brief summary of the key findings together with a handful of policy suggestions.

2 Research 'hypotheses' and approach

With the preceding objectives in mind, we explore seven main 'hypotheses', all of which are identified by catchphrases for ease of presentation. These hypotheses include the:

(i) *Authoritarian advantage hypothesis*: that authoritarian governments have greater likelihood of success in *initiating* economic reform, as they usually enjoy some dictatorial 'benefits', which are reinforced, in the case of left-wing governments, by the usual self-righteous socialist rhetoric and propaganda.

(ii) *Crisis begets reform hypothesis*: that domestic economic crisis is an important impetus for reform. However, we would not go so far as to assert categorically that domestic crises *cause* reform. We reason that domestic crisis is just one of many factors that may lead to reform. Other noteworthy triggers may include the willingness of the ruling government to pursue reform and the availability of relevant internal and external support.

(iii) *Endogenous-cum-exogenous trigger hypothesis*: that reforms are engendered and shaped by both internal and external variables. The heightened interpenetration of world trade and geopolitics, via globalisation, transnational migration and electronic mediation, makes this hypothesis virtually self-evident.

(iv) *Export sector bias hypothesis*: that export-oriented sectors, notably the production of cocoa, timber and gold, in the case of Ghana, are likely to garner more government support, at the expense of those sectors geared towards local consumption (e.g. staple food production), given the emphasis SAPs place on foreign trade, macroeconomic stability and the integration of developing nations into the global economy.

(v) *Impact variability hypothesis*: that the impacts of reforms are bound to vary on the basis of contextual variables such as geography and the level of macroeconomic (in)stability and social locations such as class, gender and ethnicity.

(vi) *Aggravated social problems hypothesis*: that the massive employment retrenchment, privatisation and government cut-backs in social services under reform are likely to exacerbate social problems such as poverty, unemployment and, to some extent, the abuse of women.

(vii) *Mixed cultural impact hypothesis*: that the openness associated with reform is likely to have a mixed impact on indigenous cultural values. On the one hand, it is likely to undermine indigenous cultural values such as the traditional reverence for the institution of marriage; while on the other hand, it is likely to promote indigenous cultural practices such as the use of traditional medicine and the reliance on informal work due to cut-backs in health services and formal employment, respectively.

Most of our stated 'hypotheses' do not lend themselves easily to quantitative testing.[3] Consequently, following Fanelli (2003) and Schmidt-Hebbel (2003),[4] we rely on descriptive documentation and a qualitative exploration of causal relationships, concentrating on the available literature on Ghana's reform. Our analysis is supplemented with information from focus group discussions with selected stakeholders in Ghana, conducted at the Ghana Institute of Management and Public Administration (GIMPA).[5] Our research approach involves a seamless combination of theory and empirical data, of description and analysis, and of ideographic and nomothetic approaches – what Robert Bates et al.

(1998: 3) call *analytic narratives*, based on the 'conviction that theory linked to data is more powerful than either data or theory alone'.

Following the works of Bates et al. (1998, 2000a, 2000b) and Fanelli (2003), our narrative pays close attention to the history and context of Ghana's reform, shedding interpretative light on the social, economic and political events that transpired in Ghana over the course of the reform. Our tale is not only grounded in hermeneutics, it is also historicist, in the belief that in order to understand current events, we need a detailed knowledge of the past. We focus on the nation's institutions and political economy, and profile both local and international events with important bearings on the design, implementation and outcome of Ghana's reform.

Like Bates et al. (1998), our approach is problem- rather than theory-driven. The problem at hand, as noted earlier, is to understand the impetus, design, implementation and results of Ghana's reform. Drawing on the techniques of institutional and political economy analyses, we identify the key players and examine the extent to which they have sought to promote, capture, block or undermine the reform process in Ghana. Invariably, the identification of key players – i.e. individuals, groups, institutions and civil society organisations – together with their respective strategies, manoeuvres, collective actions and contestations vis-à-vis Ghana's reforms is an important aspect of our approach. Our exposition, like that of Bates et al. (1998), is not unduly preoccupied with theories and meta-narratives. At the same time, the veracity, or otherwise, of our hypotheses is not ascertained through the rigidities of formal statistical testing; rather it is examined through qualitative analysis and interpretation, supported by relevant empirical data.

3   The political economy and triggers of Ghana's reform

In the years immediately following Ghana's independence from Britain in 1957, the economy was among the richest in Africa, with an annual GDP growth rate of as high as 6 per cent, a substantial foreign exchange reserve, and a strong civil service (Donkor, 1997). The republic's first government, led by Kwame Nkrumah, instituted a policy of free education and healthcare, initiated mass industrialisation and electrification programmes, and established several state corporations to compete with existing private and foreign enterprises (Mensah, 2006a, 2006b). Unfortunately, by the early 1960s Nkrumah had resorted to autocratic rule and moved Ghana into a one-party state, consolidating power in his ruling Convention People's Party (CPP). The human rights abuses, mismanagement, corruption and economic decline that ensued led to several anti-government demonstrations, which culminated in the overthrow of Nkrumah in 1966 (Mensah, 2006b).

The toppling of Nkrumah, however, did little to improve the well-being of Ghanaians, as political instability and economic mismanagement continued unabated. By 2000, Ghana's post-colonial political pendulum had swung intermittently between four military dictatorships and four democratic governments. The National Liberation Council (NLC), which overthrew Nkrumah, was replaced by the democratic government of K. A. Busia and his Progress Party in 1969, only to be toppled by Colonel I. K. Acheampong and his National Redemption Council (NRC) in 1972. Jerry Rawlings's Armed Forces Revolutionary Council (AFRC), in turn, overthrew the NRC in 1979, and handed over to the civilian government of Dr Hilla Limann in the same year, only to come back with his Provincial National Defence Council (PNDC) in yet another coup in 1981. Rawlings ruled Ghana as an elected civilian President from 1992 to 1999, when his National Democratic Congress (NDC) party was defeated in a general election by the current New Patriotic Party (NPP) headed by President J. A. Kuffour (Mensah, 2006a).

Upon his second coming into office in December 1981, Rawlings and his PNDC government plunged Ghana into political extremism. With the support of radical students, urban workers, trade unionists, and junior members of the military, the PNDC continued its 'Robin Hood politics' (Dzorgbo, 2001: 281), involving extortion, detention, confiscation of property, abduction and, sometimes, murder of the 'enemies of the revolution' – i.e. the wealthy business class, professionals and senior members of the military. The violence-soaked socialist revolution pushed Ghana into a virtual economic coma. By late 1982, it was clear that the revolution could only exacerbate the nation's economic woes, as chronic food shortages, mass poverty and astronomical inflation were prevalent (Mensah, 2006a). Drawing primarily upon a 1984 World Bank report[6] on Ghana, Boafo-Arthur (2001: 247) captures the deplorable economic situation in Ghana prior to SAPs with the following statistics:

> Between 1970 and 1982, income per capita fell by 30 percent and real wages by 80 percent; import volume fell by two-thirds; real export earnings fell by one-half, and the ratio of Ghana's export to GDP dropped from 21 to 4 percent. Furthermore, the domestic savings rate fell from 12 to 3 percent, and the investment rate from 14 to 2 percent of GDP; finally, the government deficit rose from 0.4 to 14.6 percent GDP of total government spending.

Similarly, Konadu-Agyemang (2001: 6) estimates that by the early 1980s the inflation rate in Ghana had surpassed 100 per cent, and GDP per capita had fallen by 27 per cent from its 1960 level of US$1009 to US$739. That is not all: the works of Anyinam (1994, 2001) also show that the production and earnings from the nation's leading export commodities, such as cocoa, timber and minerals, slumped considerably in the immediate pre-SAPs decade. For instance, cocoa production fell from an estimated 413 000 tons in 1970 to a mere 159 000 tons in 1983, while mineral production fell by 55 per cent between 1975 and 1983 (Anyinam, 2001: 199). Not surprisingly, a large number of Ghanaians, both skilled and unskilled, left the country in pursuit of greener pastures elsewhere – notably to Nigeria, Côte d'Ivoire and other countries such as Britain, Germany, Holland, the United States and Canada.

To aggravate the situation, Ghana's worst drought of the twentieth century occurred in 1978/9 and again in 1982/3, resulting in a high incidence of bush fire, which, in turn, undermined agriculture and food production across the country. Both drought episodes were so intense that the generation capacity of Ghana's main hydroelectric dam at Akosombo was reduced, resulting in power rationing for both industries and residences (Toye, 1990: 47). To make matters worse, more than one million Ghanaians were repatriated from Nigeria in 1983, putting more pressure on the already fragile national economy (Huq, 1989; Rimmer, 1992, Mensah, 2006a).

It would certainly be a mistake to attribute the pre-SAPs economic malaise of Ghana to 'natural' disasters and endogenous factors alone. Exogenous factors, notably the global economic upheaval sparked by the OPEC crises of the 1970s, the repatriation of Ghanaians from Nigeria, and the perennially unfavourable terms of trade for Ghana's primary export products such as cocoa, timber and gold, were equally responsible for the economic crisis (Werlin, 1994; Konadu-Agyemang, 2001). Things got so bad that Rawlings and his socialist revolutionaries were compelled to turn to the West for financial and food aid, after all attempts to garner such assistance from the so-called progressive countries of the communist bloc, including Cuba and the former Soviet Union, had failed.

While the dire economic circumstances of the 1970s and the early 1980s played a significant triggering role, we do not assert, at least not categorically, that Ghana's reform was begotten solely by crisis. For one thing, that was not the first time Ghana had faced economic crisis, and not all countries facing such circumstances embark on reform. Other factors – including the government's willingness to reform, the presumed lack of viable alternatives, the sheer ruthlessness of the government and the 'authoritarian advantage' enjoyed by the PNDC at the time, and the political dynamics and strategies of the government (e.g. its skilful use of populist coalition and populist rhetoric) – fed into the successful initiation of Ghana's reform. Clearly the preceding discussion lends support to our 'endogenous-cum-exogenous trigger hypothesis', and also to our 'crisis begets reform hypothesis', to the extent that our formulation of the latter hypothesis does not assert dogmatically that crises *cause* reform.

3.1 What accounted for the PNDC's successful implementation of reform?

In this section we examine how the PNDC managed to embark on a successful reform without much political backlash. Among other things, we identify the key players of the reform implementation and their respective support base, tactics and strategies, and highlight the 'winners' and 'losers'.

Influential interest groups in Ghana, then (and indeed now), included the Ghana Bar Association, the National Union of Ghana Students (NUGS), the Trades Union Congress (TUC), the Association of Recognised Professional Bodies, and various Christian organisations such as the Catholic Bishops' Conference, and the Christian Council of Ghana. The leading supporters of the PNDC in its early years were among students and elements of the radical intelligentsia; the urban wage-earners and organised labour; and lower-rung members of the military. During this time, the regime's opponents, by default, were those who were identified as members of the bourgeoisie by the radical revolutionaries: they included senior civil servants, senior military officers, professionals, traders and university teachers. Most of these opponents were, however, silent in their opposition, due to the obvious repercussions. In the early years of the PNDC, its functionaries and supporters used the government-controlled mass media to usher in a new discourse on the nation's development problems, which espoused anti-Western ideology, called for strict control of the activities of multinational corporations, and advocated for 'participatory democracy' entailing grassroots involvement in the social, economic and political affairs of the country.

To promote grassroots involvement, the government set up People's Defence Committees (PDCs) in villages and sub-areas of towns and Workers' Defence Committees (WDCs) in urban offices and workplaces. These organisations, modelled after Libya's *jamariya* system, were used to educate Ghanaians about the goals of the revolution. In time, the PDCs and WDCs were used to control smuggling and to foster community development, especially in rural Ghana. However, as Yeebo (1991) points out, it did not take long for many of these organisations to be used for settling personal scores and for self-aggrandisement. Also, serious concerns were raised by women about the dominance of these organisations by men. It was in response to the latter concern that, in 1983, Rawlings's wife, Nana Konadu Agyemang Rawlings, helped set up a women's organisation named after the date of the coup that brought the PNDC into power: the 31st December Women's Movement. A year later, she, the first lady, assumed the presidency of this movement (Tsikata, 2001). In 1984, both the PDCs and the WDCs were merged into the Committees for the Defence of the Revolution (CDRs) with more stringent checks and balances to reduce the abuse of power.

By the end of 1982, it was quite clear to all but the most uncompromising left-wing members of the PNDC that the revolution could not reverse the economic decline of the nation. Students were among the first groups to openly oppose the PNDC with demonstrations across campuses and beyond. With typical divide-and-rule tactics, the PNDC set the urban workers to confront the students, who were then branded 'enemies of the revolution' in the various government-controlled media outlets. By early 1983, it had dawned on the PNDC that if the nation were to survive, there was a need to reverse its socialist policies and start procuring foreign loan and development assistance from the West. In April 1983 the PNDC presented SAPs as part of the nation's budget, and shifted its political orientation towards the West.

By mid-1983, the National Union of Ghanaian Students (NUGS), which represented more than 8000 students of Ghana's then three universities, had come under a new leadership which was even more vociferous in its opposition to the PNDC. The students were particularly opposed to the PNDC's proposal to reintroduce the Student Task Force Programme[7] and to replace the existing one-year National Service Scheme[8] – under which students provided services to the nation for a relatively small stipend, in lieu of their subsidised education – with a two-year programme. The hostility between the PNDC and NUGS reached fever pitch during the 1987–8 academic year, when the government, as part of the reform, required the university students to make greater financial contribution to their education, through cut-backs in campus services and the introduction of university fees. In 1988, the nation's universities were in turmoil; students' protests and boycotts of classes were the order of the day. The government, for its part, shut the campuses down – a tactic that effectively neutralised the student protest by default.

The relationship between the PNDC and the nation's Trades Union Congress (TUC) – made up of seventeen unions, of which the most important were the Ghana Mine Workers' Union, the Railway Workers' Union and the Ghana Private Road Transport Union – became far more convoluted following the introduction of reform. Many in the TUC had a lot to lose in the harsh realities of job retrenchments, civil service reforms, and the privatisation of state-owned enterprises. However, with a skilful use of divide-and-rule tactics, the PNDC managed to sustain the reform, although not without protest from segments of the TUC. With the support of the PNDC, the Ghana Private Road Transport Union, for instance, charted an autonomous course every time the TUC clashed with the PNDC on labour issues. More importantly, the PNDC used the Workers' Defence Committees to divide the rank-and-file of the unions, thereby undermining any move towards collective labour action against the reform policies. Furthermore, the PNDC co-opted the moderate elements of the trade union leaderships to its side and offered different benefits to different unions to further subvert the negotiating power of the TUC. For instance, Tsikata (2001: 73) writes that in the mining sector the Ashanti Goldfields workers got far higher wages, due to their support for the PNDC, than their counterparts elsewhere. Notwithstanding these tactics, by early 1988, when most of the job retrenchments, cut-backs and privatisation programmes were underway, the TUC was indeed denouncing nearly all aspects of the reform, from the depreciation of the *cedi* to retrenchment, privatisation, trade liberalisation and the removal of subsidies (Rimmer, 1992).

Ninsin (1991) and Gyimah-Boadi (1990) write about the many tactics deployed by the PNDC to sustain the reform. These included: the reintroduction of the Preventive Detention Decree, used by the Nkrumah government to jail people without trial; the deployment of armed personnel against workers and student demonstrations; and the intense curtailment of freedom of association and of the press. Other such tactics included: the creation of new security agencies (e.g. the Forces Reserve Battalion and the notorious Mobisquad) to threaten and terrorise the opponents of the PNDC; the rebuilding of the command structure of the military and placing the activities of the state security apparatus under the direction of Kojo Tzikata, a long-term associate of Rawlings; and the manipulation of ethnic divisions in the military, by putting more Ewe[9] officers and troops in high and sensitive positions. These tactics engendered what the renowned Ghanaian historian Adu Boahen (1992) has called 'a culture of silence', under a government which once saw itself as a populist 'participatory democracy'. Notwithstanding, or perhaps because of, these strong-arm tactics, the survival of the PNDC was not easy; more than twenty coups were attempted between 1982 and 1987 (Haynes, 1989; Rimmer, 1992: 197).

Students and ordinary workers were among the (self-declared) 'losers' of the reform, at least in the short-run of the early years. Who were the 'winners,' then? How did the 'winners' and 'losers' influence the type of reform passed? And what was the donor community's (notably, the IMF and World Bank) position regarding the strong-arm tactics of the PNDC? Boafo-Arthur (2001: 261), who has studied the activities of associational groups, pressure groups and the donor community during the early years of Ghana's SAPs, sums up the beneficiaries of the reform as including top executives in the public services, who travelled around the world attending various conferences and seminars as part of the nation's reform; private businessmen and women, who benefited from the injection of foreign exchange into the Ghanaian economy; wealthy individuals, who had the necessary connections with the PNDC to benefit from its divestiture programmes; and commercial farmers, who benefited from higher producer prices for various cash crops.

Regarding the position of the Bretton Woods institutions on the regime's undemocratic tactics, Boafo-Arthur observed in an earlier paper that: 'the IMF and the World Bank could not have been oblivious to the various extralegal measures put in motion by the PNDC. The institutions simply turned a blind eye to the regime's excesses for the sake of the program' (Boafo-Arthur, 1999: 17). It bears stressing that until the late 1980s and early 1990s, when the Bretton Woods institutions embarked on their second and third generations of reforms, issues of democratic governance were relegated to the background of many reform initiatives, and governmental ruthlessness was a common feature of economic reforms in many developing countries (e.g. Philippines and Chile). It is quite clear from the preceding paragraphs that the PNDC's ability to initiate economic reforms in Ghana was boosted considerably by the *authoritarian advantage* it had at the time. At the same time, we must note that the relationship between 'economic reform', 'the authoritarian advantage hypothesis' and 'democracy' is dialectical (or better still 'trilectical') and not a simple linear one. The experience in Ghana suggests that economic reform sometimes requires the authoritarian advantage for its initiation, just as it may need democracy for its long-term legitimacy and sustainability.

4   Major characteristics and components of the reform

4.1   Fiscal reforms

Under the umbrella of the SAPs, efforts were made to redress the nation's fiscal imbalance through tax reforms, enhanced revenue collection, and increased fees for public services. Also, the government restructured its expenditure in favour of capital spending to help improve the nation's infrastructure. Moreover, as with nearly all IMF/World Bank-sponsored SAPs, the Ghana government was expected to reduce its involvement in direct production and provision of services, by privatising several state-owned enterprises (Kapur et al., 1991: 29; Donkor, 1997: 132).

Notable tax reforms under SAPs included: the consolidation of public sector employees' fringe benefits and allowances with their personal income, which then became taxable; the reduction of the highest marginal tax rates on both personal and corporate incomes from 65 per cent in 1983 to 35 per cent in 1995 (Appiah-Kubi, 2001); the reduction of the tax rate on dividends from 30 per cent in 1989 to 10 per cent since 1992; and the broadening of tax incentives and exemptions to attract foreign investment. Indirect taxation underwent notable changes as well. For instance, export taxes were abolished, with a few exceptions, to enhance the nation's competitiveness in the world market, and excise duties on locally made food items, with the notable exceptions of tobacco, alcoholic and some non-alcoholic beverages, were merged into sales tax with reduced rates (Appiah-Kubi, 2001). In 1995, attempts were made to convert the sales tax into a value-added tax (VAT) at a flat rate of 17.5 per cent, but stiff opposition from the public compelled the government to withdraw it after three months of implementation. The VAT was reintroduced in 1998, following intense public debate and consultation (Tsikata, 2001).

A loosely formed coalition, the Alliance for Change (AFC), emerged on the Ghanaian political scene in 1995 to mount anti-government-cum-anti-VAT demonstrations across the regional capitals in the country, starting with Accra on 11 May, and Kumasi (the second largest city) on 25 May. These public protests were met with brutal force. Indeed, four of the Accra protesters were shot dead by government security agents (Boafo-Arthur, 2001: 263). Notwithstanding, or perhaps because of, the brutalities, the AFC became even more vocal in their opposition to the VAT. On 14 June 1995, the government was forced by growing public discontent to repeal the VAT. Three years later, in 1998, with judicious planning, public consultations and educational campaigns, the government was able to reintroduce the VAT. A notable concession made by the government to facilitate the successful implementation of the tax the second time around was the simultaneous reduction of the marginal tax rates on personal and corporate incomes (Appiah-Kubi, 2001: 86). Also, it is conceivable that many people were hesitant to protest yet again, given the confrontations and brutalities meted out to those who demonstrated against the VAT the first time around.

Available research suggests that Ghana's fiscal situation improved under SAPs (World Bank, 1995; Appiah-Kubi, 2001; Tsikata, 2001). Estimates by Appiah-Kubi (2001: 83) show that government revenues increased from 5.38 per cent of GDP in 1982 to as high as 19.31 per cent of GDP by 1998; tax revenue jumped more than three times from 4.56 per cent of GDP in 1982 to 15.57 per cent by 1998; and tax on income and property also rose from 1.7 per cent of GDP in 1982 to 4.4 per cent in 1998. In a similar vein, domestic savings rose from as low as 3.62 per cent of GDP in 1983 to as high as 13.38 per cent in 1997. Government savings which stood at −1.72 per cent of GDP in 1983 increased to about 8.11 per cent in 1994, before declining to 2.34 per cent in 1997 'as a result of increases in government wages and interest payments on the national debt' (Appiah-Kubi, 2001: 87–8).

Ironically, with all the emphasis on privatisation and liberalisation, government expenditure still rose substantially under the SAPs (Amoako-Tuffour, 2001; Appiah-Kubi, 2001; Donkor, 1997). Among the noteworthy factors that contributed to this increase were the government's augmented commitments to the ECOWAS peacekeeping force (ECOMOG), the move to rehabilitate the nation's infrastructure with massive capital spending, and the creation of the District Assembly Common Fund to help implement the government's decentralisation initiatives under the SAPs – more light will be shed on the latter initiative in our section on public sector and civil service reforms.

4.1.1   Banking and other financial and monetary reforms

As part of the SAPs, the nation's banking sector was encouraged to boost its efficiency and to help expand financial services into urban and rural areas hitherto unserved by banks. The government launched its Financial Sector Adjustment Programme (FINSAP) with the financial support of the IMF, the World Bank and other bilateral aid from countries such as Switzerland and Japan (Donkor, 1997: 142). Some of the notable projects undertaken under FINSAP include the establishment of the Ghana Stock Exchange in 1990, with an initial capitalisation of about US$30 million, which increased to US$803 million in 1994 (*African Economic Digest*, 12 September 1994: 11). Additionally the National Savings and Credit Bank was placed under the Social Security Bank in 1994 to make the resulting entity more creditworthy and efficient. The establishment of quasi-banking institutions, such as private savings and loans companies, leasing companies, building societies, venture capital companies and mortgage finance companies, were also encouraged under the financial reforms (Institute of Social, Statistical and Economic Research [ISSER], 1999).

Another important banking initiative was the introduction of the Akuafo (farmers') Cheque System in rural banking earlier in 1984. Under this system, cash crop (e.g. cocoa and coffee) farmers were paid through marketing boards, using cheques instead of cash. This way, the rural farmers got to learn about banking transactions. Farmers were also encouraged through this system to save their money in the banks, instead of keeping it in their homes.

Ghana was expected to devalue its currency once it accepted the adjustment package. However, the D-word (devaluation) was so hated in the Ghanaian public and academic discourses that the government had to drag its feet on this particular conditionality. No other reform policy, in the context of Ghana, is more amenable to analytical narrative than that of devaluation. We thus find one Bank of Ghana official observing that 'Devaluation is war: you have to have a strategy',[10] and Donkor (1997: 147) noting that 'it was here (i.e. in dealing with devaluation) that the strategic brilliance was displayed by the Ghanaian leadership'. How, then, did devaluation play out in Ghana? Who were the key players? What were the tactics and strategies deployed by the government and other players involved in the devaluation? Which groups or individuals were the winners and losers?

Instead of plunging straight into a full-blown devaluation, the government initiated, in April 1983, a gradualist strategy, involving, first, a system of bonuses for exports and surcharges for imports. This technique amounted to devaluation through the back door, yielding a *de facto* average exchange rate of nearly 25 *cedis* to a dollar, when the official exchange rate was pegged at 2.75 *cedis* to a dollar (Table 3.1). The IMF chastised this manoeuvre by the government on the grounds that it was not only cumbersome, but it also created a two-tier exchange rate regime in the country. The government was forced to abolish the system by late 1983.

Once the forbidden fruit of devaluation was finally bitten with this first strategy, the government was able to adjust the exchange rate on several further occasions, with relative ease. However, the task of having to change the rate frequently due to inflation and other economic problems compelled the government to adopt a different strategy, which involved a system of foreign exchange auction in 1986. With this new strategy, the government auctioned foreign exchange to bidders on a weekly basis. The operating assumption here was that the true exchange rate for each week could be established with the interaction between the demand for and supply of foreign exchange at the auction. The main players involved in this bidding, besides the government agents, were traders and importers. As Donkor (1997) points out, with this auction, the government was relieved of the responsibility of having to set the exchange rate regularly, and also got the IMF off the back of the Finance Ministry as to when and how much the next devaluation should be. The only problem was that the government could not anticipate the manipulative tactics of the other players – i.e. the bidders. In time, the bidders were able to distort the exchange rates in their favour through underbidding.

To overcome these distortions, the government shifted to yet another tactic, with the creation of private foreign exchange bureaux (commonly dubbed

Table 3.1:   Ghana's official exchange rate
(*cedis* per US dollar)

Year	Cedis/US$
1980	2.8
1981	2.8
1982	2.8
1983	2.8
1991	367.8
1992	437.1
1993	649.1
1994	956.7
1995	1200.4
1996	1637.2
1997	2050.2
1998	2314.1
1999	2647.3
2000	5456.0
2001	7250
2002	8287
2003	8400
Annual average 1975–1984	6.1
Annual average 1985–1989	155.9
Annual average 1990–2000	1640.2
Annual average, 2001–2003	7979
Monthly average, Jan. 2004–Nov. 2005	8530

Sources: (i) World Bank, *African Development Indicators 2002* (2002b: 45) for 1980–2000 figures; (ii) www.ghanaweb.com (accessed 22 August, 2005) for 2001–2005 figures.

the *forex bureaux*) in 1988. These bureaux were able to consolidate the foreign exchange in the parallel market in competition with the government auction. It did not take long for the exchange rates at the forex bureaux and the government's auction to edge closer to each other. In fact, Donkor (1997: 149) writes that, by the August of 1990, the forex bureaux's rate was less than the auction rate by some five percentage points, and by January 1991 the forex bureaux rate had exceeded the government's by 9 per cent. The main losers with this last strategy were the currency traffickers and money launderers who made huge profits in the black market that existed prior to the introduction of the forex bureaux.

Undoubtedly the financial liberalisation pursued under SAPs yielded some benefits for the Ghanaian economy. It improved the financial sector by limiting the extent of currency trafficking, money laundering and other black market activities in the country, and helped establish a more realistic exchange rate for the nation's currency. Moreover, the financial reforms made it possible for the banking sector to assist small businesses and help educate rural farmers who were virtually neglected by the formal banks in the pre-SAPs era (Haruna, 2001).

At the same time, the numerous SAPs-induced currency devaluations have had some detrimental effects on the nation's economy. As can be seen from Table 3.1, the exchange rate of the national currency fell from 2.75 *cedis*/$ in 1983 to a whopping 8400 *cedis*/$ by 2003. This has undermined the real value of earnings, pushed the prices of most imported goods, including petroleum, medical supplies, agricultural implements and educational supplies, well beyond the reach of many Ghanaians, and augmented the rate of inflation across the country. Donkor (1997: 236) estimates that between 1983 and 1986, water rates rose by 150 per cent and electricity by as much as 1000 per cent; the standard of living of many ordinary Ghanaians was invariably compromised. While it is difficult to say for sure who the real 'winners' or 'losers' were, one can argue that urban dwellers and the middle class generally had a lot to lose from these SAPs-induced changes, assuming there were real losers here, for the rural poor, who were not benefiting much from the likes of imported goods, access to medical and educational supplies and amenities, to begin with, had very little, if anything at all, to lose.[11]

4.2   Public sector and civil service reforms

Under SAPs Ghana's public sector was steadily transformed from one of state interventionist, expansive, public administration into a business-like public management entity (Haruna, 2001: 122). It was reasoned that for the reform to be successful, the public sector and civil services needed to be overhauled to make them more efficient and profitable. As Donkor (1997: 125) points out, by the early 1980s, state-owned enterprises and the civil service 'had so underperformed . . . that the national economy had virtually become a hostage of their underperformance'. By the time the reform was introduced, the public sector had grown too big to be economically sustainable. Adda (1989: 305) estimates that by the early 1980s, there were some 235 state-owned enterprises in the nation, of which the state had a direct majority share in 181. These state-owned enterprises were heavily subsidised, with much of the subsidy going towards excessive salaries and benefits for those in top management positions.

Many of the government's reforms in the public sector were done through the Public Enterprise Reform Programme (PERP), established in 1983. With this programme, the government privatised some state enterprises and boosted the efficiency of the remainder to reduce their perennial dependence on subsidy. State-owned enterprises were forced to operate like private corporations, using the framework of corporate planning, performance contracts and annual reports to ascertain measurable production and performance targets. These changes yielded substantial positive results: by 1990, the state-owned enterprises were consuming only about 10 per cent of government expenditure, compared to 25 per cent in 1983 (Donkor, 1997: 125). In the specific case of the Ghana civil service the main reform came with the creation of the Civil Service Reform Programme (CSRP), which spanned 1987–93, followed by the Civil Service Performance Improvement Programme (CSPIP). The latter programme brought new performance appraisal systems which set targets and objectives, provided clear guidelines for workers' promotion, introduced a meritorious system of promotion, and encouraged information-sharing among various government departments, while the former was used to decompress the pay differentials in the civil service in order to attract top-notch technocrats. Many among our focus group interviewees alleged that several top officials used this opportunity to exaggerate their own pay grade to the detriment of lower-level employees. The extent to which this is true is hard to ascertain, however, in the absence of hard empirical data.

To foster management competence in the implementation of public policies, the government created a District Assembly Common Fund in 1988 to promote a massive decentralisation initiative across the country. With this programme, ten Regional Coordination Councils, a four-tier Metropolitan Assembly, and a three-tier Municipal and District Assembly of local government were instituted. In all, some three Metropolitan, four Municipal, and 103 District Assemblies were created across the country (Haruna, 2001: 127–8). These Councils and Assemblies have their own corporate powers, including the right to obtain and dispose of property, and to enforce various regulation, especially zoning and sanitation ordinances. They were also charged with the responsibility of guiding and stimulating the development of areas under their respective jurisdictions, by providing a wide range of administrative and social services.

4.3 Divestiture and privatisation

Divestiture has always been a top priority in IMF/World Bank-sponsored reforms, and the case of Ghana was no exception. With a deep-rooted conviction that state-owned enterprises tend to perform poorly, due to ingrained maladministration, corruption, nepotism and the lack of accountability and transparency, most reforming nations are encouraged to pursue divestiture as much as possible. With the help of the World Bank Group's International Development Association, the government established a Divestiture Implementation Committee (DIC) and a Divestiture Secretariat in October of 1987 to proceed with the divestiture process through consultations with the public. The rationale for the divestiture, as presented by the DIC, included the fact that many of the existing state enterprises had outlived their usefulness, and that the process would reduce the fiscal burden on the government and help provide funds for social services. It was also reasoned that the divestiture would enhance efficiency and curtail unfair competition between the public and private sectors, and, ultimately, promote market-oriented economic development (Gyimah-Boadi, 1990; Donkor, 1997). What forms of divestiture did the government pursue under SAPs? Who were the gainers? And who were the losers?

The divestiture undertaken by the government took different forms, depending on the state-owned enterprise in question. The common forms included outright sale, partnership, contracting out, and deregulation. Notable examples of Ghana's divestiture under SAPs included: the deregulation of the nation's communication sector with the establishment of the National Communication Authority (Act 524) in 1996 to open up television and radio broadcasting to the private sector; the privatisation of Ghana Telecom (in 1997) by the sale of 30 per cent of the government's share to the Gcom Consortium led by Telecom Malaysia; and the establishment of a joint venture between the state-owned Ghana National Trading Corporation's (GNTC) bottling department, Coca-Cola International, and the African Growth Fund of the USA in 1999 (Haruna, 2001: 124–5). Joint ownership was also arranged between the state-owned Ghana Afro-Food Company Limited (GAFCO) and Industrie Bau Nord AG of Switzerland, with the latter having the lion's share of 75 per cent. Available evidence indicates that by 1999, some 212 state-owned enterprises in such areas as the hotel industry, manufacturing, banking, transportation and communication had undergone a divestiture of one form or another. The annual proceeds from divestiture between 1990 and 1998 ranged from a low of 258 million *cedis* in 1990 to as high as 273 292 million *cedis* in 1993, according to estimates by Haruna (2001: 126).

To the extent that divestiture generally entails the shifting of ownership from public to private hands through direct purchase, partnership and other related arrangements, it is reasonable to assert that it invariably benefited members of the business class and community, especially those well connected with the ruling government, at the expense of ordinary Ghanaians who lacked the financial wherewithal and the connections to participate meaningfully in such a programme. Additionally, the preceding examples involving Telecom Malaysia, Coca-Cola International and the Industrie Bau Nord AG of Switzerland clearly show that some foreign businesses and transnational corporations also benefited from Ghana's divestiture.

The government's divestiture programme encountered a number of difficulties, most of which emanated from the high cost of divestiture-related retirement benefits and job (re)training programmes. It is estimated that in 1988 alone, the state's obligations in this regard amounted to more than 100 billion *cedis* – an amount almost equalling the entire internal revenue collection for that year (Donkor (1997: 130). As the works of Tangri (1991), Gyimah-Boadi (1991) and the World Bank (1996) show, divestitures in Africa have been criticised, especially in relation to the acute lack of transparency and accountability in the process. Suspicions and allegations of government officials giving away national assets to their friends, families and foreign agents under the pretext of divesture abound in nearly all the high-profile divestiture programmes in Africa. There are also serious concerns about the loss of government legitimacy (and sometimes loss of citizens' loyalty) following massive divestiture. The withdrawing of government subsidies from social services and the reduction of public employment and services are bound to generate disloyalty, especially where the government has traditionally been seen as a benevolent or paternalistic provider of jobs and social services.

4.4   Reforms in the primary economy

Like most developing countries, Ghana depends heavily on the primary economy – notably, agriculture, mining and forestry – for the bulk of its export earnings. Consequently, a number of fiscal, monetary and trade reforms were instituted not only to improve the performance of these primary sectors, but also to help align them with the broader market-oriented goals of SAPs. While we cannot examine all the SAPs-induced sectoral reforms, it is important to shed some light on what transpired in the agricultural, forestry and mining sectors, given their overarching role in the lives of Ghanaians, in terms of employment, wealth and foreign exchange generation.

4.4.1   *Agricultural reforms*

In the agricultural sector, the government, in conjunction with the World Bank, initiated a comprehensive Agricultural Development Programme in 1990 to replace the largely ad hoc policies pursued prior to the SAPs. The new programme was directed at achieving food security, creating opportunities for rural employment, diversifying the nation's agricultural exports to reduce the risks associated with commodity price fluctuation in the world market, and to enhance the links between the agriculture and manufacturing sectors (Government of Ghana, 1990). The government had provided input subsidies to farmers prior to the SAPs to help reduce the cost of production. Notable among the existing subsidies were those on fertiliser, pesticide, cost of irrigation, and agricultural machinery. Most of these subsidies were either drastically scaled back or eliminated completely under SAPs. For instance, the fertiliser subsidy that farmers had enjoyed since 1968 was reduced from 80 per cent in 1979 to 15 per cent by 1989, and completely eliminated in 1990 (Government of Ghana, 1990). Additionally, the importation and distribution of fertiliser which was solely controlled by the Ministry of Food and Agriculture was given over to the private sector as part of the agricultural reform.

Traditionally the Ministry of Food and Agriculture had provided much agricultural machinery and their related repair services at subsidised prices to farmers. As part of the reform, the government reduced its subsidies in this area as well. In 1985, for instance, pesticide sprayers were sold to farmers at a price that amounted to a mere one-third of the import price. However, since 1990, this subsidy has been eliminated. By far the most comprehensive reforms in agriculture were geared towards the cocoa industry, the leading agricultural export of the country. With the financial support of the World Bank, the government launched a five-year, $128 million Cocoa Rehabilitation Project (CRP) in 1988. This programme was used to increase the price paid to cocoa farmers; reinvigorate the nation's agricultural extension services, with emphasis on cocoa; enhance research in high-yielding, drought- and disease-resistant cocoa varieties; and to institute training programmes for farmers on the proper use of fertilisers and pesticides. Efforts were also made to improve the living conditions of farmers with rural development projects in feeder roads, healthcare and marketing facilities.

By far the leading incentive offered to cocoa farmers under the CRP was the increase in producer prices, which rose from 12 000 *cedis* per metric tonne in 1982/3 to 165 000 *cedis* in 1988/9, and increased again to as high as 840 000 *cedis* per metric ton in 1996 (ISSER, 1995). It is estimated that as of 1995 cocoa farmers were being paid 40–50 per cent of the world price, compared to the mere 25 per cent they received in 1984 (ISSER, 1995). Notwithstanding the increased producer price of cocoa, other simultaneous reform initiatives, such as the removal of subsidies on farm inputs, undermined farmers' ability to increase cocoa production. Indeed, survey data from the work of Osei-Akom (2001) suggest that to many cocoa farmers the cocoa price increases were not high enough, compared to the prevailing prices of staples such as maize, to induce them to invest in new cocoa farms. Many of the farmers interviewed by Osei-Akom (2001: 149) noted that 'a substantial proportion of their farm incomes for the last three years came from crops which were traditionally grown for subsistence consumption [and not cocoa]'. Additionally, while many observers expected the public sector retrenchment to boost agricultural labour in the farming communities, it was clear from our focus group discussions, and also from the work of Osei-Akom (2001), that this did not happen, as most of the urban workers who were laid off entered the urban informal service sector, and the few who went to the rural areas started their own agriculture ventures, mostly in staple, annual crop productions, thereby putting additional demands on the available agricultural labour in farming communities.

Evidently, the main players in the cocoa rehabilitation programme included the government, the World Bank, cocoa farmers and those who sell agricultural inputs. The gainers were not only the farmers *per se*, but also rural residents who benefited from the various rural development projects – notably, improvements in roads and transportation facilities. The traders of agricultural inputs were also among the gainers, as the reform removed subsidies on these commodities and allowed private businesses to import and distribute them. Agricultural labourers were also beneficiaries of the reform, given the inadvertent agricultural labour shortages caused by the reform. The main losers were undoubtedly the cocoa smugglers who took advantage of the price disparity to smuggle cocoa to neighbouring Côte d'Ivoire, prior to the introduction of the Cocoa Rehabilitation Programme which virtually eliminated the price gap. On the whole, one can argue that SAPs have had a positive impact on Ghana's agriculture – from the virtual elimination of the once popular incidence of cocoa smuggling to the move towards agricultural diversification, food security, rural development, and the introduction of the Akuafo Cheque System. Thus, a strong case can be made in favour of SAPs, notwithstanding the mostly negative consequences uncovered by authors such as Osei-Akom (2001), as we just saw.

4.4.2   Forestry reforms

Noble Donkor noted (2001: 182) that 'Ghana's forest cover had dwindled from 8.3 million hectares at the turn of the twentieth century to 1.6 million hectares now, and the rate of exploitation of her forests in the last two decades has been extremely fast'. Similarly, the World Bank (2002a: 146) estimates Ghana's average annual deforestation rate, between 1990 and 2000, at 1.7 per cent. While it is almost impossible to ascertain the exclusive impact of SAPs on the nation's forests, due to mediating factors such as population increase and the consequent urban and agricultural encroachment on forest lands, there are some indications that the pace of forest exploitation has quickened since the introduction of the SAPs (World Bank, 2002b; Donkor, 2001). For instance, World Bank (2002b: 89) data show that Ghana's total forest product exports, which stood at 183 000 cubic metres in 1980, increased to 361 000 cubic metres in 1990 and increased again to 1.07 million cubic metres by 1996 – albeit with some fluctuations in between. Also, Donkor (2001: 186) found that logging for export increased considerably during the SAPs period, and specifically noted an increase in the exports of veneer, sawn wood and plywood.

The impact of SAPs on forest resources emanates not only from the government's zeal to promote exports in the forest industry, but also indirectly from other SAPs-induced pressures. For instance, the lack of urban employment, following the drastic privatisation and labour retrenchment in the public sector, compelled some urban dwellers to move to rural communities for farming, thereby putting additional pressure on the available land. Furthermore, many farmers expanded their farms to boost production of both traditional export crops, such as cocoa and coffee, and non-traditional ones, such as cashew, sunflower and other food crops, in line with the government's export promotion programmes. Evidence even points to the penetration of farms and squatter settlements into some of the nation's forest reserves, including the Bodi and Manzan reserves in the western region and the Desiri forest reserve in the Brong Ahafo and the Ashanti regions (Forest Department of Ghana and the International Institute for Environment and Development, 1993).

In all fairness, though, one cannot blame SAPs for the ongoing deforestation in Ghana – as critics such as Donkor (2001) seem to suggest – for with or without SAPs, it would not be implausible to expect a reduction in the nation's forest and land resources in the face of high population growth, and the consequent urban and agricultural encroachment on forest land, especially in a situation where limited attention is paid to reforestation programmes, as was the case in Ghana until recently. One can even make the argument that SAPs have been good for the forest lands with the recent introduction of a number of government policies to alleviate forest degradation, and to encourage sustainable forest practices in the country. For instance, as Donkor (2001) himself acknowledges, by 1997 the government, as part of SAPs, had introduced the Timber Resources Management Act (Act 547), under which forest firms and their contractors are required to sign a Timber Utilisation Contract with the government, stipulating their willingness to manage the nation's forest resources in a sustainable manner. To qualify for the contract the prospective firm is expected to present a comprehensive reforestation plan to the newly established Timber Rights Evaluation Committee (TREC). Another legislative instrument, solidified under Act 547, seeks to reduce wasteful practices in the forest industry by increasing both stumpage fees and royalties (Donkor, 2001). Evidently, the government is now actively pursuing measures to relieve the intense pressures on the nation's forests.

4.4.3   Mining reforms

Ghana's mining industry was in a deep slump in the decade before the SAPs, with production dropping by as much as 55 per cent between 1973 and 1983 (Anyinam, 2001: 199). With the onset of SAPs, the mining industry received a considerable boost through new mining legislation such as the Minerals and Mining Law (PNDC Law 153, 1986), the Mineral Royalties Regulation (1986), Small Scale Mining Law (1989) and the Precious Minerals Marketing Corporation Law of 1989 (Asa, 2001: 157). The most far-reaching of these laws, to date, in terms of the provision of incentives and benefits, is the Minerals and Mining Law. With this law, mining royalties were reduced, mining companies were granted allowance on capitalisation expenditure for field reconnaissance and prospecting, and machines for the mining sector were exempted from import duties. The incentives in the gold mining sector, in particular, were broadened to include permission to export gold directly without passing through the government, and also to transfer dividends or net profits without any government restrictions.

Not surprisingly, by the end of 1986, a total of 77 foreign companies and 126 local ones had procured gold reconnaissance and prospecting licences from the Ministry of Mines and Energy (Anyinam, 2001: 204). And by 1995, exports in the nation's primary minerals, including gold, diamond, bauxite and manganese, had increased by 179 per cent from a 1990 value of US$243 million to US$679 million (Asa, 2001: 157). Gold production has witnessed by far the most dramatic increase since the introduction of the reform. Asa (2001) estimates that between 1983 and 1997 the gold sector grew by about 500 per cent. However, due to the usual instabilities in commodity prices, the increase in mineral production has not generally translated into a corresponding increase in export earnings. The work of Asa (2001) suggests that, perhaps, no other mineral output exhibits this instability in the Ghanaian context more than manganese, the price of which dropped from $72 per metric ton in 1991 to as low as $32.5 in 1997. At the same time, increases in the prices of gold, for instance, during most of the 1990s, is a positive counterfactual ingredient that needs to be taken into account here.

Somehow, unlike forestry, the mining sector has not yet attracted many environmental protection programmes since the SAPs. Consequently, mining-related environmental degradation is increasingly becoming a matter of great concern in places such as Obuasi and Prestia. What makes the situation even more serious is the fact that many of the mines in Ghana are located in the most environmentally sensitive and agriculturally productive lands of the western, central and Ashanti regions. The rudimentary exploitation and ben-eficiation procedures used in the mines, mostly by the small-scale local min-ers, have combined precariously with the lack of environmental protection policies to wreak havoc on water resources and agricultural lands in mining communities. For the most part, the modern, large-scale mining operations in Ghana are much more environmentally friendly, at least per unit of output, than their small-scale counterparts, most of which are run by Ghanaians themselves in more or less unregulated environments. Thus, it would be unfair to blame for-eign miners for the mining-related environmental problems, even though their operations in Ghana have increased since the inception of the SAPs.

What are the major revelations in this subsection? First, the preceding paragraphs lend some support to the 'export sector bias hypothesis', to the extent that the government steered most of its incentives towards the export-oriented extractive sectors with such programmes as the Minerals and Mining Laws of 1986, the Precious Mineral Royalties Regulations of 1986 and the Cocoa Rehabilitation Project of 1988. Second, while the forestry programmes were for the most part environmentally sensitive, the same cannot be said of the mining reforms. And finally, while rural communities benefited immensely from these export-oriented incentives, and their attendant spin-offs – perhaps more so than from any other reform programmes – many of these same rural commu-nities may have conceivably borne the brunt of the environmental damages wrought by the intensification of primary resource extraction on watersheds, forest and farmlands.

5 Accomplishments and consequences of the reform

While the available reviews on Ghana's SAPs have been mixed, only a few observers, if any, would deny that several of the nation's macroeconomic indicators have improved under the reform. For instance, Ghana's real GDP, which declined at an annual rate of −1.1 per cent between 1975 and 1984, grew by 5.2 per cent between 1985 and 1989 and by 4.3 per cent between 1990 and 2000 (Table 3.2). Even with an annual population growth rate of 2.9 per cent between 1980 and 2000 (World Bank, 2002a: 48), Ghana's GNI per capita increased (albeit quite modestly) during the SAPs period. As Table 3.2 shows, the average GNI per capita of Ghana was US$355 between 1975 and 1984, com-pared with US$404 for 1985–9 and US$390 for 1990–2000. The SAPs period also saw a substantial improvement in Ghana's infrastructure, with gross public investment, as a percentage of GDP, increasing from an annual rate of a mere 2.5 per cent from 1975–84 to 7 per cent in 1985–9, and again to 11.0 per cent

Table 3.2:   Ghana: macroeconomic indicators for selected years

Year	Real GDP constant @ 1995 US$	GDP growth (%)	GNI per capita US$	Consumer price index 1995 = 100	Govt revenue % GDP[1]	Current account balance millions US$[2]	Govt deficit/ surplus % GDP[3]
1980	4231	0.5	430	0.8	–	−54	–
1991	5513	5.3	410	33.4	17.7	−454	−1.4
1992	5726	3.9	430	36.8	15.2	−592	−9.4
1993	6004	4.8	410	45.9	19.2	−559	−9.8
1994	6209	3.4	370	57.4	18.7	−376	−12.4
1995	6457	4.0	370	100.0	20.4	−140	−10.0
1996	6755	4.6	380	146.6	17.6	−358	−12.1
1997	7038	4.2	390	187.5	18.7	−1132	−10.3
1998	7369	4.7	390	223.7	20.5	−522	−8.1
1999	7694	4.4	400	246.1	21.8	−1058	−4.3
2000	7978	3.7	350	261.8	17.7	−605	−10.0
1975–84 av.	−1.1%	−1.1	355	67.9%	8.0	−154	−3.1
1985–89 av.	5.2%	5.2	404	27.7%	13.2	−254	−5.1
1990–2000 av.	4.3%	4.3	390	29.0%	18.2	−566	−8.5

[1]Excludes grants and 1980 figure is unavailable.
[2]Current prices; excludes net capital grants.
[3]Excludes grants; 1980 figure is unavailable.
Source: World Bank, 2002b.

between 1990 and 2000. Even inflation, which hit an astronomical height of 123 per cent per annum in 1984, declined to 29 per cent by 1997 and further down to 10 per cent by 1999 (Konadu-Agyemang and Baffour-Takyi, 2001: 25).

Not surprisingly, the IMF and World Bank (and many sympathisers) have touted Ghana's case as a success story (Devarajan et al., 2001). In addition to the preceding statistics, these supporters are quick to assert that the reform has helped resuscitate the nation's cocoa, mining and forestry industries, and helped restore the confidence of international financial institutions in the nation's economy.

Notwithstanding these laudable accomplishments, several critics, including Konadu-Agyemang (2001), Amoako-Tuffour (2001), Oxfam (1999), Owusu (1998) and UNICEF (1986), have criticised Ghana's SAPs for increasing the nation's dependence on foreign aid, worsening its international debt situation, and undermining its environmental sustainability. In addition, there are serious concerns that the reform is imposing significant economic hardships on vulnerable groups such as women, children and the poor, through higher taxes, public sector retrenchment and the removal of subsidies (UNICEF, 1986; Oxfam, 1999). Many of our focus group interviewees raised similar issues, arguing that Ghana's SAPs have concentrated too much on *growth*, as measured by macroeconomic yardsticks, to the virtual neglect of real *development,* which entails a qualitative improvement in human welfare. While some amongst

Table 3.3:   Ghana's external public debt and debt service payments, 1994–2002[1] (in millions of US dollars, unless otherwise specified)

National debt	1994	1995	1996	1997	1998	1999	2000	2001	2002
Total external debt[2]	5703	5875	6174	6324	6605	6796	6908	6967	6925
Of which									
Multilateral[3]	4226	4298	4662	4752	4971	5083	5134	5126	5014
Bilateral	1302	1400	1484	1532	1633	1713	1773	1842	1910
Other[4]	175	178	28	40	0	0	0	0	0
External debt service									
Principal	270	438	328	424	466	450	406	389	358
Interest	106	128	144	127	141	150	125	126	134
Total									
Including IMF	376	566	473	551	607	600	532	515	492
Excluding IMF	282	447	337	377	463	520	489	477	473
Debt service ratio[5]									
Including IMF (%)	27.4	35.8	27.4	32.9	33.2	28.9	23.4	20.8	18.6
External IMF (%)	20.5	28.3	19.5	22.5	25.3	25.0	21.5	19.3	17.8

Notes
[1] The figures for 1997 to 2000 are estimates.
[2] Includes total external public debt and publicly guaranteed debt.
[3] Includes debt to the IMF.
[4] Consists of short-term oil credits, Cocoa Board debt, and Bank of Ghana debt.
[5] Represents the percentage of exports of goods and non-factor services.
Source: IMF (2003: 10–11).

our focus group acknowledged that with the SAPs, legal and other institutional arrangements, as well as programmes for capacity building, political freedom and freedom of the press have improved, others were concerned about what they see as a widening gap between the nation's rich and the poor. In what follows, we highlight some of the empirical data and theoretical arguments commonly espoused in conjunction with these concerns.

5.1   Reform and the national debt

One aspect of the contemporary Ghanaian economic scene that can hardly escape even the most cursory observer are the rising levels of national debt. What is ironic about Ghana's debt is the fact that it has accrued in peacetime, and under a reform programme couched in terms of privatisation, economic austerity, and limited government involvement in the economy as a whole (Amoako-Tuffour, 2001). Available records show that between 1955 and 1959, Ghana's national debt amounted to a mere 5 per cent of GDP, a figure which increased to 50 per cent by 1964, and again to about 60 per cent by the mid-1970s (Amoako-Tuffour, 2001); indeed, since 1994, the nation's external debt has always been over US$5.5 billion a year (Table 3.3).

Examined against the backdrop of its historical progression, it would be unfair to attribute the worsening debt situation in Ghana in its entirety to the reform. At the same time, there are indications that the reform has exacerbated the debt problem, in the light of the massive external borrowing it has engendered over the years, as we saw earlier on. Not surprisingly, Ghana now finds itself among the infamous list of Heavily Indebted Poor Countries (HIPCs), together with thirty-six other African nations (World Bank, 2002b: 365).

5.2   The social cost of reform

5.2.1   Health

During the 1970s, Ghana spent an average of 3–4 per cent of its GDP on health; the corresponding figure for the 1980s and 1990s stood at 1.7 per cent (World Bank, 2002a), due to SAPs-induced cutbacks and privatisation in the provision of social services. These cutbacks have led to poor maintenance of healthcare facilities, acute understaffing and the reduction of pay and benefits, all of which have, in turn, undermined the morale of healthcare practitioners and increased absenteeism and the brain drain in the health sector. Vogel (1988) notes that the number of physicians dropped by 52.9 per cent from 1700 in 1981 to 800 in 1984. And according to the World Bank (1990, 1999), the physician–population ratio, which stood at 1:13 740 in 1965, decreased to 1:22 000 by 1998. The introduction of user-fees has compelled many low-income people to routinely postpone medical treatment or resort to self-treatment and alternative medicine, most of which are provided by untrained and unregulated traditional healers and spiritualists (Oppong, 2001; Waddington and Enyimayew, 1989; Anyinam, 1989). There are even indications that some healthcare providers extort money from clients to make ends meet. Oppong (2001: 363), for instance, writes about a newspaper account of nurses in the Korle Bu Teaching Hospital, the nation's biggest hospital, charging new mothers unauthorised fees to have their babies bathed.

A disturbing aspect of the cut-backs in healthcare that resonated throughout our focus group discussions relates to the growing rural–urban divide in service provision. Many people expressed serious concerns about the deplorable state of rural healthcare in Ghana. It appears that rural communities across the country have borne a disproportionate share of the cut-backs, a trend that is increasingly making self-treatment and reliance upon traditional medicine the norm in rural Ghana. This finding lends support to that of Batse et al. (1999) who estimate that some 8.36 million rural dwellers (in a nation of about 19 million people), have little or no access whatsoever to government hospitals or clinics. The spatial disparity in healthcare delivery is not only limited to the rural–urban divide; there are discernible regional differences as well. The work of Batse et al. (1999) shows that the greater Accra region, where the nation's capital, Accra (and, consequently, the seat of the government), is located, has more healthcare personnel per capita than the regions of the north, including the upper west, upper east, and northern regions. While this geographic disparity is traceable to the legacy of colonial regional development, and therefore cannot be blamed exclusively on the reform, it appears that SAPs have done little to redress the imbalance.

5.2.2 Education

In the African context, Ghana has long been a leader in education, producing more than its proportionate share of primary, secondary and university graduates over the years. In 1985, for instance, whereas the illiteracy rate of Africa (as a whole) and sub-Saharan Africa were both 56 per cent, the comparable rate for Ghana stood at 49 per cent. By 1999, Ghana's illiteracy rate had dropped to 21 per cent, with those of Africa and sub-Saharan Africa at 40 per cent and 39 per cent, respectively (World Bank, 2002b: 322).

From the time of independence, in 1957, until the mid-1980s, Ghana's basic education system followed the British primary and secondary school system, entailing Ordinary Level (O Level) and Advanced Level (A Level) examinations (before entering one of the nation's universities). During the 1986/7 academic year, the government introduced sweeping changes under its Education Reform Programme. These changes included a replacement of the British system with a new junior secondary school (JSS) and senior secondary school (SSS) format, which was placed on top of the existing six-year primary school system, reducing the number of years of schooling prior to university by some three to five years. Furthermore, the government terminated its free university education programme and introduced fees for tuition, books and other supplies at the primary and secondary levels. Available data indicate that government expenditure on education dropped from 4–6 per cent of GDP in the immediate pre-SAPs period to 2–3 per cent by the 1990s (Konadu-Agyemang and Baffour-Takyi, 2001: 33). In the belief that university education in Ghana was too expensive and yielded dwindling social benefits, compared with primary and secondary education, the cut-backs in the nation's universities were even more pronounced (Panford, 2001).

The impacts of these changes are worth noting. For instance, the gross enrolment ratio for primary schools dropped from 79 per cent in 1980 to 75 per cent by 1990; the corresponding ratio for secondary schools also dropped from 41 per cent in 1980 to 36 per cent in 1990. While Panford's (2001: 233) assertion that the cut-backs in education have adversely impacted females' enrolment more than males' is intuitively appealing, given the traditional 'preference for educating males when there is some financial cost involved', the available empirical data seem to suggest that both male and female enrolments suffered under the reforms. For instance, whereas the primary school gross enrolment ratio for males dropped from 88 per cent in 1980 to 82 per cent in 1990, that for females dropped from 71 per cent to 68 per cent. At the secondary school level, the drop for males was from 50 per cent to 45 per cent, compared to 31 per cent to 28 per cent for females. Clearly, the statement that females have lower enrolment ratios remains true.

No other issue yielded more emotional outburst in our focus group discussions than the impact of SAPs on the nation's education. Most of our participants were visibly upset about the austerity facing secondary and tertiary students (especially the latter) across the nation, due to cut-backs and the attendant shortages of educational supplies and deterioration in educational infrastructure. One participant queried: 'How on earth are these university students expected to learn when many of them do not have access to affordable housing or even food to eat?' From what we were able to gather from our focus group discussions, the cut-backs in primary and secondary education, as in the health sector, have affected rural areas more than the urban centres, where reasonably good private schools have sprung up in recent years. Anecdotal evidence from our discussions suggests that students of urban private schools tend to do better in the Basic Education Certificate Examination (BECE) with which students gain access to senior secondary schools (SSS) and then to universities.

5.2.3 *Poverty and other social consequences*

Ghana's SAPs, like many others around the world, involved massive public sector job retrenchment and privatisation, as we saw earlier on. This inevitably added to the number of unemployed Ghanaians. Konadu-Agyemang and Baffour-Takyi (2001: 29) report that the unemployment rate jumped from about 10 per cent in 1980 to 18.9 in 1987, and again to as high as 21.3 per cent by 1993. Available records show that as many as 200 000 public sector employees endured retrenchment between 1983 and 1992 as a result of the reform, with the bulk occurring in the nation's Cocoa Marketing Board and the Ghana Education Services (Konadu-Agyemang and Baffour-Takyi, 2001: 28; Panford, 2001: 220). Also, the government estimates that in the five-year period between 1985 and 1990, employment in both the public and private sectors shrunk by 50.4 per cent from 464 000 to 230 000 (Government of Ghana, 1995b: 6). In a similar vein, Tutu (1994: 10) notes that there were a total of 312 000 formal sector jobs in Ghana at the onset of the reform in 1983, of which the vast majority (254 300, or 81.5 per cent) were in the public sector. By 1990 the total number of formal sector jobs had declined by 26.4 per cent to 229 600, of which some 189 400 (or 82 per cent) were in the public sector.

The layoffs did not occur in the public sector alone, as the private sector took advantage of the precarious employment situation and reform-induced trade union deregulation to engage in its own retrenchment. Panford (2001: 227) notes that 'the only sectors of the economy that grew were the informal sector and the service sector. [Yet] both sectors do not provide secure and good paying jobs.' With so many layoffs in the formal sector, it is quite natural that many people would seek employment in the informal sector. However, in a 1995 discussion paper prepared for the International Labour Office (ILO) in Geneva, S. D. Barwa observed that the effect of the reform on the urban informal sector was not all that positive. His study shows that while some entrepreneurs were able to carve out a niche in such areas as petty-construction, non-traditional exports, and soap and cosmetics production, the informal sector as a whole faced intense competition as a result of import liberalisation, which ended up flooding the domestic market with consumer goods, especially from Asian countries such as Malaysia, Taiwan and South Korea.

The public sector retrenchment had a devastating effect on trade unions in Ghana, as the vast majority of union members were government employees, most of whom were effectively silenced with the cut-backs. The Trades Union Congress (TUC), which is by far the biggest and most influential union in the country to date, estimates that its membership of 635 000 in 1985 dropped to 520 936 by 1996 (TUC, 1996: 54). In a bold and innovative response to the job cut-backs, the TUC and its seventeen affiliates launched the Workers Enterprise Trust in 1997 to raise some 25 billion *cedis,* through membership dues, to help create jobs for some of its retrenched members (*West Africa,* 19–25 May 1997). In addition, the TUC initiated programmes to aggressively recruit more members by spreading its influence among professionals and senior officers in banks and other institutions (Panford, 2001).

The employment cut-backs have undoubtedly worsened the unemployment situation in Ghana, with more and more workers thrown into part-time, temporary and other precarious labour market situations. However, the available data on the extent of poverty engendered by these layoffs remains mixed, if not inconsistent. The work of Kunfaa and Dogbe (2002: 18) seems to suggest that poverty has reduced 'from 52 per cent of the population in 1991–92 to just under 40 per cent in 1998–99'. They also noted that 'Another feature of poverty in Ghana is that it remains quite severe despite overall declines' (2002: 18). Other analysts, including Dzorbgo (2001), Konadu-Agyemang (2001), Manuh (1997) and Husain and Faruquee (1995), found poverty to be on the rise in Ghana. Some of these apparent inconsistencies are attributable to disparities in the timeframe of research and the use of different measures of poverty.

Notwithstanding these mixed conclusions, both the Ghana government and the World Bank, with pressure from concerned citizens and international observers (e.g. Oxfam and UNICEF), acknowledged that the reform has inadvertently worsened the economic circumstances of vulnerable groups such as the unemployed, women and children – an admission which culminated in the establishment of the Programme of Action to Mitigate the Social Costs of Adjustment (PAMSCAD) in 1987/8. Even though Ghana's reform policies, like many others in the developing world, have been implemented as though they were gender-neutral, many of the female participants in our focus group discussions were quick to point out that the programmes have generally favoured men over women. For one thing, they noted that most of the retrenched workers in education and healthcare were women; meanwhile most of the jobs created in the construction, transportation, manufacturing, and the primary export sectors (e.g. mining, cocoa production and forestry) were dominated by men, due to culturally imposed gender roles in Ghanaian society. These concerns chime with Brydon and Legge's (1996: 116) lamentation that 'With the withdrawal of subsidies for food, fuel, healthcare and education and the more assiduous collection of taxes, rates for water, electricity charges and so on . . . women's work and the drains on their purses increase.' Also, Manuh (1997: 278) contends that the nation's SAPs not only reduced women's chances of getting employment, but also raised the price of social services (e.g. healthcare and childcare provision), which are normally provided by women in their respective households, again, as a result of culturally imposed gender roles.

The work of Manuh (1997) also indicates that, for the most part, women became the 'shock-absorbers' in many of the families that were adversely impacted by the structural adjustment. According to her, even though real family incomes shrunk, especially in the early years of the reform, many men expected domestic services as usual, without participating much in household chores. No wonder domestic conflicts, divorces, gender violence and female-headed families increased under SAPs (Manuh, 1997; Kunfaa and Dogbe, 2002). On this same issue, a woman reported to Kunfaa and Dogbe (2002: 41) in their study of poverty under SAPs that tensions in the family increase when men cannot find jobs to provide for their families; this then leads to 'dissatisfaction, quarrels, and beatings'. Even a man admitted that 'it's because of unemployment and poverty that most men in this community [i.e. Teshie, a suburb of Accra] beat their wives. We have no money to look after them' (2002: 41). While it is virtually impossible to establish a direct causal link between the economic austerities of the nation's reform and the increase in gender violence, it would be unreasonable to discount any indirect relationship on the basis of such personal accounts.

The incidence of poverty exhibits discernible geographical variations. The various Ghana Living Standards Surveys (notably in 1988 and 1992) have all documented that poverty is more pervasive in northern than in southern Ghana. For instance, whereas the northern, upper west and upper east regions have only 12 per cent of the national population, they are home to 18 per cent of the nation's poor and about 35 per cent of the extremely poor. Also, according to the World Bank (2002a: 68) the incidence of poverty in rural Ghana stood at 34.3 per cent in 1992, compared with 26.7 per cent in urban areas. This is hardly surprising, given the long-standing neglect of rural economies by successive national governments.

These findings, set in juxtaposition with the earlier revelation that increasing numbers of Ghanaians are resorting to traditional medicines and to informal and traditional economic activities due to the cut-backs in healthcare and formal employment, respectively, lend some support to our 'mixed cultural impact hypothesis' with which we anticipated that SAPs would undermine and reinforce traditional cultural practices simultaneously. In addition, with our revelation of a widening rural–urban gap in the provision of healthcare and education, of regional variations in poverty, of gender variations in the negative consequence of SAPs-induced job retrenchment, and with females bearing a disproportionate share of the burden, one can reasonably assert that the 'impact variability hypothesis' has considerable support. In a similar vein, to the extent that problems such as unemployment, poverty, gender violence and divorce were found to be on the rise, our 'aggravated social problem hypothesis' has some level of support in the Ghanaian context.

6 Conclusion

We have explored three main questions in this report: What were the triggers of Ghana's reform? What kind of reform was undertaken in Ghana? And how did the reform perform? We noted that since the early 1980s, Ghana has solicited considerable amounts of policy- and non-policy-based loans from the Bretton Woods institutions and other bilateral sources for its structural adjustment. While many factors instigated the nation's SAPs, it was found that by far the most important trigger was the economic crisis that prevailed at the time. As we saw, the economic situation got so bad that Jerry Rawlings's government, which came into office under the banner of socialism and did little to hide its abhorrence of the West and the free-market capitalism it stands for, was compelled to seek help from the IMF, the World Bank and Western countries for Ghana's economic reform. Like SAPs elsewhere, Ghana's reform entailed currency devaluation, trade and financial liberalisation, privatisation, removal of subsidies, and the retrenchment of public sector employment.

While the accomplishments of Ghana's SAPs remain a matter of debate among analysts, the fact that the adjustment programmes have helped improve many of Ghana's macroeconomic indicators cannot be readily overlooked. As we saw, Ghana has witnessed a growth in terms of real GDP, industrial capacity, domestic investment, and infrastructural development under the SAPs. Also Ghana's agriculture, mining and forestry sectors have all been resuscitated under the SAPs, not to mention the renewed confidence that the international financial institutions, notably the IMF and the World Bank, now have in Ghana's economy and its management. Despite these accomplishments, it was noted that the SAPs have aggravated Ghana's debt situation and, arguably, increased poverty, unemployment and income polarisation among Ghanaians. Placed in the context of SAPs' emphasis on government cut-backs and on the development of the tradable sector, with mining, forestry and cocoa production gaining so much government support in Ghana under SAPs, it is not easy to account for the nation's growing debt situation and its continued dependence on foreign aid. Could it be that the emphasis on the tradable sector was not strong enough? Or could it be attributable to worsening terms of trade? Or could it be that government spending so outstripped revenue, either justifiably or unjustifiably, that possible gains from the tradable sector were overshadowed in the final analysis? These are all possible issues for future research.

Our findings lend some support to all our stated hypotheses – 'authoritarian advantage', 'crisis begets reform', 'endogenous-cum-exogenous trigger', 'export sector bias', 'impact variability', 'aggravated social problems', and 'mixed cultural impact'. For instance, we found that the urge towards reform was precipitated by socio-economic and environmental crises, some of which were endogenous, while others were exogenous. Moreover, we noted that the PNDC enjoyed considerable 'authoritarian advantage', especially during the early years, relying on both secret and public tribunals, ruthless security apparatus, a government-controlled press, intimidations, repression and the attendant 'culture of silence' to move its reform agenda forward. Evidently, the successful implementation of SAPs in Ghana has a lot to do with the 'authoritarian advantage hypothesis', at least until 1992, when the illegal mandate of the PNDC (acquired through the barrel of the gun) was legitimised by the electorate in a national election.[12] At the same time, a cautionary note is in order here: it would be simplistic, if not utterly erroneous, to attribute the successful implementation of reform in Ghana solely to the 'authoritarian advantage'. For one thing, many other African nations (e.g. Nigeria, Côte d'Ivoire and Liberia) were under fairly similar authoritarian regimes at the time, but did not embark on reform then. In the specific case of Ghana, one needs to acknowledge the fact that the Rawlings government made conscious efforts to build a populist coalition for his policies, which ensured some semblance of popular participation that most of the other African authoritarian regimes never even attempted. Also, we should not forget that authoritarian advantages generally accrue in the initial stages of the reform, and have very little to do with the sustainability of reform, which normally requires popular support and legitimacy – or democracy. For Ghana, such popular support and authenticity came about following the 1992 elections, which set the stage for the concurrent pursuance of both economic reform and democratisation. It is also important to stress that, unlike the case of many other African countries, the Rawlings government and most Ghanaians went through a protracted policy learning process – a trial-and-error period – from which the government and people of Ghana came to accept the need for IMF/World Bank-sponsored reforms, in part because of the depth of the economic crisis the country faced in the early 1980s, and in part because the other unorthodox reform experiments, especially those based on socialism and extreme traditionalism, had essentially failed miserably.[13]

There are certainly many scholars, including several Ghanaians, many of whom have been cited in this chapter, who share the view of the influential development analyst Susan George (2001: 210) that 'structural adjustments have cured nothing at all (in the developing world)'. In her view 'they have, rather, caused untold human suffering and widespread environmental destruction while simultaneously emptying debtor countries of their resources; rendering them each year less able to service their debts, let alone invest in economic and human recovery.' Notwithstanding the popularity of such sentiment, a closer and an objective look at Ghana's case suggests that Ghana has gained some substantive benefits and structural changes for the better from SAPs over and above the enhancement of its macroeconomics. These include the virtual elimination of cocoa smuggling with the increase in producer prices for local farmers; the overhaul of the nation's civil service, transforming it from a bloated, expansive, public administration system to a business-like public management entity, with performance appraisal and a meritorious system of hiring and promotion; and the elimination of black market transactions in foreign exchange, with the creation of the forex bureaux and the introduction of the *Akuafo* system in rural Ghana. This is certainly not to assert that structural adjustment is a paragon of virtue; it has its problems, but it is patently unfair to paint it solely in negative terms, as many opponents of the World Bank and IMF seem to do. At the end of the day, we must reiterate Susan George's (2001: 212) own observation that '[r]arely in human affairs can one show a linear, one-to-one causal link between events', and the impact of the SAPs on developing economies is no exception.

Since the early 1990s, Ghana has become reasonably stable, at least politically. The nation has also embarked on a number of poverty-reduction programmes under its *Vision 2020* (which seeks to alleviate poverty by 2020), with the support of funds from the HIPCs initiative. While poverty, unemployment, corruption and bureaucratic inefficiencies still persist, all indications point to an increased democratisation in Ghana. Now, more civil society organisations, professional associations, voluntary groups and NGOs are springing up across the nation. Unlike the pre-SAPs and early SAPs eras, people are now free to express their opinions and engage in informed (and sometimes uninformed) political debates and discussions, without any fear of political repercussions. This is certainly a praiseworthy development for any West African nation, given the prevalence of political repression and civil conflicts ravaging that part of the world. However, more needs to be done to shift the emphasis of the reform away from macroeconomic growth to human-friendly development, with more attention paid to the distributional ramification of SAPs and their outcomes. Indeed, the distributive and regulatory roles of the government need to be reinserted in the discourse on SAPs. In as much as free market enterprise is laudable, it is our deep conviction that a nation can hardly pursue unbridled trade and financial liberalisation without exposing itself to economic instability, polarisation and the loss of basic sovereignty to some extent.

Notes

1. We would like to thank the Global Development Network (GDN) for its generous financial support for this research project. Additionally we are very grateful to José María Fanelli and Gary McMahon for their insightful and constructive suggestions on earlier drafts of this chapter.
2. These objectives draw upon insights from Fanelli and Popov (2003) and the Final Terms of Reference (FTOR) produced by Klaus Schmids-Hebbel, under the auspices of the Global Development Network (GDN) for this global research on understanding reform.
3. Hence the use of quotation marks around the word hypotheses.
4. In the Final Terms of Reference (FTOR) for the country studies and the thematic papers for this project, Klaus Schmidt-Hebbel and José María Fanelli urged authors to adopt more qualitative (rather than quantitative or high level econometric modelling) techniques of analysis, and we couldn't agree with them more.

5. The focus group discussions were conducted in July of 2003. The participants of the group discussions were drawn from a variety of government institutions and departments and private businesses and organisations.
6. Boafo-Arthur (2001) relied on the World Bank's *Ghana: Policies and Program for Adjustment* (1984) for these data.
7. The Student Task Force was a programme initiated by the university students, in conjunction with the PNDC, during the early months of the PNDC, in which the students went home for about two terms and organised themselves for various national and community development projects (notably carting cocoa from farms to the coast for shipment) to show their support for the PNDC in particular, and for national development in general.
8. As of now the National Service Scheme covers a total of two years, half of which is served prior to entry into university and the other half after graduation.
9. Ewe is one of ethnic groups in Ghana; Jerry Rawlings hails from this ethnic group.
10. Quoted in Donkor (1997: 147).
11. This point was raised by Gary McMahon in his review of an earlier draft of this chapter, and we would like to acknowledge that.
12. The Provisional National Defence Council (PNDC) was transformed into the National Democratic Congress (NDP) for the 1992 election; the NDC campaigned under a platform of 'continuity for SAPs' and won the elections.
13. These two crucial points/reminders were suggested by Nic van de Walle who reviewed an earlier draft of this chapter.

References

Adda, William (1989) 'Ghana', in V. Ramandham (ed.), *Privatization in Developing Countries* (London: Routledge).

Amoako-Tuffour, Joe (2001) 'The Growth of Public Debt in a Reform Economy', in Kwadwo Konadu-Agyemang (ed.), *IMF and World Bank Sponsored Structural Adjustment Programs in Africa: Ghana's Experience, 1983–1999* (Burlington, USA: Ashgate), 41–76.

Anquandah, James (1982) *Rediscovering Ghana's Past* (Essex: Longman).

Anyinam, Charles (1989) 'The Social Cost of the IMF's Adjustment Programs for Poverty: the Case of Health Care in Ghana', *International Journal of Health Services*, 19: 531–47.

Anyinam, Charles (1994) 'Spatial Implications of Structural Adjustment Programs: the Ghanaian Experience', *Tidjdschrift voor Economische en Sociale Geografie (Journal of Economic and Social Geography)*, 85, 5: 446–60.

Anyinam, Charles (2001) 'Structural Adjustment Programs and the Mortgaging of Africa's Ecosystems: the Case of Mineral Development in Ghana', in Kwadwo Konadu-Agyemang (ed.), *IMF and World Bank Sponsored Structural Adjustment Programs in African: Ghana's Experience, 1983–1999* (Burlington: Ashgate), 197–218.

Appiah-Kubi, Kojo (2001) 'Fiscal Impacts of Structural Adjustment', in Kwadwo Konadu-Agyemang (ed.), *IMF and World Bank Sponsored Structural Adjustment Programs in Africa: Ghana's Experience, 1983–1999* (Burlington: Ashgate), 77–109.

Aryeetey, Ernest, Harrigan, Jane and Nissanke, Machiki (eds) (2000) *Economic Reforms in Ghana: the Miracle and the Mirage* (Oxford: James Currey).

Asa, Eric (2001) 'Structural Adjustment Program and Ghana's Mineral Industries', in Kwadwo Konadu-Agyemang (ed.), *IMF and World Bank Sponsored Structural Adjustment Programs in Africa: Ghana's Experience, 1983–1999* (Burlington, USA: Ashgate), 157–80.

Barwa, S. D. (1995) *Structural Adjustment Programmes and the Urban Informal Sector in Ghana*, discussion paper no. 3 (Geneva: International Labour Office).

Bates, Robert H. Greif, Avner, Levi, Margaret, Rosenthal, Jean-Laurent and Weingast, Barry R. (1998) *Analytic Narratives* (Princeton, NJ: Princeton University Press).

Bates, Robert H. et al. (2000a) 'Analytic Narratives: Revisited', *Social Science History*, 24, 4: 685–9.

Bates, Robert H. et al. (2000b) 'The Analytic Narrative Project', *American Political Science Review*, 75, 2: 696–702.

Batse, Z. K. M., Botschie, G. and Agyemang, M. M. (1999) *Integrating Capacity Building within the Context of Social Policies for Poverty Reduction in Ghana* (Dakar, Senegal: IDRC).

Bello, W., Kinley, D. and Elinson, E. (1982) *Development Debacle: the World Bank in the Philippines* (San Francisco: Institute for Food and Development Policy).

Boafo-Arthur, Kwame (2001) 'Structural Adjustment, Policies and Democracy in Ghana', in Kwadwo Konadu-Agyemang (ed.), *IMF and World Bank Sponsored Structural Adjustment Programs in African: Ghana's Experience, 1983–1999* (Burlington: Ashgate), 241–71.

Boafo-Arthur, Kwame (1999) 'Structural Adjustment Programs (SAPs) in Ghana: Interrogating PNDC's Implementation', *West African Review*, 1, 1, available at http://www.icaap.org/iuicode?101.1.1.3 (accessed on 20 August 2003).

Boahen, Adu (1992) *The Ghanaian Sphinx: Reflections on the Contemporary History of Ghana: 1972–1987* (Accra: Academy of Arts and Sciences).

Brydon, Lynne and Legge, Katen (1996) *Adjusting Society: the World Bank, the IMF and Ghana* (London and New York: I. B. Tauris Publishers).

Cardoso, Eliana and Galal, Ahmed (2003) 'External Environment, Globalization and Reform', paper prepared for the 4th Annual Global Development Conference, Cairo, Egypt, 15–21 January.

Chamlee-Wright, Emily (1997) *The Cultural Foundations of Economic Development: Urban Female Entrepreneurship in Ghana* (New York: Routledge).

Cornia, A. G., Jolly, R. and Stewart, F. (1987) *Adjustment with a Human Face: Protecting the Vulnerable and Promoting Growth* (New York: Oxford University Press).

Dessler, David (2001) 'Analytic Narrative: a Methodological Innovation in Social Science?' *International Studies Association* (Oxford: Blackwell): 176–9.

Devarajan, Shantayanan, Dollar, David R. and Holmgren, Torgny (eds) (2001) *Aid and Reform in Africa: Lessons from Ten Case Studies* (Washington, DC: World Bank).

Donkor, Noble T. (2001) 'Impact of Structural Adjustment Policies on Forests and Natural Resources Management', in Kwadwo Konadu-Agyemang (ed.), *IMF and World Bank Sponsored Structural Adjustment Programs in African: Ghana's Experience, 1983–1999* (Burlington: Ashgate), 181–96.

Donkor, Kwabena (1997) *Structural Adjustment and Mass Poverty in Ghana* (Aldershot: Ashgate).

Dornbusch, R. (1993) *Stabilization, Debt, and Reform: Policy Analysis for Developing Countries* (Upper Saddle River, NJ: Prentice Hall).

Dzorgbo, Dan-Bright, S. (2001) *Ghana in Search of Development: the Challenge of Governance, Economic Management and Institutional Building* (Aldershot: Ashgate).

Edgar, Andrew (2002) 'Institution', in Andrew Edgar and Peter Sedgwick (eds), *Cultural Theory: the Key Concepts* (London: Routledge), 194.

Evans, P. (1995) *Embedded Autonomy: States and Industrial Transformation* (Princeton: Princeton University Press).

Fanelli, José María (2003). 'On Analytic Narratives and Reforms', a thematic paper for the GDN Understanding Reform Project.

Fanelli, José María and Popov, Vladimir (2003) 'On the Philosophical, Political, and Methodological Underpinnings of Reform', a paper prepared for the 4th Annual Global Development Conference, Cairo, Egypt, 15–21 January.

Folasade, Ayonrinde (2002) *Trade Liberalization and Technology Acquisition in the Manufacturing Sector* (Nairobi: African Economic Research Consortium).

Forest Department of Ghana and International Institute for Environment and Development (1993) *Study of Incentives for the Sustainable Management of the Tropical High Forest of Ghana* (Accra: Forestry Department).

George, Susan (2001) 'How the Poor Develop the Rich', in Majid Rahnema (ed.), *The Post-Development Reader* (London and New Jersey: Zed Books), 207–13.

Government of Ghana (undated) *Civil Service Performance Improvement Programme* (Accra: Government Printer).

Government of Ghana (1987) *Programme of Action to Mitigate the Social Cost of Adjustment* (PAMSCAD) (Accra: PAMSCAD Secretariat).

Government of Ghana (1988) *Ghana Living Standard Survey* (Accra: Ghana Statistical Service).

Government of Ghana (1990) *Medium Term Agricultural Program: an Agenda for Sustained Growth and Development* (Accra: Ministry of Food and Agriculture).

Government of Ghana (1992) *Ghana Living Standard Survey* (Accra: Ghana Statistical Service).

Government of Ghana (1995a) *Ghana-Vision 2020: the First Step: 1996–2000* (Accra: Government Printer).

Government of Ghana (1995b) *The Pattern of Poverty in Ghana* (Accra: Ghana Statistical Services).

Graham, Elspeth (1997) 'Philosophies Underlying Human Geography Research' in Robin Flowerdew and David Martin (eds), *Methods in Human Geography: a Guide for Students Doing Research Projects* (Harlow, Essex: Longman), 6–30.

Green, J. A. (1995) 'Toward a Détente with History: Confronting Canada's Colonial Legacy', *International Journal of Canadian Studies*, 12 (Fall): 85–105.

Gyimah-Boadi, E. (1990) 'Economic Recovery and Politics in PNDC's Ghana', *Journal of Commonwealth and Comparative Studies*, 28, 3: 328–43.

Haggard, S. and Kaufman, R. R. (1989) 'Economic Adjustment in New Democracies', in Joan Nelson (ed.), *Fragile Coalitions: the Politics of Economic Adjustment* (Oxford: Transaction Books), 59–60.

Haruna, Peter F. (2001) 'From Developmental to a Managerial Paradigm: Ghana's Administrative Reform under Structural Adjustment Programs', in Kwadwo Konadu-Agyemang (ed.), *IMF and World Bank Sponsored Structural Adjustment Programs in African: Ghana's Experience, 1983–1999* (Burlington: Ashgate), 111–39.

Haynes, J. (1989) 'Ghana: Indebtedness, Recovery, and the IMF, 1977–87', in T. W. Parfitt and S. P. Riley (eds), *The African Debt Crisis* (London: Routledge).

Healey, J. and Robinson, M. (1992) *Democracy, Governance and Economic Policy: Sub-Saharan Africa in Comparative Perspective* (London: ODI).

Healey, J. and Robinson, M. (1995) *The Design of Economic Reforms in the Context of Political Liberalization* (London: ODI).

Husain, I. and Faruquee, R. (1995) *Adjustment in Africa: Lessons from Country Case Studies* (Washington, DC: World Bank).

Hutchful, Eboe (1997) 'Military Policy and Reform in Ghana since 1966', *Journal of Modern African Studies*, 35, 2.

Huq, M. M. (1989) *The Economy of Ghana: the First 25 Years since Independence* (New York: St. Martin's Press).

Institute of Social, Statistical and Economic Research (ISSER) (1999) *The State of the Ghanaian Economy in 1998* (Lagon, Accra: ISSER).

ISSER (1995) *The State of the Ghanaian Economy* (Lagon, Accra: ISSER).

International Development Center of Japan (1992) *Structural Adjustment in Ghana: an Evaluation* (Tokyo: Ministry of Foreign Affairs, Government of Japan).

IMF (2003) *Ghana-Enhanced Structural Adjustment Facility: Economic and Financial Framework Paper, 1998–2000* (Washington, DC: IMF).

James, Mary (1999) 'Impact of the Programme of Action to Mitigate the Social Cost of Adjustment (PAMSCAD) Projects on the Rural Poor in Ejisu Juaben District, Ghana', MA thesis, Kwame Nkrumah University of Science and Technology, Kumasi, Ghana.

Jonah, K. (1989) 'Changing Relations between IMF and the Government of Ghana: 1960–1987', in E. Hanson and Y. A. Ninsin (eds), *The State, Development and Politics in Ghana* (London: CODESRIA), 94–115.

Kapur, I., Hadhjimichael, Michael T., Hilbers, Paul, Schiff, Jerald and Philippe Szymczak (1991) *Ghana: Adjustment and Growth, 1983–1991* (Washington, DC: International Monetary Fund).

Konadu-Agyemang, Kwadwo (ed.) (2001) *IMF and World Bank Sponsored Structural Adjustment Programs in Africa: Ghana's Experience, 1983–1999* (Burlington: Ashgate).

Konadu-Agyemang, Kwadwo and Baffour-Takyi, Kwaku (2001) 'Structural Adjustment Programs and the Political Economy of Development and Underdevelopment in Ghana', in K. Konadu-Agyemang (ed.), *IMF and World Bank Sponsored Structural Adjustment Programs in Africa: Ghana's Experience, 1983–1999* (Burlington: Ashgate), 17–40.

Kunfaa, Ernest Y. and Dogbe, Tony (2002) 'Ghana: Empty Pockets', in Deepa Narayan and Patti Petesch (eds), *Voices of the Poor from Many Lands* (New York and Washington, DC: Oxford University Press and the World Bank), 17–49.

Leechor, Chad (1994) 'Ghana: Front-runner in Adjustment', in Ishrat Husain and Rashid Faruqee (eds), *Adjustment in Africa: Lessons from Country Case Studies* (Washington, DC: World Bank).

Libby, R. L. (1976) 'External Cooptation of a Less Developed Country's Policy Making: the Case of Ghana', *World Politics*, 1, 10: 67–89.

Liew, Leong H., Bruszt, Laszlo and He Liping (2003) 'Causes, National Costs, and Timing of Reforms', a paper prepared for GDN Workshop, Cairo, January.

Manuh, Takyiwaa (1997) 'Ghana: Women in the Public and Informal Sectors Under the Economic Recovery Programme', in Nalini Visvanathan, Lynn Duggan, Laurier Nisonoff and Nan Wiegersma (eds), *The Women, Gender and Development Reader* (London: Zed Books), 277–84.

Mensah, Joseph (2006a) 'Ghana', in Thomas M. Leonard (ed.), *Encyclopaedia of the Developing World*, vol. 2 (New York and London: Routledge), 699–702.

Mensah, Joseph (2006b) 'Nkrumah, Kwame', in Thomas M. Leonard (ed.), *Encyclopaedia of the Developing World*, vol. 2 (New York and London: Routledge), 1145–7.

Mkandawire, T. (1992) 'The Political Economy of Development with Democratic Face', in A. G. Cornia, R. van der Hoeven and T. Mkandawire (eds), *Africa's Recovery in the 1990s* (London: St. Martin's Press).

Narayan, Deepa (2002) *Voices of the Poor: Can Anyone Hear Us?* (New York and Washington, DC: Oxford University Press and the World Bank).

Narayan, Deepa, Chambers, Robert, Shah, Meera Kaul and Petesch, Patti (eds) (2000) *Voices of the Poor: Crying Out for Change* (New York and Washington, DC: Oxford University Press and the World Bank).

Ninsin, K. A. (1989) 'State, Capital and Labour Relations, 1961–1987', in E. Hansen and K. A. Ninsin (eds), *The State, Development and Politics in Ghana* (London: CODESRIA).

Ninsin, K. A. (1991) 'The PNDC and the Problems of Legitimacy', in Donald Rothchild (ed.), *Ghana: the Political Economy of Recovery* (Boulder: Lynne Rienner), 49–67.

Noury, Abdul G. and Fidrmuc, Jan (2002) 'Interest Groups, Stakeholders, and the Distribution of Benefits and Costs of Reform', a paper presented to the GDN Workshop on Understanding Reform, Cairo, Egypt, 15–21 January.

Olukoshi, Adebayo (1992) 'The World Bank, Structural Adjustment and Governance in African', mimeo.

Oppong, J. R. (2001) 'Structural Adjustment and the Health Care System', in Kwadwo Konadu-Agyemang (ed.), *IMF and World Bank Sponsored Structural Adjustment Programs in Africa: Ghana's Experience, 1983–1999* (Burlington: Ashgate), 357–70.

Osei-Akom, Kwaku (2001) 'Cocoa Production under Ghana's Structural Adjustment Programs: a Study of Rural Farmers', in Kwadwo Konadu-Agyemang (ed.), *IMF and World Bank Sponsored Structural Adjustment Programs in Africa: Ghana's Experience, 1983–1999* (Burlington, USA: Ashgate), 141–55.

Owusu, J. H. (1998) 'Current Convenience, Desperate Deforestation: Ghana's Adjustment Program and the Forestry Sector', *Professional Geographer*, 50, 4: 418–36.

Oxfam (1999) *IMF: Wrong Diagnosis, Wrong Medicine* (Oxford: Oxfam).

Panford, Kwamina (2001) 'Structural Adjustment Programs, Human Resources and Organizational Challenges facing Labor and Policy Makers in Ghana', in Kwadwo Konadu-Agyemang (ed.), *IMF and World Bank Sponsored Structural Adjustment Programs in Africa: Ghana's Experience, 1983–1999* (Burlington, USA: Ashgate), 219–39.

Pereira, Sérgio et al. (2000) *Ghana: Economic Development in a Democratic Environment* (Washington, DC: International Monetary Fund).

Przeworski, Adam and Limongi, Fernando (1997) 'Modernization: Theories and Facts', *World Politics*, 49: 155–83.

Ray, Donald I. (1989) *Ghana: Politics, Economics and Society* (London: Francis Pinter Publishers).

Riddel, Barry (1992) 'Things Fall Apart Again: Structural Adjustment Programs in Sub-Saharan Africa', *Journal of Modern African Studies*, 30, 1.

Rimmer, Douglas (1992) *Staying Poor: Ghana's Political Economy 1950–1990* (Oxford: Pergamon Press).

Rostow, W. (1960) *The Stages of Economic Growth: a Non-Communist Manifesto* (Cambridge: Cambridge University Press).

Ruis, Andres and Walle, Nicolas van de (2003) 'Political and Cultural Institutions and Economic Polity Reform', paper presented to the GDN Workshop on Understanding Reform, Cairo, Egypt, 16–17 January.

Schmidt-Hebbel, Klaus (2003) 'Panel on Final Terms of Reference', presented at GDN Workshop on Understanding Reform, Cairo, Egypt, 17 January.

Sirrowy, L. and Inkeles, A. (1990) 'The Effects of Democracy on Economic Growth and Inequality: a Review', *Studies in Comparative International Development*, 25, 1 (Spring).

Tangri, Roger (1991) 'The Politics of State Divestiture in Ghana', *African Affairs*, 90.

Toye, John (1990) 'Ghana's Economic Reform, 1983–1987: Origins, Achievements and Limitations', in J. Pikett and H. Singer (eds), *Towards Economic Recovery in Sub-Saharan Africa* (London: Routledge).

Trades Union Congress of Ghana (1996) *Report of the Executive Board*, 5th Quadrennial Delegates Congress (Accra: TUC).

Tsikata, Yvonne M. (2001) 'Ghana', in Shantayanan Devarajan, David R. Dollar and Torgny Holmgren (eds), *Aid and Reform in Africa* (Washington, DC: World Bank), 45–100.

Tutu, K. (1994) *Structural Adjustments and Their Effects on Ghanaian Workers* (Accra: Friedrich Ebert Stiftung).

UNDP (1992) *Human Development Report 1992* (New York: Oxford University Press).

UNDP (1996) *Human Development Report 1996* (New York: Oxford University Press).

UNDP (1999) *Human Development Report 1999: Globalization with a Human Face* (New York: United Nations Development Program).

United Nations Economic Commission for Africa (ECA) (1989) *Africa's Alternative Framework to Structural Adjustment Programmes for Socio-Economic Recovery and Growth in the 1980s* (Addis Ababa: ECA).

United Nations Economic Commission for Africa (ECA) (2002) *Economic Report on Africa 2002: Tracking Performance and Progress* (Addis Ababa: ECA).

UNICEF (1986) *Ghana: Adjustment Policies and Programmes to Protect Children and Other Vulnerable Groups* (Accra: UNICEF).

Vogel, R. J. (1988) *Cost Recovery in the Health Sector: Selected Country Studies in West Africa,* Technical Paper No. 82 (Washington, DC: World Bank).

Waddington, C. J. Enyimayew (1989) 'A Price to Pay: the Impact of User Charges in Ashanti-Akim District, Ghana', *International Journal of Health Planning and Management,* 4: 17–47.

Werlin, Herbert H. (1994) 'Ghana and South Korea: Explaining Development Disparities', *Journal of African and Asian Studies,* 3–4: 205–25.

World Bank (1984) *Ghana: Policies and Program for Adjustment* (Washington, DC: World Bank).

World Bank (1989) *Sub-Saharan Africa: From Crisis to Sustainable Growth. A Long-Term Perspective* Study (Washington, DC: World Bank).

World Bank (1990) *World Development Report* (New York: Oxford University Press).

World Bank (1994) *Adjustment in Africa: Reform, Result, and the Road Ahead* (Washington, and New York: World Bank and Oxford University Press).

World Bank (1995) *Ghana Growth, Private Sector, and Poverty Reduction,* a Country Economic Memorandum, Country Operations Divisions, West Central Africa Department, Report no. 14111-GH (Washington, DC: World Bank).

World Bank (1996) *Reports on Ongoing Operational, Economic and Sector Work* (Washington, DC: Knowledge Networks).

World Bank (1999) *World Development Report* (New York: Oxford University Press).

World Bank (2002a) *World Development Indicators, 2002* (Washington, DC: World Bank).

World Bank (2002b) *African Development Indicators, 2002* (Washington, DC: World Bank).

Yeebo, Zeya (1991) *Ghana, the Struggle for Popular Power: Rawlings: Saviour or Demagogue* (London: New Beacon Books).

4
Understanding Reforms: a Country Case Study of Morocco

Brahim Mansouri, Brahim Elmorchid, Mustapha Ziky and S. Mohamed Rigar[1]

Like many African countries, Morocco adopted macroeconomic and structural reforms, following the international debt crisis of the early 1980s. In spite of increasing theoretical and empirical work on reforms, we contend that, at least in the case of Morocco, the available literature has significant shortcomings. First, many of the previous studies deal only with specific components of reforms; second, the existing studies are excessively descriptive; third, several of the available studies have ideological undertones, doggedly supporting or rejecting reforms undertaken within the framework of the Structural Adjustment Programmes (SAPs); and, finally, in the case of Morocco, there is practically no serious work on the political economy and the role of extra-economic factors in the reform process.

Our research seeks to fill some of these gaps, using an approach that combines political economic analysis with interviews with policy-makers, leaders of political parties and scholars. Our analysis divides the Moroccan reform blueprint into three main episodes. The first deals with the macroeconomic stabilisation and the initial structural reforms undertaken over the period 1983–93. The second episode relates to the reinforcement of structural reforms (e.g. privatisation and financial sector reforms) undertaken in the period 1993–8; this reform episode is also characterised by the 1995 partnership agreement signed between Morocco and the European Union (EU). The third reform episode concerns the period 1998–2004, characterised by the reinforcement of the second generation of reforms, namely political, institutional and social reforms. This last episode also entailed the accession of the ancient political opposition to political power in March 1998. Also important was the enthronement of the young King Mohamed VI in July 1999, following the death of his father King Hassan II. For each reform episode, we try to analyse why reforms were initiated (the 'why' question), the factors shaping them (the 'what' question) and the reform outcomes (the 'how well' question). The remainder of the chapter is organised as follows. Section 1 addresses the why, what and how well questions in relation to the first episode of reforms, while sections 2 and 3 deal with the same questions, regarding the second and third episodes of reform, respectively.

1 The first episode of reforms 1983–93: a period of macroeconomic stabilisation

1.1 Why reforms in the first episode were initiated

The Moroccan pre-adjustment crisis was multifaceted, entailing difficult macroeconomic, political and social problems. We propose here to test the hypothesis that 'crisis is the main driving force behind the initiation of structural reforms'. We will then focus on the role of uncertainty and external factors. Historically, economic crises in Morocco have been followed by some kinds of reforms, but reforms in the framework of the Structural Adjustment Programmes (SAPs) have been deeper, dealing with practically all aspects of the Moroccan economy and society. Even though crises have generally been followed by reforms, it is important to test whether or not such crises are sufficient, or necessary, for the adoption of reforms. The hypothesis that 'crisis triggers reforms' is not that different from the supposition of Al-Muaqqit (1934), a Moroccan thinker who proposed that the justification of reforms in Morocco relied upon the apocalyptic description of a generalised crisis. In light of Al-Muaqqit's view, our analysis of the pre-reform crisis becomes very pertinent.

Crisis not only introduces turbulence into the functioning of the economic system, but may also threaten the stability of the political regime. As Williamson and Haggard (1994: 565) argue, 'crisis is clearly neither a necessary nor a sufficient condition to initiate reforms. It has nevertheless played a critical role in stimulating reforms.' And according to Bates and Krueger (1993: 454), 'in all cases, of course, reforms have been undertaken in circumstances in which economic conditions were deteriorating'. At the same time, we must note that Morocco has experienced sharp crises, especially since 1977, but no concerted efforts were made to address the issues involved.

In Morocco, especially by the end of the 1970s, there was generally a political unanimity on the need to pursue territorial integrity, by reintegrating the Moroccan Saharan provinces – what has been called the 'Saharan fact'. In the face of the 'Saharan fact', the Moroccan government delayed the necessary reforms. Interviews with King Hassan II revealed that Morocco had been in a war economy, with major resources being channelled not only towards financing the war, but also to the financing of the physical and social infrastructure (interviews with Hassan II, 1980a, 1980b).

We argue that historically the Moroccan government has not been willing to internalise 'social learning' from crisis. The question is why the Moroccan government did not take the right decisions to solve problems even before embarking on the nation's major SAPs, which started in 1983. We think that the Moroccan political regime is often so concerned with partial reforms that wider and deeper macroeconomic and structural reforms are generally delayed.[2] The government routinely reacted to economic crisis by adopting timid measures, such as its Stabilisation Triennial Plan of 1978/80 and the voluntary adjustment of 1980–3 – an adjustment without the backing of the IMF or the World Bank. However, the fact that crisis may trigger reforms does not mean that the initiation of reform invariably results in a successful outcome. As Tommasi (2002: 26) points out, an economic crisis may result in right, wrong, or no reforms at all. Reforms adopted in Morocco in the pre-adjustment period may be considered in Tommasi's terms as 'bad reforms'. In this sense, pre-adjustment reforms were episodic policies, which suffered from shortcomings at various stages of the policy process: at the stages of problem definition, design, implementation and evaluation/monitoring.

The claim[3] that the Moroccan government had a short-term approach to development planning may be correct, but the real question is: why did a monarchy, with a king who is not subject to re-election, take a short-term perspective on development? It is possible to understand this paradox in the particular context of Morocco by analysing the existing mechanisms of the political game as well as the nature of legitimacy of the Moroccan political system. During the 1956–62 period the Moroccan political regime pursued a modernisation process by which the cycle of religious legitimacy was removed. This process was strengthened in 1962, following the promulgation of the constitution which promoted political rationalisation. However, the constitution appeared then as a legal framework devoted to what can be considered a 'conflicting coexistence' (Lagroye, 1985) of legitimacies rather than a means to consecrate Weberian rational legitimacy. In this sense, the constitution of 1962 reflects two types of legitimacy: civil and religious.

The conflicting coexistence of legitimacies instituted by the constitution of 1962 was not inspired by the Islamic system but by the objective facts that shaped the Moroccan political system during the period 1956–62. There were tensions between tradition and modernity, especially at the political level, with two conceptions of authority emerging: the first is linked to religion, while the second is linked to civil society. The conflicting coexistence of legitimacies stopped once the Nationalist Movement was weakened and the exception status was announced in 1965 in conformity with the constitution. In 1965 the king ended the conflicting coexistence of legitimacies and replaced it with the traditionalist religious legitimacy reflected in the 1970 constitution. Political instability in 1970–2 led the political regime to see the dangers of relying on religious legitimacy. Civil legitimacy re-emerged in the framework of the 1972 constitution, but as a mere support to religious legitimacy. Such ideology of traditionalist legitimacy may partly explain why the Moroccan political regime tends to give little importance to the utility of economic policy actions and even tends to make policy mistakes and to favour short-term actions to the detriment of long-term ones. The acceptance of short-term measures among the population may be due to the bounded rationality of the people in a context of widespread illiteracy.

Also, the political patterns of the opposition in Morocco were not sufficiently pragmatic. The opposition was very ideological and less constructivist in terms of economic, social, political and institutional changes. Instead of improving proposals put forward by the ruling political parties, the opposition often tries to block them. Another hypothesis which may be plausible in the case of Morocco is that crisis stimulates reforms because it threatens the political regime (Liew, Bruszt and He 2003). Multifaceted crisis and the resulting mass disaffection might lead the political regime to fear the instability of the system. In this framework, it seems that the regime learned from past experiences and interactions with the people, especially when popular dissatisfaction led to the exception status in 1965, and when King Hassan II experienced failed putsches in 1971 and 1972. Even though the Moroccan government had initiated voluntary reforms before 1983, the fear that the multifaceted crisis may threaten political stability led the government to initiate deeper reforms under the aegis of the IMF and the World Bank. The government often exploited existing information asymmetries and attributed the causes of the crisis to exogenous factors, and not to its own policy mistakes. Hunger, unrest and other social turbulence have sometimes been attributed to external interference.

1.2   Factors shaping reforms and reform outcomes during the 1983–93 episode

As in many developing countries, initial economic reforms include macroeconomic stabilisation and structural reforms. While macroeconomic stabilisation relies on demand management and aspires to reduce fiscal deficits, money creation and current account deficits, structural reforms seek price liberalisation, trade openness and privatisation. In what follows, we examine the speed of adjustment regarding price liberalisation and trade openness. We will then try to assess the reform outcomes, and the role of stakeholders and interest groups in these reform areas.

1.2.1   *Speed of macroeconomic stabilisation and initial structural reforms*

The debate on the timing and sequencing of reforms is particularly crucial. It has received much attention, especially following the failure of economic reforms in Latin America in the second part of the 1970s and early 1980s. As argued in Cardoso and Galal (2003), Fidrmuc and Noury (2003) and Liew and Bruszt (2003), reform outcomes depend, to some extent, on their timing and sequencing.

The adjustment speed (or timing of reforms) can be defined as the timeframe between the move from an initial set of macroeconomic variables to a targeted set of such variables (Nsouli et al., 2002: 4). Generally, it refers to the total time required to move from one set of macroeconomic variables to another or to introduce economic reforms and make them operational. As in many developing and transitional countries, Moroccan decision-makers had to make a choice between two competing approaches. The first approach is commonly termed the shock, cold-turkey or big bang therapy approach. The second is the gradual or incremental approach. Whereas the shock approach uses programmes of rapid, surprising and far more austere reforms, the gradual approach is based on a package of incremental and multistage reforms. Proponents of the gradual approach argue that it is better to cut incrementally the tail of a dog than to cut it entirely and immediately: as the farmer may reason: 'Oh! My poor dog, I must dock your tail, but, so as you suffer less, I will cut a small piece each day.'

What is more important to note in the case of Morocco is that macroeconomic stabilisation – notably, fiscal austerity and monetary restriction – generally followed a shock approach.[4] Moroccan decision-makers and the international financial institutions recognised the sharpness and the destabilising nature of the financial and monetary crisis of the early 1980s, and this pushed them to choose a relatively big bang approach to macroeconomic stabilisation. The aim of such an approach was to restore confidence for international creditors as well as for domestic economic and social operators.

There is no doubt that fiscal deficits were decreasing, especially after the early 1980s. However, available data suggest that the fiscal surplus was stabilised only by the end of the 1980s (see Table 4.1). Indeed, the fiscal deficit was estimated to be around 11.5 per cent of GDP in 1982. Even though it improved during the subsequent year, it experienced some increases after 1984, reaching 7.3 and 6.7 per cent of GDP in 1985 and 1986, respectively, and amounting to about 5.2 per cent of GDP in 1989. Over the period 1982–9, the fiscal deficit annual average stood at about 6.6 per cent of GDP (Table 4.1). In 1990, the budget deficit was stabilised at a level of less than 3 per cent of GDP, and continued thereafter to decline, reaching only 2.2 and 1.5 per cent of GDP in 1992 and 1993, respectively. The budget deficit annual average over the period 1990–7 was estimated to be only 2.6 per cent of GDP. However, fiscal surplus experienced an annual average deterioration of about 3.52 per cent of GDP over the period 1998–2000. Nevertheless, it is important to note that fiscal deficits in Morocco have experienced a tendential decrease during the whole period (see Table 4.1).

What is more important is to know why budget deficits in Morocco became stable and sustainable only after a period of fiscal adjustment of about seven years, even though Moroccan decision-makers used a shock approach to fiscal adjustment. We think that the reason behind this relatively slow speed of adjustment is that the big bang approach to fiscal austerity relied heavily on cutting public investment expenditures. By contrast, other components of public expenditures were cut only slightly or even maintained over time. In addition to subsidies (which were cut gradually) and current public consumption (which was slightly reduced or even maintained in some cases), interest payments have remained a constant burden for the government budget and even accumulated as a consequence of previous deficits. Another component of macroeconomic stabilisation is the so-called monetary restriction. While Morocco is known as a country characterised by fiscal expansion and higher public debt stocks, it is important to stress that historically Moroccan decision-makers did not resort to the monetisation of public deficits.

There seems to be a general agreement among Moroccan decision-makers that there was a big trade-off between inflation and money creation and decided accordingly not to resort to money creation to finance fiscal deficits. According to Mansouri (2001, 2003a), the relationship between money creation and inflation may be analysed as a typical Laffer curve of seigniorage, where money creation (as a ratio to GDP) increases in a first period in relationship to inflation, and, as inflation increases, money creation begins to fall because money holders are very sensitive to the eroding value of their money balances.

Let us move now to the speed of adjustment in the case of inflation. Our data suggest that inflation began to be stabilised in the early 1980s. However, the rate of inflation began to be comparable with those of European countries at the end of 1987, standing at a mere 3 per cent or less. From that year through 1997, the annual average inflation rate was estimated to be about 4 per cent, against an annual average inflation rate of about 8 per cent over the period 1969–86 when inflationary pressures were particularly destabilising (see Table 4.1). Over the period of 1974–86, when inflationary tensions were more destabilising and more detrimental to the economy of the country, the rate reached an annual average of about 10 per cent.[5]

Concerning external surpluses, it is important to emphasise that they were also improving, following the macroeconomic stabilisation of the early 1980s. Available data suggest that current surpluses as well as surpluses on goods and services continued to improve during the 1980s and beyond. Decreases in external deficits may have had some links with fiscal adjustment in line with the budgetary approach to the balance of payments. From values of about −12.3 and −15.0 per cent of GDP, respectively, for current account and goods and services surpluses in 1982, they improved in 1983 to be only about −6.5 and −10.7 per cent of GDP, respectively. After some deterioration in 1984 and 1985, they began to improve henceforth, even reaching a positive current surplus of about 2 per cent of GDP in 1988. From that year onwards, external deficits became relatively sustainable. What is surprising is that budget and external sector surpluses were stabilised following similar speeds of adjustment. This would probably give support to proponents of the Keynesian twin-deficit proposition according to which fiscal and external deficits are linked (Table 4.1).

It is interesting to link the shock therapy in macroeconomic stabilisation to the degree of credibility of the Moroccan government and its policies. Moroccan decision-makers, on the basis of a shock approach, limited the

Table 4.1:　Macroeconomic data over the adjustment period until the end of the debt rescheduling

Year	Fiscal deficit	Public investment	Current public consumption	Current account surplus	Inflation (%)	Economic growth rate (%)
1980	9.70	10.32	18.34	−7.47	9.41	3.64
1981	13.35	12.84	19.08	−11.96	12.49	−2.76
1982	11.44	12.83	18.30	−12.10	10.53	9.62
1983	7.75	7.94	16.77	−6.35	6.21	−0.58
1984	6.02	6.44	15.56	−7.72	12.45	4.34
1985	7.28	5.86	15.84	−6.92	7.73	6.32
1986	6.67	6.84	15.35	−1.23	8.73	8.30
1987	4.48	6.12	15.72	0.97	2.70	−2.54
1988	3.20	7.08	15.38	2.13	2.37	10.42
1989	5.13	7.86	15.68	−3.45	3.14	2.36
1990	2.23	8.04	15.50	−0.78	6.91	4.03
1991	2.10	6.16	15.55	−1.48	7.98	6.90
1992	1.40	6.86	16.82	−1.52	5.74	−4.03

Source: World Development Indicators, the World Bank, CD-ROM, 2002; Direction de la Statistique, Rabat, Morocco.

hiring of additional graduates and postgraduates. The objective was to gradually eradicate the excessive numbers of staff in central government, public enterprises and local government. Because people were used to massive over-hiring in the public sector, by way of nepotism, clientelism and corruption, decision-makers and their adjustments lost credibility and adjustment costs, especially in terms of unemployment, intensified rapidly.

Another example concerns the proclamation of wage increases among labour unions in the Moroccan public sector. When decision-makers reacted negatively to such labour demands, arguing that Morocco is in a phase of adjustment, labour unions ironically retorted that 'the government has money just to make wasteful expenditures as well as to pay big salaries for highly placed bureaucrats'. This explains why public employees did not align their behaviour with the authorities' explicit or implicit announcements in the reform process. It also explains the magnitude of adjustment costs in terms of strikes, diminishing production and the blocking of administrative activities. The government finally decided to satisfy some of the demands of the labour unions by, for instance, increasing public wages and indemnities in 1987, but without significantly reforming the environment in which the bureaucracy operated. For example, the government did not make major changes to curtail wasteful expenditure, bad governance, corruption or the big salaries awarded to powerful and highly placed bureaucrats.

In contrast to the shock approach to macroeconomic adjustment, initial structural reforms during the 1983–93 episode may be described as a gradual, incremental or multistage process. Even though price liberalisation was adopted during the 1980s, reinforced reforms in this area were undertaken during the 1980s and beyond. These measures led to increases in prices, including those of basic goods, largely consumed by less well-off people at the bottom of Moroccan society. These price increases culminated in violent popular unrest in 1984, which was vigorously repressed by the Moroccan regime. In this sense, it is interesting to emphasise that Moroccan decision-makers were apparently undertaking a relative shock approach to price liberalisation at the beginning of the Structural Adjustment Programme. Facing serious popular and political dissatisfaction, they reoriented their price liberalisation therapy towards a more gradual approach.

Concerning foreign exchange policy, the government undertook three successive devaluations of the dirham in 1984, 1985 and 1990. The objective was to encourage exports and limit imports. While the devaluation of the dirham boosted exports, it arguably contributed to increased prices for imported investment and intermediate goods as well as an increase in national debt service. In a reform sequencing perspective, it seems that the government was willing to accelerate devaluation in line with a big bang approach before undertaking gradual trade liberalisation. To limit the negative impact of devaluation on imports, import liberalisation was undertaken in conformity with an incremental approach. A gradual approach was also followed to remove exchange controls, through incremental easing of exchange regulations.

Concerning the gradual trade policy liberalisation, Moroccan policy-makers had some success in eradicating barriers to international transactions, especially through reducing export taxes and, less vigorously, through decreasing import taxes and duties. As early as 1983, the government began to steadily cut import taxes and duties. However, especially with the institution of a special tax on imports, public revenues from imports started to increase before experiencing a net decrease in 1994. The institution of a special tax on imports in 1987 may be considered as the government's attempt to improve public revenues in the context of fiscal adjustment.

1.2.2   *Stakeholders, interest groups and reform outcomes*

Stakeholders dominating the Moroccan stabilisation process were essentially bureaucrats and public servants, labour associations in the public sector, sector-based trade unions, and the opposition political parties. Among these stakeholders, there were those who constituted true powerful interest groups, especially bureaucrats, labour associations and sector-based trade unions. In what follows, we highlight the outcomes of macroeconomic stabilisation and the initial structural reforms in relation to the activities of the above-mentioned stakeholders and interest groups.

As already pointed out, macroeconomic stabilisation in Morocco resulted in fiscal and current account deficits and kept inflation at lower levels at the end of the debt rescheduling in 1992–3. However, these macroeconomic stabilisation outcomes were realised to the detriment of economic growth and social well-being. Stakeholders and interest groups contributed to some of the inefficiency in the nation's macroeconomic stabilisation process. In a political economy perspective, to restore the budget balance, Morocco relied heavily on cutting public investment expenditures in accordance with a big bang approach whereas some public subsidies and transfers were readjusted only gradually, and current public expenditures were cut only slightly and even maintained constant in some cases. In 1983, when the implementation of the Structural Adjustment Programme started, the shock therapy in cutting public investment spending resulted in about 5 percentage points in GDP decrease in public investment against 1.5 and 0.75 percentage points of GDP for current public consumption and subsidies, respectively.

This approach to transforming the structure of public expenditure had something to do with the fact that the shock therapy adopted in Morocco aimed at balancing the nation's budget without exacerbating popular and political disaffection, especially among trade associations in the public sector, less favoured private consumers who benefited from subsidies, and some bureaucrats who can be considered as a powerful interest group in the Moroccan case (Mansouri, 2003b). As the works of Mansouri (2001, 2003a, 2003b) indicate, public investment is an important catalyst for capital accumulation in the private sector as well as for overall real economic growth.

Facing a sharp fiscal, financial and monetary crisis, the government was obliged to resort to a shock approach, at least on the macroeconomic stabilisation front. But fearing popular and political dissatisfaction, the government limited its big bang therapy to what was politically feasible, and thus avoided cutting public expenditures which may exacerbate popular and political disaffection, especially among labour associations, public servants and the poor. In the area of public consumption and subsidies, for example, the government used a gradual and multistage approach rather than a shock therapy. The former director of taxation in the Moroccan Ministry of Finance and Economy noted in an interview with us that it is better to adopt a gradual long-run approach to reduce current public consumption than to do it rapidly in line with a shock approach.

In addition to their opposition to the cutting of current public consumption, bureaucrats also opposed currency devaluation and trade reforms. Devaluation, for one, increased the prices of imported goods largely consumed by high-level bureaucrats. As for the new trade policy, it went against the interests of many employees of the administration who benefited from rents due to the provision of licences. To justify their opposition to free trade, they argued that it would result in losses to tariff revenues.

The government was generally unable to raise taxes because of the power of some sector-based trade unions. In particular, the large agricultural sector was exonerated from tax not only because the government wanted to favour the powerful agricultural trade union, but also to solidify its support in the rural areas, following intense displeasure in the urban areas. Unsurprisingly, in the Moroccan agricultural sector the large landowners wield far greater political power than their small landowner counterparts. Even political parties with high levels of rural support (e.g. the Parti National Démocrate, the Mouvement National Populaire and the Mouvement Démocratique Populaire) tend to defend the interests of large landowners. The political clout of large landowners may explain certain public choices in the agricultural sector, especially those dealing with tax exemptions and subsidies, all of which contributed to the slow decreases in fiscal deficits. It is important to note that the agricultural trade union also supported the government's trade liberalisation, not only because of the government's favour to the union, but also because the liberalisation boosted the exports of citrus fruits and other agricultural goods, especially those produced by large landowners.

The corporate trade union in the manufactured sector also played a major role in weakening tax return and therefore slowing down the reduction of the national deficit. In this sector, we also find a predominance of large enterprises in terms of their ability to influence policy-makers. The existing association of small and medium enterprises is not as influential as the one comprising large companies. As Benali and Cherkaoui (2002) pointed out, 'the historical development of the Moroccan bourgeoisie influenced the ability of large companies to defend their interests and influence policy makers'. Following the Moroccanisation programme in the early 1970s, a minority of Moroccan capitalist families gained control over a significant share of the capital involved, accelerating the economic and financial concentration of private capital in the hands of a minority of Moroccan families. This minority has an advantageous relationship with the political regime and their political and economic power is strong. As Berrada (1992) argued, following the Moroccanisation programme, private capital relied on the state apparatus in order to strengthen its position and redefine its relations with foreign capital. In return, private capital had to support the political regime. Such a connection of interests often led to the adoption of policies in favour of large companies. This may explain why such companies benefited not only from low taxes but also from the possibility of tax evasion and fraud. In such an environment, the government continued to rely heavily on indirect taxes, preventing the country using direct taxes as a catalyst to improve the *redistributive intensity*. Without cutting public investment expenditures, budget deficits would have remained higher and fiscal adjustment would have been sacrificed. The interconnection of interests between the private sector oligarchy and the administration may also explain why exchange rate devaluations and trade reform were initiated relatively rapidly during the 1980s, because the minority of capitalist families had a control over exporting firms. Exporting firms, as a powerful interest group, supported the trade liberalisation and exchange rate devaluations, taking advantage of their proximity to

Europe. Even though the new trade policy was seen by import-substitution industries as detrimental to their growth, trade liberalisation was also considered as a means to increase imports of inputs necessary to their expansion. Such import-substitution companies were also informed by the powerful business association about the orientations of the new trade policy and, probably, had pointed to a horizontal diversification across industrial groups. This means that the existing 'inside information' might allow the investors to transform the trade policy changes to their advantage (Benali and Cherkaoui, 2002).

The opposition political parties can also be seen as important stakeholders within the Moroccan macroeconomic stabilisation process of the 1980s. In Morocco, the multiparty system has a long history, but it is difficult to accept the idea that changes in electoral rules would significantly enhance competition among political parties. Since the nation's independence, the electoral process has never facilitated political competition deserving the name of democracy (Benali and Cherkaoui, 2002). With regard to SAPs, one can identify two main political parties: pro-administration political parties, which agree with the administration with practically no criticism of its SAP policies, and the 'anti-administration' political parties, which criticise virtually all aspects of the nation's SAPs. And since the 'anti-administration' political parties stayed in opposition for decades, their power was very strong. However, instead of using such power to contribute to the debate on how macroeconomic stabilisation should be conducted to influence the structure of public spending and, consequently, foster economic growth, these opposition political parties tended to criticise, quite dogmatically, the reform project as a whole. Concerning trade liberalisation, for instance, both the Parti du Progrès et du Socialisme (PPS) and the Union Socialiste des Forces Populaires (USFP) were against it, and focused much of their attention on the expected negative impacts of liberalisation on employment. They also rejected liberalisation as something non-Moroccan, but imposed by the international financial institutions, notably by the World Bank and the IMF. As for the Parti de l'Istiqlal (PI), its arguments against the new trade policy focused on nationalistic considerations. Such arguments are, however, unrealistic given the fact that the PI is led by the Fassi family (from the imperial city of Fez), which is strongly involved in big companies.

2   The second episode of reforms, 1993–8

Even though structural reforms started in the first half of the 1980s, they were reinforced and sustained only in the first half of the 1990s in the context of a relatively stabilised economy. Although the emerging Moroccan democracy experienced some improvement during this period (e.g. the reform of the constitution in 1992 and 1996), the old political regime continued to dominate national politics, economy and society. In what follows, we examine why deeper structural reforms and initial extra-economic reforms were undertaken, to highlight the factors that shaped them, analyse the role of stakeholders, and explore the reform outcomes during this period. To examine why deeper structural reforms were undertaken, we try here to highlight the contribution of the following factors: the role of external factors in political and institutional reforms; and the role of lower fragmentation of the political power and the Euro-Mediterranean Free Trade Zone as a coordination device for reforms.

2.1 The role of external factors in the initial political and institutional reforms

In spite of the importance of some domestic factors, such as the less encouraging outcomes of macroeconomic stabilisation and initial structural reforms and the clear conscience of the political opposition about political reforms, external factors seem to have played a major role in the initiation of earlier political and institutional reforms in Morocco. Such external factors may be summarised as follows:

- The increasing demand by the IMF and the World Bank to couple economic reforms with political and institutional reforms. In 1995, the World Bank published a new report on the prevailing economic and social situation in Morocco and concluded that extra-economic reforms should be adopted to improve economic and social performance in the country.
- Pressure from international NGOs (e.g. Amnesty International, France Liberty, etc.) for political liberalisation in Morocco.
- Renewed push by powerful Moroccan allies, such as the United States and France, for the country to clean up its political environment, especially following the publication of the American State Department's 'alarming report' on human rights abuses in Morocco in 1991. These external pressures were, however, reduced, following the involvement of Morocco in the second Gulf War, in spite of the opposition of a large segment of the Moroccan public. Moreover, the nomination of two Jewish personalities at the top of the political hierarchy (André Azoulay, as the economic adviser of the king, and Serge Berdugo, as Minister of Tourism) helped Morocco to win the support of the Jewish lobby in Washington. These factors seemed to have reduced the push for a speedy implementation of political and institutional reforms in Morocco.

2.1.1 *The roles of centralised political power and the Euro-Mediterranean Free Trade Zone in the implementation of reform*

Following Liew, Bruszt and He (2003: 11), 'a regime will not embrace reform if reform weakens the basis of its power but will embrace reform, or at least elements of it, if they provide the regime with opportunities to strengthen its power and weaken its opposition.' However, strengthening power and weakening opposition will not happen if the electoral system leads to frag-mented political power. As Liew, Bruszt and He (2003: 11) hypothesised: 'a decision to reform depends on the degree of centralized power – the higher the degree of centralized power the greater the likelihood of a decision to reform.'

Our analysis of the Moroccan political regime during the reform episode of 1993–8 reveals that political power was relatively less fragmented. Indeed, during this period, the polity and the economy were controlled by political parties which were elected and enjoyed a comfortable majority in the national parliament. Such lower fragmentation of political power may explain why the authorities were able to embark on structural reforms such as privatisa-tion and financial sector reforms during this period. It may also explain why the Euro-Moroccan Partnership Agreement was finally signed in 1995.

The translation of some major elements of reforms into laws (e.g. laws concerning trade, privatisation and financial sector reforms, for instance), international agreements (the free trade association agreement with Europe), constitutional clauses, and the role of King Hassan II certainly reinforced the government's commitment to economic liberalisation during the 1993–8 reform episode. It is now known that partnership agreements are often accom-panied by certain conditions, including those related to macroeconomic stabilisation and structural reforms. This is particularly plausible because (co)partners need some reforms in order to benefit fully from these partner-ship agreements. In the case of Morocco, the partnership agreement with the European Union and the scheduled Euro-Mediterranean Free Trade Zone motivated the initiation of reforms. The free trade agreement with the European Union included commitments with respect to political discipline, the free movement of goods, rights of establishment, payments, capital flows, competition policy, economic and financial cooperation and other general measures. The Barcelona Declaration explicitly noted that the Southern part-ner countries should initiate and activate reforms at the political, institu-tional and social levels in order to adapt the environment to economic cooperation and regional integration. Thus, Morocco adopted extra-economic reforms in 1996 to provide its institutions with more credibility and demys-tify the political system. It seems that regional integration played a major role in accelerating certain reforms in Morocco. Perhaps, without such regional integration, reforms would have taken more time to be initiated.

A restructuring of the Moroccan economy cannot yield satisfactory out-comes without the privatisation of public sector enterprises. Privatisation tends to improve productive and allocative efficiency and, therefore, facili-tates the regional integration of the Moroccan economy through the reinforce-ment of national corporate capacity to face international competition. Regarding financial sector reforms, it is important to note that they were par-ticularly needed to enhance the financial structure of firms and, conse-quently, to boost their ability to compete in a context of a more liberalised global economy. To benefit from regional integration, Morocco needed to attract foreign direct as well as portfolio investments, especially from Europe. This was virtually impossible without deeper reforms of direct and indirect finance. This partly explains why Morocco reformed its financial market with an improved stock market, banking and money market. Also, the convertibility of the national currency, the dirham, on current transactions was set up as a strong signal towards foreign investors and international financial markets.

2.2   Factors shaping reforms and reform outcomes during the 1993–8 episode

Deeper structural reforms during 1993–8 dealt with privatisation, extended trade liberalisation, financial sector reforms and industrial restructuring in the framework of the scheduled Euro-Mediterranean Free Trade Zone. In addition to deeper structural reforms, initial political and institutional reforms were initiated during the 1993–8 reform episode. The major political and institutional reforms undertaken during this period may be summarised as follows:

- The national constitution was revised twice under the reign of King Hassan II, in 1992 and 1996. The objective was to confirm and strengthen the separation between the legislative and executive powers as well as to provide the parliament with legal tools to control the government. Two supreme councils were created: the Constitutional Council with the mission to respect constitutional institutions and to ensure the good functioning of elections, and the Economic and Social Council with the objective of boosting economic and social development and ensuring transparency among various sectors of the economy. A second parliamentary chamber (Chambre des Conseillers) was created in order to better ensure the representativeness of professionals within the parliament.
- The legislative elections in 1997 resulted in the *consensual* nomination of a new coalition government under the direction of the socialist Abderrahmane Youssoufi.
- Actions were undertaken to free political prisoners and to encourage those living in exile for political reasons to come home.
- A new territorial division and a reform of local governments were adopted in 1996 with the aim of consolidating decentralisation efforts and ensuring more autonomy and prerogatives in the process of management of local affairs. The objective was also to create more homogeneous jurisdictions in terms of geography, demography, ethnicity and wealth.

2.2.1   *The political economy and the speed of major structural reforms*

Reforms in the financial area used a gradual approach. It seems that the government had learned much from the failures of the shock approaches to financial reforms in Latin America and, henceforth, resorted to incremental decision-making in financial reforms and liberalisation. Interest rate liberalisation was undertaken very slowly until 1996. Even since then interest rates have not been completely liberalised.[6] Even though bank reforms were implemented relatively rapidly, there is currently a project to reinforce reforms in this area. Stock market as well as monetary and exchange markets were also reformed gradually (Mansouri, 1997a, 1997b).

A useful indicator to measure the speed of adjustment in the financial sector would be the real interest rate, measured here as the annualised monthly real interest rate on time deposits with maturities less than eighteen months (see Easterly et al., 1994). In spite of a partial liberalisation of interest rates since 1974, real interest rates became steadily positive only since 1985, corresponding to a sounder, even though partial, interest rate liberalisation. The policy of positive real interest rates reflected the willingness and the effectiveness of policy-makers to boost domestic savings, especially through promoting time bank deposits, which are the main channel through which the domestic economy can be financed in the long run.

Another channel through which long-run economic growth can be financed more efficiently is the stock market. In a reform sequencing perspective, simultaneous launching of privatisation and stock market reforms in 1993 induced an increasing stock market capitalisation, increasing from 5 per cent of annual average GDP over the period 1986–93 to more than 10 per cent of GDP, following the privatisation process of 1993, and jumping to more than 25 per cent of GDP in 2003. However, due to the lack of substantial privatisation transiting through the stock market, and given the refractory mentality of the Moroccan people, stock market capitalisation and the number of listed companies remain particularly stationary.

Even though the law on privatisation had been adopted earlier in 1989, implementation of the process only started in 1993, because of the necessity to prepare legal and juridical regulations as well as to permit the operations of privatisation to transit through the financial markets, which began to be reformed and restructured in 1993. The privatisation process started through privatising the most profitable public sector enterprises. Therefore, it seems that the objective of the Moroccan government was to address fiscal issues rather than to improve efficiency. Public sector enterprises were privatised only gradually, resorting to privatising a set of them simultaneously. The process was not only gradual but also delayed until the end of the 1990s and the beginning of the 2000s. This reveals how privatisation of less profitable enterprises, regarded in Morocco as 'lame ducks', is difficult to undertake. Even with the recovery of the privatisation process at the end of the 1990s and the beginning of the 2000s, big public corporations, like the Maroc Telecom and Public Tobacco Corporation were only partially privatised.

In conformity with the partnership agreement with the European Union in 1995, Morocco had to conduct industrial restructuring within the framework of cooperation between the Moroccan private and public sectors on the one hand and the European Union on the other hand. In accordance with the Euro-Mediterranean Free Trade Zone rescheduled to be set up in 2010, a programme of industrial restructuring was designed and has to be implemented gradually and hand-in-hand with the gradual removal of import duties.

To better understand the gradual approach to structural reforms in Morocco, it is important to examine the debate between proponents of the shock therapy and the supporters of an incremental approach to reforms. Here, we centre the debate on the issues of the costs of adjustment and the credibility of the reform programme. In an 'unreal' world where immediate adjustments of prices and non-costly reallocation of resources are possible, the optimal policy would be a simultaneous removal of all existing distortions. Unfortunately, this is not the case in the real world, because reallocation of resources generates adjustment costs among different sectors of the economy. Moreover, different markets cannot adjust at the same speed to policy changes and price signals.

Two main hypotheses are necessary for the supporters of the idea that a shock approach to reforms is associated with lower adjustment costs through increasing reallocation of resources: presence of rational expectations and absence of distortions. In contrast, proponents of gradualism in the field of reforms emphasise that the big bang approach is costly in terms of adjustment costs to the extent that fast reforms may generate short-term losses, especially those associated with unemployment and income distribution effects, thereby accentuating political opposition to the reform process. Following this argument, an incremental approach to reforms would create less severe losses of gains for owners of factors of production. Concerning the case of Morocco, it seems that it is difficult for the two hypotheses of rational expectations and absence of distortions to completely hold on the macroeconomic as well as structural fronts. First of all, individualism is lacking, especially because of the persistence of old communal economic and social formations. Indeed, one can observe that collective styles of life inherited from pre-colonial eras are still predominant in Moroccan society, especially in the rural areas. Moreover, the weakness of a modern civil society may be considered a serious obstacle to the emergence of individualism. The latter is also hindered through the lack of an efficient educational system, generating ignorance. This explains what is generally called the 'neo-patrimonial nature of the state'. This means that in addition to its economic role, the Moroccan state should play a patrimonial role, especially through distributing advantages and benefits amongst the population.

We think that the unsuitability of the hypothesis of rational expectations to the reality of Morocco supports a gradual approach to implementing structural reforms in the Moroccan context. This partially explains why even the big bang approach to macroeconomic stabilisation contains a grain of gradualism and incrementalism. In spite of a certain dose of gradualism within the big bang therapy, however, short-term adjustment costs occurred and were sufficiently accentuated that the hypothesis of rational expectations lacked favour. For instance, in 1984, a popular and widespread unrest emerged in Morocco, following a generalised increase in prices. This can be considered, in contrast with the neo-classical theory, as a reaction of the population against self-regulating mechanisms of the market. This also means that people did not refer to the principle of equilibrating supply and demand to prices which can emerge from this balance. The popular unrest of 1984 may be theoretically associated with the 'irrational' behaviour of the Moroccan people. However, if we can consider Moroccan people as irrational, there is a reason to term the Moroccan state an irrational agent as well. Indeed, due to complete or bounded rationality, Moroccan decision-makers decided to resort to a general increase in prices, without paying attention to the behaviour of the population in the early stages of reform. We conclude that the 'cold-turkey approach' seems to be inappropriate in the Moroccan economic, social, political and cultural context, even for macroeconomic stabilisation. Meanwhile, the Moroccan government was forced, after the popular unrest of 1984, to abandon the generalised increases in prices and the big bang decreases in public subsidies to consumer goods.

The second hypothesis concerning the absence of distortions also cannot hold in the Moroccan case. In an underachieved liberal economy, as already emphasised in our diagnosis, multiple distortions destabilise the system. From administration of prices of goods and services, salaries and interest rates to that of exchange rates, distortions are detrimental for the optimal reallocation of resources, generating higher costs for the Moroccan economy. The problem is that the Moroccan government multiplied distortions within the economy and economic agents were sufficiently used to such distortions to the extent that the existing system was seen as the real world situation for many people.

In sum, we think that because the two hypotheses of rational expectations and absence of distortions do not hold in the Moroccan case, structural reforms, and even some aspects of macroeconomic stabilisation, cannot be implemented in line with big bang therapy approaches. So important in this framework is the cultural context in which reforms are designed and implemented. We agree with the political scientist, Mohamed Darif, when he affirmed in an interview with us that macroeconomic stabilisation and structural reforms need, above all, what he called a 'true cultural change'. However, since such cultural changes are long and exacting tasks, we think that gradual and multistage approaches to the structural reform process are needed.

Success of reforms depends also on the degree of credibility of the government policy and the reforms themselves. As Nsouli et al. (2002) pointed out, the credibility of government policy as well as that of the reform process is particularly crucial for the success of reforms and the control of adjustment costs. Feasibility is also essential for the reform process. Other factors, such as the specificity of the sector to reform, initial conditions and costs of failure, also matter greatly for reform outcomes and results. As Edwards (1989: 40) noted, 'the absence of credibility is equivalent to distortion'. But, what is important is not that credibility may be assimilated to a distortion; more interesting is that the degree of credibility determines the magnitude of adjustment costs. The problem of such adjustment costs arises when economic agents do not align their behaviour with explicit or implicit policies; that is, when they consider the state as untrustworthy. In the relationship between approaches to reforms and speed of adjustment, the more credible the reforms, the more rapid the reallocation of resources will be, and, therefore, the faster the speed of adjustment. By contrast, when credibility is lacking, there will be a reluctance of agents to adhere to announced reforms and, consequently, the process of adjustment will be longer, more specifically in highly distorted economies. It is also interesting to note that credibility may be reinforced in the case of broad-based reforms, especially if agents view them as a clear signal by authorities to break with past traditions (Nsouli et al., 2002). However, a gradual and incremental approach to reforms can improve credibility if the results achieved in the short term are sufficiently favourable in the sense that initial success in reforms can improve the reputation of decision-makers and, consequently, may encourage implementation of subsequent reforms. In this situation of enhanced credibility, decision-makers may even implement several reforms simultaneously, but, for efficiency purposes, without necessarily tackling them completely in one go.

We view credibility – a situation where the public's behaviour is aligned with that of the decision-makers – as a crucial question for the Moroccan case. As Tanzi (1994: 517) argued, 'a government that has not been sincere in the past about the real macroeconomic situation and has made major mistakes will not have a good reputation.' Morocco would probably be a very expressive example of diminishing government credibility, mainly because of decision-makers' past mistakes in public policies and income distribution. Even before the launching of the Structural Adjustment Programme in 1983 and the undertaking and reinforcement of the second generation of reforms in the 1990s and 2000s, the public had often viewed reforms as a partial manoeuvre or as a piecemeal game. When Moroccan decision-makers were engaged in wider and broad-based reforms, beginning with the implementation of the Structural Adjustment Programme, perhaps with good intentions, agents still considered the process as unreliable. The problem is not only that of past policy mistakes but also that of falsified electoral operations, widely criticised by opposition socialist political parties.

In line with Aesop's fable, the Moroccan government may be likened to a 'boy who cried wolf too many times when there was no wolf, (and) was not believed when he finally told the truth' (Tanzi, 1994: 517). The Moroccan government would probably have learned from past mistakes, but, because it is a slow learner, by the time it has done so, it has lost much of its credibility. Generally speaking, it is no accident that the major part of the recent literature on the timing of reforms stresses that the degree of credibility determines the magnitude of adjustment cost: that is, when credibility is lacking, agents will be reluctant to stick to reforms. Unlike previous scholars who have investigated the credibility of policy-makers and their policies only according to the point of view of private agents, we also view it from the point of view of bureaucrats themselves, especially those who are in charge of implementing public policies and reforms. Indeed, it is important to stress that policy-makers have a 'control deficit', resulting from the fact that they do not implement the policies and reforms themselves. For one reason or another, implementation of policies and reforms may not necessarily result in expected outcomes or may not achieve stated objectives. We argue that the level of *in-house credibility* of policy-makers and their reform programmes is important. This means, especially in the Moroccan case, that even with good intentions at the top of the hierarchy, how bureaucrats from the top right down to the lower levels of the governmental hierarchy appreciate the policies matters greatly in shaping reforms, independently of the approaches adopted in the timing of reforms. Thus, in Morocco, even the street-level bureaucrats may be able to block some aspects of reform, especially if they view policy-makers in the top of the hierarchy as less credible and particularly if they pursue rent-seeking objectives.

2.2.2   Stakeholders, interest groups, and the outcomes of the deeper structural reforms

In addition to farmers who continue to benefit from tax exemptions, we argue that the main stakeholders and interest groups operating during the 1993–8 reform episode were the bureaucrats, labour unions in the public sector, the banking sector lobby, and the opposition political parties. We argue that such stakeholders played a major role in the wider structural reforms and the launching of the second generation of reforms during this period. They were even able to determine the speed of reforms and reform outcomes in areas such as privatisation and financial sector reforms, as well as the launching of political, institutional and social reforms. While extra revenue from privatisation of the most profitable enterprises allowed the government to alleviate some of the burdens of the fiscal adjustment on public investment, it is expected that subsequent privatisations would be accelerated to complete the liberalisation of the economy.

While the privatisation of less profitable public sector enterprises is extremely urgent, it is very important to know why the privatisation process was delayed. In this context, we rely on Campos and Esfahani's framework which posits that:

Policy reform can be interpreted as a renegotiation of contracts that entail direct government involvement in production toward more efficient, market-oriented ones. But to consent to a reform package, interest groups that currently support or could support the ruling coalition must know what they will gain from the reform, how the gains will be distributed, and whether the distribution of rewards will indeed be honored by the government. Thus, the reform decision is hampered by the usual contracting problems, that is the problem of information and opportunism.

(Campos and Esfahani, 1996: 452)

Retaining power, while embarking on privatisation, requires establishing sufficient political support from the polity. Also, as pointed out by Campos and Esfahani (1996: 254), 'government interventions cannot be divorced from issues of redistribution, because it is partly through redistribution that a regime sustains itself'. In the real world of politics, redistribution does not necessarily mean a transfer of wealth from rich to poor: it usually means transfer of wealth from less powerful to more influential groups. In Morocco, for instance, when the Moroccanisation process was conducted in the early 1970s, firms previously owned by foreigners were given to powerful groups and individuals in the private and public sector, therefore creating quasi-feudalities operating around the political regime. No vigorous efforts from the government had been made to promote the sharing of ownership among different people within the Moroccanisation process. When decision-makers decided to privatise public sector enterprises, multiple interest groups, such as landlords and trade unions, resisted the reforms. What is perhaps more important in the privatisation process is that the Moroccan political regime can be considered as the most powerful 'interest group' in the sense that the regime would have likely resisted early efficient privatisations because of the importance of public sector enterprises in ensuring political support. In addition to resistance from trade unions and other interest groups, it seems that the public sector, as a source of political support for government, may explain why privatisations are delayed and, consequently, why performances in this reform area are relatively poor in terms of the number and the nature of privatised enterprises.

It is also important to stress that efficiency and rationality through privatisation are closely linked to the notion of 'enterprise spirit'. Furthermore, official discourses in Morocco highlighted the role of privatisation in promoting the sharing of ownership among different people. Can privatisation be considered as a factor for promoting enterprise spirit to shared ownership? This is the question we try to answer in what follows. Do Moroccan entrepreneurs have the necessary qualities to allow them to efficiently manage 'lame ducks' which subsist only through the 'generous manna' of the state? In fact, in Morocco, in various situations, one can observe the manifest shortage of a true 'entrepreneur culture' as well as of 'a taste and liking for business'. Moroccan entrepreneurs usually prefer investment in immediately profitable activities such as tertiary transactions, landed property and real estate, where they can be protected against foreign competition, allowing them to get higher annual returns (Berrada, 1992). Thus, we think that within the framework of the subsequent privatisations, in addition to complementary measures like sector-based incentives and training activities for future managers of privatisable enterprises, deeper cultural changes and institutional reforms should be undertaken to transform people's mentalities. Without such changes and reform efforts, privatisation cannot be considered as the magic panacea to enhance the productive and allocative efficiency of the domestic economy.

Based on the principle of 'property rights', the aim of ownership-sharing was to avoid the concentration of economic power in the hands of a minority of owners and to facilitate the emergence of a new dynamic capitalist social class. In fact, such argumentation seems to neglect multiple structural blockages of the underdeveloped Moroccan capitalist economy, rendering shared ownership ideals a real utopia (such an argumentation may have an ideological connotation; on this issue, see Mansouri, 1992: 99). The shared ownership ideology experienced a manifest failure even in the developed world where shared ownership remains limited even with existing adequate institutional and legal frameworks. Furthermore, in spite of financial sector reforms, shared ownership remains hindered by the narrowness and weakness of financial markets. In Morocco, the role of the stock market remains weak, especially because of the familial structure of Moroccan capitalism. Hence, even though most of the privatisation process transited through the stock market and some shares were sold to some small investors, the 'cake' of privatisation seems to be mainly profitable for the bigger local and foreign capitalists.

Bureaucrats constitute an important stakeholder within the privatisation process. Since privatisation allows the government to get high amounts of financial resources, bureaucrats tend to accept the transfer of public sector enterprises to the private sector. Such financial resources are needed to permit bureaucrats to continue to benefit from high rents within the administration. Such rent-seeking behaviour may also explain why profitable public sector enterprises were privatised first. Labour unions within the public sector, including those operating in privatisable public sector enterprises, also constitute an important stakeholder and powerful interest group within the Moroccan privatisation process. In coordination with opposition political parties, such labour unions virtually opposed all attempts to privatise certain public sector enterprises. The privatisation delays in Morocco since the early 1990s are largely due to the opposition from the public sector labour unions. During the period, many strikes were organised against privatisation and financial and/or employment compensations were made in favour of employees to allow them to comply with the privatisation process. Opposition political parties also opposed certain aspects of privatisation even before the launching of the programme in the early 1990s. Intense debates on this issue were conducted within the parliament before the promulgation of the privatisation law in 1989. In addition to the required preparations to implement privatisation, the influence of public sector labour unions and opposition political parties largely explained late implementation of privatisation in Morocco.

Let us now move to the outcomes of the financial sector reforms in Morocco. In this reform area, one can observe that the efforts of decision-makers yielded relatively better results in comparison with neighbouring countries like Algeria and Tunisia. Indeed, monetary policy became increasingly liberalised, as multiple controls on banks and on stock and exchange markets were removed, although sometimes only partially. Following Loayza and Soto (2003), we consider the ratio to GDP of a broad monetary aggregate as a relevant outcome indicator for the banking sector. From 1960 through to the end of 1983 (the date when financial reforms were started) the sum of money and quasi-money was estimated to be around 40 per cent of annual average GDP, with 36 per cent for money and only 4 per cent of GDP for quasi-money. Over the period 1984–2000 the sum of money and quasi-money was estimated to be around 64 per cent of annual average GDP, with 48 per cent for money and 16 per cent of GDP for quasi-money. This distinction between money and quasi-money is very interesting, especially in developing countries. As in many developing countries, monetary aggregates in Morocco are characterised by the predominance of money, which is more liquid, in comparison with quasi-money, which constitutes the main determinant of savings in the banking sector. While relatively liquid money dominated the monetary aggregates in Morocco before the initiation of incremental financial sector reforms in the early 1980s, quasi-money experienced relatively more substantial growth afterwards, suggesting that financial reforms contributed to enhancing, even though not strongly, financial depth. Another outcome indicator concerns the size and liquidity of the Casablanca stock exchange. Even though the number of listed companies remained relatively stable from the early 1980s until the beginning of the 1990s, the stock market capitalisation experienced a real big bang, increasing from an annual average of 5 per cent of GDP during the period 1986–93 (Mansouri, 1997a) to nearly 25 per cent of GDP in 2003, and most of the boom in stock market capitalisation is due to privatisation. Stock market liquidity, as measured by the ratio to GDP of the volume of transactions, has also experienced significant increases, suggesting that financial market reforms, coupled with privatisation, are good news for the stock market. Nevertheless, in spite of these important stock market developments, outcomes in this reform area remain below what is expected (Mansouri, 1997a, 1997b).

Another reliable outcome indicator in the financial reform area may be the levels of real interest rates, which have generally tended to be positive, suggesting that financial sector reforms, especially through eradicating financial repression, resulted in a 'liberated' financial market, and, consequently, to more reliable incentives to savings, especially in the long run; this has also fostered the growth of quasi-money and financial depth. As Loayza and Soto (2003: 8) argued, 'in the case of banking, a good indicator of financial depth that focuses on the private sector is domestic credit allocated by private commercial banks to the private sector, divided by GDP.' In the Moroccan case, the ratio to GDP of the credit stock available to the private sector is estimated to be around 38 per cent of GDP per annum for the period 1960–83. During the period from 1983 to 2000, characterised by bank reform efforts, the credit stock available to the private sector jumped to about 63 per cent of GDP. Even though the time-series data of the credit have sometimes experienced sharp fluctuations over the period (and no control has been done for the contribution of other factors), our analysis suggests that the reforms in the banking sector have yielded relatively good performances.

In spite of some good performances in the financial sector reforms, the process of financial liberalisation has been slow. For instance, interest rate liberalisation has not yet been completed. The slowness of interest rate liberalisation seems to be largely due to the powerful influence of the banking sector lobby, that is the influential banking sector trade union (i.e. the Groupement Professionnel des Banques Marocaines). While financial sector reforms aspire, among other objectives, to foster competition, the banking lobby tends to let the sector function like a quasi-cartel, especially through the manipulation of interest rates. There is also a coalition of interest between the banking sector and the ruling elite. Over-liquidity of the Moroccan banks is often encouraged by the government, notably because such over-liquidity ensures financial resources are devoted to the purchase of government bonds.

3   The third episode of reforms, 1998–2004

In the past, the ruling elite in Morocco did not attach any importance to domestic democratic demands. The Moroccan political regime was even violating citizens' civic and political rights without fearing international protest. The government benefited from considerable latitude from Western governments in a situation where the main enemy was communism and its local alliances. With the Cold War over, such international leeway has died down, and Western governments are now pushing for democracy and human rights reforms in Morocco, in particular, and in developing countries, in general. This push is also reinforced by pressures from public opinion and local and international human rights organisations, and from international financial institutions. It is important to note that since the first part of the 1990s, the international financial institutions and governments of developing and transitional countries recognised the importance of non-economic factors in the success or failure of economic reforms. They recognised that political, institutional, social and cultural factors may hinder the efficiency of macroeconomic stabilisation and structural reforms. It is reasoned that reforms in these areas should go hand-in-hand with economic reforms.

Political and institutional reforms include the reinforcement of popular participation through the development of a true democratic system, the emergence of a system of accountability and transparency, the fight against corruption, freedom of information and human rights, free and legislative deliberation, the rule of law, decentralisation, and a stronger state capacity (Guessous, 2003a). All these were considered urgent in developing and transitional countries under the influence of the ongoing global neo-liberal hegemony. This hegemonic model predominates not only at the theoretical level, but also in the practical policy arena. It is extended and reinforced especially through conditionality and consent-building mechanisms. After several attempts by King Hassan II to get the opposition political parties involved in a new government, a government of coalition, including opposition political parties, was finally constituted in March 1998, about one year before the death of Hassan II. Even though the coalition government was composed of a mosaic of left and centre-left political parties, the event was considered very significant in a country where past governments had always been technocratic or constituted by members of right-wing political parties.

We must note that sovereignty-related ministers, such as those concerned with justice, foreign affairs, interior and Islamic affairs, remained apolitical and subjugated to the direct power of the royal palace. Some conditions regarding macroeconomic stabilisation (lower fiscal deficits, lower inflation, etc.) were also imposed on the new government under Prime Minister Abderrahmane Yousoufi, who was chosen from the USFP – an opposition political party. Confidence in the Moroccan political regime was particularly restored after the appointment of the new coalition government. The move was described as a 'consensual government changeover' in the sense that, as the king wanted, it emerged not from elections, which were often criticised by the opposition parties as involving voting irregularities and falsifications, but by way of appointments. However, integrating opposition political parties into the new government was considered, in and by itself, as the expression of the political regime's willingness to favour political, economic and social changes. Indeed, the new government exhibited some willingness to carry on with the reform agenda, especially with regard to political, institutional and social reforms.

3.1   The emerging new concept of governance after the enthronement of King Mohamed VI

Even though major improvements at the political level were observed even before the death of King Hassan II, it is interesting to note that the reign of the king was characterised by disaffection among national political parties, human rights movements and democratic nations, especially during the 1960s and 1970s. The enthronement of King Mohamed VI in July 1999 opened a new era of political development, especially following the declarations of the new king's willingness to pursue, sustain and reinforce the democratic transition already announced, notably after the 'consensual government changeover' of March 1998. King Mohamed VI is highly regarded as a man of dialogue, a democrat and a humanist.

Considerable changes were observed following the enthronement of the new king. In particular, just after his enthronement, he announced his famous 'New Concept of Governance' for Morocco. He declared in an official speech: 'This democracy, if it is practised by democrats, would be an important leverage for overall development. By contrast, if it is affected by irregular electoral practices, it would become a burden for the Nation.' Under the reign of Mohamed VI, Moroccans increasingly became 'true citizens', and not simply subjects. The powerful Minister of the Interior, Driss Basri was dismissed; civil society and the public were jubilant, given Basri's violations of human rights, falsification of elections, nepotism, clientelism and bad management of public resources.

The newly enthroned king is also known as a man who worked hard to improve social conditions when he was the prince-heir to the throne. Moroccan people even considered him as the 'king of the poor'. His willingness to pursue social objectives after his enthronement added much to the legitimacy of the Moroccan political regime and accelerated the adhesion of the people to the whole effort of reforms and changes. The new king expressed his willingness to reinforce reforms, especially the second generation of reforms which involved political, institutional and social measures. Improvements in electoral processes, the fight against corruption, press freedom, poverty alleviation programmes, and the advancement in areas such as judicial reforms, democracy and governance are signals of the willingness and ability of the new king to accelerate reforms of the second generation.

It is important, however, to note that the political openness experienced under the reign of King Mohamed VI faced some obstacles following the events of 16 May 2003. On the pretext of fighting against terrorism, the regime started to oppress public liberties. We now find even Islamist political parties hesitant to support the recent decisions of the political regime, especially those which are opposed to their ideology (e.g. the new family status adopted in 2004). In addition, the intellectual and academic class has abandoned its zeal for constructive opposition. Some individuals, (such as certain journalists, for example) who have criticised the political regime have been imprisoned only to be freed after an amnesty from the king. Moreover, the new electoral code (election by listing) has resulted in the balkanisation of the political map. This has led to politically unusual and ideologically strange alliances (alliances between socialists and Islamists, for instance). Such alliances have resulted in a loss of legitimacy for certain political parties and a reinforcement of the legitimacy of the monarchy.

Obviously, economic reforms cannot induce expected outcomes without changes to the institutional and political environment. In the Moroccan case, the changes that have occurred include: the moralisation of public life, public sector rationalisation and the creation of conditions for good governance; the setting up of the Consultative Council for Human Rights and a ministerial department specialising in human rights; and the introduction of a judicial reform designed to create an environment that is favourable to the proper functioning of the market economy. Other changes were the creation of a national programme to improve and modernise public sector management, rationalise public expenditures, increase transparency, and strengthen the rule of law; and, in an acknowledgement of the cultural diversity of the Moroccan people, the Moroccan government recognised the Berber language (*Tamazight*) in education and the media, and created the new Royal Research Institute on Amazigh Culture in October 2001 to boost people's knowledge on the nation's culture, especially through research efforts from the Amazigh elite.

3.2   The need for a second generation of reforms and the role of extra-economic factors

Morocco experienced poor performances on several macroeconomic stabilisation and structural adjustment fronts. While macroeconomic domestic and external accounts seem to be stabilised, there are counter-performances in other reform areas. From an accounting perspective, the macroeconomic indicators present a stable picture, with lower inflation and firm fiscal and balance of payments current account deficits, etc. (Table 4.2). At the same time, economic growth continues to rely heavily on rainfall, standards of living are worsening and social inequalities are widening.

Table 4.2:   Macroeconomic data over the post-debt rescheduling period

Year	Fiscal deficit	Public investment	Current public consumption	Current account surplus	Inflation (%)	Economic growth (%)
1993	2.61	7.24	18.08	−1.94	5.18	−1.01
1994	3.19	6.41	17.13	−2.38	5.14	10.35
1995	4.70	6.98	17.40	−3.59	6.12	−6.58
1996	2.97	6.42	16.85	0.09	2.98	12.22
1997	0.70	6.30	17.78	−0.26	1.04	−2.23
1998	2.13	6.39	18.02	−0.40	2.75	7.67
1999	2.46	7.26	19.17	−0.47	0.68	0.04
2000	5.94	6.35	19.14	−1.42	1.90	0.87
2001	1.50	6.18	19.22	−0.55	1.54	6.50
2002	4.18	5.68	19.78	−2.05	2.32	4.50

Source: World Development Indicators, the World Bank, CD-ROM, 2002; Direction de la Statistique, Rabat, Morocco.

In fact, what matters more is not to 'reform for the sake of reform' but to 'reform to improve'. In addition to inadequacies and mistakes in timing and sequencing, bad performances of the Moroccan reforms seem to be attributable to the fact that institutional, political, social and cultural reforms had not accompanied macroeconomic stabilisation and structural measures. The Moroccan government and the international financial institutions and partner countries in Europe and elsewhere know by now that the outcomes of economic reforms depend on the institutional, political, social and cultural context, suggesting that reforms in these areas are particularly urgent. As noted through our interviews with decision-makers in Rabat, real reforms in Morocco are those which started later in the 1990s and early 2000s (we refer mainly to our interviews with the Central Directors in the Ministry of Finance and Privatisation, the Director of Statistics and Plan, advisers of ministers, political scientists, leaders of political parties, etc.).

Ruis and van de Walle (2003: 2) noted that 'there has been a growing recognition over the course of the last twenty years that institutional, cultural and managerial factors weigh heavily on the course of economic reform programs in developing countries.' In a situation of autocracy, political repression, weak state capacity, bad governance and weak civil society, economic reforms cannot yield successful results. Not surprisingly, all reforms of the second generation are linked to the concepts of democracy, state capacity and governance. It is essential to underline that the quality of governance depends on the stage reached in the field of democracy (African Institute for Democracy, 1997). Reform is certainly a political act and, consequently, there is no sense in dealing with reforms without taking into consideration the role of democracy. Interviews with some members and leaders of political parties in Morocco indicate that democracy in Morocco is a 'democracy of façade'. It is not unreasonable in the Moroccan case to say that bad administrative and political governance is largely due to the absence of real democracy, even though the Moroccan democratisation process is perhaps the best in the region of the Middle East and North Africa. Successful economic reforms inevitably involve some form of political reform towards the maximisation of aggregate social welfare. To reach this goal, the state should have the capabilities to identify specific problems, to explore the necessary reform programmes, and to implement them efficiently.[7]

3.3   Stakeholders, interest groups and outcomes of the second generation of reforms

During the 1998–2004 reform episode, in addition to multilateral institutions, the main stakeholders and interest groups were the bureaucrats, the ruling elite, labour unions, political parties, including those with religious inclination, and other components of civil society. The bureaucracy in Morocco is the main stakeholder in the ongoing, second generation of reforms because it is a player which may influence and be influenced by the political, institutional and social reforms as well as cultural changes to a considerable extent. Among the components of the second generation of reforms, it is important to acknowledge the efforts to enhance governance and promote civil society as well as administrative and judicial reforms. Since these reform components have an impact on the ability of bureaucrats to continue to extract rents and to benefit from corruption and bribes, the bureaucracy has generally blocked the reform process in these areas.

The ruling elite is also a powerful stakeholder. Even though a coalition government was set up in 1998, some key ministerial departments, known as sovereignty ministries, such as the Ministries of the Interior, Justice, the Foreign Office, Religious Affairs and the powerful General Secretariat of Government, remained under the direct control of the royal palace. The same division of ministerial responsibilities continues to hold under the current government nominated by King Mohamed VI, following the legislative elections of September 2002. In spite of the willingness and ability of the young king to embark on reforms of the second generation, the powerful ministerial departments tend to block and delay reforms. Following the legislative elections of September 2002, the 'Institution of the Prime Minister' was annexed to the royal palace after the king had nominated the Prime Minister, the former Minister of the Interior, Driss Jettou. Even though we observe some improvements in democratic transition and freedom of information, weak coordination between the sovereignty ministries and those ruled by politicians may partially explain the slowness in some of the second generation reforms such as judicial and administrative reforms. On the administrative front, for instance, a national programme to improve and modernise public sector management, started in 1990s, is still dragging on.

Other important stakeholder and powerful interest groups within the process of second generation reform are represented by the labour unions. Labour unions in Morocco, as in many other countries, have often been in conflict with employers. Even though the estimated share of employees belonging to labour unions remains around only 5 per cent of the workforce, the unions have recently gained enormous power as a result of the ongoing democratic change in the country. Political life in Morocco is currently influenced by labour unions, primarily because of their concentration in large cities and their close links to political parties. Despite agreements between the government, the labour unions and business associations in 1996 and the adoption of a new labour code by the government in 2000, many general strikes and unrest have occurred in Morocco during recent years. Any attempt to rationalise the public sector, particularly through the cutting of wages or the reduction of the number of employees, cannot be implemented in the face of powerful trade unions. Even merit-based remuneration in the public sector is generally rejected by labour unions, undermining efforts to improve administrative efficiency. Certain privatisation programmes have also been recently delayed because labour associations have vigorously resisted them.

In general, the Moroccan government has not embarked on important reforms (e.g. administrative and judicial reforms) because it has not been able to come up with the necessary compensatory mechanism for the reform 'losers'.

Political parties are also important stakeholders within reforms of the second generation. The proliferation and continuous sub-divisions of political parties and their inefficiency in designing innovative and operational economic, social and political programmes are the main features of political parties during the 1998–2004 reform episode. Proliferation of political parties in Morocco may be due to ideological factors (Santucci, 2001; Benali and Cherkaoui, 2001) in addition to regional and generational considerations.

Representatives of political power within the government continue to consider themselves as holding the right of parliamentary 'impunity' if not parliamentary 'immunity' (Elbadaoui, 2004). People are generally suspicious of certain candidates who work for their individual interests, instead of working for the design and implementation of growth-induced economic and social programmes. The problem is that political parties, instead of contributing to the setting up of a true democratic system, tend to use political liberalisation as a means to continue to extract rents. In such a situation, democracy becomes a system for enriching the rent-holders and impoverishing the poor.

Civil society (other than labour and business associations) is another important stakeholder in the ongoing second generation of reforms. In the situation of economic liberalisation and decreasing state intervention, a strong civil society is urgently needed. Its potential for replacing the role of the state in responding to people's needs as well as its active role in influencing public policies are of a great importance. For instance, a strong civil society is needed for efficient privatisations and the promotion of 'entrepreneurship spirit'. Also crucial would be its role in influencing public decisions in political and institutional reforms. Unfortunately, at least in the Moroccan case, the emergence of a real civil society is facing major hurdles, including: the neo-patrimonial nature of the Moroccan state; the lack of civic education; and the traditional nature of Moroccan society. One can easily observe how the Moroccans still behave as simple individuals not as true citizens.

The neo-patrimonial nature of the Moroccan state is due to the resistance of old 'collectivist' economic and social formations inherited from pre-capitalist modes of production. While the construction of a market-oriented economy is crucial in the reform process, the cultural environment may be a resisting factor. A market-oriented economy system needs a situation where economic agents do not expect government to respond to all their needs. Paradoxically, this is not the case in Morocco. For instance, people tend to associate increasing prices not with demand and supply mechanisms but with the fact that the state does not assume responsibility in regulating prices. In the imagination of the Moroccan people, the state should play a role in regulating not only the economy but also the social sphere: distribution of benefits, clientelism, etc. Hence, instead of organising themselves into civil society associations, Moroccan people often expect the state to fulfil all their needs. This cultural reality constitutes an obstacle to reforms (on the effects of cultural factors on the reform process see, for example, Ruis and van de Walle, 2003).

As the work of Bernoussi (2000: 4) shows, many Moroccans have virtually nothing to do with any form of institutional contracting. Research by the Conseil National de la Jeunesse et de l'Avenir' (CNJA) in the 1990s, found that only 18 per cent of the interviewed urban youth understood the meaning of the term 'association'; the comparable figure for the rural youth was even smaller – at 10 per cent. Moreover, only 14 per cent of urban youth compared with 6 per cent of rural youth belonged to any associations. This passive situation is unlikely to change, at least in the short and medium term, even if there were some political willingness to after the situation. The traditional nature of Moroccan society also hinders the emergence of civil society. The concept of 'tradition' among sociologists who study Moroccan society refers to the geographical and value space where certain institutions are set up to respond to people's needs within the framework of a political regime characterised by traditionalism and 'holiness'. Paul Pascon (1967), the famous Moroccan sociologist, studied the nature of Moroccan society and wrote about the robustness of resistance against political modernisation and civil society.

In the framework of civil society, among the emerging associations, one can mention feminist groups. After efforts to defend women rights in the 1990s, feminist organisations obtained some timid amendments to the *Mudawana* in 1997. The poor performances in this reform area are due primarily to religious resistance. Following the enthronement of King Mohamed VI, a new relatively revolutionary familial code has been promulgated. Without the arbitrage of the king, such a code would have been impossible.

As already noted, macroeconomic stabilisation and structural reforms in Morocco did not result in successful performances on the social front. While the widening social inequalities and increasing poverty may be explained by the negative effects of inefficient reforms on economic growth, social inequalities may also be due to less public efforts to fight against poverty and gender inequalities. It is now well established that the cultural context also affects the reform path. As the Moroccan political scientist Mohamed Darif declared in an interview with us, 'Reform is not a simple promulgation of laws. This is insufficient. Culture should change. The cultural condition has considerable impact on the success of the reforms.'

4   Concluding remarks

We have divided the Moroccan reform process into three main phases or episodes: the first from 1983–93; the second from 1993–8; and the third from 1998–2004. We have shown that the main reasons behind the initiation of the first reform episode were the multifaceted crisis of the early 1980s, the quality of political debate, and external factors such as the transformation of economic paradigms abroad and international contagion effects. In the case of the second reform episode, we noted that the main reasons had to do with some specific external factors, the centralisation of political power, and the Euro-Mediterranean Free Trade Zone. Finally, for the third reform episode, 1998–2004, we noted that the main impetus for reform were the international contagion effects of political, institutional and social reforms, restored confidence after the government changeover of March 1998, and the emergence of a new concept of governance, following the enthronement of the young King Mohamed VI.

In addition to the speed and sequencing of reforms, we argue that stakeholders and interest groups played a major role in the Moroccan reform. Because of the uncertainties about the reform and its outcomes, stakeholders and interest groups often resisted reforms. For each reform episode, we tried to identify the main stakeholders and interest groups. Concerning the first episode (1983–93), the main stakeholders and interest groups were the bureaucrats and public servants, labour associations in the public sector, sector-based trade unions, and the opposition political parties. Among these stakeholders were various powerful interest groups, including bureaucrats, labour associations and sector-based trade unions. In addition to farmers, who continued to benefit from tax exemptions, we argue that the main stakeholders and interest groups operating during the second episode of reform (1993–8) were the bureaucrats, labour unions in the public sector, the banking sector lobby, and the opposition political parties. We contend that such stakeholders played a major role in the structural reforms and the launching of the second generation of reforms. They were even able to determine the speed and the outcome of the reform programmes, such as the privatisation initiatives, financial sector reforms, and the launching of political, institutional and social reforms. In all the reform episodes analysed in this chapter, we found that only powerful stakeholders and interest groups were compensated. The best examples are the large landowners, business associations and labour unions, especially within the public sector. Indeed, the failure of some of the major reforms undertaken in Morocco is attributable to the resistance of influential interest groups. For instance, inefficiency of fiscal policy reform has something to do with the strong power of bureaucrats and labour unions within the public sector. Such powerful groups finally forced the government to maintain and even expand current public consumption and other wasteful expenditures to the detriment of public investment. The Moroccan economy seems to be one of 'rent extraction'. The nexus between the interests of powerful groups and the political regime largely explains why the nation's reforms have underperformed over the years.

Notes

1. The full text of this chapter was written by Dr Brahim Mansouri, the leader of the Moroccan team working on 'Understanding Reforms'. The leader of the group would like to thank the other collaborators to this research. The members of the Moroccan team would like to thank the GDN for its support. They would also like to thank the coordinator of the GDN Programme on Understanding Reforms, Professor Dr José Fanelli, for his interesting comments, the Principal Economist at the GDN, Professor Dr Gary McMahon, for his support and comments, as well as Professor Dr Hadi Esfahani for his useful remarks on earlier drafts of this study. We would also like to thank Mr Sidi Mohamed Rigar, member of the management department in Marrakesh University, for his help and assistance. For comments: contact@mansouribrahim.com.
2. Official discourses in early 1980s did not often use the term 'crisis' to characterise the economic situation. Generally, they used notions such as 'financial difficulties'. Furthermore, financial difficulties have been often attributed to exogenous developments such as oil shocks, decreasing prices of phosphates, and recession of the world economy (see Hassan II, 1979, 1985).
3. This claim was made by Professor Hadi Esfahani who commented on an earlier draft of this chapter.
4. The remaining structural reforms in the second reform phase have been generally designed and implemented in line with a gradual and multistage process.
5. It is, however, interesting to stress that inflation in Morocco, in comparison with other countries with an inflationary tradition, has never reached the level of inflation-maximising seigniorage, estimated to be around 20 per cent, corresponding to a maximum of money creation (seigniorage) of about 4 per cent of GDP (Mansouri, 2001).
6. However, 'social learning' from past reforms in other countries cannot be considered as the sole reason for a gradual approach to financial reforms. Resistance of bank trade unions, as powerful interest groups, may also have something to do with slow reforms in this area.
7. Another factor that may affect the process of reforms, as well as their outcomes, failure or success, is the credibility of laws. If this is the case, poor credibility of laws may undermine prospects for long-run economic growth. 'It would be expected that a business environment characterized by incredible rules such as unclear property rights, constant policy surprises and reversals, uncertain contract enforcement, and high corruption would translate into lower investment and growth' (Brunetti et al., 1998: 353).

References

African Institute for Democracy (1997) *Bonne Gouvernance et Développement en Afrique*, 'Démocraties Africaines', Dakar, Senegal.

Alesina, R. and Drazen, A. (1990) 'Why are Stabilizations Delayed?' *Papers in Political Economy* (Canada: University of Western Ontario).

Al-Muaqqit, Mohamed Ibn Abdellah (1934) *Les Gens du Navire*, translated in 1998 from Arabic to French by Abdellah Saaf and A. Roussillon (Casablanca, Morocco: Afrique/Orient).

Bates, R. and Krueger, A. (1993) 'Generalizations Arising from the Country Studies', in R. Bates and A. Krueger (eds), *Political and Economic Interactions in Economic Policy Reform: Evidence from Eight Countries* (Oxford: Basil Blackwell).

Benali, Driss and Cherkaoui, Mouna (2002) 'The Political Economy of Growth in Morocco', first draft, GDN Global Research Project on 'Explaining Growth', Economic Research Forum, Cairo, Egypt (www.erf.org.eg.).

Bernoussi, Omar (2000) 'About the Hypothesis of Civil Society in Morocco', article in Arabic, *Wijhat Nazar Review* (Review of Point of View), 6, Winter.

Berrada, Abdelkader (1992) *Etat et Capital Privé au Maroc de 1956 à 1986*, State Doctoral Thesis, Faculty of Law and Economics, Mohamed V University, Rabat, Morocco.

Bicanic, I., Gligorov, V. and Krastev, I. (2003) 'State, Public Sector and Development', *Thematic Paper*, No. 6, GDN Workshop on Understanding Reforms, 16–17 January, Cairo, Egypt (www.gdnet.org).

Brunetti, A. et al. (1998) 'Credibility of Rules and Economic Growth: Evidence from a Worldwide Survey of the Private Sector', *World Bank Economic Review*, 12, 3.

Campos, Jose Edgardo and Esfahani, Hadi Salehi (1996) 'Why and When Do Governments Initiate Public Enterprise Reform?', *World Bank Economic Review*, 10, 3, September.

Cardoso, E. and Galal, A. (2003) 'External Environment, Globalization and Reform', *Thematic Paper* No. 8, GDN Workshop on Understanding Reforms, 16–17 January, Cairo, Egypt (www.gdnet.org).

Darif, M. (1987) 'The Legitimacy Issue in Morocco', *Moroccan Review of Political Sociology*, 4, Autumn.

Easterly, William, Rodrigùez, Carlos Alfredo and Schmidt-Habbel, Klaus (eds) (1994) *Public Sector Deficits and Macroeconomic Performance* (Oxford: Oxford University Press).

Edwards, S. (1989) 'On the Sequencing of Structural Reforms', *Economics and Statistics Department, Working Paper* No. 22147 (Paris: OECD).

Elbadaoui, Abderrahim (2004) *Les Rentiers du Maroc Utile*, Faculty of Law and Economics, Hassan II University, Casablanca, Morocco.

Fanelli, José Maria and Popov, Vladimir (2003) 'On the Philosophical, Political and Methodological Underpinnings of Reform', *Thematic Paper* No. 10, GDN Programme on Understanding Reforms, Global Development Network, January (www.gdnet.org).

Fidramuc, J. and Noury, A. G. (2003) 'Interest Groups, Stakeholders, and the Distribution of Benefits and Costs of Reforms', *Thematic Paper* No. 2, GDN Workshop on Understanding Reforms, 16–17 January, Cairo, Egypt (www.gdnet.org).

Guessous, Mohamed (2003a) *Approaches on Sociological Issues in Morocco* (in Arabic), editions of *Al-Ahadath Ul-Maghribia* (Casablanca, Morocco).

Guessous, Mohamed (2003b) *Challenges of the Sociological Thought in Morocco* (in Arabic), Editions of the Moroccan Ministry of Culture, Rabat, Morocco.

Hajji, Nasr, Jaidi, Larabi and Zouaoui, Mekki (1992) *Prix et Concurrence au Maroc*, Ministère chargé des affaires économiques, Imprimerie Najah El Jadida, Casablanca Morocco.

Hall, Peter (1990) 'Policy Paradigms, Experts and the State: the Case of Macro-economic Policy-Making in Britain', in S. Brooks and A.-G. Gagnon (eds), *Social Scientists, Policy and the State* (New York: Praeger).

Hassan II, the King of Morocco (1979) 'Discourse to the Participants of the Second Workshop on Local Jurisdictions', 24 November, *Inbiaath Ummah*, 28, publication of the Royal Palace, Rabat, Morocco.

Hassan II, the King of Morocco (1980a) Interview with Monte Carlo Radio Station, 28 May, reproduced in *Inbiaath Ummah*, 25, publication of the Royal Palace, Rabat, Morocco.

Hassan II, the King of Morocco (1980b) Interview with *Le Figaro* magazine, 7 January, reproduced in *Inbiaath Ummah*, 25, publication of the Royal Palace, Rabat, Morocco.

Hassan II, the King of Morocco (1985) Official Discourse, 3 March, reproduced in *Inbiaath Ummah*, 30, publication of the Royal Palace, Rabat, Morocco.

Ibn Khaldoon, Abderrahmane, *Al-Muqaddima*, a manuscript of the fourteenth century.

Kornai, Janos (1986) 'The Hungarian Reform Process: Visions, Hopes and Reality', *Journal of Economic Literature*, 24, December.

Lagroye, J. (1985) 'La Légitimation', in M. Crawtz and J. Luca (eds), *La Science Politique: Science Sociale* (Paris: PUF).

Liew, L. H., and Bruszt, L. (2003) 'Causes, National Costs and Timing of Reforms', *Thematic Paper* No. 1, GDN Workshop on Understanding Reforms, 16–17 January, Cairo, Egypt (www.gdnet.org).

Liew, L. H., Bruszt, L. and He, L. (2003) 'Causes, National Costs and Timing of Reforms', *Thematic Paper*, No. 1, GDN Workshop on Understanding Reforms, 16–17 January, Cairo.

Little, I., Scitovsky, T. and Scott, M. (1970) *Industry and Trade in Some Developing Countries: a Comparative Study* (Oxford: Oxford University Press).

Loayza, N. V. and Soto, R. (2003) 'On the Measurement of Market-oriented Reforms', *Thematic Paper* No. 9, GDN Workshop on Understanding Reforms, 16–17 January, Cairo, Egypt (www.gdnet.org).

Lora, Eduardo (2000) 'What Makes Likely Timing and Sequencing of Structural Reforms in Latin America?', *Working Paper* No. 424, Inter-American Development Bank.

Mansouri, Brahim (1992) *Libéralisme Economique et Développement: Quelques Elements sur l'Evolution Récente de l'Economie Marocaine*, Third Cycle Doctoral Thesis, Faculty of Law and Economics, Mohamed V University, Rabat, Morocco, July.

Mansouri, Brahim (1997a) 'Développement des Marchés Boursiers et Développement Economique: Quelles Relations?', *Annales Marocaines d'Economie*, 21, Autumn.

Mansouri, Brahim (1997b) 'Indicateurs Simples et Indices Agrégés du Développement des Marchés Boursiers: Cas du Maroc', *Annales Marocaines d'Economie*, 20, Summer.

Mansouri, Brahim (2001) *Macroeconomic Implications of Public Deficits in Developing Countries: the Case of Morocco*, research funded by the Ford Foundation, Middle East Research Competition, Lebanese Center for Policy Studies (LCPS), Beirut, Lebanon, June.

Mansouri, Brahim (2003a) *Soutenabilité, Déterminants et Implications Macro-économiques des Déficits Budgétaires dans les Pays en Développement: Cas du Maroc*, State Doctoral Thesis, Faculty of Law and Economics, Hassan II University, Casablanca, Morocco, 9 January.

Mansouri, Brahim (2003b) 'Why the Moroccan Government Does Not Use Reliable Research When Implementing Fiscal Policy Reforms: the Driving Role of Governance and Interest Group Pressures', GDN Programme on 'Bridging Research and Policy', *RAPNET* (www.gdnet.org).

Neilson, Stephanie (2001) 'IDRC-Supported Research and its Influences on Public Policy', chapter in *Knowledge Utilization and Policy Processes: a Literature Review*, International Development Research Center, Evaluation Unit, Ottawa, Canada.

Nsouli, Saleh, Mounir Rached, M. and Funke, Norbert (2002) 'The Speed of Adjustment and the Sequencing of Economic Reforms: Issues and Guidelines for Policymakers', *IMF Working Paper*, No. 132, International Monetary Fund, Washington DC, August.

Pascon, Paul (1967) 'The Composite Nature of Moroccan Society', translated to Arabic from French, *Baït Ul-Hikmah*, 3, October 1986.

Perktold, J. and Tommasi, M. (1994) 'Ideas, State Capacity and Policy Variability: the Shift to Markets as the Outcome of Learning Process', unpublished manuscript, University of California, Los Angeles, USA.

Rodrik, Dani (1992) 'The Limits of Trade Policy Reform in Developing Countries', *Journal of Economic Perspectives*, Winter.

Rodrik, D. (1994) 'The Rush to Free Trade in the Developing World: Why So Late? Why Not? Will it Last?' in S. Haggard and S. B. Webb (eds), *Voting for Reform: Democracy, Political Liberalization, and Economic Adjustment* (Washington, DC: World Bank).

Ruis, A. and van de Walle, A. (2003) 'Political and Cultural Institutions and Economic Policy Reform', *Thematic Paper* No. 3, GDN Workshop on Understanding Reforms, 16–17 January, Cairo, Egypt (www.gdnet.org).

Santucci, J. C. (2001) 'Les Partis Politiques Marocains à L'Epreuve du Pouvoir', REMALD, Rabat, Morocco.

Tanzi, Vito (1994) 'The Political Economy of Fiscal Deficits', in W. Easterly, C. A. Rodrigùez and K. Schmidt-Hebbel (eds), *Public Sector Deficits and Macroeconomic Performances* (Oxford: Oxford University Press and the World Bank).

Tommasi, Mariano (2002) 'Crisis, Political Institutions and Policy Reform: the Good, the Bad and the Ugly', paper presented at the annual World Bank conference on development economics, session on 'The Political Economy of Crisis and Reform', Oslo, Norway, June.

Williamson, J. and Haggard, S. (1994) 'The Political Conditions for Economic Reform', in J. Williamson (ed.), *The Political Economy of Policy Reform* (Washington, DC: Institute for International Economics).

Part II
Late Reformers

Introduction

Joseph Mensah

The three chapters that constitute Part II of the book deal with basically the same themes as those of Part I. What unites the countries in Part II and, indeed, sets them apart from those in Part I, is the fact that they all embarked on their major IMF/World Bank- sponsored SAPs since the second half of the 1980s. Chapter 5, which opens Part II, is on Burundi. It is written by two economists, Floribert Ngaruko and Janvier-Désiré Nkurunziza, who set out to explore the internal and external impetus for Burundi's reform, account for its failures and successes, and discuss the role of various agents and stakeholders in the design and implementation of the nation's reform. The strategies used by policy-makers to include, co-opt or alienate different stakeholders are given particular attention in this chapter. The authors note that Burundi's economic reform was an integral part of a vicious political cycle in the country by which the distributive policies and politics of the government fed into the nation's socio-economic polarisation, which, in turn, increased the risks of violent conflict, ethnic and regional political segmentation and domination, and then led back to the government's distributive politics once again. The analysis in this chapter suggests that Burundi's reform programmes were implemented mostly by way of compromises reached through a complex, multifaceted and often non-cooperative and dynamic game involving anticipation, expectation and subjective perceptions about both internal and external (f)actors. Drawing upon the relationships that developed between donor organisations and the government, as well as between the democratically elected, Hutu-dominated government and the army, Ngaruko and Nkurunziza demonstrate how reforms in Burundi have not been much different from any game-like transactions among participating groups and stakeholders.

Chapter 6, 'Understanding Economic and Politcal Reforms in Tanzania', was written by Haidari Amani of the Economic and Social Research Foundation (ESRF) and four of his colleagues: Samuel Wangwe, Dennis Rweyemamu, Rose Aiko and Godwill Wanga. Perhaps more than any other African nation, Tanzania has been through an array of political and socio-economic policy experiments, the most notable of which was the programme of African socialism – *ujamaa*. Dwelling mostly on the review of relevant records and files from the government, the donor community, and non-governmental organisations, together with interviews, informal discussions and consultations with key policy analysts and stakeholders, the chapter examines Tanzania's reform and identifies the challenges and responses undertaken to counter them. The chapter also explores the differential impacts of the nation's SAPs on the various classes and stakeholders. Among other things the authors note that since poverty in Tanzania is predominantly a rural phenomenon, and to the extent that most of the people still depend on rural agriculture for their livelihood, an agriculture-based growth strategy is, perhaps, the best option for sustainable growth and poverty reduction in the country.

Given the chronological order by which the book is organised, it comes as no surprise, then, that the last substantive chapter of the book, Chapter 7, is devoted to the youngest nation – Zimbabwe – by the development economist Takawira Mumvuma and his co-authors, Charles Mujajati and Bernard Mufute. The chapter, like the case of Burundi, in particular, provides pertinent insights into why economic reforms in Zimbabwe have generally failed, and discusses the role of various interest groups in the design and implementation of reforms in Zimbabwe. Additionally, the authors identify the 'losers' and 'winners' of SAPs and draw out the key lessons for the enhancement of future reforms in the country. Quite expectedly, the message that comes out most forcefully from this chapter is that 'architects of policy reforms should pay greater attention to the issue of skewed assets, wealth and income distribution before and during the implementation of policy reforms if distributional conflicts and policy reversals are to be avoided.'

5
The Political Economy of Reform in Polarised and War-Prone Societies: the Case of Burundi[1]

Floribert Ngaruko and Janvier-Désiré Nkurunziza

1 Introduction

Burundi is a small country, landlocked between Tanzania to the east and the south, the Democratic Republic of Congo to the west and Rwanda to the north. With a population of about 6.5 million people living on 27 834 square km of land, Burundi has one of the highest population densities in Africa. There are many competing theories about the process of populating the area currently known as Burundi, but the most consensual hypothesis contends that until 2000 years ago Twa hunter and gatherer pygmies sparsely inhabited this area. Since then, waves of Bantu Hutu farmers originating from central Africa immigrated to the area, and between the eleventh and fifteenth centuries Tutsi herders from the East African region settled here (Chrétien, 2000). Added to these categories was another group that emerged as a result of political organisation: the Ganwas, a group of high-ranking nobles who dominated Hutus, Tutsis and Twas, but this group was *de facto* assimilated to Tutsis since the overthrow of the monarchy in 1966.

Attempts to adapt socio-economic structures to make them more conducive to desired social situations are not new in Burundi, but such experiences in the past have had uneven outcomes. While pre-colonial changes resulted in land productivity increases, which in turn enabled Burundi to bear the second highest African population density after Rwanda, those undertaken by the colonial authority set the basis for sharp socio-economic problems that undermined Burundi's development, especially since independence in 1962. Presently, some forty-four years after independence, the picture of Burundi's social, political and economic structures is typical of many low-income African countries. Half of Burundi's population is under the age of 18. Agriculture employs 90 per cent of the labour force and accounts for more than 50 per cent of GDP. The industrial sector and manufacturing represent only about 18 per cent and 9 per cent of GDP, respectively. Public monopolistic companies geared towards agro-processing dominate the industrial sector and manufacturing. While manufacturing industries rely heavily on agriculture as a supplier of inputs, the sectoral pricing and distribution policies mean that agriculture has barely represented a significant market for industry. This in turn explains why agricultural productivity has recorded little progress over the past decades.

As regards Burundi's state, it conforms to the description of a typical post-colonial African state (Herbst, 2000). Burundi's past state policies have resulted in a distrustful relationship with the bulk of the population. The weakness of its legitimacy has undermined its capacity for fiscal extraction, increasing its reliance on indirect taxes, mostly levied on agricultural exports including coffee and tea. These produces have accounted for more than 80 per cent of total exports since independence and have mainly been taxed through public monopsonies, often offering a small share of market prices to producers. Together with cotton until the early 1980s, these produces have dominated Burundi's exports, especially since the end of the economic and monetary integration between Burundi, Rwanda and eastern Congo in the 1960s. Until then, Burundi's agricultural exports were directed to Europe and North America, while the regional market absorbed industrial exports. Following the independence of these three countries, this integration was ended, while policies overly marked by nationalism have prevented Burundi from engaging effectively in any sound scheme of regional integration.[2]

Also consistent with Herbst's analysis, this low capacity of fiscal extraction explains Burundi's structural dependency on external assistance for its viability. This dependency has in turn contributed to the shaping of policy and politics, as the discourse around Burundi's ethnic conflict illustrates. Given the sensitivity of donors to human rights violations, Burundi's successive Tutsi-dominated regimes have developed a discourse intended to diffuse responsibilities for past pogroms to escape from condemnation by the international community, and thereby maintain external assistance. Together with Hutu propaganda intended to reduce donors' support to these regimes, this discourse has resulted in a 'meta-conflict', which Lemarchand (1994) defines as a conflict between Hutus and Tutsis about the origins of Burundi's ethnic conflict. As later analysts will argue, such attempts at manipulating external donors have been commonplace in Burundi.

Overall, the outcomes of post-colonial changes have been consistent with an environment rather inimical to economic and political progress. Compared with the early 1960s, most of the post-colonial period has been marked by a higher external debt burden, higher inflation, lower income per capita, lower life expectancy at birth, while political changes have resulted in five major civil wars, which have caused about 600 000 casualties to date.

While this broad picture makes it clear that explaining reform in Burundi essentially requires exploring the reasons for failure more than success, it raises many questions at the same time. What has been the rationale for post-colonial changes in Burundi? What were the cultural, social and political underpinnings of these changes? Who championed them? Was there any room for opposition to policy decisions regarding these changes? What was the role of external agents, especially donors, in these processes? And so on.

The following sections attempt to provide insight into these issues. This study's aim is to examine why and what kind of reforms were undertaken in Burundi over the past twenty-five years or so, and how well these performed. Using a political economy approach and an analytic narrative method, it combines theory and empirical analysis in an iterative process.[3] It relies on rational choice and game theories, and captures the importance of sequences, uncertainty, the capacity of people to manipulate and strategise, and the limits of their ability to do so. It considers that like most policies, reform (and its absence) is an outcome of existing institutions, which in turn reflect individual preferences, interests and strategies as well as the way these variables aggregate for collective action.[4] The distribution of the negotiation of power throughout society is viewed as a key factor of this aggregation, given that it determines the extent to which individuals contribute to shaping institutions and thus to including their preferences in public policy.

The rest of this chapter proceeds as follows. Following this introductory section, section 2 focuses on the rationale for, and context of, reform in Burundi. Section 3 deals with reform design, implementation and performance, and section 4 provides a view of the reform process in prospect.

2   Motivation to reform and reform equilibrium

2.1   The role of neo-patrimonialism

The patrimonial character of Burundi's state can be illustrated from many perspectives.[5] The state's functioning appears to be based on modern values, but in fact it is undermined by informal archaic practices, which often have dominance over formal modern values. The logic underlying this archaism in part refers back to pre-colonial practices and the way these evolved under colonial and post-colonial polities. Before colonisation, the Mwami (i.e. the king) was an absolute monarch and a central religious and political figure, with proprietorship of everything valuable in the kingdom, including people.[6] Considered sacred and of divine essence, he was part of a mystique that everyone shared. This system and its associated myths officially ended in 1966, when the monarchy was abolished, but the style of governance, the overcentralisation of power, and the sentiment that the president had virtually unlimited prerogatives over citizens barely changed.

Burundi largely meets the anthropological characteristic that Bayart (1999) finds to be central to African patrimonialism: power rests on both material wealth and symbols. Manirakiza (1992) argues that for Micombero, the president who came to power after the overthrow of the monarchy, the exercise of power meant a style of governance based on both enjoyment and sycophancy.[7] This style largely conformed to the vulgar perception of the routine functioning of the royal court and of the exercise of the monarch's power: endless feasts and the arbitrary and abusive exercise of a virtually unconstrained authority.

Yet the grandeur-related conception and exercise of power meant more than just a matter of style under the Micombero regime. Avenging past injustices against Himas – the president's clan, essentially established in Bururi province, and which was traditionally considered as an inferior caste by the rest of the Tutsis – accounted for a great deal in this conception. In the political and administration area, the regime undertook to centralise power in the hands of a tiny group of Tutsi-Himas from Bururi since 1966. Within months, the democratic changes that had marked the course to independence were reversed. The multiparty system and the parliament were abolished, while selective promotions in the army resulted in the control of the military apparatus by Himas from Bururi. In the economic area, distributive politics privileging Tutsi-Himas from Bururi were favoured over growth-enhancing policy. More tragically, the new regime and its supporters used violent conflicts, which broke out in large part due to disastrous governance, to redistribute properties (including land and houses) of Hutu victims' families to Tutsis, especially Hima dignitaries from Bururi.

In this context, the economy plummeted, especially during the first half of the Micombero's regime (Nkurunziza and Ngaruko, 2002). By the mid-1970s, the president suffered physical deterioration, essentially due to alcoholism, and by 1976 his shaky regime was overthrown in a military palace coup led by Colonel Bagaza, another Tutsi-Hima from the Rutovu commune.

To differentiate itself from the previous polity, the Bagaza regime promoted a new style of governance based on discipline and rigour, at least until the early 1980s (Reyntjens, 1994). The new regime undertook an ambitious programme of investment through the creation of infrastructures and public enterprises often aimed at import substitution (Ngaruko, 1993). It also carried out some changes in the land area. However, as later discussion will show, these changes basically reinforced the privileges for Tutsi-Himas of Bururi. The Bagaza regime abolished the four-century-old clientage system, sought to weaken the role of churches in the society, and improved the status of women. Under the Bagaza regime, Burundi's economy expanded, thanks to investment made possible more by massive external borrowing than by improvement in the allocation of resources, and by grants provided by donors. This expansion benefited non-agricultural professions, which included Tutsis – especially those from the south – disproportionately more than Hutus.

In 1987, the Bagaza regime was overthrown in a palace coup that brought Major Buyoya to power. A Tutsi-Hima military officer from the Rutovu commune of Bururi province, Buyoya ruled Burundi until 1993. Amidst raging civil war, a new military coup brought him back to office in 1996, but he left in 2003 as a result of international pressures attempting to push the implementation of a peace plan that had been agreed to by Hutu-dominated rebels and the government. Under Buyoya's rule, there were notable changes. These were mainly due to international pressures in an attempt to force Tutsis to concede a minimum inclusion of Hutus in public institutions. However, these changes were superficial. They were not underpinned by any commitment to changing the style of governance. As Ndikumana (1998) notes, after three Tutsi-Hima presidents from one commune out of 114 ruled Burundi for nearly 85 per cent of the post-independence period, things have long been as if the state had been privatised to the benefit of Tutsis, especially those from the south.

2.2   Present-day reform equilibrium in Burundi

Whereas the privileges devoted to Tutsi-Himas by Micombero were his personal choice, the subsequent empowerment of this group enabled it to resist any change affecting its privileges negatively. This resulted in a path dependency that has characterised later change processes. The type of external equilibrium that results from such reforms has been acknowledged. Typically, in African countries where leaders have sought to use reform to derive discretionary benefits, they have learned how to protect their own interests even as they implement just enough reform to maintain donor support (van de Walle, 2001).

The underlying transaction between the government and donors is characteristic of a reform equilibrium, which Husain (1994) clearly confirms. As Husain points out, Burundi leaders typically have tried to extract the maximum amount of resources with as few changes in policies as they could get away with, while international financial institutions (IFIs) and donors typically have tried to place as many conditions as possible and to tranch their releases of funds on pre-specified actions in policy changes.

From a static perspective, four variables have been involved in the resulting equilibrium (Figure 5.1). The first has consisted of biased distributive policies. These have been leveraged through the pricing of export produces, especially coffee, which accounts for more than 80 per cent of total exports and for a similar share of public revenue.[8] The second variable is the degree of socio-economic polarisation stemming from these distributive policies.[9] This polarisation has in turn accounted for a large part of the violent conflicts that Burundi has encountered since the 1960s.[10] The fourth variable is the extent

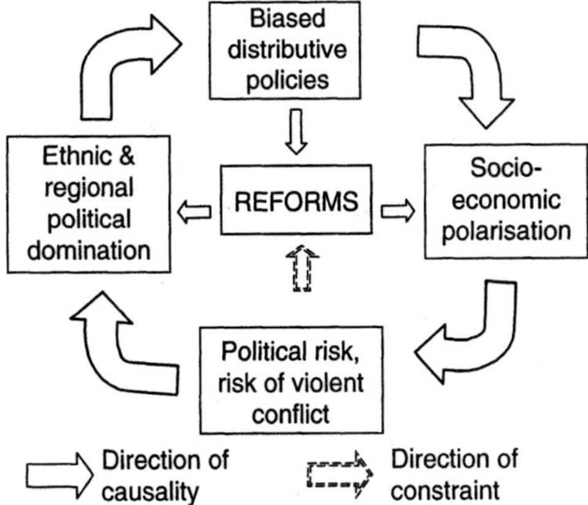

Figure 5.1:   Reform and politics

of ethnic and clan control over institutions.[11] This has been both the cause and the consequence of the repetitive violent conflicts.[12] Policies stemming from these institutions have in turn played an important role in the design of biased distributive policies since independence (Ngaruko and Nkurunziza, 2005).[13] The static equilibrium has prevailed to the extent that the risk of conflict resulting from socio-economic polarisation and underlying distributive policies was consistent with the extent of the grip of the ruling group over institutions, especially the army, which has acted as a deterrent against rebellion on the part of victims of these distributive policies.

From a dynamic viewpoint, the risk of conflict has exerted some constraint on the inequity of the biased reforms. These have in turn served as a tool for distributive politics to adjust to the equilibrium from a double perspective. On the one hand, economic reforms have typically been an instrument for distributive politics to adjust polarisation to the rest of the variables involved in the equilibrium, while, on the other hand, political reforms have served to adjust the grip over institutions to the aforementioned equilibrium (Figure 5.1). In this process, the government has used external support for reform to leverage its own reform agenda. Information asymmetries between donors and the government have played an important role in this process. Typically, donors have faced a problem of adverse selection, as the government has prompted them to support reforms and projects that did not necessarily present the highest growth-enhancing and poverty-reducing impact but that had substantial benefits for politically powerful groups. Illustrating this, a recent study estimated that by the late 1980s, about 60 per cent of the total external aid given to Burundi for education financing benefited Bururi, one province out of fifteen (Jackson, 2000).

Considered in the long run, the aforementioned factors particularly raise the question of why the pre-colonial reform recorded large success since, prima facie, a number of factors responsible for reform distortions today (little distinction between public and private domains, little accountability and control over the executive, etc.) were already present. One possible explanation is the way the colonial polity altered the balance of power that prevailed until colonisation. Before colonisation, the aggregation of individual interests and preferences shaped institutions that seemed to be dominated by so few Tutsis and Ganwas that Belgian colonisers overlooked the power of Hutus.[14] For instance, a Hutu clan's members were entrusted with the task of choosing the future king among eligible Ganwa pretenders. Also, before the so-called modernisation colonial reform of the 1930s eliminated Hutus from any significant public authority, there were roughly as many Hutu, as Tutsi, chiefs. The changes of the 1930s durably altered the balance of power upon which Burundi's society was built, as it sought to turn institutions and power into a Tutsi monopoly. Since independence, this process of power concentration in the hands of Tutsis continued, and during the post-monarchic period the executive faced little democratic control and accountability, even by African standards.

2.3   The decision to embark on externally led reforms

Viewed in the light of the notion of reform transaction mentioned earlier, the move towards stabilisation and structural adjustment policies in 1986 appears to have been in part a readjustment to a new understanding of development and the subsequent change in reform policy, as well as to the difficulties that Burundi's economy experienced due to the deterioration of domestic and international conditions, even though there was a long lag period between the time most African countries facing similar international conditions embarked on externally led reforms and the time Burundi initiated similar reforms.

In the 1980s, a broad change in the understanding of development occurred. While until the late 1970s the availability of financial capital and engineering resources were thought to be sufficient to secure development, by the early 1980s it had become apparent that the efficiency rather than the quantity of investment was the key to sustainable growth, and that the incentives that result from economic policy were crucial determinants of investment efficiency. Economic policy reform then moved to the centre of development strategy, paving the way for structural adjustment programme (SAPs).[15]

The framing of problems, policy alternatives and recommendations underlying reform were generally based on the Washington Consensus. To stabilise the economy, the macroeconomic reform focused on the restoration of both internal and external balances. The main instruments that the reform used to achieve these objectives were those generally recommended by the monetarist economic approach as it had evolved since its inception by Polak in the 1950s.[16] That is, restrictions in the supply of money were the main instrument used to fight inflation, while monetary devaluations were the main tool used to restore the balance of payments, as this instrument was meant to discourage imports while enhancing exports and foreign direct investment.

As for structural reforms, whereas nationalism, protectionism and import-substitution motives underpinned Burundi's domestic economic policy in the period 1976–86, the new reform strategy emphasised liberalism, openness and export promotion. The analytical approach focused on efficiency on a neo-classical microeconomic and sectoral basis, whereas the former reforms rested on a holistic and quantitative view of investment. As for the aim, structural adjustment reforms were meant to set the basis for sustainable growth.

By the early 1980s, Burundi was at the peak of the expansionary cycle that had begun in the late 1970s and had continued through the end of the decade, in spite of a drastic decline in the terms of trade (deterioration by 45 per cent between 1978 and 1981) brought about by the decline of coffee prices and higher oil prices. But since 1983, this changed dramatically. The international context since the oil counter-shock of the late 1970s, the subsequent hardening of borrowing conditions on international markets, and the collapse of international coffee prices all resulted in increasing difficulties for Burundi's economy.

This situation was particularly critical since Burundi's past lax investment policy, which relied on the creation of public enterprises heavily dependent on imports for their inputs, aggravated the crisis in the balance of payments. Together with adverse climatic conditions, these difficulties precipitated a rapid change in economic performance. GDP, which had grown by more than 6 per cent a year during the period 1978–81, declined in real terms in 1982–3. The external current account balance moved from a surplus during 1977–8 to a deficit of 12.4 per cent of GDP in 1983, and foreign exchange reserves fell from eleven months of imports equivalent in 1977 to less than one month in 1982.

As regards the budget deficit, it reached an all-time high of 16 per cent of GDP, compared with 6.8 per cent in 1978. Inflation then amounted to 15 per cent a year, nearly twice the level at which it reduces growth.[17] The exchange rate of the national currency, pegged to the US dollar since 1977, appreciated considerably. Public external debt was ten times as high as in 1977, while domestic arrears amounted to 30 per cent of total expenditures. The ratio of external debt service over exports was rising exponentially: from 4.6 per cent in 1978 to 12.5 per cent in 1983, and again to 38.4 per cent in 1987. Faced with these difficulties, the government asked the World Bank and the IMF for help in 1984.

Yet, a closer look at the uneven distribution of the costs entailed by this situation sheds more light on the reason why the government, which barely cared about social welfare, decided to embark on reform. This unevenness owed a great deal to the structure of the economy. First, in Burundi the average household consumes 88 per cent of its own produce, but the figures are 20 per cent for a typical non-agricultural household.[18] Second, until the abolition of the clientage system, much investment was made in land and cattle, typically acquired through non-monetary exchange. Third, while industry and manufactures rely heavily on agriculture as a supplier of inputs, the sectoral pricing and distribution policies mean that agriculture has barely represented a significant market for industry. In 1988, for example, only 0.4 per cent of industrial production was used in agriculture as input, amounting to only 0.2 per cent of agriculture sector output and 5 per cent of non-imported intermediate agriculture consumption (Ngaruko, 1993). In 1994–5, the agricultural sector received an average of only 1.9 per cent of the total credit to the economy (IMF, 2000: 39).

Another key feature of Burundi's economic structure relates to the private sector. In manufacturing, services, commerce and imports, the firms of the private sector are small compared with international standards. Even the largest ones correspond to what are generally considered 'small and medium-sized enterprises', as only a handful of them have 1000 employees or more. The underdevelopment of the private sector owes a great deal to the industrial policy, which consisted in the creation of public corporations to respond to virtually any solvable demand. As for the process of capital accumulation, it illustrates the weakness of the private sector in Burundi by shedding light on the influence of neo-patrimonialism.

At independence, Burundi did not have a national bourgeoisie. Since then, the process of capital accumulation has largely relied on one's connections and/or position in the public sector. This made it difficult to separate politics and business. A typical businessman is a former public official who has accumulated capital through various means, legal or otherwise. The viability of his business largely relies on connections with politicians, to such an extent that the overthrow of a regime has often meant the replacement of a whole fringe of formerly prosperous businessmen with a new one (Nkurunziza and Ngaruko, 2002).

These factors implied that an increase in inflation, for instance, hit urban dwellers and all those relying on monetary exchange the most. Likewise, the exhaustion of international reserves and monetary devaluations threatened those who relied on imports the most, while credit restrictions intended to mitigate inflation would hit those who had access to credit the most, and so on. Also, the unwholesomeness of the dependency of private sector entrepreneurs on politicians and the state implied that stabilisation reforms hit businessmen more than other economic operators, as these reforms sought to make policy more transparent, to instil competitiveness, to limit public deficits, to restrict credit, and to improve public financial management – this undermined the basis of the profitability of many businesses. Thus, the profiteers of the regime's biased policy faced higher marginal costs compared with ordinary people. For these groups, the costs of continuing with existing policies had come to exceed those that could follow from reform, which therefore was tolerated (Husain, 1994). Still, the reluctance to really reform the economy was likely to result in a low-achievement equilibrium consistent with the notion of transaction over reform laid out earlier.

2.4   The enabling environment of reform

The neo-patrimonial environment affected reform design and implementation in many ways. Over-centralisation of decision-making led to a high propensity to design reform in a top-down, command-and-control fashion resulting in a tendency to skip important stages of the reform processes, thereby undermining reform ownership. The participation of key actors in project design was such that stakeholders as central as teachers and parents were barely consulted for basic education reform design. Coupled with reform mongering – especially in favour of conservative reforms presenting a leftist-like appearance – the strong disincentives to criticism and even to fair discussion of policy had resulted in a situation whereby technocrats made little effort to investigate problems that prospective reforms were likely to face. In the light of the analytical framework proposed earlier, it is arguable that this attitude was a result of a long learning process whereby technocrats had internalised the attitudes that the government would tolerate.

Understandably, donors sought to reform the institutional capacity in Burundi as an attempt to improve the enabling environment of the broad reform process. Overlooking the neo-patrimonial character of Burundi's state, they misdiagnosed its institutional dysfunctions and undertook reforms that barely affected them. Likely for dogmatic reasons, they considered the private sector as a model for an efficient public management system. Accordingly, IFIs sought to use businessmen to champion the public sector reform. Given the very nature of private sector operators in Burundi, especially the unwholesomeness of their ties with politicians, this decision was ill advised.[19]

The strategic approach to institutional reforms also emphasised support of existing or the creation of new public agencies, committees and offices in charge of various tasks. This implied the third pillar of the strategy: the need to reinforce capacities. This was mainly done through the focus on improving technical capacity, typically through training. One major problem with this approach was one of irrelevance, given the neo-patrimonial nature of Burundi's institutional environment. IFIs concentrated their efforts on designing technically sound reforms whose chances of working and being sustainable were politically undermined. Of six projects that were implemented over the period 1988–2003, and which were evaluated by the World Bank's independent Operations Evaluation Department, the institutional development impact was rated negligible for four projects and modest for two. Only one project was found to have yielded likely sustainable benefits. Only one had a satisfactory overall outcome, while four were rated unsatisfactory, and one moderately satisfactory.

Since North (1990) popularised it, the definition of institutions has turned out to be increasingly viewed as 'the rules of the game'. Guerrien (1993), however, emphasises the need to distinguish between the goals and the means – that is, between the rules of the game and the machineries (also, and confusingly, called institutions) aimed at enforcing these rules. On the basis of this distinction, it becomes clear that in spite of their frequent use of the term 'institutions', externally led reform designers focused on 'public machineries' more than on the rules of the game.

In total, this section depicts an environment rather inimical to sound reform in many respects. On the government's side, reform was undertaken as best of a bad lot. The government embarked on reform without real commitment to improving social welfare, but rather to best protect the interests of a tiny group threatened by increasing problems arising from past lax policies. On the international community's side, reform was undermined by ideological bias, which the next sections will illustrate extensively. In Burundi's broad society's understanding, reform was just one more policy that the government was intending to implement to the benefit of a few and to the detriment of the majority. As such this bad reputation and the resulting low credibility of the government to stage sound reform intended to improve the well-being of all were additional challenges posed to the process of reform. The next section illustrates the impact of these factors.

3   Reform process and outcomes

3.1   Structural adjustment reforms

Focusing on which structural reforms were implemented and how these fared provides an insight into how interactions between ideology, special interests, government's negative reputation and lack of credibility undermined reform in Burundi. Indeed, ideological bias sometimes caused the principles underlying structural adjustment reforms to be antagonistic. For example, while externally led reforms explicitly claimed the intention of restoring well-functioning markets, they distorted them in order to foster their outward orientation, as some of the reforms aiming at restoring the balance of payments and at containing the budget deficit would show. To promote exports while containing public deficits, the World Bank's strategy recommended applying a concessionary tax rate of 5 per cent to the profits attributable to export sales and a rate of 45 per cent to the proportion of profits attributable to local sales (World Bank, 1988: 71).

In other instances, market-oriented reforms were pushed forward despite the fact that markets did not work very well. For example, the strategy proposed by the World Bank to raise agricultural productivity with a view to improving food security and increasing agricultural exports emphasised the use of fertilizer. But after having diagnosed the 'uncertainty about fertilizer demand due to its high cost given the low purchasing power of farmers' – clearly, fertilizer price being higher than the reservation price for farmers – the strategy stressed without further explanation, that 'it is important for the short-term agricultural reform agenda that early promotion efforts price fertilizer at full cost' (World Bank, 1988: 39). Eventually, this strategy was abandoned, and fertilizer was purchased and allocated through non-market mechanisms, essentially to the benefit of export crops. As a result, fertilizer use rose from an annual average of 1.5 kg per hectare in the period 1976–85 to 4.0 kg per hectare in 1986–93.

Such pragmatism did not prevail in all instances, though, as the programme of privatisation of public enterprises would show. From the outset this programme was faced with the weakness of savings. In Burundi, the average ratio of domestic private savings over GDP amounted to only 2 per cent during the period 1981–6, suggesting that few people were capable of acquiring significant equity shares of public companies. One possible strategy was to compensate this lack of savings through a targeted, limited programme of monetary system credit. Although such policy conflicts with macroeconomic stabilisation, some reasonable compromise more favourable to privatisation would have been reached. In fact, such a heterodox option was not even envisaged. Unsurprisingly, apart from public enterprises closed because of financial problems, the programme recorded modest achievements. From 1986 to the end of 1998, the government's privatisation programme yielded only US$11 million (World Bank, 2000). Over the period 1991–2001, privatisation revenue amounted to only US$4 million (UNECA, 2003).[20]

The ideological background of IFIs is not the sole factor explaining the limited outcome of structural reforms, though. Warfare also played a role. Table 5.1 shows the performance of some structural reforms, by major reform period. It confirms the improvement in fertilizer use over the period 1986–92 compared with the period 1976–85. It also suggests that the situation improved during

Table 5.1:   Performance of structural reform

	Average 1976–85	Average 1982–85	Average 1986–92	Average 1993–99	Average 2000–2
Real effective exchange rate index	161.9	176.6	113.5	88.6	93.0
Terms of trade index, 1995 = 100	173.4	137.8	107.7	80.5	51.9
Fertilizer consumption (kg/ha)	1.5	2.3	3.8	3.4	3.9
Real agricultural GDP per capita growth rate (%)	0.3	−1.2	0.0	−4.4	1.9
Accumulation of arrears (net, current US$ mil)	n.a.	n.a.	0	15.2	n.a.
GDP per capita (const 1995 US$)	184	188	205	159	141.0

Source: World Bank (2003).

the 1986–92 period compared with the period 1982–5, especially in terms of real agricultural GDP growth and GDP per capita. As Table 5.1 shows, performance declined during the war period 1993–9, and improved slightly in the post-war period 2000–2, except for the terms of trade whose trend is decreasing regardless of the prevailing peace versus war situation, and GDP per capita growth rate, which takes more time to recover from warfare.

Factors such as bad reputation and lack of credibility of the government as well as subjective beliefs played a key role as well. As regards reputation and credibility of the government, a closer look at the aforementioned case of fertilizer use provides some insight into their influence. Along with the promotion of the use of fertilizer, the World Bank's strategy emphasised a series of supply-driven measures involving governmental agencies (provision of improved varieties and of cost-reducing and yield-increasing innovations to farmers, storage facilities, diffusion of information to help rationalise marketing circuits, soil mapping, techniques to control soil erosion and maintain soil fertility, updating and use of aerial photos and satellite imagery, etc.). These reforms suffered from a double weakness. First, they were too sophisticated for farmers, and so barely resulted in real improvement of farming techniques. Second, by putting state agencies at the core of its strategy, the World Bank overlooked a central feature that has marked the relationship between the state and peasants for decades – namely, the profound distrust that has developed throughout Burundi's colonial and post-colonial history (Ndarishikanye, 1994).

Indeed, past experience has made peasants avoid using chemical fertilizer in spite of government encouragement, based on a widespread belief among Burundi farmers that chemical fertilizer exhausts soils. Peasants believe that if chemical fertilizer is used once, it takes several years for the soil to recover its former level of fertility unless it is used thereafter on a regular basis. As farmers barely trust the government on the question of continuing to provide fertilizer, this negative reputation and the lack of credibility on the part of the government made this strategy fail. As a result, the use of fertilizer has remained negligible except for export crops.[21]

3.2   The role of special interests: the case of state-owned enterprises (SOEs)

While the failure of structural adjustment reforms confirms that subjective beliefs and other irrational factors like ideology affected reform, it should be made clear that the impact of rational, opportunistic behaviour was important as well. This is hereafter illustrated using the case of the state-owned enterprises sector. Like many issues related to the crisis of the 1980s, and which led to the reforms under scrutiny in this study, Burundi's SOE sectoral policy recorded a major turning point under the Bagaza regime. Yet, this episode of Burundi's economic history is controversial. The supporters of the Bagaza regime today praise its pro-active orientation, arguing that this regime did much to modernise Burundi's economy through the creation of public enterprises, among other things.[22]

From the outset, the Bagaza regime used a huge share of external resources to create public companies. From 1977 to 1982, more than 100 public enterprises were created (Nyamoya, 1998). Claiming a pseudo-socialist orientation, but undermined by neo-patrimonialism, the government's policy was to respond to virtually any domestic demand through public corporations. This resulted in the state becoming virtually the sole provider of employment and sole agent of economic distribution from the 1970s through the 1980s. Public monopolies and monopsonies were created in agricultural produce purchasing, processing, transportation and commercialisation. Major public monopolies and monopsonies dominated consumer good imports, telecommunications, house construction, banking, pharmacy, insurance, etc.

Most admirers of the Bagaza regime omit to consider these enterprises' inefficiencies, though, most of which stem from the biased distributive role that marked their creation from the outset. Retrospectively, two main goals seem to have underpinned the expansion of the public enterprises sector: the extraction of revenue and the subsidising of employment to the benefit of the regime's fellows. The former goal was typical of those public companies in charge of buying cash crops. One prominent feature of the four state corporations controlling agricultural major cash produces (coffee, tea, sugar and cotton) is their high contribution to public revenue. These are the *Office des Cultures Industrielles du Burundi* (OCIBU), *Office du Thé du Burundi* (OTB), *Société Sucrière du Mosso* (SOSUMO) and *Compagnie de Gérance du Cotton* (COGERCO), respectively.

Over the period 1998–2002, for example, these four agencies accounted for 12 per cent of the net flows of subsidies from the government, and they represented 40 per cent of the loans to state-owned enterprises. However, they accounted for 45 per cent of repayments of SOEs to the government. As Table 5.2 shows, OCIBU – the public monopoly present in the coffee sector – outstandingly appears to be a taxation tool for the government, as this company ensured

Table 5.2: The public enterprise sector

		Indicators of SOEs, mil of Burundi francs (Fbu), 1997					Total public financial flows to SOEs over period 1998–2002, Fbu mil		
SOEs	Equity share*	Wages	Total assets	Debts	Value added	Earnings before subsidies	Net flows from govt. to SOEs	On-lending to SOEs	Repayments by SOEs
Major crop buyers									
[1] OCIBU	78	246	32 314	20 041	3795	3337	−648	2981	3630
[2] OTB	100	631	4091	6979	676	−845	755	1484	729
[3] SOSUMO	99	661	3238	2921	2534	574	1588	1653	65
[4] COGERCO	100	152	407	1359	152	56	−1275	462	1736
[5] = [1] + [2] + [3] + [4]		1690	40 050	31 300	7157	3122	420	6580	6160
Major employers									
[6] REGIDESO	100	1011	4000	21 070	2511	−1700	1390	6160	4770
[7] ONATEL	100	749	5093	6031	3528	174	−359	1596	1954
[8] COTEBU	100	795	2414	6277	541	−1076	NA	NA	NA
[9] = [6] + [7] + [8]		2555	11 507	33 378	6580	−2602	1031	7756	6724
[10] SOE sector		6482	89 539	96 188	18 591	−316	3601	16 483	13 605
[11] = [5]/[10]		0.26	0.45	0.33	0.38	−9.88	0.12	0.40	0.45
[12] = [1]/[10]		0.04	0.36	0.21	0.20	−10.56	−0.18	0.18	0.27
[13] = [9]/[10]		0.39	0.13	0.35	0.35	8.23	0.29	0.47	0.49
[14] = [6]/[10]		0.16	0.04	0.22	0.14	5.38	0.39	0.37	0.35

*Direct or indirect equity participation of government.

Note 1: OCIBU = Office des Cultures Industrielles du Burundi; OTB = Office du Thé du Burundi; SOSUMO = Société Sucrière du Mosso; COGERCO = Compagnie de Gérance du Cotton.

Note 2: REGIDESO = Régie de Production d'Eau et d'Electricité; ONATEL = Office National des Télécommunications; COTEBU = Complexe Textile de Bujumbura.

Source: Indicators of SOEs: IMF (2000). Financial flows to SOEs: IMF (2004).

27 per cent of the repayments to the government. Furthermore, the financial flows that go from the government to SOEs are negative in the case of OCIBU, meaning that additional net flows accounting for 18 per cent of the total flows that the government directed to the SOEs actually went from OCIBU to the government.

The government has long justified these earnings as surpluses to be deposited in the OCIBU-controlled stabilisation fund and to be used to increase the payment of operators in the coffee sector during periods of low sales. In times of tight budgetary funds, however, the government has merely appropriated these surpluses to the expense of producers and other operators of the coffee sector (IMF, 1997). Given the limited role of OCIBU in terms of value-added and employment, the picture for 1997 suggests that the large assets and debts that the government provided OCIBU did not have any clear rationale other than to procure huge earnings, even though these may fluctuate depending on various parameters like climatic conditions, international market prices and the like.

As regards the distributive role of SOEs, it has been achieved through employment. The public enterprise sector has represented a high share of formal employment. In the 1980s, for instance, this share oscillated between 27 per cent and 35 per cent. Tutsis – especially from the south – represented so high a share of this sector's employment that, retrospectively, a number of observers believe that the creation of public enterprises was a strategy to subsidise jobs for them. Such a belief may be correct, at least for some SOEs.

First, as Table 5.2 shows, by the late 1990s, the top three wage payer SOEs (the Régie de Production d'Eau et d'Electricité (REGIDESO), Office National des Télécommunications (ONATEL) and the Complexe Textile de Bujumbura (COTEBU)) accounted for 39 per cent of the total SOEs' wages, 35 per cent of the sector's total debts, and more than eight times as much as the sector's losses before subsidies. These enterprises' low assets (only 13 per cent of the sector's total assets) suggest that the bulk of the high value-added (35 per cent of sector's total value-added) went to wages and salaries, as returns to capital accounted for a negligible share of these three enterprises' value-added. Second, as a reflection of the place devoted to Tutsis from Bururi in SOE employment, the ethnic and regional background of the top managers of public corporations is telling. By the late 1990s, Tutsis from Bururi managed 60 per cent of the largest thirty-seven public corporations, while 29 per cent, 3 per cent and 8 per cent of these corporations were managed by non-Bururi Tutsis, Bururi Hutus and non-Bururi Hutus, respectively (International Crisis Group, 2001).

Other effects of the SOE policy affect key reform goals like growth and privatisation. In the 1980s, the SOE sector accounted for 30–50 per cent of gross domestic investment, but SOEs' share of output was never over 10 per cent. The fact that so much investment effort was directed to a sector with so low a potential for growth was responsible for part of the weakness of growth, substantiating the hypothesis that goals like economic development and the like are collateral rather than the central goal of reform, especially compared with distributive motives. Indeed, from this viewpoint, the aforementioned misallocation is not a surprise, insofar as predation and redistribution to the benefit of the ruling groups' cronies were the real goals pursued through the creation and the expansion of SOEs.

3.3 The case of required reforms that never happened

While understanding reform in Burundi requires us to look at those reforms that were undertaken, the way these were designed and implemented, and how they performed, focusing on reforms that were required in terms of the weakness of Burundi's enabling environment, but which never happened, may be equally insightful. Like reforms that were undertaken, omitted ones had a consistent context, both external and internal. In this regard, two different categories of omitted reforms are identifiable. The first includes reforms that were envisaged and ultimately cleared away through the reform transaction process. This was the case of the reform of university learning funding and the attempt to privatise REGIDESO – the public quasi-monopolistic corporation producing and distributing power and water nationwide.

Soon after the launch of externally led stabilisation and structural reforms, IFIs pushed for the change of the costly system of public grants for university students into loans, as part of the effort to bring the public deficit down to sustainable levels. What these institutions overlooked was that this system was a tool for the government to redistribute revenue and opportunities to the benefit of Bururi dwellers then representing the majority of university students. Unsurprisingly, the students resisted this reform. Together with the low incentive for the Bururi-dominated government to implement it, this caused the reform to be abandoned.

Illustrative is the attempt at privatising REGIDESO as well. REGIDESO is the largest company in Burundi in terms of employment, and it has hosted large numbers of personnel from the Bururi ruling group. The ethnic and regional background of REGIDESO's managers reflects this bias. From independence (in 1962) to 2003, REGIDESO had one Hutu Director General, for two years only. For the rest of the period it had nine Tutsi Directors General, seven of whom were from Bururi. Of eight top managers directly reporting to the Director General by mid-2003, five were from Bururi, and so were fifteen out of twenty-seven lower level managers.

Since the late 1980s, IFIs have been pushing towards the privatisation of REGIDESO, due in part to its enormous deficits. Officially, the government has been committed to this privatisation. In large part to satisfy IFIs, and with IFI support, the government undertook to rehabilitate REGIDESO in 1990 as a prelude to its privatisation. For this task, Hydro-Québec International, a Canadian company that was believed to be interested in acquiring REGIDESO, assisted the government. But when conflicts broke out between the Canadian firm and REGIDESO personnel who feared job losses under privatisation, the government did not make the expected and fair arbitrage. The privatisation operation failed, as Hydro-Québec International eventually withdrew in 1993. Starting from zero, the government has allegedly been devising a new scheme of privatisation since then, substantiating the jump-started character of the privatisation process of REGIDESO.

With regard to the required reforms that were not even envisaged, a consistent context exists for them as well. An illustration of this is the case of property rights-strengthening reforms, especially viewed in relation to the need to attract foreign investment. Attracting foreign investment is one of the most important objectives of externally led reforms, and one area where past reform efforts have recorded limited success in Burundi. The weakness of property rights may be one of the factors that explain this situation. Strengthening property rights is particularly critical for several reasons. Not only does it have the potential to make up for the savings weakness, which has hampered reforms like privatisation for decades. The failure to strengthen property rights also means that even the little domestic savings may have been drawn up by capital flight, presumably to the benefit of those of Burundi's partner countries that have sounder property rights, and where the resulting inflows are recorded as foreign investment.[23]

In the specific case of Burundi, the balance between inward and outward flows of capital in Burundi is telling. Over the period 1985–95, the balance has been negative, except for 1990. Estimates suggest that from 1985–96, foreign direct investment amounted to just 0.1 per cent of GDP, while capital flight represented about 5.6 per cent of GDP.[24] These figures particularly help us to understand reform in Burundi, as they show how important potential social benefits of reform can be without any effort on the part of the government to stage change. In the case of the relationship between capital flight and property rights, things appear as if political decision-makers deliberately maintained a weak domestic property rights regime to facilitate their appropriation of domestic assets and thereby guarantee their proprietorship on these assets by placing them to countries enjoying sounder property rights;[25] this implies that, other things – for instance, external financial inflows – being equal, putting constraints (administrative or otherwise) on the transferability of assets abroad would result in the shift of the political economic equilibrium towards improved domestic property rights and so less embezzlement of public assets, as political decision-makers would trade off large but unsafe embezzlements with smaller but safer ones.

In total, this section shows that structural adjustment reforms had limited achievements. In fact, it is a complex combination of three types of factors that ultimately determined reform outcomes, quite apart from reform design and technical soundness. The three types of factors include ideology and subjective beliefs, negative reputation and lack of credibility of the government, and special interests. The first two factors basically reflected the population's learning from its long experience in interacting with the government. The third factor suggests that the resulting attitudes were pragmatic, even though they may not always have been consistent.

3.4 Stabilisation reforms

The main tools used by IFIs to stabilise the economy were those generally recommended by the monetarist economic approach: restrictions in the supply of money and monetary devaluations. Whereas the foreign exchange rate had dropped by 30 per cent between 1980 and 1985, it was devalued by 68 per cent between 1986 and 1991. At the same time, the supply of money rose at the average rate of 3 per cent from 1987 to 1989, compared with the rate of 9 per cent in 1986, and 18 per cent from 1983 to 1985 (for these periods, the average growth rates of GDP were 5 per cent, 3 per cent, and 2 per cent, respectively).

Designed so as to achieve the goals of both price stability and reduction of public expenditure, this policy resulted in a dramatic decrease in the ratio between net domestic credit to government and net domestic credit to the economy. Whereas this ratio had increased from 28.2 per cent in 1980 to 57.3 per cent in 1985, it dropped to 19.6 per cent in 1991. As for the reduction of public deficits, the strategy proved to be consistent with a neo-conservative agenda, as it focused on reducing public consumption relatively more than on raising public revenue. Comparisons of some key revenue and expenditure posts of the budget over the six-year periods preceding and following the initiation of reform are illustrative of this evolution.

For example, the government's wage bill, which had averaged 49 per cent of recurrent budget during the period 1980–5 dropped to 43.6 per cent during the period 1986–91. Likewise, whereas subsidies had averaged 10 per cent of total expenditures and net lending during the former period, this ratio dropped to an average 5.2 per cent during the latter period. In contrast, the ratio amounted to 18.1 per cent over the period 1986–91, whereas the government's revenues (excluding all grants) represented an average 17.3 per cent of GDP during the former period. During the same periods, figures for the tax revenues over total expenditures (including grants) ratio were 105.6 per cent and 51.4 per cent, respectively, while figures for taxes on international trade over total revenue (excluding grants) ratio amounted to 25.2 per cent and 24.6 per cent, respectively. As for the total tax revenues over GDP ratio, the figure rose from 12.8 per cent during the pre-reform six-year period to 13.6 per cent during the first six-year reform period.

Indirect taxes was one of the few variables to follow a different pattern, as net indirect taxes (in constant local currency) rose by an average 23 per cent per annum from 1987–9, compared with an average of 5 per cent per annum from 1983–5. Yet, this was still consistent with the philosophy of the macroeconomic stabilisation reform, given that indirect taxes affect domestic consumption relatively more than business, conversely to direct taxes. Overall, the result in terms of reduction of public deficits was mitigated, though, suggesting that taxes were reduced too much (or did not increase enough) compared with public expenditure needs. For example, whereas the overall surplus/deficit (excluding grants) over GDP ratio averaged 4.9 per cent of GDP during the period 1980–5, this ratio averaged −8.7 per cent during the period 1986–91. As regards the overall surplus/deficit (including grants) versus GDP ratio, it dropped from an average 8.9 per cent in the former period to an average −5.2 per cent in the latter period.

Comparing performance by major reform period, Table 5.3 provides a broader view of the outcomes of macroeconomic stabilisation reforms. The period 1986–99 is split in three sub-periods corresponding to peacetime (1986–92), warfare (1993–9), and post-wartime. As regards the 1976–85 and 1982–5 periods, they correspond to the internally led changes and to the macroeconomic crisis that compelled the government to initiate externally led reforms, respectively. As Table 5.3 shows, stabilisation reform effort recorded mixed results. On the one hand, it improved international reserves and reduced inflation, but the achievements in the latter area were reversed in the war period 1993–9. Even the improvement in international reserves over the period 1993–9 was in large part due to the international community's embargo, introduced to force the army to step back after a military coup in July 1996. This reduced imports drastically, mechanically making the ratio of reserves high. By the same token, the end of the embargo in 1999 resulted in the deterioration of international reserves.

In areas like budget surplus/deficit and parallel market premium, success was limited, though. This variable particularly suggests that positive results that held in the short term have not been sustainable in the medium term. The reversal of macroeconomic stabilisation reforms in the period 1993–9 resulted from the civil war, which eroded fiscal taxation (Ndikumana, 2001a), and increased capital flight,[26] at a time when reforms had been reduced drastically because of insecurity, and external interventions focused on providing humanitarian aid to alleviate the suffering of the population. For their part, donors cut their aid to Burundi by half, forcing the government to turn heavily to monetary taxation, which in turn raised inflation and undermined macroeconomic stability (Nkurunziza, 2003). Unsurprisingly, the end of the war had converse effects on foreign direct investment and capital flight, surplus/deficit over GDP ratio, and inflation. The parallel market premium was the only notable exception until recently.

Table 5.3:   Performance of stabilisation reform: period annual averages

	76–85	82–85	86–92	93–99	00–02
Foreign direct investment /GDP (%)	n.a.	0.1	0.1	0.0	1.0
Reserves (in months of imports)	4.6	1.5	4.1	7.7	2.8
Surplus/deficit, including grants /GDP (%)	8.9	8.3	−4.8	−4.4	−0.8
Consumption Price Index annual change (%)	11.9	8.0	6.9	16.8	10.7
Parallel market to official exchange rate ratio	1.34	1.27	1.29	1.41	1.45

Source: Rough data are from World Bank (2003).

The macroeconomic evolution during the period of war was not a smooth process, however. For instance, the embargo was a significant macroeconomic shock, which led the government to trade off macroeconomic discipline with public revenue on a large basis. Figure 5.2 suggests that credit restrictions loosened more in the wake of the institution of the embargo than they did following the outbreak of war – even though the deterioration has been considerable since 1993 – and that by the same token, the end of the embargo resulted in renewed restrictions, in contrast to the end of war. Similarly, the public deficit deepened more in the year the embargo was decided than in the year civil war broke out, while the public deficit decreased following the end of the embargo in 1999 more than after the end of war in 2001.

The figures above show that the embargo was a more severe shock compared with the war, reflecting the deep dependence of Burundi's economy on external factors. Yet, as discussed earlier, civil conflict is endogenous to politics in Burundi, as the risk of conflict is part of the reform equilibrium. On the other hand, it was structural factors pertaining to Burundi's institutions and politics that triggered the embargo, as it was a consequence of the 1996 coup d'état intended to restore the political prominence of southern Tutsi-Himas. Therefore, reform reversibility may just be a reflection of the constraint that Burundi's institutional and political environment puts on reform sustainability.

Overall, macroeconomic stabilisation reforms have recorded modest success. Yet, they seem to have fared better than structural adjustment reforms, confirming the widespread finding according to which donor-supported reforms have succeeded more in stabilising than in changing structures in recipient economies.[27] In Burundi, success has been dependent on how specific and transaction-intensive the concerned programmes were. The higher

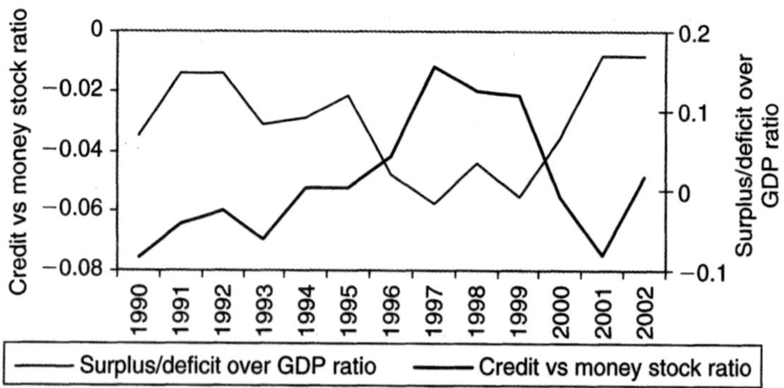

Notes: (i) Surplus and deficit include grants; (ii) credit relates to the monetary system credit; and (iii) the stock of money relates to the stock of money and quasi-money.
Source: Rough data are from the World Bank (2003).

Figure 5.2:   Public deficit and credit in the 1990s

the transaction intensity and the lower the specificity the harder it has been to bring about improvement.[28] Stabilisation reforms focused mainly on the central bank, thus allowing for the maintenance of reform momentum throughout the period 1986–2003 – including the sub-period of warfare to some extent. In contrast, structural adjustment reforms were faced with interests, views and beliefs of many more antagonistic groups, each of which could lead reform to fail, as the experience of fertilizer use illustrated. Yet, special interests did not spare stabilisation reforms. Using the foreign exchange rate reform policy, the next sub-section illustrates how stabilisation reform momentum was maintained during warfare, but argues that special interests undermined its performance.

3.5   Reform and socio-political stability

As hypothesised earlier, reforms in Burundi have been the outcomes of institutions, which in turn reflected individual preferences, interests and strategies as well as the way these aggregated for collective action. Ethnic, clan, regional and professional aggregation of interests and strategies has characterised Burundi's institutions, and socio-political stability has prevailed only when the distribution of reform-related benefits matched the distribution of power among these various groups. In this regard, the reforms were politically destabilising. Not only did they imply costs unevenly distributed across the Burundi society, but also – and more importantly – these costs were distributed irrespective of the distribution of power.

A number of observers have compared Burundi to South Africa under apartheid. Among others, Nelson Mandela made this comparison in 1999, some thirty-two years after it was first publicly expressed when Martin Ndayahoze, the Minister of Information, warned against the risk for Burundi's political system of turning into apartheid, antagonising Tutsis and Hutus. In the light of subsequent developments, it appears that Burundi's political system differed from apartheid in at least two respects. First, the divide between Hutus and Tutsis has never been as clear as it was between Whites and Blacks in South Africa. Even though Tutsis as a group have benefited from the discriminatory system in Burundi, large numbers of them have not received any notable benefit from it. Second, severe as it has been, ethnic discrimination has never been codified in formal rules, as apartheid was in South Africa. Even the mention of ethnic group on identity cards was ended in the 1960s, meaning that discrimination followed informal patterns pertaining to patrimonialism, and that it differed depending on personal relations.[29]

Thus in contrast to the South African apartheid system, which included a democracy-like system restricted to the White minority, the Tutsi-Hima minority members never attempted to establish an egalitarian political system among Tutsis, or even among Tutsi-Himas. Instead, as Prunier (1994) argues, since this group seized power in 1966 it built mafia-like hierarchies.[30] The opacity and the harshness of competition inherent in such organisations explain the palace revolutions mentioned earlier. Particularly, the military staff responsible for the palace coup of 1987 included Tutsi-Hima militaries unhappy with their pay and those on the list of an early retirement plan seeking to downsize the army, as part of the effort at reducing budgetary deficits (Ntibazonkiza, 1993). Thus it was the ruling group's members facing relatively higher reform costs – either real or perceived ex ante – who staged the coup that overthrew the Bagaza regime and brought Buyoya to office. Hence, while institutions and politics affected IFI-supported reforms, there was a two-way impact, as these reforms in turn contributed to regime change. The next section provides a wider view of how external aid has affected Burundi's institutions, and concludes with a discussion of the implications of this impact for future institutions and reforms.

4   Reform and institutional change in retrospect and prospective

4.1   External factors and institutional change since the 1980s

The hypothesis that aid may be, or has been, a strong driving force for change in Burundi is not new. Even though the views about how aid should be used as a tool to leverage change differ among authors, most observers agree that aid has played an important role since the mid-1980s.[31] For instance, the reaction of the international community to the outbreak of ethnic violence in 1988 in the northern communes of Ntega and Marangara was an illustration of this. Having learned from the massacres of 1972, the international community spoke up to deter new anti-Hutu pogroms, and forced Buyoya's regime to open up public institutions to Hutus and to stage democratic reforms by threatening to suspend aid in case of abuses.[32]

As a result, in October 1988, a National Commission with twelve Hutus and twelve Tutsis was set up to study the question of national unity. A Hutu prime minister was appointed, while a cabinet where Hutus and Tutsis held the same number of portfolios was created. These appointments could hardly be considered a real recasting of power, though. Indeed, Hutus were co-opted in a scheme referring more to a redistribution of posts and associated privileges.[33] However, given the situation prevailing until then, this was a considerable change.

In 1991, a new constitution designed to open up the political process to direct democratic participation was approved by referendum. In 1992, the multi-party system was restored, some twenty-six years after its suppression by the Micombero regime. In June 1993, free and fair presidential and legislative elections were held and won by Ndadaye, the first Hutu president, while his party, FRODEBU (Front pour la Démocratie au Burundi), won 80 per cent of the seats in the National Assembly. It is largely consensual in Burundi that these changes owed a great deal to the way donors used aid to get concessions on reform at the time. Since the crisis of 1988, the international community realised that aid was a powerful tool to exert pressure for change. Again, aid was used in 1993 to deter the reversal of the democratic reforms.

Given its vulnerability to the nation's military, the new regime had no other strategic choice than to try to cooperate with the army and, more generally, Tutsis, which the new president co-opted with some 40 per cent of the ministerial portfolios, including the prime ministry. In a context where virtually all Hutus had been victims of terrible injustices and brutalities at the hands of the army, this goodwill could hardly be credible, though. Unsurprisingly, whereas the regime sought to promote cooperation, the army opted for confrontation. In October 1993, it sought to interrupt the process of change by assassinating President Ndadaye and a number of his closest collaborators. This triggered the 1993 civil war that has continued until recently. The decision of major donors to reduce aid if the democratic government were not restored played a central role in the failure of the 21 October 1993 coup. Indeed, after the condemnation of the coup by donors, panic spread among plotters, who knew that if external aid were suppressed they could not provide the elites with the usual privileges and, therefore, could hardly govern the country.[34]

In the aftermath of the coup attempt, the army did not return to being under the legal authority of the government attempting to control the situation, though. Instead, in a subtler strategy to undermine the power of FRODEBU and to finally take power back without alienating the goodwill of the international community, it started a long process of sabotage of government efforts. The pressure on FRODEBU prompted a series of negotiations out of which this party lost substantial prerogatives to the benefit of the Tutsi-dominated opposition. One core argument of the latter was that democracy was not appropriate for a society like Burundi, where it allegedly tended to generate violence. Another argument – which particularly seemed to be legitimate in the wake of the massacre of Tutsis by Hutus in Rwanda in 1994 – was the quest for a scheme that would ensure safety for Tutsis. Essentially developed by the politico-military groups' members who sparked the 1993 war by the decapitation of the elected government, these arguments were largely part of tactics intended to convince donors of the need to reverse the democratic reforms.

By September 1994, the pressure on the surviving government members led to the appointment of a prime minister from the opposition, as well as to the representation of the opposition in sensitive sectors like intelligence, media and police. The opposition also received 40 per cent of positions for provincial governors and municipal administrators. The share of the opposition in ministerial positions increased to 45 per cent. The constitution was suspended and replaced with a lopsided convention, which provided the Tutsi-dominated opposition with the prerogative to designate the president and to agree on the appointment of the prime minister. A National Security Council was instituted, with the majority of its ten members coming from the opposition. The unrest continued until July 1996, when the army reinstalled Buyoya in office.

During this troubled period, 1993–6, the economy plummeted. Annual real growth of GDP fell by 6.5 per cent on average, while income per capita dropped from US$203 to US$163. The agriculture share of GDP fell to an unprecedented low of 44.8 per cent, due to disruptions caused by military operations and subsequent population displacements. Thanks to generalised smuggling to neighbouring countries by individuals who crossed to Rwanda and Tanzania through virtually any point of the border, the volume of exports was less affected than imports, which in contrast had to be shipped through more vulnerable routes.

Soon after the 1996 military coup, it became clear to the international community that the goal was more about power than safety despite allegations of those seeking to restore the Tutsi political domination. To force the military junta to step back, Burundi's neighbours decided on an embargo on trade to and from Burundi, while the international community decided to reduce foreign aid drastically (Figure 5.3). This weakened the Tutsi-Hima oligarchy relatively more than the rest of the society. For example, while incomes from agricultural exports were barely affected – in part thanks to the aforementioned smuggling – manufactured exports, which are controlled by Tutsi-dominated operators, dropped from 8 per cent to only 0.8 per cent of total exports from 1994–6 to 1997–9.

At the same time, the tolerance of Hutu-dominated rebel bases by neighbouring countries prevented the army from defeating them. The army-controlled government opted for a long war of attrition, whereby it attempted to use the increasing misery of the population as an argument to get aid resumed and the embargo ended. But this strategy did not fare any better than previous attempts. Eventually, the government and satellite Tutsi parties agreed to participate in negotiations with FRODEBU and other Hutu parties in Arusha, Tanzania. On

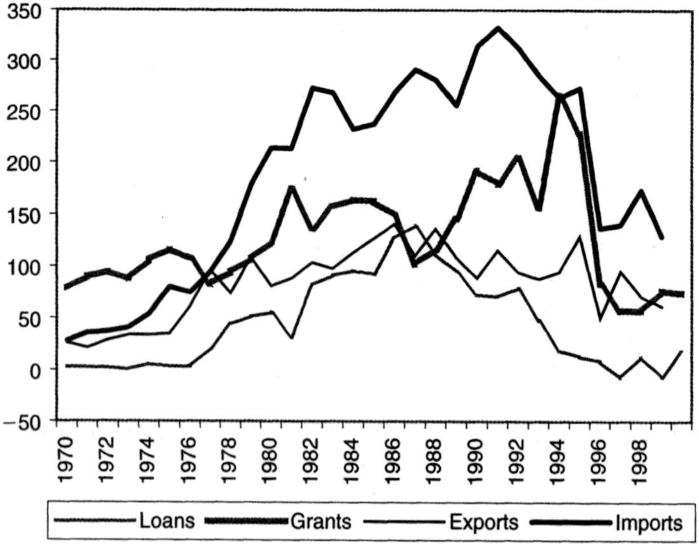

Figure 5.3:   Official development aid flows, 1970–99 (US$ m)

28 August 2000, the government and the representatives of FRODEBU agreed on a peace accord, which was signed by nineteen political parties in a high-profile ceremony attended by heads of state, including US President Clinton. Yet most people knew the signatories had not really agreed to peace. As it sought to avoid massacres like those in Rwanda in 1994 and to compensate for its failure in preventing genocide there, the international community supported the Arusha negotiation patiently. But eventually tired of the two-year wrangling among the negotiators, the mediation – led by Nelson Mandela – decided to force them to sign a text that most of them had not even read due to last-minute modifications (Sindayigaya, 2002).

Not surprisingly, the implementation of the accord raised many difficulties. Violence increased as the Hutu rebel wings, which were at odds with the FRODEBU, sought to show that no agreement was viable without them. A resurgence of violence hardened political positions, putting immense pressure on the government. As a result, the government made implementation of the agreement conditional on prior signature of a ceasefire, but it was bound to additional concessions as the international community made it clear that aid would not resume until peace was restored. This decision was an additional incentive for the government to accept more concessions, which led to the signature of the decisive peace agreement between the government and the major rebel group, the CNDD-FDD (Conseil pour la Défense de la Démocratie and its armed wing, the Forces de Défense de la Démocratie, led by Peter Nkurunziza). This agreement has resulted in the restoration of peace over the quasi-totality of Burundi's territory.

Although the 2000 peace accord did not end the war, it provided a minimum political agreement, particularly with regard to the origins of the Hutu–Tutsi dispute, questioning openly the 'meta-conflict' mentioned earlier. It also resulted in some agreement on the path to reconstruction and on the role and composition of the army and its relation to civil power (International Crisis Group, 2001). The document recognised that acts of genocide, war crimes and other crimes against humanity had been perpetrated in Burundi for decades. It provided for an inquiry by an international judicial commission on human rights abuses since independence.

The accord also recognised the need to establish a new political, economic, social, cultural and judicial order based on the principles of democracy and the rule of law. It included the commitment to fight all forms of discrimination in access to education, the administration of justice, and the management of public services and to adopt a multiparty political system. It emphasised the need to establish an independent electoral commission, a senate with two delegates from each province, the elimination of ethnic dominance in the army, the need to reconsider the cases of political prisoners, and the involvement of an international peacekeeping force to help stabilise the country.

In the economic area, this accord contributed to notable improvements. Together with the end of the embargo, it stopped the decline of real GDP per capita, allowed for the restoration of fertilizer consumption to its pre-1996 level of 3.9 kg/ha, and brought back the real agriculture GDP per capita growth rate into positive territory. Drawbacks were recorded in the current account. International reserves dropped from an equivalent six to three months of imports from the period 1997–9 to the period 2000–2, as imports resumed on a large basis.

5   Conclusion: institutions and reform in prospect

By using aid and embargo as a tool to leverage reform, the international community at large has affected power relations throughout society, with important implications. This has affected transactions about new rules, and thus shifted the internal reform policy equilibrium. Although some economic reforms were reversed as a result of political instability, changes that were unthinkable before the crisis became feasible as the conflict weakened both the Tutsi-Hima-dominated government and the centrifugal forces that determined the former modes of aggregation of preferences and interests. The civil society that had long been suffocated by totalitarianism and authoritarianism gained impetus; the army, which virtually included only Tutsi elements before 1993, is now reported to have 40 per cent Hutus in its low-ranking staff; higher education, formerly centralised in the capital city and tightly controlled by the central government, now includes private universities established in several provinces.

These changes are not a reflection of any real conversion of the still Tutsi-dominated government to values like equity, though. Rather they reflect a readjustment to a new political economic equilibrium, taking into account the new balance of power and donors' pressures for inclusiveness of Hutus in public institutions. In light of the analytical framework laid out earlier in this chapter, it is arguable that the crisis that broke out in 1993 has shifted reform towards equilibrium favourable to sounder reform, in the sense that it has resulted in relatively more balanced power relations between groups. However, the signature of the peace accord that formalised this balance of power owed more to tactics than to real commitment to peace. As a result, the changes rest on a fragile basis, and their sustainability remains an issue.

The first major source of uncertainty lies with the role that donors will be playing in the new context. Until recently, donors influenced Burundi's institutions by suspending aid and setting progress in the inclusiveness of Hutus in public institutions as a condition of aid resumption. As such, the impact has been a result of deliberate omission more than of a pro-active policy. Now this pattern has changed, as donors have decided to resume development assistance. Whether they will manage to channel fungible resources through Burundi's institutions without affecting negatively the fragile balance of power that arose from the peace process remains an open question. The risk is considerable since past interventions do not seem to have reflected a strong political economic understanding of social interactions in Burundi, while Burundi politicians' attempts to manipulate donors in order to achieve their hidden agendas are quasi-permanent, as the 1994–6 episode illustrated.

Second, the uncertainty surrounding Burundi's future institutions also owes a great deal to the still prominent place of people with strong incentives to prevent the emergence of democracy and justice – the two basic changes on which long-lasting peace and genuine political and economic reforms depend. For instance, the changes that the peace process has staged have barely affected the structure of the army. As of October 2004, officers from the south controlled 73 per cent of senior operational positions in the army; commanders of four in the five military districts are Tutsis from the south; and officers from the south control thirty-nine of the fifty-six battalions of the Burundi army.[35] Although the present balance of power among politico-military actors is such that the army can hardly stage a coup d'état successfully, the resulting ability of the army to easily overcome problems of collective action is particularly an incentive to stage such action since the democratic elections in 2005 weakened it even more. Whether the army, traditionally so conservative and dedicated to special interest, will resign itself to losing its privileges and restrain from causing chaos as a means to escape from being held accountable for past atrocities remains an issue.

The constitution that the executive and legislative have approved for the post-transitional period is a reflection of the influence of forces opposed to the advent of an egalitarian system. This draft proposes the automatic inclusion of former presidents in the Senate without any election, and provides for the prominence of non-elected bodies, many of which were created and staffed under the Buyoya government, over elected ones. It also provides for an equal representation of Hutus and Tutsis in various state bodies, despite the fact that these groups represent respectively 85 per cent and 14 per cent of Burundi's population. As Ndayongeje (2004) has recently pointed out, this constitution seeks to prevent the emergence of any clear majority – presumably believed to be favourable to Hutus.

The issue of justice is central as well. There is a consensus that it will be extremely difficult to build sound institutions in Burundi as long as a judicial process has not sidelined the politicians responsible for the disastrous post-colonial governance (Nindorera, 2001). Yet justice will likely be the most difficult change to bring about for many reasons. First, it is those most involved in the troubled past of Burundi who have the most power. An illustration of this power is the way negotiation facilitators have been compelled to concede temporary amnesty for past atrocities in order for various peace accords to be accepted. This is also why many politicians oppose the advent of true democracy, since it would result in the empowerment of the victims' families, and eventually in the prosecution of past crimes and assassinations. Thus the problems of justice and democracy overlap one another in a vicious circle: the blocking of democracy is a means to prevent justice, while the blocking of the prosecution of past abuses impedes democracy.

A well-advised support of the international community may help break this vicious circle, though. Ngaruko and Nkurunziza (2000) have modelled how a justice-based and internationally led strategy can help achieve this change. A solution based on democracy would be effective as well, thanks to the interdependence between justice and democracy.[36] Sidelining politically (through the restoration of democracy) or judicially those who take Burundi people hostage is currently the hope of Burundi people. It is also a necessary – though not sufficient – condition for a minimum of common goals to emerge and to receive adequate political support, as was once the case for centuries before colonial rule. What is at stake is the emergence of a developmental state and future reforms. Whereas neo-patrimonialism has turned past reforms in heuristic opportunities for the government to extract resources from donors for the benefit of a tiny group, the sidelining of these people is necessary to strengthen the nascent civil society, whose empowerment is required for donor-led reforms to be more equitable, and to enjoy minimum local ownership and sustainability.

In light of the analytical framework developed earlier in this chapter, it is arguable that what is at stake with this support is not only future institutions but also future economic reforms. Sidelining the few profiteers of past regimes is required to achieve structural reforms in many areas including state-owned enterprises, trade, foreign exchange, etc. Yet, as for democracy and justice, this would likely not be a sufficient condition to get sound economic reforms on track. Regarding stabilisation reforms, for example, it is the tension between two forces that would likely determine the reform equilibrium. The first is the pressure that the government may come to face due not only to the immense social demands that a decade of warfare and impoverishment has exacerbated, but also to the fact that a democratic government will likely be bound to respond to demands of crowds of Hutu pariahs. The second force is the need for the government to maintain a good relationship with the international community, especially IFIs, on which Burundi's state and economy will continue to depend financially for a long time.

Notes

1. This study was developed as part of the Global Development Network (GDN) project on 'Understanding Reform'. The GDN's financial assistance is gratefully acknowledged. The study has greatly benefited from comments by Gary McMahon and José Maria Fanelli on an earlier draft. The authors also wish to thank without implicating Hanaa Kheir-El-Din and Barbara Stallings for their valuable comments when an earlier version of this study was presented at the GDN Workshop in New Delhi, India in 2004.

2. In the 1970s, Burundi participated in some regional organisations, though. The Communauté Economique des Pays des Grands-Lacs (CEPGL), including Congo, Rwanda and Burundi; and the Kagera River Basin Organisation (KBO), including Uganda, Tanzania, Rwanda and Burundi, were two of these. However, poor governance and ethnic rivalries, especially between Rwanda, then controlled by Hutus, and Burundi, ruled by Tutsis, have undermined these organisations. Only the participation in larger organisations like the Preferential Trade Area (PTA), including the quasi-totality of eastern and southern Africa, has remained fairly and durably

effective, but Burundi's transactions within the PTA remain limited compared with the total volume of Burundi's exports.

3. The 'analytic narrative' method was developed by Bates et al. (1998).

4. This assumption follows from Bates and Devarajan (1999).

5. Max Weber originally defined patrimonialism as both the confusion of public and private domains in the exercise of public authority, and the personalisation of public authority, especially in societies without any bureaucracy. In patrimonial political settings, the political leader is considered as the owner of his constituency, and public servants are *de facto* personal servants. In its use by present-day political scientists, this concept refers to the dominance of personalised and informal rules, institutions and groups like family, ethnic group, and the like, over formal ones, and with little control and accountability in the use of public office and in public management, in addition to the conflation between public and private domains (Schacter, 2000). Neo-patrimonialism has been defined in specific reference to Africa, as one of the sub-categories of patrimonialism where patrimonial and bureaucratic practices coexist and are mutually enforcing. Neo-patrimonialism corresponds to a dual institutional system where both formal and informal rules coexist, and where the former rules are instrumented to leverage the latter. This results in the institutional system displaying the format of a modern state, but just *en façade*. Another key distinctive feature between patrimonialism and neo-patrimonialism is that in a neo-patrimonial system, most people – especially public officials – know what a (modern) state should be and should do. This is often referred to demagogically by the official discourse, and the gap between modern norms and actual practices is a result of a deliberate policy. In this sense, one can speak of corruption in neo-patrimonial institutional settings, but not in patrimonial regimes, where this knowledge is limited (Médard, 1998).

6. As an illustration, Burundi's national motto under the monarchy – 'God, *Mwami*, Burundi' – placed the king just below God, but above the nation.

7. The president and his ministers – often chosen among his courtiers – would hold feasts several days in a row, at the expense of their work duties. One anecdote states that while the president was delivering a speech on national celebration day, the audience applauded enthusiastically. For this reason, he decided that the next day would be a holiday. As the audience applauded even more heavily, the president declared the next second day a holiday too. In the sexuality area – specifically emphasised by Bayart (1999) as one in which power is manifested the most in Africa through the multiplication of mistresses – the president publicly exerted unlimited prerogative over the wives of leading citizens, who faced the risk of imprisonment and confiscation of their properties if they protested. To illustrate a more recent manifestation of this symbolism, Prunier (1994) mentions that for Hutu grassroots populations, the Hutu candidate in the 1993 presidential election symbolised both a king and a god, for whom women took off their dresses to spread the cloth on the ground for him to walk on.

8. For a detailed account of the impact of politics on income distribution in Burundi, see Nkurunziza and Ngaruko (2002).

9. With a Gini coefficient of 0.33 in the second half of the 1990s (World Bank, 2003), Burundi appears to be an egalitarian society. However, as Ngaruko (2003b) and Ngaruko and Nkurunziza (2005) argue, this apparent egalitarianism conceals profound inequalities between ethnic groups and among regions that are barely captured by usual measures.

10. Ngaruko and Nkurunziza (2005) show that the predicted probability of war in Burundi is three times as high compared to a typical developing country.

11. Data presented in Ngaruko and Nkurunziza (2005) suggest that 47 per cent of high-ranking political and administrative leaders were from Bururi in 1967, while 71 per cent were Tutsis. By 2000, these figures were 70 per cent and 100 per cent, respectively, confirming that the discriminatory policies resulted in a self-reinforcing process.

12. Part of the process of power concentration in the hands of Tutsi-Himas took place through violent crises. The main turning points of this process include the physical elimination of all Hutu political leaders in 1965, the political elimination of non-Bururi Tutsis from leadership in 1971, and the end of participation of Hutus in any administrative authority in 1972. In 1988, new ethnic massacres occurred, but the subsequent outcry of the international community limited the massacres and forced the government to open up public institutions to Hutus. Yet the hierarchies bequeathed by previous discriminations still hold, and as Ndikumana (2001b) argues, being a Tutsi military officer from Bururi still presents the best opportunity for social and economic promotion.

13. For an overall view of these causalities, see Oketch and Polzer (2002).

14. Such a misperception also existed in other African countries. For a view of this, see Isichei (1997).

15. Levy and Kpundeh (2004).

16. Khan et al. (1990) propose a recent version of this model.

17. Collier and Gunning (1999) argue that when inflation is over 8 per cent in Africa, it affects economic growth negatively.

18. These figures are drawn from a survey carried out in 1985 in the northern province of Ngozi by the Société Nationale d'Etudes Statistiques (SNES), now the Institut de Statistique et d'Etudes Economiques du Burundi (ISTEEBU).

19. Hirschman's typology of human behaviour when individuals come to deal with authority in social hierarchies may help explain this mistake. Hirschman (1970) identifies three basic attitudes, which may help explain the inconsistency of the strategy that relied on businessmen to champion reform: *loyalty* (when individuals choose to cling to existing rules), *exit* (when they abandon these rules), and *voice* (when they seek to change these rules). In light of this typology, it becomes clear that IFIs believed the attitude of businessmen vis-à-vis the government to be voice, while it was really loyalty (and exit for peasants). Put differently, IFIs believed that the relevant social divide existed between the government and the civil society, especially economic operators, which they sought to empower and to use to reform the state. Actually, the most significant divide was between the elites and the masses.

20. By 1997, the non-weighted average of the government's equity share of the thirty-three largest public and partly privatised enterprises amounted to 87 per cent. The total assets of these companies were then estimated to US$255 million (data from IMF, 2000).

21. The use of fertilizer and pesticides is forced for export crops, and the government makes a particular effort to make it available on a regular basis, probably thanks to the role of these crops in public revenue.

22. See, for example, Kururu (2002).

23. A number of economists consider cross-border private capital flows as a result of portfolio adjustments to property rights differentials. For example, Deppler and Williamson (1987) define capital flight as an 'acquisition or retention of a claim on non-residents that is motivated by the owner's concern that the value of his asset would be subject to discrete losses if his claims continued to be held domestically', while Jacquemin and Schrans (1970) present the risk of expropriation as one form

of such losses: 'the risk of expropriation from a possession represents a decrease in the utility provided by this possession'.
24. Ndikumana and Boyce (2002).
25. Supportive of this view is recent work showing that in African countries profoundly marked by neo-patrimonial dysfunctions, external aid tends to delay reform rather than fostering it (van de Walle, 2001).
26. Ndikumana and Boyce (2002) found that from 1985 to 1996, Burundi recorded US$820 million of capital flight.
27. See Easterly (2001), for example.
28. *Specificity* measures how readily output performance can be monitored and, therefore, improvement measures identified and tracked. *Transaction intensity* describes how complex/conflictual the decision process is to get from inputs to outputs, including the number and strength of relevant interest groups and steps. This explanation is drawn from the recent work by Fukuyama (2004).
29. Actually, some Hutus, especially from the south, benefited from this discriminatory system through co-optation, even though, overall, Hutus as a group have suffered from the system.
30. In the mid-1980s, the divide between Bayanzi and Bashingo clans of Tutsi-Hima elites from Bururi crosscut another divide between Vyanda and Rutovu, two sub-localities of this province.
31. See Beleli (2001), International Crisis Group (2001), and Van Eck (2001).
32. In 1972, the army and Tutsi operatives hunted down and killed most Hutu business-men, civil servants, university students and secondary school students throughout the country, in what the United Nations (1996) and other independent observers (Lemarchand and Martin, 1974) qualified as genocide. Hundreds of thousands of Hutus were killed while hundreds of thousands more fled to neighbouring countries, representing a loss of about 14 per cent of the total population. These events were a watershed in Burundi's history. During and after these massacres, the international community barely reacted (Du Bois, 1972). The fear that the Micombero regime would turn to the communist bloc if the West condemned these massacres is gen-erally advanced as the explanation to this attitude.
33. For a view of the privileges of public servants in Burundi, see Ngaruko and Nkurun-ziza (2000).
34. Besides, uncontrollable killings of Tutsis by Hutus avenging the assassination of President Ndadaye had rapidly spread throughout the country, compelling the army's chief of staff to condemn the coup.
35. Rukindikiza (2004).
36. In 1994, Ahmed Abdallah, the United Nations special envoy in Burundi, estimated that the exclusion of only 200 politicians who were the most involved in stirring up violence could have led to the end of war. This figure also shows the extent of power concentration, as the interests of so few – but well organised – people prevail over those of the masses.

References

Bates, R. and Devarajan, S. (1999) *Framework Paper on the Political Economy of African Growth*, mimeo (Washington, DC: World Bank).
Bates, R., Greif, A., Levi, M., Rosenthal, J.-L. and Weingast, B. (1998) *Analytic Narratives* (Princeton, NJ: Princeton University Press).
Bates, R. and Krueger, A. O. (eds) (1993) *Political and Economic Interaction in Economic Reform* (Cambridge, MA: Blackwell).

Bayart, J. F. (1999) *The State in Africa: the Politics of the Belly* (New York: Longman Group).

Beleli, O. (2001) 'Aid as a Peacemaker: a View From Burundi', Justice & Peace Certificate Senior Thesis, Georgetown University, Washington, DC.

Chrétien, J. P. (2000) *L'Afrique des Grands-Lacs. Deux Mille Ans d'Histoire* (Paris: Aubier).

Collier, P. and Gunning, J. W. (1999) 'Explaining African Economic Performance', *Journal of Economic Literature*, 37: 64–111.

Deppler, M. and Williamson, M. (1987) 'Capital Flight: Concepts, Measurement and Issues', *Staff Studies for the World Economic Outlook*, IMF, Washington, DC.

Du Bois, V. (1972) 'To Die in Burundi', *Central and Southern Africa Series*, 16, 4.

Easterly, W. (2001) 'The Effect of International Monetary Fund and World Bank Programs on Poverty', *Policy Research Working Paper* No. 2517, World Bank, Washington, DC.

Fukuyama, F. (2004) *State-Building: Governance and World Order in the 21st Century* (New York: Cornell University Press).

Guerrien, B. (1993) *Dictionnaire d'Analyse Economique* (Paris: Repères-La Découverte).

Herbst, J. (2000) *State and Power in Africa: Comparative Lessons in Authority and Control* (Princeton: Princeton University Press).

Hirschman, A. O. (1970) *Exit, Voice and Loyalty* (Cambridge, MA: Harvard University Press).

Husain, I. (1994) 'Why Do Some Economies Adjust More Successfully Than Others? Lessons from Seven African Countries', *Policy Research Working Paper* No. 1364, World Bank, Washington, DC.

International Crisis Group (2001) *Burundi: Breaking the Deadlock: the Urgent Need for a New Negotiating Framework*, Africa Report No. 29, 14 May, Brussels/Nairobi.

International Monetary Fund (2000) 'Burundi: Statistical Annex', IMF Staff Country Report No. 00/58, Washington, DC.

Isichei, E. (1997) *A History of African Societies to 1870* (Cambridge: Cambridge University Press).

Jackson, T. (2000) 'Equal Access to Education: a Peace Imperative for Burundi', International Alert, London. http://www.international-alert.org/pdf/pubgl/burun_ed_en.pdf.

Jacquemin, A. and Schrans, G. (1970) *Le Droit Economique* (Paris: Presses Universitaires de France).

Khan, S., Montiel, P. and Haque, U. (1990) 'Adjustment with Growth', *Journal of Development Economics*, 32.

Kururu, S. (2002) 'L'ère Bagaza', http://www.abarundi.org/actualite/national/bdinet_260602_bagaza_retour.html.

Lemarchand, R. (1994) *Burundi: Ethnic Conflict and Genocide* (Cambridge, UK: Woodrow Wilson Centre Press and Cambridge University Press).

Lemarchand, R. and Martin, D. (1974) *Selective Genocide in Burundi*, Minority Rights Group Report No. 20, London.

Levy, B. (2004) 'Governance and Economic Development in Africa: Meeting the Challenge of Capacity Building', in B. Levy and S. Kpundeh (eds), *Building State Capacity in Africa: New Approaches, Emerging Lessons*. World Bank Institute Studies (Washington, DC: World Bank), pp. 1–42.

Manirakiza, Marc (1992) *Burundi, de la Révolution au Régionalisme 1966–1976* Paris-Bruxelles: Le Mât de Misaine.

Médard, J.-F. (1998) 'La Crise de l'Etat Néo-Patrimonial et l'Evolution de la Corruption en Afrique sub-Saharienne', *Mondes en Développement* 26, 102: 55–67.

Ndarishikanye, B. (1994) 'Quand Deux Clientélismes s'Affrontent', *Komera* 3 (March–April).

Ndayongeje, L. (2004) *Observations Critiques sur le Projet de Constitution de la République du Burundi pour la Période Post-Transition*, Burundi Réalités International Inc., 14 March.

Ndikumana, L. (1998) 'Institutional Failure and Ethic Conflict in Burundi', *African Studies Review*, 41, 1: 29–48.

Ndikumana, L. (2001a) 'Fiscal Policy, Conflict and Reconstruction in Burundi and Rwanda', WIDER Discussion Paper No. 62, World Institute for Development Economics Research, United Nations.

Ndikumana, L. (2001b) *Making the State Relevant in Burundi*, mimeo, University of Massachusetts.

Ndikumana, L. and Boyce, J. K. (2002) 'Public Debts and Private Assets: Explaining Capital Flight from Sub-Saharan African Countries', PERI Working Paper, University of Massachusetts, Amherst.

Ngaruko, F. (1993) 'L'Industrie et l'Accumulation au Burundi', *Mondes En Développement*, 21, 92: 85–91.

Ngaruko, F. (2003a) 'Political Economy of Reform for Service Delivery', *Nordic Journal of African Studies*, 12, 2.

Ngaruko, F. (2003b) 'Agricultural Export Performance in Africa: Elements of Comparison with Asia', *ESA Working Paper* No. 03–09, FAO, Rome.

Ngaruko F. and Nkurunziza, J. (2000) 'An Economic Interpretation of Conflict in Burundi', *Journal of African Economies*, 9, 3: 370–409.

Ngaruko, F. and Nkurunziza, J. (2005) 'Explaining the Duration of Civil Wars: the Case Study of Burundi', in Paul Collier and Nicholas Sambanis (eds.), *Understanding Civil War (Volume 1: Africa): Evidence and Analysis* (Washington, DC: World Bank).

Nindorera, E. (2001) 'Le Long Chemin de la Réconciliation au Burundi', in *Au Coeur de l'Afrique*, special issue: 72–111.

Nkurunziza, J. D. (2003) *War, Inflation Tax and Policy in Burundi*, mimeo, CSAE and St Antony's College, University of Oxford.

Nkurunziza, J. D. and Ngaruko, F. (2002) 'Explaining Economic Growth in Burundi 1960–2000', CSAE *Working Paper* WPS/2002–3, Oxford University.

North, D. (1990) *Institutions, Institutional Change and Economic Performance* (New York: Cambridge University Press).

Ntibazonkiza, R. (1993) 'Au Royaume des Seigneurs de la Lance: Une Approche Historique de la Question Ethnique au Burundi. Tome 2 – De l'independence à Nos Jours (1962–1992)', La Louvière: Centre d'Animation en Langues.

Nyamoya, P. (1998) 'Pour un Modèle Original de Privatisation des Entreprises Publiques an Burundi', RIDEC, Vol. 2, September, Bujumbura.

Oketch, J. S. and Polzer, T. (2002) 'Conflict and Coffee in Burundi', in J. Lind and K. Sturman (eds), *Scarcity and Surfeit: the Ecology of African Conflicts* (Pretoria: Institute for Security Studies).

Prunier, G. (1994) 'Burundi: a Manageable Crisis?' Writenet, UK http://129.194.252.80/catfiles/2505.pdf.

Reyntjens, P. (1994) *L'Afrique des Grands Lacs en Crise* (Paris: Karthala).

Rukindikiza, G. (2004) 'Curieuse Répartition des Commandants d'Unité dans l'Armée Burundaise', http://burundi.news.free.fr, 19 November.

Schacter, M. (2000) 'Sub-Saharan Africa: Lessons from Experience in Supporting Sound Governance', *ECD Working Paper Series* No. 7, February.

Sindayigaya, J.-M. (2002) *La Saga d'Arusha* (Bruxelles: ARIB).

United Nations (1996) *Rapport de la Commission d'Enquête Internationale Chargée d'établir les faits concernant l'assassinat du président du Burundi, le 21 octobre 1993, ainsi que les massacres qui ont suivi*, document S/1996/682, August.

UNECA (2003) *Economic Report on Africa* (Addis Ababa: United Nations Economic Commission for Africa).

Van Eck, J. (2001) *Polarisation of Parties Into 'Win Power' and 'Keep Power' Camps Threatens the Collapse of Peace Process*, Burundi Report No. 2001/1 (April), Centre for Conflict Resolution, Cape Town, South Africa.

Walle, N. van de (2001) *African Economies and the Politics of Permanent Crisis, 1979–1999* (New York: Cambridge University Press).

World Bank (1988) *Burundi: Structural Adjustment and Development Issues. Background Papers*, Report No. 6754-BU, 20 January.

World Bank (2000) *African Development Indicators*, Washington, DC.

World Bank (2003) *African Development Indicators*, CD-ROM.

6
Understanding Economic and Political Reforms in Tanzania

Haidari K. R. Amani, Samuel M. Wangwe, Dennis Rweyemamu,
Rose Aiko and Godwill G. Wanga

1   Introduction

Tanzania has gone through an array of political and socio-economic policy experiments in the last four decades with diverse impacts on the trajectory of its development.[1] In 1986 Tanzania embarked on IMF/World Bank-sponsored economic reforms, which essentially meant a shift from the nation's centrally planned socialist economy to a market-oriented one led by the private sector. The first generation of reforms, implemented from 1986 to 1992, were dominated by the will to 'get prices right', while the second generation of reforms, from 1993 to 2004, have been devoted to institutional changes.

The immediate post-independence period (i.e. 1961–6), which could be characterised as a market-oriented development era, was marked by fast rates of economic growth. Nonetheless, it was also a period of discernible income disparity, which the socialist approach to development, adopted from 1967 to 1985, was supposed to address (Nyerere, 1967). While the socialist policies were well-intentioned, the strategies that were adopted paid little attention to incentives for performance – this situation eventually undermined the success of the socialist project. With time, the socialist experiment experienced serious trouble, with the economy sliding into a crisis, which could only be addressed by a major policy swing, but which the government was not prepared to undertake for some time until 1986 (Bigsten et al., 2000).

As the initial responses to counter the crisis failed and the crisis deepened, the country agreed to implement conditionality-based adjustment programmes under the aegis of the World Bank and the IMF in 1986. This chapter examines the Tanzanian reform episode and highlights the main challenges and the responses undertaken to counter them. More specifically, we explore the triggers or motivations for Tanzania's reforms at the time of their initial implementation; describe the major reforms that have been undertaken in the country to date; analyse the reform implementation process with respect to its breadth, depth, speed and path dependency; document the role of different stakeholders and interest groups in the design and implementation of the reforms; and assess the outcomes of the reforms that have been implemented over the years. Our ultimate aim is to shed light on the Tanzanian reform experiment, with the aim of drawing out the options available for the way forward, taking key economic, social and political institutional factors into consideration.

2   Analytical framework and research hypotheses

In explaining the Tanzanian reform episode, context matters. Accordingly, we review the documented accounts of the initial conditions and the policies implemented, together with their outcomes, dwelling primarily on the records of the government, donor community and non-governmental organisations (NGOs). It addition, our study is informed by field data from guided interviews, meetings, informal discussions and consultations with key policy analysts, and various reform stakeholders at the central and local government levels, including the private sector and civil society organisations.

The literature on institutional economics and political economy has revealed that institutions and the interactions with stakeholders are a major factor for the successful implementation of reforms. Available studies (e.g. Tommasi, 2002; Ruis and van de Walle, 2003) suggest that economic reforms are generally influenced by the formal procedures by which politicians accede to power (Ruis and van de Walle, 2003). Consequently, our analysis pays more attention to institutional reforms. We reason that to better understand economic reforms, one needs to consider the operations of higher-level institutions which invariably determine who has the power, and under what procedures, to make policies or to set the regulations that influence the functioning of the market. In undertaking this study we set out to test the following seven hypotheses which posit that:

- economic crises in Tanzania were important for reforms to occur;
- gradual policy reforms generate better results in terms of 'high quality growth' and minimising the discrepancy between macro-stability achievements and micro-level impacts on livelihoods and well-being;
- broader participation in the reform process leads to better technical content in policies;
- national ownership of reforms is essential for a nation's commitment to, and the ultimate success of, reforms;
- the impetus for the policy changes usually comes, to a large extent, from the influence of the donor community;
- the nature and the extent of civil society participation in the reforms are generally conditioned by the legacy of the government;
- reforms need to be backed by strong institutions and human capacities to be able to cope with the challenges that emerge in the reform process.

3   Why Tanzania chose to reform

Between 1961 and 1966, Tanzania's economy was largely driven by the private sector. The development strategy adopted soon after independence was based on the principles of a mixed economy in which private investment (including foreign direct investment) was encouraged. However, Tanzania declared, through the Arusha Declaration of 1967, that it would follow a socialist ideology, couched in *ujamaa*. With this ideology, the Nyerere government sought to incorporate issues of equity and justice in the development process. Conspicuous among the objectives of the Arusha Declaration were the gradual creation of a dominant public sector and the evolution of a socialist income policy. Among other things, this policy promoted equitable income distribution through various measures, including the provision of free social services to all; and the nationalisation of all strategic economic activities in manufacturing, commerce, banking, mining, construction, export and import trade, and crop marketing. Other major control instruments that were adopted to facilitate the efficient management of the economy included:

(i)   a central control of investment planning, together with restrictive codes on domestic and foreign investments;

(ii)   a confinement policy in which the wholesale trade for specified goods (imported and domestically manufactured) could only be done by state-owned enterprises (SOEs);

(iii)   a price control system, for which the National Price Commission was established in 1974, to regulate and control prices and interest rates;

(iv)   compensation policy controls, instituted as part of the socialist income policy, by which wages were regulated in the economy by the government through a permanent labour tribunal;

(v)   a credit rationing system under which credit was deliberately rationed in favour of state-owned enterprises; and

(vi)   a foreign exchange and import licensing mechanism which gave preference to public consignees and public enterprises.

The government at the same time adopted a development strategy which emphasised investments in human development in line with its objective to develop the people by helping them attain their basic needs. Major investments were made in social services, such as education, health, water and sanitation. This was done through central government investment programmes underpinned by the basic needs approach to development and facilitated by considerable inflows of aid, especially in the 1970s. Laudable achievements were recorded in school enrolment, adult education and health development. Perhaps the most remarkable accomplishment was in the literacy rate, which was only about 33 per cent in 1970, but rose to about 90 per cent by 1985. Notably, the results of Universal Primary Education intertwined with adult education programmes to facilitate this achievement. These achievements, however, were not sustained for long, partly because there was not enough growth in output to maintain the flow of the required resources for the upkeep of the social sector. The government also formulated an industrial strategy to go with its import substitution industrialisation policy, which sought to make the economy self-reliant and to facilitate sustainable development. From this point onwards, the government's intervention took the form of creating and promoting new public sector institutions and consolidating existing ones. Socialism and self-reliance became the foundation upon which the Tanzania's egalitarian political economy rested.

Initially, many socialist-minded nations, including the Nordic countries, the former Soviet Union, China and Cuba, welcomed the Tanzanian socialist experiment. In fact, Tanzania received massive foreign aid and technical assistance from these countries (Bigsten et al., 2000; Helleiner, 2001). Foreign aid became the major source of foreign exchange for the importation of capital goods for the state-owned enterprises and other industrial ventures in Tanzania (Bigsten et al., 2000). Even though Tanzania made considerable strides in human development during this period, the progress was interrupted by the economic crisis of the late 1970s. And as the nation's dependence on aid increased, in the face of dwindling foreign exchange, industrial operations became inefficient and under-utilised (Wangwe, 1983). At the same time, the government's interventions in the production and distribution of goods intensified: price control mechanisms were tightened, taxes were hiked, and the tax structure became even more complex. It is fair to note, though, that exogenous economic shocks of the 1970s (notably the OPEC crisis) imposed additional constraints on the nation's economy, all of which contributed to the failure of the socialist experiment.

In the course of building a socialist Tanzania, the government also undertook various measures to ensure political stability and cohesion, and to counter any opposition to its policies. After making Tanzania a one-party state in 1965, the major groups in society, such as workers' organisations, women's organisations, the youth and cooperatives, were all co-opted into, or subordinated to, the ruling party as affiliates.

President Nyerere, at least in his rhetoric, favoured the participation of the people in the development process. According to the socialist ideals that President Nyerere embraced, the political system had to be organised to give people an opportunity to voice their concerns from the village councils to the party system and, ultimately, to the central government. The private sector was, however, on the defensive, given the political atmosphere that was essentially hostile to private sector development. With the branding of private sector investors as exploiters and undesirable elements in a socialist regime, the local business community could not organise itself as a socio-economic force and, consequently, lost its position as a potential pressure group that could influence public policy.

Tanzania went under a bi-partisan government, constitutionally, with the Tanganyika African National Union (TANU) ruling in the mainland and the Afro Shirazi Party (ASP) ruling in the Zanzibar islands. In 1977 the two parties merged to form Chama cha Mapinduzi (CCM), which has continued to be the ruling party in Tanzania. Political stability, however, remained the major strength of the country, even when Tanzania entered a period of economic and social crisis.

The size of the public sector, both in terms of employment and total spending, increased, as more state-owned enterprises were established from the nationalised private enterprises and through new investments in the public sector. The overall result was a dramatic growth of parastatals, increasing from about 43 in 1966 to 380 in 1979 and again to 425 by the mid-1980s (Bagachwa and Limbu, 1995). The government established a leadership code of ethics for all civil servants, politicians and technocrats, preventing them from running parallel businesses in the private sector.

Although the government intended to create a strong and efficient public sector in the country, the instruments used (nationalisation and forcible reorganisation of people into villages) could not sustain growth. The government's nationalisation and villagisation policies contributed to the erosion of private development initiatives. By and large, credit and foreign exchange were allocated in favour of the public sector, resulting in the crowding-out of the private sector. Excessive government intervention created further problems: inefficiency in public enterprises, mismanagement, corruption and rent-seeking behaviour at many public enterprises, coupled with inadequate compensation packages for public sector employees, led to low morale and, eventually, to a decline in productivity. A culture of accountability in the public sector was being eroded at an alarming rate, but there were no institutional mechanisms to counter the situation (Bigsten et al., 2000; Mtatifikolo, 1998; Maliyamkono and Bagachwa, 1990).

Due to low productivity, fiscal and foreign exchange strains began to emerge. There was, however, a short-lived real economic growth to the tune of some 2.8 per cent per year, due to the 1976–8 coffee export boom, but the rate of inflation continued to increase, as can be seen from Table 6.1. The temporary gains from the coffee boom postponed the government's urge to change its policy, despite the apparent emergence of structural weaknesses and macroeconomic imbalances (Bigsten et al., 2000). Also, the slight recovery recorded between 1976 and 1978 was disrupted by the break-up of the East African Community in 1977, the war with Idi Amin in Uganda, the second oil shock, and the failure to make the necessary policy adjustments to address the crisis. The import bill for Tanzania rose sharply without a corresponding rise in exports at a time when aid fatigue was beginning to set in. Inflation was very high, the budget deficit deepened, balance of payment deficits persisted, shortages of goods became widespread, and the productive capacities of many industries were under-utilised, due to the scarcity of foreign exchange to

Table 6.1:   Tanzania: selected economic indicators, 1960s–2003

	1966–70	*1971–5*	*1976–80*	*1981–5*	*1986–92*	*1993–7*	*1998–2002*	*2003*
Real GDP growth rate (per cent)	3.9	3.8	2.8	0.7	4.1	3	5	5.6
Gross Capital Formation/ GDP ratio	24.2	26.8	28	18.1	24.6	23	20	22.8
Gross Domestic Savings/GDP ratio	17.1	12.9	15.3	10.5	5.1	5	9	11.8
Current Account Balance (US$ mill)	−4.7	−157.7	−256.9	−241.9	−231.6	−374.4	−214.7	−384.2
Current Account Balance/GDP ratio (per cent)	−1.3	−7.7	−6.4	−5.8	−13.3	−15	−8	−4.1
Recurrent Budget Balance/GDP ratio	0.3	0.8	−0.4	−4.1	−4.8	−6	−7	−5.6
Fiscal Balance (excluding loans, grants and import support)/GDP	−1.6	−4	−5.5	−3.3	−7.9	−5.8	−4.72	−9.0
Overall Fiscal Balance/GDP (including external finance)	−3.7	−4.8	−7.1	−8.2	−3	−5.2	−6.7	−2.51
Inflation rate (per cent)	2.8	13.7	13.7	30.2	26.2	25	7.3	4.4

Source: Economic Surveys and the Bank of Tanzania, various publications, 2003.

finance the importation of inputs. As a result of the economic crises, access to, and the quality of, basic social services declined, precipitating the need for reforms by the mid-1980s.

There were signs in the late 1970s and early 1980s that the legitimacy of the state was at stake as the socialist policy regime was failing to deliver goods and services to meet the expectations of the people. The donor community upon which the Tanzanian government had relied so heavily for finance began to demand a major policy change. During this period, the rise of the ideologically conservative regimes in Reagan's United States, Margaret Thatcher's United Kingdom, and Chancellor Kohl's Germany contributed to the shaping of what came to be known as the Washington Consensus, articulated by the Bretton Woods institutions, making it the dominant theoretical paradigm informing economic reforms worldwide. The central theme of the Consensus was an emphasis on the virtues of a free market, which invariably require a reduction in government intervention in the economy and the maintenance of macroeconomic stability (Lodewijks, 2006; Stiglitz, 2003).

President Nyerere led the resistance to the demanded policy shift. The reluctance of the government to the World Bank and IMF reform policies persisted for several years, even though the economic stagnation and the crises in social services were becoming more and more visible. Helleiner (2001), a sympathiser of the Tanzanian development model, notes that although President Nyerere was a great leader, he lacked a complete grasp of macroeconomic principles and some of his respected advisers did not help with good advice, either. The international financial institutions (IFIs) withheld their financial assistance to Tanzania, although several more friendly and sympathetic bilateral donors, particularly the Nordic countries, maintained their financial support to Tanzania (Bigsten et al., 2000). Also, pressure from local constituencies was minimal, as the major groups in society had by then been incorporated into the ruling party machinery and, consequently, lacked any independent capacity to organise themselves as pressure groups against the prevailing government ideology. The private sector producers and the peasantry withdrew into subsistence activities, producing surpluses for the open market, parallel to the parastatal system represented by the various crop authorities. Even though the private sector was not organised into any formidable pressure group, with time, the peasantry, in particular, proved to be very slippery in the government's attempt to sustain its co-optation into the ruling ideology (Hyden, 1980).

As the crisis became very severe, the government entered into a standby credit agreement with the IMF in 1979, but when the government failed to observe the loan conditionalities, notably its budget ceiling, the agreement was cancelled. During the discussions for the release of the second tranche, the government ordered the head of the visiting IMF mission out of the country. The Minister of Finance, Edwin Mtei, was perceived by the president to be too close to the IMF and had to resign. He was replaced by Amir Jamal, who was regarded as more loyal to Nyerere's position. In a public speech in 1981, President Nyerere expressed his now-famous query: 'Who appointed the IMF to be the Finance Minister of every country in this world?' With this, Nyerere fired, perhaps, the first African salvo in the great debate over the role of the IMF in Africa (Maliyamkono, 1995; Bigsten et al., 2000). The government decided to take its own initiatives in an effort to turn around the declining economy; these efforts are examined in the next section.

3.1   Early attempts to reform through home-grown programmes, 1980–1985

By the early 1980s the country had slid into a deep economic crisis. The failure of the economic system to deliver the promised progress undermined the credibility and legitimacy of the political regime. The government found itself in a dilemma: yielding to pressure from the international community would not only amount to losing the accomplishments it had made along the socialist path, but would also erode its sovereignty, independence and autonomy in policy-making. However, by holding on to an economic system, which continues to lose support among its own people, the government risked losing its legitimacy on the domestic front. The government resorted to an extensive internal debate, which culminated in the design of home-grown economic programmes (Wangwe, 2004).

Amidst the disagreements with the Bretton Woods institutions, Tanzania undertook three main initiatives to solve its economic crisis without adopting IMF and other donor policy-based conditionalities. First, the government formulated its own home-grown recovery programme (1981–2) with the help of an independent group of experts; second, the government intensified its solicitation of funds from friendlier donors and continued to resist pressure from the Bretton Woods institutions, their supporting donors; and, finally, the government engaged in intensive national debates on whether to agree with the policy options offered by the donor community or not.

3.1.1   National Economic Survival Programme (NESP)

After resisting the pressure from the Bretton Woods institutions, the government resorted to its home-grown programme – the National Economic Survival Programme (NESP) – from 1981–2, with the hope, ultimately, of selling it to the Bretton Woods institutions for support. Indeed, the NESP, conceived and adopted by the National Executive Committee of the ruling party in May 1981, became part of the government's aid application to the IMF. The goals of the NESP were to increase export revenue, to eliminate food shortages through various supply-side measures, and to reduce public expenditures. This was to be achieved by a tighter state control of public expenditure and increased production. The government overvalued the domestic currency and retained monopoly over external trade and production in key sectors of the economy. Though the plan had many good intentions, it lacked workable, strategic instruments for its implementation. It lacked clarity about what was to be done, how it was to be done, and who had to do it. Two other factors contributed to its failure. First, there were very few senior officials in the central government ministries then capable of undertaking independent macroeconomic and sectoral policy analysis to generate new ideas and develop new programmes. Second, the NESP was prepared in haste and with too little consultation even to be realistic and feasible. The programme not only fell short of what the IMF could approve, but also failed to address the country's pressing economic problems. The IMF was not ready to support the implementation of the proposed home-grown programme and, quite expectedly, most donors followed suit.

The country entered into a very desperate situation after the breakdown of negotiations with the IMF as the crisis deepened. The exchange rate continued to be overvalued, balance of payments and shortages of goods in the market worsened, and the rate of inflation continued to rise (Mtatifikolo, 1998; Maliyamkono, 1995). The World Bank and Tanzania's bilateral donors, trying to find some compromise solution, took the unusual step of funding an independent group of experts acceptable to both sides to study the situation and give advice on the way forward. A group of well-known economists, which came to be known as the Tanzania Advisory Group (TAG), prepared a much more comprehensive programme than the NESP and proposed more substantial changes in policy direction, content and practice, giving the government several policy options. The programme had two major components – a macroeconomic policy and a sectoral policy. The macroeconomic policy aimed at improving the public sector finances, reducing inflation and improving external balances by way of initiatives such as devaluation; while the sectoral component included measures to revive key sectors of the economy, particularly agriculture and industry.

The government, especially the Ministry of Planning under Kighoma Malima, was, however, not ready to make the policy changes proposed by TAG even though those proposals were more moderate compared to changes that the IMF had proposed earlier. The government and the IMF ended up at odds on the plausible adjustment programme for Tanzania. The situation remained grave, and there was increasing public criticism of the regime, largely on grounds of widespread shortages of consumer goods in the economy.

3.1.2   Outcomes of home-grown reforms

In spite of the many efforts that the government made to improve the economic situation, the crisis persisted, with imbalances in macroeconomic variables becoming even worse. For instance, annual GDP growth declined from an average of 2.8 per cent between 1976 and 1980, to 0.7 per cent from 1981 to 1985. Similarly, real per capita GDP growth decline from 1 per cent to −1.6 per cent in the same period. Even though there was some tightening of fiscal and monetary policies, the measures were still insufficient to reverse the increasing inflation, which jumped from an annual rate of 13.7 per cent from 1976–80 to 30.2 per cent between 1981 and 1985 (Table 6.1).

Around this time the government made some moderate skirmishes in response to some of the demands of the IFIs for fiscal austerity and for the correction of the foreign exchange misalignment. For instance, the fiscal year 1984–5 budget included devaluation of the Tanzanian shilling by 26 per cent and the removal of subsidies on maize and fertilizers. The government also took a more compromising policy stance and permitted partial trade liberalisation, by which those who had their own funds could import goods without inhibitions. The success of the partial import liberalisation scheme led to the scheme's extension to other goods in 1985 and 1986. In addition, cost-sharing was introduced in the financing of basic social services, as parents were required to contribute towards secondary education, and a development levy was reintroduced for all those who were eligible (i.e. 18 years and above). This partial 'success' was important in alleviating some of the commodity shortages and in helping to shift the balance of power between reformers and non-reformers in favour of the former. The changes formed the first step towards the restoration of government–donor relations. From the standpoint of the IFIs, these new reform programmes were at least a basis for some discussions with the Tanzanian government.

3.1.3   *State and non-state actors' interaction during home-grown reforms*

Initially the government was under the illusion that its policies were correct, and that the Bretton Woods institutions and some unfriendly donors did not appreciate the gravity of the external constraints facing the Tanzanian economy. But at this time most donors were losing faith in Nyerere and his macro-economic management abilities, as the economy continued its downward spiral. The government turned to the Nordic and other pro-socialist countries for support, but most declined to help until the government mended its ties with the IMF. To the dismay of Nyerere and his government, virtually all the donors had agreed to take one stand on pressing the government to change its policy stance and adopt the IMF package. Apparently, the government had underestimated the role of the IMF in providing the seal of approval for most bilateral and multilateral donors. Furthermore, some of the countries that had been very supportive – notably, the former Soviet Union and China – were already experiencing their own internal economic and political problems, and had to drastically scale down their assistance to countries such as Tanzania.

As partial liberalisation alleviated the shortages of goods to some extent, the legitimacy of the state interventionist and control-oriented regime started to erode and the balance of power shifted more in favour of reformers. The reformers used their newly gained power to put forward more reform ideas to the ruling party hierarchy and the cabinet, despite stiff resistance. Msuya, the Minister of Finance, together with the Governor of the Bank of Tanzania, Gilman Rutihinda, and other cabinet members within the government tried to push for additional reforms.

The ideological struggles and debates that ensued involved not only the contestation between the government and the international community, but also between internal reformers and non-reformers. Quite expectedly, the government was doggedly resisting any change to its policies, while the donors, led by the Bretton Woods institutions, were insisting on major shifts in the nation's domestic policies. During this period, the interactions between the academics at the University of Dar es Salaam and policy-makers took place in two ways. First, the university scholars, led by economists, organised annual policy workshops in which discussions essentially focused on alternative policy options that would address the country's crisis. The workshops organised in 1984 and 1985 were particularly influential. Second, selected economists from the university were invited to join the team that negotiated the policy change along with experts from the government. The role of the experts from the university was to supplement the technical capacity within the government, especially in discussions and negotiations with the IFIs.

The workshops attracted a broad range of participants, including policy-makers, representatives of the ruling party, trade unions and the private sector. Initially the debate consisted of three identifiable groups. The first group advocated a continuation of the existing domestic policies and blamed the economic crisis on external factors, rather than on failures in domestic policies; they argued for what amounts to a total rejection of the IMF package. The second group called on the government to adopt the IMF package as it was proposed, while the third group advocated a major policy shift, but with a substantial modification of the proposed IMF package. The debates became polarised to the extent of undermining efforts to formulate an alternative policy package. Much energy was spent arguing whether the domestic policies needed to be changed according to the IMF package or not. In fact, as the debate raged on, the second and third groups combined their forces and came together to form a more forceful group advocating a major policy shift.

In the meantime (in late 1985) a technical group was working with the technical staff of the government and IMF on modifying the policy package, with the aim of softening the hard stance of the IMF. For instance, while the IMF was proposing devaluation from 17 shillings to the dollar to 57 shillings, the local technical group came up with a lower figure of 40 shillings to the dollar, based on models which they deemed more appropriate for the Tanzanian economy at that time.

The failure of the efforts made by the government to improve the economy without making any substantial policy shifts, the failure of the government's efforts to split the donors and go ahead with the friendlier donors, and the thrust of internal debates reinforced by the role of the technical groups in reducing the gap between the hard stands by the government and IMF, all contributed to reaching an agreement with the IMF in 1986. This policy package is examined in the next section.

4   The first phase of the structural adjustment programme, 1989–1995

Negotiations between the government and the IFIs resumed in 1985, the same year that Nyerere decided to leave office. When President Mwinyi took office in late 1985, some steps had already been taken in the context of partial liberalisation, as a prelude to the major market-oriented reforms contained in an IMF-World Bank-sponsored adjustment package – locally dubbed Economic Reform Program (ERP I) – agreed upon in August 1986. The ERP I was a typical first generation reform package that sought to promote economic growth through the dismantling of economic controls with the active participation of the private sector in the economy. A broad range of ERP I policies were adopted to help liberalise internal and external trade, unify the exchange rate, revive exports, stimulate domestic saving, and restore fiscal sustainability. The ERP I covered a three-year period (1986–9) for which the government agreed to undertake the following specific measures to achieve macroeconomic stability and to correct the structural problems in the country's economy:

- deregulation of both imports and local trade and the reduction of domestic price controls;
- sufficient devaluation of the shilling to eliminate the exchange rate overvaluation by mid-1988, with a subsequent shift towards a market-based allocation of foreign exchange;
- control of public expenditure through the continuation of the austerity measures started in 1984/5, by limiting government recurrent expenditure, reducing deficit financing from the banking system, and rationalising and reducing parastatals' activities and subsidies to them;
- tightening monetary policy to raise the interest rate until it is positive in real terms; adopting tight credit ceilings; and limiting the growth of money supply to 15–20 per cent per year;
- improving the revenue collection system through efficient monitoring and an increased tax base.

Among other things, these measures fostered the participation of the erstwhile suffocated private sector in the nation's economy and helped restore donor confidence in Tanzania, which, in turn, enhanced the country's access to additional external support. Moreover, the ERP I boosted the utilisation of the nation's productive capacity, with output growth recovering to about 4 per cent, per annum. However, towards the end of the 1980s, the adverse impact of the reform measures on social indicators started to raise concerns among many observers.

The government entered into a new agreement with the IMF[2] and the World Bank, covering the period from 1989 to 1992. This agreement culminated in the second phase of the nation's adjustment programme, locally called ERP II (1989–92). The flagship of ERP II was an Economic and Social Action Programme (ESAP), instituted to deal with people's concerns over the social consequences of ERP I; for this reason, many analysts use ERP II and ESAP interchangeably. The nation's ERP II was specifically supported by the IMF's Enhanced Structural Adjustment Facility (ESAF) together with three other World Bank projects, including:

- the Tanzanian Agricultural Adjustment Credit (TAAC), which started in 1990 with the aim of liberalising the marketing of agricultural inputs and outputs. Finances were channelled through the Open General Licensing (OGL) scheme;
- the Financial Sector Adjustment Programme (FSAP) of 1991, aimed at the restructuring and privatisation of the banking system to allow foreign banks and foreign exchange bureaux into the financial system of the country;

- the Structural Adjustment Credit of 1991, focusing on the restructuring and privatisation of parastatals; civil service reform; and further restructuring of markets for agricultural exports.   .

ERP II (ESAP) basically maintained the same macroeconomic objectives as ERP I, and thus concentrated on trade liberalisation through the revival of producer incentives, exchange rate liberalisation and management, macroeconomic stabilisation, credit and money supply policies, and balance of payments management. Also, ERP II covered institutional reforms in the parastatal sector, banking system, agricultural marketing, the civil service, and the social sectors. Critics of ERP I had noted that the programme was not addressing the social dimensions of adjustment and that the reforms were not making any notable dent in the poverty and livelihood situations of the neediest citizens.[3] Nevertheless, in what came to be known as a vintage 'second-generation reform', the ESAP explicitly acknowledged the lapses in the social sector and, consequently, included measures to reverse the erosion of social services and to redress the concerns of the vulnerable groups in society. The inclusion of social safety nets for the poor and attention to issues surrounding their growing vulnerability to economic shocks became an important feature of ESAP (ERP II). The programme set objectives for designing appropriate strategies and programmes that would enhance people's participation in the operation and management of these services. Sectoral priorities and programmes covering the agricultural sector (the mainstay of the economy), transport and communication, manufacturing, mining and energy were also set for implementation.

The measures succeeded in improving some macroeconomic indicators. For instance, the current account balance improved from -6.4 per cent in 1976–80 to -5.8 per cent during 1981–5 (Table 6.1). However, a worsening trend in the quality and provision of social services (education, health, water and nutrition) was not arrested, a situation which posed a long-term threat to the whole society. The major weakness of ERP II, however, was the fact that measures to address the deteriorating social conditions were only introduced as 'add ons' rather than being integrated in the policy-making process. The fact that poverty and social challenges are multidimensional and cross-cutting was not appreciated at the time.

4.1   State, non-state actors and donors' interaction

Although the 1986 agreement between the government and the Bretton Woods institutions helped restore donor confidence and improved cooperation between the two entities, the implementation of the reforms did not occur as smoothly as anticipated. The government cabinet still included some non-reformers, and the pro-reform faction had a daunting task not only to convince the anti-reformers of the necessity to change, but also to gauge the commitment from government officials to implement the reforms, especially when it came to the more demanding second generation of reforms which involved major structural and institutional changes.

The purging of non-reformers into ambassadorial positions was a big step forward in promoting the reform agenda in Tanzania. Nevertheless, some elements of resistance remained in the party as reflected in the lip service paid to the reforms: policy changes would be agreed upon but when it came to implementation, positions in the party hierarchy were manipulated to slow down the implementation of reform policies. As with other economic reform measures, which were viewed to be inimical to the socialist ideology, political liberalisation was also resisted from within the ruling party, even though the need for, and the inevitability of, political pluralism was realised as early as the mid-1980s. The legislation to allow other political parties to contest in elections was only passed in 1992. Between 1990 and 1992, however, reforms progressed more smoothly than in the earlier periods.

Bigsten et al. (2000) write that during this time the opposition to reforms had taken a new turn and became more issue-based rather than ideology-based. Former President Nyerere who had remained as the chairperson for the ruling Chama cha Mapinduzi also made his views on the direction of the reform known from time to time, but seldom intervened directly. When issues of non-state domestic constituents in reforms are invoked, it is clear that throughout the early 1980s the non-state actors in Tanzania displayed little interest in reforms. Policy decisions were mostly made in a top-down format and without consultation with the general public. However, as the negative social consequences of the reform started to surface and became known to the public, the population was reluctant to bear the costs of the structural changes. For instance, the introduction of cost-sharing in education under the World Bank Higher Education Credit Project at a time when the poor were already facing hardships, due to the deterioration of government funding for social services, sent university students on a protest demonstration in 1992. Cost-sharing contributed to the consequent decline of enrolment in basic education (primary and secondary schools) and in the transition rates to higher levels of education.[4] Also, the drastic cuts in social spending (education, healthcare and water) adversely affected the quality of these services.

Social and political liberalisation started to pick up with the rise of an independent mass media. Independent newspapers were allowed for the first time in 1988, thus opening the door that had been closed since 1960s for the development and expansion of free media. Non-governmental organisations and community-based associations also started to come into the picture. Limited public debate was allowed on human rights violations in 1991 and 1992. The government also started reducing its supervisory powers over labour and cooperative unions, which gained some autonomy after 1990. These changes allowed debates over policy issues. For the most part, public debate in the early 1990s was mainly about the deterioration in the quality of social services and over the lack of democracy in the country.

In terms of the debate between donors, on the one hand, and government and other domestic constituencies on the other, it has been argued that the voice of the state and local constituencies was lowest during the early years of the economic recovery programmes. The state, it seems, eventually conceded defeat to the donor community, as its capacity to determine the course of policy developments eroded. The government was locked in a three-year programme, which had tight implementation schedules based on conditionality and close monitoring procedures which were linked to conditional release of resources from the donor community. The period 1986–92 was essentially one of 'a rolling back of the state' and a 'rolling forward of the donor community' led by the IFIs (Wangwe, 2004). The level of autonomy and sovereignty of the state was at its lowest. The government became enormously preoccupied with meeting conditionalities, which were needed to renew its funding agreement from time to time. These developments brought into the open the realities of the challenges faced by a weak and aid-dependent economy and its implications for sovereignty and autonomy of the public machinery in policy-making.

4.2   Reforms off-track, 1993–1995

President Mwinyi, who had been largely instrumental in carrying forward the reform agenda in his first term of presidency and in convincing the hardliners of the necessity to adopt the conditionality reforms, seemed less emphatic as a reformer in his second term in office that started in 1991. This was apparent at a time when the more difficult structural and institutional reforms required strong political leadership. At this time, starting in 1991, the multilateral donors' approach to tackling the reform agenda had changed drastically. Donor emphasis now encompassed not only macroeconomic stabilisation, but also institutional aspects, geared towards improved accountability and enhanced performance in the public sector. These institutional reforms required civil service restructuring, privatisation, financial sector reforms, and tighter fiscal controls.

Some scholars argue that Mwinyi simply lost control (Bigsten et al., 2000; Maliyamkono, 1995). The president was subjected to all sorts of advice from various competing factions in the party, which eventually made him succumb to confusion (Maliyamkono, 1995). As a result, between 1993 and 1995, the reforms veered off-track: the fiscal policy went out of control as government spending and the national deficit shot up. At this time, there was a general feeling that corruption and tax evasion were becoming rampant. For instance, Kighoma Malima, the former Minister for Planning, using his position, granted large tax exemptions to politically influential people. Also, the government failed to collect all the counterpart money emanating from the use of the OGL scheme. Not surprisingly, government revenue fell sharply, and faced with the constraints of financing its deficit, the government resorted to borrowing from the central bank again. Indeed, the fiscal discipline that had been developed since the mid-1980s was lost (Bigsten et al., 2000).

The failure of the government to collect counterpart funds under the Commodity Import Support (CIS) and OGL schemes and to increase tax revenue led the donor community to feel that the resources it was giving to the government were not being utilised effectively. The government, for its part, felt that the donors' demands were unrealistic and too intrusive in matters that were essentially domestic. The erosion of autonomy in policy-making and in determining the development agenda was also manifested in the suspension of the traditional five-year development planning in favour of shorter-term economic recovery programmes. Key policy documents such as the nation's policy framework papers and the public expenditure reviews came under greater influence from the IFIs. The government felt that the shift of its accountability from its own people to the donor community had gone beyond tolerable limits, to the extent of causing a real threat to the government's position in the eyes of local constituencies. The donor community on the other hand, it seemed, had overestimated the ability of the government to undertake meaningful institutional changes. State capacity in economic management had deteriorated tremendously during the crisis period and with the onset of reforms the demand for such capacity had become greater than ever. The weak capacity of the state and its related institutions to effectively coordinate and implement the reforms thus became a major constraint to the success of the reforms (Maliyamkono, 1995; Bigsten et al., 2000; Helleiner et al., 1995).

4.3   Multiparty democracy in Tanzania

Relatively speaking, the single-party regime in Tanzania was more democratic than other such regimes in Africa. The airing of complaints against TANU (1961–76) and CCM (from 1977) was at least tolerated to some degree, and regular elections were held every five years since 1965. But like many other authoritarian single-party states, the ruling party monopolised politics to the extent that it left no political space outside the TANU/CCM party apparatus. As a result, while citizens' complaints were heard, alternative views that countered the legitimacy of the single-party rule and socialism were generally not well received by CCM. Single-party rule practically promoted political apathy and the fear of expressing opposing views.

Even the regularised elections turned out to be less meaningful in outcome to a large degree, because even though voters had the right to vote and decide who held political positions, they did not really have the ability to change the outcome of the polity process since all political candidates were from the one party – TANU (1961–76) or CCM (1977–92) – and therefore were homogeneous in their outlook. Personalities and patronage turned out to be more important virtues than ideas and merit, and the regular elections turned out to be avenues for contest of personalities rather than policy platforms; this further eroded accountability and increased apathy. Most Tanzanians would concur that party supremacy, the lack of separation of power between the party and the instruments of the state, and the party's entry into executive functions (which included direct trading) played a significant role in alienating the masses from their party and making it difficult for the government to be held accountable to its people.

Growing realisation that liberalisation could not be carried out effectively by a single-party state, coupled with the collapse of Gorbachev and his *perestroika* ideology in Eastern Europe and the introduction by the Bretton Woods institutions and Western democracies of the idea of good governance which became a global agenda in the 1990s, created discontent about Tanzania's single-party system. Events taking place in neighbouring countries also played an important role in the trajectory of political developments in the country. For instance, in Zambia, Kenneth Kaunda had lost dreadfully, and in Kenya there was strong pressure put on President Arap Moi by influential groups (including some heads of diplomatic missions) to allow multipartyism. Moi, however, was adamant because he feared that if multiparty politics were allowed in Kenya people would be divided along tribal lines. Of course the ethnic conflicts in Burundi and Rwanda reinforced his position at that time (Maliyamkono, 1995). In a positive way, however, the developments in Rwanda and Burundi provided a strong reason for other African governments to think about putting up measures to ensure that multiparty politics do not lead to the eventual destruction of their countries. Nonetheless, during this period multiparty democracy was increasingly becoming a loan conditionality. Not only that, there was a build-up of internal pressure for a change by human rights activists that was applauded by scholars in local universities and some urban elites.

Although the ruling party continued to have exclusive monopoly of political power, some underground opposition parties had already been formed in the country even before political liberalisation and pluralism were formally endorsed in 1992. As demands for multiparty democracy mounted, the government formed a Presidential Commission on Multiparty Democracy to inquire into the readiness of Tanzanians to enter into a multiparty system. This was the first attempt made towards public consultation on political matters since the mid-1960s. The findings of the Commission revealed that among the Tanzanians whose views were solicited, only 23 per cent were in favour of multiparty democracy. However, Nyerere, quite surprisingly, threw his support behind the introduction of multiparty democracy. The argument was that while single-party politics would not give any space for the 23 per cent who wanted alternatives, multiparty politics would give everybody a choice of which party they wanted to belong to. In fact, it was argued that even the 77 per cent who did not want multipartyism were free to continue membership in the party they preferred. It is important to note that, even though at this time Nyerere had already resigned from the chairmanship of the ruling party, he maintained considerable influence over its leaders. Nyerere openly supported competitive elections in a multiparty system, and the CCM, under the chairmanship of President Mwinyi, succumbed to external pressure and growing opposition from the domestic constituents and legalised the registration of opposition parties in 1992, which became the turning point in the political arena.

Maliyamkono (1995) observes that the opposition parties in Tanzania turned out to be very weak, as they were apparently created for many reasons, some of which undermined their ability to come up with policy agendas worth selling to the public and to mobilise adequate support from the masses. According to Maliyamkono (1995), some people who established new political parties perceived them as sources of employment and income generation; this was evidenced by regular quarrels within and between political parties over resources. Secondly, some parties were formed by people who had long been dissatisfied with the ruling party or with Nyerere himself as a person. And, of course, there were other parties which were started as genuine alternatives to the CCM, tapping into the growing dissatisfaction over some of their key policies articulated in the Arusha Declaration.

By 1995, thirteen opposition parties had been registered and all participated in the first multiparty election. Being young and vulnerable, the new political parties found it difficult to out-compete the CCM in the 1994 local government elections and the 1995 presidential elections. They were also not able to out-compete the CCM in the 2000 presidential elections. In the 1995 parliamentary elections, the CCM won 80 per cent of the seats and had the highest representation in parliament. In the presidential elections the CCM candidate Benjamin Mkapa won 62 per cent of the votes, which allowed the CCM to maintain power. The remaining 38 per cent was distributed among the opposition parties (Whitehead, 2000). In 1995, speaking of the challenges faced by the opposition parties in Tanzania, Mtei observed, 'You cannot let a two-year-old fight a grown up and expect a surprise' (Maliyamkono, 1995).

The major agenda of most new political parties in the country was to enhance freedom of political choice and promote multiparty democracy, but beyond that they hardly distinguished themselves from the ruling party in terms of the policy options they stood for. To date, the opposition parties have not been able to develop policy frameworks which could constitute alternative policy options for the country. Furthermore, in spite of multiparty democracy, there continues to be a vacuum in terms of the ability of political constituencies to respond to alternative policy options. And to make matters worse, many of the new parties lack genuine internal democracy. The balance of power between local and foreign constituencies also continues to raise concern in politics. The power imbalance between local and foreign constituencies in influencing political decisions has been demonstrated on various occasions, especially during times of conflict between opposition parties and the ruling party. The tendency among opposition parties has been to appeal to donors to intervene instead of mobilising the support of local constituencies to argue for a change and to let their voices be heard.

This suggests that political parties attached considerable weight to the influence of donors on the government and the ruling political party. Many politicians approached donors individually and requested them to fund specific projects in their own constituencies. This situation reinforced the imbalance of power in favour of external entities, and undermined the government's accountability to the Tanzanian electorate. It is in this context that scholars like Mafeje, cited in Mpangala (2002), have argued that liberal democracy can give rise to 'compradorial democracy' by creating a political faction that benefits from both its position of power and its relationship with international capitalism (or the donor community).

5   A new era of deepening institutional reforms, 1996 and beyond

By the early 1990s, the reforms that started in the 1980s were stalling. Towards 1995 various institutional reforms were beginning to take shape (e.g. investment promotion, financial sector reforms, civil service reforms and privatisation) but the tempo of their implementation was slow. When President Mkapa came to power in November 1995, one of his first challenges was to restore Tanzania–donor relations that had deteriorated during the first half of the 1990s. The Mkapa government also put a high priority on pursuing reforms, fighting corruption and mobilising domestic resources. The government's commitment to reforms was reflected in initiatives taken to ensure that the new cabinet and top civil servants understood the challenges of the reforms through seminars on various aspects of the government's economic programme.

In terms of performance, however, Tanzania's macroeconomic conditions deteriorated, largely because of deficiencies in the financial sector and budgetary management, weak tax administration, weakening political will, and dwindling commitment to tackle the demanding institutional and structural reforms. Capacity to manage change had been overstretched, yet it was a time when deeper institutional reforms and greater institutional capacities were required for successful management of a new market-oriented economy.

The government initiated a shadow programme with the IMF, for the period January–June 1996, focusing primarily on eliminating the main impediments to sound budgetary management, and on reforming the financial sector. In order to enhance revenue collection, efforts to establish a revenue authority were accelerated such that by July 1996 the government had established the Tanzania Revenue Authority. A mini-budget was passed in February 1996, in which budget expenditure was curtailed considerably and a cash budget was introduced. Performance of the shadow reform programme was generally satisfactory, although progress with restructuring the financial sector was slower than envisaged (IMF, 1996). Reforms were back on track and the IMF came back with a new three-year ESAF loan for 1996–9 and other donors followed suit. The ESAF loan was followed by a three-year loan under the Poverty Reduction and Growth Facility for Tanzania from 2000 to 2002.

5.1   The new development partnership

The virtual breakdown of relations between the government and the donors in 1994 was, indeed, part of a long roller-coaster ride in Tanzania's aid relationship since the late 1970s. The IFIs laid the blame for policy reversal on the government's lack of commitment to reform and rampant corruption in its machineries. The government, on the other hand, blamed the IFIs for interfering with its sovereignty. The Danish government, in agreement with the government of Tanzania, sponsored a fence-mending operation in 1995, the result of which was the *Report on Development Cooperation between Tanzania and its Aid Donors*, well-known as the Helleiner Report. This report questioned the reasonableness of the donor criticisms, and placed some of the blame on the 'government's half-heartedness' in complying with conditionalities. The operational prescription from the exercise was to pay serious attention to local/government ownership of the reform programmes. The government was to improve governance while both parties worked together to make the reforms sustainable. Concerted efforts to improve dialogue between the government and donors were initiated in 1996. A set of 'agreed notes' (in the form of eighteen points) stated, among other things, that there was a need to ensure enhanced government leadership in development programming and increased transparency, accountability and efficiency in aid delivery. Following the government–donor agreement of January 1997, it was decided that developments in implementing the agreed actions would be monitored, and reports on progress would be presented to the meetings of the Consultative Group (CG) in Tanzania. To set the ball rolling, Professor Helleiner was asked to evaluate and present evaluation reports to CG meetings in December 1997, March 1999 and May 2000. In 1999 Helleiner made a comprehensive review of the status of the government–donor relations, which identified several problems, including the parallel donor systems and procedures; uncoordinated project support and country assistance strategies; channelling of aid outside the exchequer; overdependence on technical assistance; and inadequate government capacity. In February 2002 the government and the donors jointly appointed an Independent Monitoring Group (IMG) to review progress in aid relations and report to the next CG meetings. The IMG presented its first report to the CG meeting in December 2002.

Gould and Ojanen (2003) observed that such a change of approach in practice hinges on the way the Bank and other donors shifted their position on the management of state governance. The Bank reorganised its mode of consultation with Tanzania in policy matters: 'decentralising' Tanzania's Country Director, hitherto based in Washington, to Dar es Salaam, and recruiting economist Professor Benno Ndulu as deputy to the Country Director, thus providing the Bank with a Tanzanian face, palatable to both donors and the government. The donor community started supporting Tanzania's efforts to formulate domestic policies, such as the National Poverty Eradication Strategy (NPES), the Tanzanian Assistance Strategy (TAS) and, later on, the Poverty Reduction Strategy (PRS) – all of which were formulated in a participatory manner depicting a new turn in the policy-making process and the evolution of the partnership between the government, the state and non-state actors.

The first account of the business community's influence in policy came in its 1996 response to the government's tax reform. The government had just established the Tanzania Revenue Authority (TRA) in July 1996 and introduced some tax reform measures. The business community organised itself to convince the government that high taxes were inimical to both private sector expansion and the government revenue mobilisation objective, and that to increase compliance, the tax rates needed to be reduced. In the 1996–7 budget the government gave in to some of the demands. In order to blunt the influence of the IMF on the government, the business community representatives arranged to meet the IFIs' representatives for a discussion.

Genuine efforts to promote civil society's role in Tanzania's development were not made until the onset of multiparty democracy. For representatives of civil society, meaningful participation in policy-making started with an informal Consultative Group Civil Society shadow meeting in Dar es Salaam in 1997, which later on led to their participation, albeit in an ad hoc manner, in the formulation of the Poverty Reduction Strategy Paper (PRSP) at zonal and national workshops organised in 2000 (Bigsten et al., 2000). Since then civil society participation in policy-making in Tanzania has grown substantially. The fast growth of civic organisations in recent years[5] has made it possible for these organisations to assert themselves more forcefully in national debates. The consultation conditionality invoked by the donor community in the second half of the 1990s also created more room for the civic organisations to voice their views directly or through the media for the government, donor community and citizens to hear and take action. In 1998, for example, gender activists in the women-led NGOs lobbied for the reform of laws pertaining to inheritance, domestic violence, land, children's rights and child abuse and managed to make a dent in national policies in these matters.

Political space has indeed widened in the country for private and other non-state[6] actors to articulate their interests or those of their local constituencies through a participatory policy-making process. Also, there are trends towards increased openness, transparency and accountability in the conduct of government business, and specifically in the administration of the national budget. The Poverty Reduction Strategy (PRS), Public Expenditure Review/Medium Term Expenditure Framework (PER/MTEF) preparation, Poverty Monitoring System (PMS) and Participatory Poverty Assessment (PPA) processes stand out as important instruments for a more transparent, goal-oriented and integrated budgetary process. The computer-based Integrated Financial Management System (IFMS), designed to raise the efficiency and integrity of public finance management, has also contributed to increased donor confidence.

With regards to political reform at the national level, we must note that despite the Multi-Party Act of 1992, constitutional reforms set in place to allow for a fair play in the new multiparty system have been very haphazard. Mwesiga, for one, has described the constitutional reforms in Tanzania as 'a hesitant and disjointed reform'.[7] Because of the shallowness of the constitutional reforms, what has developed between political parties in Tanzania is an antagonistic political system, seeking the self-interest of individual parties in the name of democracy. A number of scholars (e.g. Ewald, 2002; Whitehead, 2000; Maliyamkono, 1995) have noted that while administrative reforms could be said to have somehow strengthened the technocratic capabilities at the central government, similar capacity has not been developed in the parliament (where the opposition has some representatives) and at the local government level where true democratic participation is still too constrained to influence public policy in any appreciable manner.

With due cognizance of the lessons learned from the past, the government formulated its long-term development goals, expressed in its Vision 2025, to include the attainment of high-quality livelihoods, through the alleviation of poverty and the creation of a strong and competitive economy and good governance based on the rule of law. To realise these goals, the government has made efforts to ensure price stability; to mobilise higher levels of domestic savings and investment; and to promote a broad-based human resource development. With the financial backing of an ESAF, from 1996/7 to 1998/9, the government sought, among other things, to achieve: a real GDP growth rate of 6 per cent; an average rate of inflation of 5 per cent; an external current account deficit, excluding grants, of 13.3 per cent of GDP, compared with 20.6 per cent of GDP in 1994/5; and to increase gross official reserves to the equivalent of three months of imports by the end of June 1999.

Fiscal and monetary policy formed the key instruments in achieving these objectives with the government making efforts to boost government savings, and to improve revenue mobilisation through the rationalisation and harmonisation of taxes, and to widen the tax base. Efforts were also directed towards strengthening the budget process to ensure that government spending is reorganised to give social services (health, education and water supply) adequate funding to facilitate their revival. Tight monetary policy was also used to curtail the supply of money in the economy, while at the same time ensuring that sufficient bank credit is available to the private sector. Building on the success of the restructured financial sector, the government expanded the privatisation programme, by accelerating the disposal of public assets already placed under the Parastatal Sector Reform Commission (PSRC). The external and domestic debt situation for Tanzania was still grim[8] but through a firm implementation of the adjustment measures, together with some debt

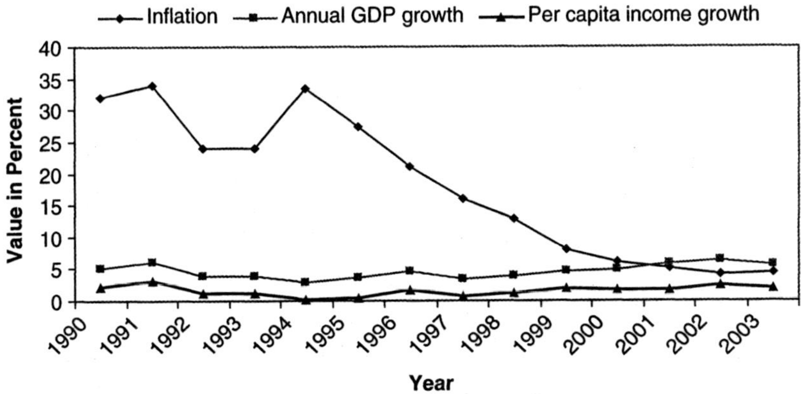

Figure 6.1   Tanzania: trends in some macroeconomic indicators, 1990–2003
Source: *Economic Survey* (various issues); Bank of Tanzania Quarterly Economic Bulletins.

concessions, Tanzania managed to improve, albeit very slightly, its macro-economic outlook (Figure 6.1).

Structural and institutional reforms, however, turned out to be more challenging than expected. For instance, redefining the role of government to give greater space for the private sector required not only the willingness of the government to give up some of the activities it had always been doing but it also required adequate private sector involvement. Appropriate provisions for capacity building in the private sector had, however, not been made. Private sector response continued to be inhibited by problems such as red-tapism, unfavourable tax regime, poor and inadequate infrastructure, weak institutional support systems, outdated or inadequate legal and regulatory framework, and insufficient access to finance due to limited financial sector reform.

Generally, public attitudes towards the business community were slow to change. Too often, private initiatives were presented in the public media as self-serving and unethical, and business achievements were not yet seen as an admirable trait. The principle of 'Smart Partnership' was endorsed, but not adhered to in practice. The responses to economic reforms, notably those relating to trade liberalisation, from the private sector have been mixed, with some units gaining from the liberalisation programmes and others struggling to survive. Investment resources have also shifted, to a large extent, from long-term investments in manufacturing to shorter-term investments in trade and commerce. With major new investments – mainly by foreign direct investors – going into the extraction of natural resources, particularly mining and to the services sectors (e.g. telecommunications and travel and tourism), the nation's export structure has gradually shifted in favour of minerals and other non-traditional exports as shown in Figure 6.2.

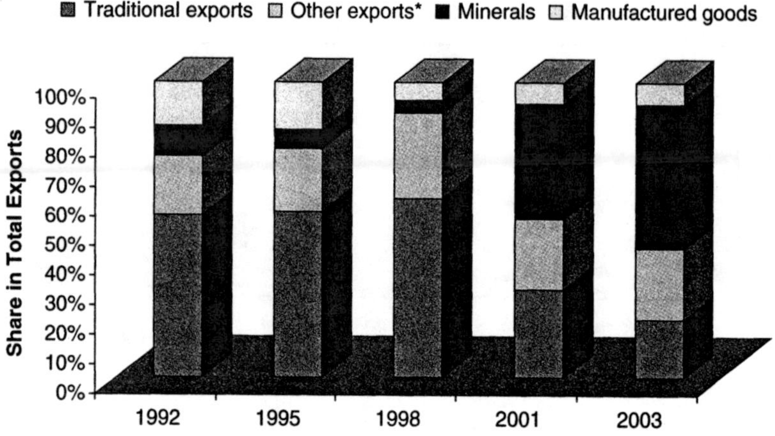

Figure 6.2   Tanzania: change in export earnings structure
*Other exports include petroleum products.
Source: *Economic Survey* (2002), Bank of Tanzania Quarterly Economic Bulletin (various).

The impact of the reforms on the livelihoods of the nation's poor has been mixed and quite uncertain, as well. The 2000/1 Household Budget Survey (HBS), for example, confirms that poverty in Tanzania is still deep and pervasive. It also shows that there are still large income differentials between different groups and between urban and rural areas. Tanzania experienced only a slight decline in income poverty, of about 3 per cent over the 1990s. According to the nation's poverty headcount ratio, more than one third (36 per cent) of Tanzanians still fall below the basic needs poverty line and 19 per cent are below the food poverty line, which is only a slight improvement from 39 per cent and 22 per cent respectively in 1991/2. Nevertheless, in absolute terms, poverty seems to be on the increase: for instance, there were 11.4 million Tanzanians below the basic needs poverty line in 2001 compared with 9.5 million in 1991/2. In 2001 the HBS estimated that the richest 20 per cent of households in the country accounted for 44 per cent of household consumption spending compared with 43 per cent[9] in 1991/2 showing a slight increase in inequality. Though incomes in Tanzania remain more equal than one finds in many sub-Saharan African countries, poverty and deprivations continue to be a matter of great concern, especially in rural areas of the country.

Though macroeconomic fundamentals have been restored, somewhat, the poor section of the population has not benefited much from these achievements due to weaknesses in institutions as well as continued existence of structural impediments to growth of economic activities. Reforms have led to sharp increase in foreign direct investment (FDI) (through the privatisation of former state parastatals) and growth of new economic activities in the mining and tourism sectors, but the net impact on employment and poverty reduction is still small. The most recent estimate (2001) of the unemployment rate stood at 12.9 per cent (United Republic of Tanzania [URT], various), which is an increase from 3.7 per cent in 1991. Employment in the public sector declined considerably due to its restructuring, yet expansion of employment in the private economy has not grown fast enough to match the growth of the working population. According to the Integrated Labour Force Survey (2001/2) the total labour force (age 15 years and above) has increased from 11.2 million in 1990/1 to 17.8 million in 2001. This implies that about 650 000 new people have been entering the labour market every year. Wage and salary employment has been expanding at a much lower rate, estimated at some 40 000 persons per annum.[10] That leaves the majority of the new entrants into the labour market with no option other than either being unemployed or entering the labour market through self-employment largely in agriculture and other informal economic activities.

Furthermore, despite the reforms, the structure of the Tanzanian economy (in terms of employment and sectoral contribution to GDP) has not changed much. The agricultural sector continues to be the main source of livelihoods for over 74 per cent of the Tanzanian population, most of which is living in rural areas. The informal economy has also grown to absorb some of those who lost their jobs or failed to get jobs in the formal economy. The 1991 Labour Force Survey estimated that about 21 per cent of the Tanzanian active labour force was employed in the private informal sector (excluding agriculture). This figure has risen in recent years to an estimated 55 per cent by 2001 (HBS, 2002), with the sector contributing as much as a third of GDP. However, the informal sector has only served as a survival mechanism rather than as a developmental economy. The institutional foundations that have been laid for the private sector to develop have not been sufficient enough to allow fair play in the liberalised market and for the benefits of economic liberalisation to trickle down. The enforcement of regulations for fair competition also continues to be weak.[11] Thus, the efficacy of reforms in Tanzania has been hampered by institutional limitations, which have, in turn, made it difficult for the government to correct market failures inherent in the economic transition.

Towards the end of the 1990s, Tanzania started to address poverty as a major policy concern. These initiatives coincided with the World Bank's Comprehensive Development Framework, which essentially recognised that development had to be pursued in a comprehensive manner, taking into account economic as well as social and political concerns. It is in this context that the IFIs came up with the Poverty Reduction Strategy Paper, which was tied to debt relief funds for highly indebted poor countries (HIPCs). The Tanzanian government responded quickly to the demand to prepare the PRSP in order to gain access to the HIPCs' debt relief resources. The PRS initiative, known as the National Strategy for Growth and Reduction of Poverty

(NSGRP), has, since the end of 2003, contributed significantly towards the promotion of a more participatory approach to public policy-making and to economic growth (Wangwe, 2004).

Since poverty in Tanzania is predominantly a rural phenomenon, and to the extent that the majority of the poor derive their livelihood in agriculture, an agriculture-focused growth strategy stands out as the best option for sustainable economic growth and poverty reduction in Tanzania. The challenge is to facilitate growth in agriculture in a way that will be inclusive of the majority of the poor within that sector. Modernisations of agriculture and productivity increases in that sector are given high priority in Tanzania's Development Vision 2025 (1998), in PRSP (2000), as well as in the revised poverty reduction strategy. The NSGRP is, therefore, a step in the right direction. Development of agriculture is seen as an effective strategy for poverty reduction, addressing food security and contributing to the growth of the economy. The government is thus implementing an agricultural development strategy with the intention of building an environment favourable to private investment in agriculture. The Agricultural Sector Development Strategy is accompanied by the Rural Development Strategy, which provides a strategic framework meant to facilitate a coordinated implementation of policies and strategies for the development of rural communities.

6   Conclusion

In the Tanzanian context, economic crises were important for market-oriented reforms to occur. Yet, the impetus to rigorously implement the policy changes came from external pressure exerted by the donor community on the government of Tanzania. As Tanzania's home-grown efforts failed to garner foreign support, due to their inadequacy in addressing the fundamental economic problems of the country, the government was forced to agree to market-oriented reforms advocated by the Bretton Woods Institutions (BWIs). Reform efforts, particularly since the second half of the 1990s, have been gradual, more cautious, and comprehensive, compared with the way they were implemented during the early years (1986–92). Lessons learned in the past were instrumental in changing the momentum and pace of reforms. And with these developments, Tanzania has been able to achieve some semblance of macroeconomic stability.

Issues surrounding sequencing of reforms in Tanzania show that the theoretical distinction between stabilisation and structural adjustment did not apply in practice in the greater part of the first decade of the reforms. The two were considered together, contrary to the experience in some developing countries where stabilisation has been considered as a prerequisite for deeper structural reforms. The question of sequencing of the policies that were part of the first two reform packages (ERP I and ERP II) is a subject for which theory has few answers. The government did not consider or make decisions, when it agreed to the reform packages, about what should come first between macroeconomic stabilisation and structural adjustment. Neither was there an analysis of possible constraints or benefits to be expected from undertaking the reforms with alternative sequencing. Donors did not propose a particular sequence, either, so Tanzania found itself doing everything at the same time – trying to curb the deficit, devalue the currency, reform trade and pricing policies, privatise state-owned corporations, save money for the social sector, and embark on civil service reform. And most likely, due to capacity weaknesses for policy analysis in government, nobody dared to stand up and question the sequencing, timing or the speed of the adjustment policies.

Also it appears that neither the donors nor the government paid much attention to the speed and timing of the adjustment in the early years. For the government it appears that the urge to maintain the status quo was very strong, and this, together with ideological conflicts within the ruling party, took up most of the time that could have been used for analysing policy issues. Much of the ruling party's attention was also directed towards maintaining public support and support from the donor community at the same time. The government went ahead with many reforms without consideration of its own capacity for implementing the proposed measures. With too many things going on at the same time, the government lost direction and found itself at odds with both its aid donors and the general public in the early 1990s. But the donor community could not escape criticisms over the failure of 'their' reforms, either. Viewed in retrospect, the timing, sequencing and speed of the adjustment adopted in the first years do not seem to have been the first best solution, and with the 'learning through mistakes approach' it would be naive to expect that a different and perhaps more optimal equilibrium would have been achieved. Nevertheless, one can argue that a gradual policy reform process would have generated better results as it has a potential to minimise mistakes by allowing a longer period for the learning process to occur.

The political feasibility of reforms was not a major issue in the beginning, at least not until very late in the 1980s when external pressure and some indication of domestic dissatisfaction with the lack of democracy forced the government to adopt multiparty democracy. It is nevertheless clear that when certain reform packages threatened sovereignty of the ruling party, they were considered more carefully and their implementation dragged. For example, although Tanzania accepted price deregulation, it maintained price control on some highly sensitive products or services (e.g. petroleum and public utilities). And while privatisation was accepted in principle in 1990 the government did not set any time for privatisation of what were considered strategic enterprises (i.e. public utilities). Having learned from experience after the setback in the early 1990s, the government and the donor community chose a different approach – gradualism in the implementation of reform, once the principles have been agreed upon, so as to allow consultation with local interest groups and room for learning. This has been the major achievement of the new development partnership in Tanzania.

The political context does matter in several ways for ownership and success of reforms. Groups of winners and losers are to be expected in any game, and their emergence in the reform process can strengthen or weaken the pace of reforms depending on their ability to influence decisions or the balance of power. Where the gains accrue to influential groups with which the government is well aligned, open, official acceptance of government moves is to be expected (regardless of what happens to the less privileged) except where the latter (losers and the less privileged) can organise into coalitions and argue their case for a better deal. Though the opening up of the political space for participation has been a significant step in promoting democracy and accountability in the state machinery, evaluation of politics of inclusion in the country points to the fact that Tanzania can at best be described as a country in transition to democracy. The responses on the political front have been different from those in the economic arena. In the political arena we see intense struggle to maintain the status quo. In the economic arena, on the other hand, due to the inability of the state to meet the demands of the people, there has been a proliferation of policy advocacy and lobby groups (NGOs and private business associations in various sectors) to argue for change. There have also emerged many community social support programmes to provide safety nets for the poor to cushion them from the negative impacts of reforms (loss in incomes, decline in welfare spending) particularly where state support is inadequate or unavailable.

Reform is not a mechanistic process, but rather an interactive one, requiring negotiation, modification of views, compromise, concessions and management of risks. The key to success is the ability of government and stakeholders to forge consensus, deal with opposition, and develop reform strategies and sequencing that soften negative impacts on the most vulnerable, while increasing the chances for intended long-term benefits. Broader participation in the reform process becomes more likely when affected groups can translate their economic interests into political pressures. More participation in policy reform leads to better technical content in policies; it also leads to greater sustainability, because more affected interests can be included. However, more participation is harder to manage, and requires a flexible, strategic approach. This calls for new management skills; thus, institutional capacity building is needed not just for public agencies, but also for local non-state actors, including NGOs, private sector groups, political parties, and the media.

Despite the initial starts and stops, the reforms have created a new and more rewarding environment for the private sector and a relatively fairer political space in Tanzania. Trade has been liberalised and, overall, business activities now transpire more freely than they did two decades ago. Taken as a whole, the private sector has, without doubt, benefited from the reform. But advantages to individuals have varied with their ability to capitalise on the opportunities of the reforms. Much remains to be done to facilitate the development of a vibrant economy and better living conditions for the people. Poverty in Tanzania has been strongly rooted in rural areas and this structure has not changed despite the reforms. How the government should go about fighting poverty, particularly in rural areas, and to bring lasting benefits is still a challenge. Economic liberalisation and price deregulation have opened up markets and more opportunities for people to invest in all forms of trade, including agricultural marketing and processing. But it is apparent that there has not been fair and efficient competition within the liberalised environment in Tanzania. Some have lost out in the game and others have failed to take advantage of the opportunities arising to better their conditions. Since a market economy needs to be backed up by reasonably strong institutions, a macroeconomic setting and a supportive environment, the tasks left with government are both critical and complex. The gaps in the institutional arrangements for both political and economic participation are also still great. The need for constitutional reforms, judicial and legal reforms, state welfare reforms, and the enforcement of regulations cannot be overlooked. Equally important is the need to maintain macroeconomic stability and to solve the country's growing external debt problem.

Notes

1. The country moved from a market-oriented economy (1961–6) to a centrally planned and public sector-led economy (1967–85) with a one-party political regime (1965–92), and to a transition to market-oriented economy with multiparty democracy since 1992.
2. The agreement with the IMF was renewed in 1987, 1988 and 1990.
3. Adjustment with a human face.
4. Decline in quality of education, continuing declining enrolment rates and increasing drop-out rates, particularly in primary schools, led the government to abolish the cost-sharing in primary schools in 2002 under World Bank financial support for the Primary Education Development Programme (PEDP).
5. In the mid-1980s there were some 200 NGOs and CBOs together. The number of these organisations had, however, increased to 8400 by 1997.
6. As Gould and Ojanen (2003) points out, 'non-state actors' is a term that can be used more clearly than the subtle term 'civil society' in analyses of interaction of interest groups and the state in the policy process.
7. Mkapa seems to have been more adept in ensuring that economic reforms work, yet in terms of political reforms Mkapa seems to have been conservative and as a result there does not seem to have been any significant transformation. In fact, the constitution still vests too much power in the president and, as a result, the presidential system lacks essential checks and balances for accountability.
8. The 1997/8 Country Policy Framework Paper discusses the Tanzanian domestic and external debt situation and medium-term targets in more detail.
9. These are point estimates and do not tell us anything about happened in the whole ten-year period between the two surveys. Therefore, it is possible that income disparities might have been larger.
10. Assuming that the distribution of the new entrants in various avenues of employment is along the lines of the findings of the Integrated Labour Force Survey of 2001/2.

11. CUTS (2002) observes that Tanzania still ranks low in enforcement or rules and regulations for fair competition and, as a result, small and micro enterprises have found it difficult to grow. The lack of anti-dumping regulation and poor enforcement of quality and standards have also led to significant loss of market opportunities for emerging local manufacturing enterprises.

References

African Development Bank [ADB] (1996) *African Development Report for 1995* (Abidjan: ADB).

Bagachwa, M. S. D. and Limbu, F. (1995) *Policy Reforms and Environment in Tanzania* (Dar es Salaam: Dar es Salaam University Press).

Bank of Tanzania (1996) *Economic Bulletin*, 24, 3 (Dar es Salaam: Bank of Tanzania).

Bigsten, A., Mutalemwa, D., Tsikata, Y. and Wangwe, S. (2000) 'Tanzania', in Shantayanan Devarajan, David, R. Dollar and Torgny Holmgren (eds), *Aid and Reform in Africa: Lessons from Ten Cases* (Washington, DC: World Bank), pp. 289–360.

Centre for Development Research [CDR] (1995) *Structural Adjustment in Africa: a Survey of the Experience* (Copenhagen: CDR).

Consumer Unity and Trust Society [CUTS] (2002) *Tanzania Investment Policy and Performance*, Policy Brief.

Economic and Social Research Foundation [ESRF] (1995) *Children and Women in Tanzania: a Situational Analysis*, report submitted to UNICEF, Dar es Salaam.

Economic and Social Research Foundation [ESRF] (1996) *Transitional Economic Policy and Policy Options in Tanzania*, report submitted to the government of Tanzania, Dar es Salaam.

Ewald, J. (2002) 'Economic Reforms and Democratisation in Tanzania: the Case of Election 2000 and the Need to go Beyond Elections', paper presented at the Conference on Democratisation and Conflict Management in East Africa, February–March.

Ferreira, L. (1993) *Poverty Profile in Tanzania* (Washington, DC: World Bank).

Ferreira, L. (1995) *Poverty and Inequality during Structural Adjustment in Rural Tanzania*, World Bank Transitional Economies Department Research Paper Series No. 8.

Gould, J. and Ojanen, J. (2003) *Merging in the Circle: the Politics of Poverty Reduction Strategy* (Helsinki: Institute of Development Studies, University of Helsinki).

Helleiner G. (2001) *Local Ownership and Donor Performance Monitoring: New Aid Relationships in Tanzania?* (Dar es Salaam: Government of Tanzania Printer).

Helleiner, G. K., Killick, T., Lipumba, N., Ndulu, B. and Svendsen, K. (1995) 'Report of the Group of Independent Advisors on Development Cooperation Issues between Tanzania and its Aid Donors', DANIDA.

Hyden, G. (1980) *Beyond Ujamaa in Tanzania: Underdevelopment and an Uncaptured Peasantry* (London, Ibadan and Nairobi: Heinemann Educational Books Ltd.).

IMF (1996) *Tanzania 1–1 Staff Report for 1996*, Article IV Consultation (October) (Washington, DC: International Monetary Fund).

National Bureau of Statistics [NBS] (2002) *Integrated Labour Force Survey (2000/01)* (Dar es Salaam: Government of Tanzania Printer).

Ishumi, A. G. (1994) 'Higher Education in Tanzania: Past Trends and Challenges for the Future', in L. A. Msambichaka, P. B. Moshi et al. (eds), *Development Challenges and Strategies for Tanzania: an Agenda for the 21st Century* (Dar es Salaam: Dar es Salaam University Press).

Kishimba, M. A. and Mkenda, A. (1994) 'The Impact of Structural Adjustment Programs on Urban Population and Sanitation: Empirical Evidence from Tanzania's Major

Urban Centres', paper presented at the 9th National Economic Policy Workshop on SAP and Environment in Tanzania, 28–30 November, Dar es Salaam.

Kulindwa, K. and Sechambo, F. (1993) 'Structural Adjustment Energy Use and the Environment: Some Evidence from Brazil/Tanzania', paper presented at the 9th National Economic Policy Workshop on SAP and Environment in Tanzania, 28–30 November, Dar es Salaam.

Lodewijks, John (2006) 'Structural Adjustment Programs (SAPs)', in Thomas M. Leonard (ed.), *Encyclopaedia of the Developing World*, Vol. 3 (New York and London: Routledge), pp. 1498–1500.

Maliyamkono, T. L. (1995) *The Race for Presidency: the First Multi-party Democracy in Tanzania* (Dar es Salaam: Tema Publishers Co. Ltd.).

Maliyamkono, T. L. and Bagachwa, M. S. D. (1990) *The Second Economy in Tanzania* (London and Athens: James Currey and Ohio University Press).

Mpangala, G. P. (2002) 'Growth of Corruption in Zanzibar Elections of 1995 and 2000', in S. E. Chambua, V. Kihiyo and G. P. Mpangala (eds), *Multi-party Elections and Corruption in Tanzania with Special Reference to the 2000 Elections* (Dar es Salaam: Dar es Salaam University Press).

Msambichaka, L. A., Kilindo, A. A. L. and Mjema, G. (1995) *Beyond Structural Adjustment Programs in Tanzania: Successes, Failures and Perspectives* (Dar es Salaam: Economic Research Bureau).

Mtatifikolo, F. P. (1998) *The Content and Challenge of Reform Programs in Africa: the Case of Tanzania* (Bremen, Germany: University of Bremen Press).

Ndullu, B. J. (1994) *Tanzania Economic Development: Lessons from Experience and Challenges for the Future* (Dar es Salaam: Government of Tanzania Printer).

Ndullu, B. J. and Wangwe, S. M. (1997) 'Managing the Tanzania Economy in Transition to Sustainable Development', paper submitted for a Workshop on Economic Management, 20–31 March, Kilimanjaro Hotel, Dar es Salaam.

Nyerere, J. K. (1967) 'After the Arusha Declaration', Presidential Address to the National Conference of the Tanganyika African National Union, 16 October, Mwanza Tanzania.

Patricia, H. (1994) 'Women Empowerment: the Only Way Out', in L. A. Msambichaka, H. P. B. Moshi et al. (eds), *Development Challenges and Strategies for Tanzania: an Agenda for the 21st Century* (Dar es Salaam: University of Dar es Salaam Press), pp. 325–37.

Reed, D. (ed.) (1992) *Structural Adjustment and the Environment* (London: World Wildlife Fund (WWF); International Earth Scan Publications Ltd.).

Ruis, Andres and Walle, Nicolas van de (2003) 'Political and Cultural Institutions and Economic Polity Reform', paper presented to the GDN Workshop on Understanding Reform, 16–17 January, Cairo, Egypt.

Sechambo, F. and Kulindwa, K. (1994) 'Policy Impact of Agricultural Activity on the Environment in Tanzania', paper presented at the 9th National Economic Policy Workshop on SAP and Environment in Tanzania, 28–30 November, Dar es Salaam.

Semboja, H. and Kweka, J. P. (1997) 'Import Liberalization, Industrialization and Technological Capability in Sub-Saharan Africa: the Case of the Garment Industry in Tanzania', ESRF Discussion Paper Series Research Paper, Dar es Salaam.

Stiglitz, Joseph (2003) *Globalization and its Discontents* (New York and London: W. W. Norton & Company).

Tinois, P. (1993) *Household Consumption and Poverty in Tanzania: Results from a 1991 Household Survey*, Cornell University Food and Nutrition Policy Program, mimeo.

Tommasi, Mariano (2002) 'Crises, Political Institutions and Policy Reforms: the Good, the Bad and the Ugly', paper presented at the annual World Bank Conference on Development Economics, Session on the Political Economy of Crisis and Reform, June, Oslo, Norway.

Toye, J. (1995) *Structural Adjustment: Issues and Experience – Employment Policy* (Geneva: International Labour Organisation).

United Republic of Tanzania [URT] (various), *Economic Surveys*, President's Office Planning and Privatisation (Dar es Salaam: Government of Tanzania Printer).

URT (1982) *The National Economic Survival Program* (Dar es Salaam: Government of Tanzania Printer).

URT (1990) *Economic Recovery Program II* (Dar es Salaam: Government of Tanzania Printer).

URT (1994) *Policy Framework Paper for 1994/95–1996/97* (Dar es Salaam: Government of Tanzania Printer).

URT (1996) 'National Poverty Eradication Policy (DRAFT)', Vice President's Office (Dar es Salaam: Government of Tanzania Printer).

Wangwe, S. M. (1983) 'Industrialization and Resource Allocation in a Developing Country: the Case of Recent Experience in Tanzania', *World Development*, 2, 6.

Wangwe, S. M. (1996) 'Economic Reforms and Poverty Alleviation in Tanzania', a paper prepared for ILO, Geneva.

Wangwe, S. M. (1997a) 'The Management of Foreign Aid', a paper submitted for a Workshop on Economic Management 20–31 March, Kilimanjaro Hotel, Dar es Salaam.

Wangwe, S. M. (1997b) *Exporting Africa: Technology Trade and Industrialization in Sub-Saharan Africa* (London, New York: Routledge Publishers).

Wangwe, S. M. (2004) 'The Politics of Autonomy and Sovereignty: Tanzania's Aid Relationship', in Simon Bromley et al. (eds), *A World of Whose Making? Making the International: Economic Interdependence and Political Order* (London: Open University Press).

Whitehead, R. L. (2000) *The Institutionalisation of the Tanzanian Opposition Parties: How Stable are They?* (Postterminalen, Stockholm: CMI Development Studies and Human Rights).

World Bank (1996a) *African Development Indicators 1996* (Washington, DC: World Bank).

World Bank (1996b) *Tanzania: the Challenge of Reforms: Growth, Incomes and Welfare*, 2 vols, Country Operation Division, Eastern Africa Department, Africa Region.

Wuyts, M., Mackintosh, M. and Hewitt, T. (1992) *Development Policies and Public Action* (London: Open University Press).

7
Understanding Economic Reforms: the Case of Zimbabwe

Takawira Mumvuma, Charles Mujajati and Bernard Mufute

1 Introduction

Policy reforms undertaken in many African countries are not working. Indeed, only a handful of countries have so far taken a sound macroeconomic policy stance. While it is true that in the majority of African countries policy reforms followed many years of economic decline, in some cases reforms were implemented primarily in response to the international debt crises. Just as many policy reform episodes across Africa are preceded by economic crisis, in many of those countries reforms have undergone policy reversals. There are only few cases where policy reforms have been sustained for any protracted period of time, or where reforms have registered measurable success. To help us understand economic reforms in Africa, this chapter examines the specific case of Zimbabwe. It starts by looking at the key triggers of policy reforms in Zimbabwe; this is then followed by an extensive analysis of the reform programmes undertaken in the country from 1991 to 1995, shedding light on the policies implemented and their outcomes, and on the 'losers' and 'winners'. After this, we examine the phenomenal economic crisis, conflicts of interest, resistance and policy reversals that took hold in Zimbabwe from 1996 until 2001, when the government formally abandoned its reform package. The chapter concludes with some general assessment of the factors behind Zimbabwe's unsuccessful attempt at IMF/World Bank-sponsored economic reforms. Before moving on to the discussion, it bears stressing that the division of the timeframes (or periodisations) used in the chapter – i.e. 1991–5 and 1996–2001 – is not cast in stone: it is just used to facilitate our presentation. Indeed, there is considerable overlap between what transpired in the two periods stipulated, as our discussion will soon show.

2 The main triggers of policy reforms

At the heart of most policy reforms is the need to move an economy from an economically inferior position to a superior one, where a society enjoys a higher standard of living through the creation of quality employment, reduction of poverty, enhancement of equity and the protection of the environment. This also entails the expansion of certain freedoms in society and the maintenance of an environment that enables the enjoyment of a high quality of life.[1] In order to bring about such superior economic and social outcomes, a whole range of institutional changes are required. These institutional changes may range from those governing the interaction amongst economic and social agents to those governing the interaction between economic and social agents, on the one hand, and the state, on the other.

According to Liew et al. (2003), policy reforms require that the 'rules of the game' be changed so that economic and political agents are able and willing to respond to market prices. Among economists a widely held view is that economic crisis is a major trigger of policy change (Martinelli, 1993; Rodrik, 1996; Drazen and Easterly, 2001). The work of Martinelli (1993: 9) suggests that crisis usually occurs in countries, such as Zimbabwe, experiencing distributive struggles, and that generally the economy tends to get worse before significant support and decisive actions are taken to stabilise the economy. Indeed Zimbabwe's reform seems to support the hypothesis that 'crisis induces policy reforms'.

Although the inward-looking, statist development strategy adopted by the Zimbabwean government in the immediate post-independence era initially served the interests of the emergent Black elite, foreign investors and the White population very well, by the late 1980s a crisis was already in the making. Despite some achievements, the 1980s, for the most part, were characterised by increasing economic gloom and a growing uncertainty about the thrust of economic policy. The six years from 1982 to 1987 witnessed very low and volatile economic growth, stagnant employment, foreign exchange shortages, inadequate investment, and a large and rising structural budget deficit (Table 7.1). The boom of the early years could not be sustained mainly because of the shortage of foreign currency and drought. The main cause of the drop in foreign currency allocations was the growing burden of foreign debt. With the stagnation and decline in world commodity prices, exports were not able to earn sufficient foreign currency to pay off the country's debts. In 1987, for example, the Confederation of Zimbabwe Industries (CZI) estimated that import allocations for production for the domestic market were below 40 per cent of their value in 1980 (Rushinga, 1987). In fact, such a level of import reduction was impossible to sustain without hurting output.[2] Another major contributor to the foreign currency shortage was the allocation system, which sold foreign exchange at an unrealistic price.

The difficulties which the economy was facing towards the late 1980s were most vividly shown by shortages of basic commodities. The foreign currency shortage adversely impacted both local and foreign business interests, and engendered considerable loss of business opportunities. This was worsened by the problems of low profitability due to price controls,[3] low productivity

Table 7.1:   Zimbabwe: key macroeconomic indicators, 1980–90

	1980	1981	1982	1983	1984	1985	1986	1987	1988	1989	1990
Aggregate indicators											
Real GDP growth (1990 prices %)	10.6	12.5	2.6	1.6	−1.9	6.4	2.1	1.1	7.6	5.2	7.0
Manufacturing GDP growth	14.7	9.4	−0.7	−2.6	−4.5	9.9	3.6	2.7	4.9	5.6	5.6
Inflation (%)	5.4	13.2	10.6	23.1	20.2	8.5	14.3	12.5	7.4	12.9	17.4
Treasury bill rate (%)	3.4	5.7	8.5	8.5	8.5	8.5	8.7	8.7	8.4	8.3	8.4
Deposit rate (%)	3.5	7.5	14.5	12.8	10.3	10.0	10.3	9.6	9.7	8.9	8.8
Composition of expenditure (% of GDP)											
Private consumption	64.5	67.0	64.7	72.5	59.2	61.3	58.7	58.7	50.7	65.4	63.4
Government consumption	19.7	17.2	19.7	19.3	21.3	20.1	20.6	23.3	27.6	18.9	19.5
Gross fixed capital Formation	15.3	18.7	19.9	20.7	18.5	14.2	15.0	16.0	15.6	14.2	18.3
Change in stocks	3.5	4.4	1.2	−3.9	0.4	3.5	3.0	−1.2	3.1	1.0	−0.8
Exports of goods and services	30.3	25.2	21.9	22.5	26.7	22.0	24.0	23.9	23.9	23.6	23.0
Imports of goods and services	33.3	32.5	27.8	25.7	26.1	21.8	21.5	21.2	20.5	22.0	22.9
Government finance											
Government deficit/GDP	−10.9	−5.9	−10.5	−6.6	−10.1	5.6	−6.2	−8.7	−7.2	−6.4	−5.3
Revenue/GDP	24.1	25.5	29.0	31.2	31.7	23.3	24.1	26.3	25.1	24.6	24.3
Expenditure/GDP	34.8	29.4	36.1	34.7	39.7	28.6	29.7	33.6	30.4	28.7	27.4
Total domestic debt/GDP	40.5	34.0	31.1	31.0	36.0	26.4	28.7	32.2	31.8	31.2	29.8
Total foreign debt/GDP	12.6	12.9	16.1	16.5	22.4	18.5	21.4	22.4	20.1	18.7	18.9

Source: IMF, International Financial Statistics (CD-ROM) cited in Gunning and Oosterndorp, 2002.

due to labour controls and high taxation of companies. These problems created some political pressure for the government to rethink its economic policies and strategies as it was fast losing part of its political base, particularly from the urban electorate and young school leavers who could not find employment.

The process of moving to a new institutional path, although initiated in late 1990, started in earnest in 1991 when the country embarked upon trade and exchange rate liberalisation. This was triggered internally, but with some exogenous factors also coming into play. The fiscal crisis and the costs of enduring the old rules of the game became unbearable to the extent that even some of the benefits to big business – such as protection from imports through trade barriers, and the enjoyment of monopoly profits, which the status quo offered – were now being outweighed by the burdens of high taxes and price controls. Consequently, key players began gradually to see their interests as diverging from the status quo and started lobbying for policy reforms. Besides the CZI, other well-organised interest groups, such as the Commercial Farmers Union, the Chamber of Mines and the Zimbabwe Tobacco Association, had an interest in liberalisation because these sectors were now suffering from large implicit taxation caused by the exchange rate distortion (Gunning and Oosterndorp, 2002). This exchange rate distortion was negative not only for big business but also for the economy at large because it hampered export growth, which was critical for economic development to take place. From these big business interest groups' perspective, price decontrols, deregulation of labour laws, the opening up of the country for imports, and the realignment of the exchange rate would lead to important changes that were conducive for business in Zimbabwe.[4]

These economic problems weakened civil society interest groups, such as the Zimbabwe Congress of Trade Unions (ZCTU), that had the capacity to lobby against the policy reforms. The economic situation by the late 1980s was so bad that the labour body, which under normal circumstances would lobby against these policy reforms, was now in agreement with the implementation of policy reforms in principle. This weakening of civil society interest also coincided with the government's shift in ideology from Marxist-Leninist principles to neo-liberalism.

As in several African nations which pursued socialist policies (see the cases of Ghana and Tanzania in this book) and were hit by severe economic crisis, the introduction of reform, or new rules of the economic game in Zimbabwe was preceded by intense ideological debate. Commenting on the introduction of a liberal investment policy in 1989, a leading political scientist from the University of Zimbabwe had this to say: 'Something drastic had to be done to tackle unemployment before it became a social problem. This radical departure was probably overdue.' He went on to say that 'We are now moving to a situation where the important thing from the people's point of view is whether they are employed, have accommodation, health service, and it may not make much difference what we call ourselves as long as the goods are provided' (*Ziana*, 30 April 1990). Others, however, felt the adoption of the reform meant socialism was dead. As one member of the Zimbabwe Economic Society noted, 'there is nothing wrong in the Government attracting investment, but it meant that socialism was no longer on the agenda' (*Ziana*, 30 April 1989).

In some instances during the debate, there was a deliberate misrepresentation of facts in order to push for the acceptance of the new ideology by various interest groups. For example, after launching the new investment guidelines in May 1989, the Minister of Finance, Dr Chidzero, denied the suggestion that Zimbabwe's new economic thrust, based on greater recognition of the role of market forces, was a negation of socialism; rather he said it represented an adaptation to changing circumstances in the true nature of the dialectical process. He went on to say, 'Nothing is static but the direction towards socialism is clear. There is no inherent contradiction between socialism and market forces' (*Ziana*, 9 May 1989).[5] The ruling party ZANU PF did not want to accept that there had been an ideological shift, as they argued that whatever policy reforms they were introducing were being forced on them by external forces given the crisis they were in. The *Zimbabwe News*, the official publication of the ruling party, had this to say: 'It is therefore the imperatives of capitalism and not the desire of our party and government that lies beneath the policy changes' (*Ziana*, 2 October 1989).[6] This reluctance to wholeheartedly embrace reforms is not surprising. Dr Chidzero's international career and his limited participation in the country's struggle for independence made some of the leftists in the party sceptical and suspicious of his intentions. In some circles, the minister was seen as representing the interest of the World Bank and the IMF, in particular, and international capital, in general, a view which initially weakened his position on the policy reform.

Although some people in the party were ideologically opposed to the adoption of reforms, Dr Chidzero worked hard to convince them that reforms were the best option that could rescue the economy from sinking any further. This ideological swing also became acceptable because it received support at the highest political level. This is reflected in a speech that was made by President Mugabe while he was addressing a breakfast meeting organised by the Confederation of French Industries in March 1990 in Paris. He told his audience that even though Zimbabwe had at independence adopted socialism, based on Marxism-Leninism, the economy had remained largely capitalist, and that the government was now committed to liberalising the economy even further. With reference to this apparent ideological shift, the president noted that, 'We do realize that some entrepreneurs may be fearful we might change again and nationalize their enterprises. But no, we are principled and committed to certain ideals . . . We are prepared to go into agreements that promote investments' (*The Chronicle*, 8 March 1990). By this time the president had also become a true convert of the free market ideology. Of course, this initial change of heart was being driven by a tacit acknowledgment of the severity of the problems that were besieging the economy by then and therefore the need for self-preservation, politically.

As this ideological debate intensified, both the weakening and purging of civil society interest groups or individuals that had the potential to oppose the introduction of the policy reforms were further extended to cover the university and some important government departments. Some individuals who had strong socialist ideals in key institutions such as the University of Zimbabwe found themselves no longer in favour with the government. Some neo-liberal economic consultants from Australia, whose ideas and beliefs were in line with those of the reformers, were recruited into the government, while key personnel were reshuffled; generally, those with strong socialist views were either replaced by reform-minded people or moved to less important ministries.

Additionally, some exogenous events – such as the collapse of the Soviet Union in 1989, which left an ideological vacuum for the ruling ZANU PF party – were a blessing in disguise for those who were in favour of policy reforms. It allowed them to swiftly push their market-based rules of the game against a background of the weakened Marxist-Leninist ideology of the ruling party and its supporters. Dr Chidzero's success in pushing through his reform agenda was also partly attributable to his ability to engage in constituency service and to build support for his reform agenda among the institutions that were expected to implement it. In other words, the minister was himself a good political actor whose other task was also to serve and protect the interests of those in political office. Bates and Devarajan (1999: 30) concur with the latter observation when they state that:

> The dominance of economic technocrats does not signal the absence of politics; the depoliticization of economic policy making is itself a political outcome. When finance ministers and bank governors are strong, it is often because they possess the backing of the ruling elite, have cultivated and created political interests, and have thereby constructed political defences for their policy programmes. To become powerful, they anchor their programmes in structures of vested interests, structures they themselves have often helped to create.

In addition to the above internal shift in ideology, external influence, in terms of ideas coming from the World Bank and other international institutions, such as the IMF, UNDP, UNIDO and the Western donor community, was quite significant, particularly towards the time the reforms were about to be launched.[7] Speaking at a two-day CZI conference on 25 October 1990, Dr Chidzero remarked that 'we are in fact currently working with a World Bank team to recast the programme in a manner which accords with the expectations of the international community, and with a view not only to secure

World Bank financial support but also financial support from other bilateral and multilateral sources' (*Ziana*, 25 October 1990). Indeed, the emergence of the World Bank as a key player further strengthened the pro-reform stance of the Minister of Finance vis-à-vis the domestic opponents of the reforms. During this period a number of key technocrats were sent to attend economics training courses conducted by the World Bank and IMF. The surprise performance of the opposition party, the Zimbabwe Unity Movement, in the 1990 presidential elections and the Gulf crisis of 1990, which worsened the already precarious balance of payments situation, accelerated the adoption and implementation of policy reforms.

Thus, in the Zimbabwean case a shift in the institutional path did not come as a result of interest group pressure only, but also through a dialogue with the private sector and an 'ideological shift' on the part of key government technocrats and the ruling elite who began to share the concerns of big business about the shortcomings of continued protectionist policies. Apart from the consultations with big business organisations, the government did not give much attention to the issue of consensus-building during the implementation of the policy reforms. Many civil society groups representing workers, students and peasants' interests that could have provided some input into the policy reforms were left out in the cold. The failure to engage and consult the large but disorganised civil society groups on matters concerning the design of the policy reforms in Zimbabwe is quite consistent with Pierson's (2000) observation that when it comes to initiating important institutional changes, politics and ideology matter because the exercise of political power and the deployment of ideology in favour of a particular path can affect institutions or rules of the game in a manner that reinforces their power or *new* ideology or *both*.[8]

It can be concluded from the preceding paragraphs that, in addition to the influence of exogenous forces, institutional change in Zimbabwe was mainly triggered by forces internal to the system, which altered the vested interests of key economic and political players who then went on to initiate a series of changes to the existing rules of the game in order to serve or protect their own vested interests without consulting the generality of civil society. This is despite the well-known fact that wider consultation often enables interest groups with the potential to block the policy reforms to buy into them. The failure by the government to consult with all the relevant stakeholders was clearly a mistake; credibility could have been enhanced by wide-ranging consultations with the relevant interest groups before and during the policy reform process. As Husain (2003: 3) argues, when the affected interest groups participate in designing the policy reforms after negotiations, consultations and consensus, the chances of the policy reforms being implemented are brighter. This lack of consultation and failure to raise awareness about the policy reforms in Zimbabwe resulted in ignorance and the lack of ownership on the part of many relevant interest groups.[9]

3   Policy reforms, 1991–5

In response to these internal and external pressures, Zimbabwe undertook policy reforms in 1991, which were referred to as the Economic Structural Adjustment Programme (ESAP). This policy reform fundamentally changed the rules of the game, as it essentially replaced the old policy regime, which emphasised government interventions and controls with a market-oriented policy regime. The major policy changes that were implemented during this period are summarised in Table 7.2.

3.1   Outcomes

Internal reviews of the policy reforms conducted in early 1996 noted that some of the goals set in 1991 have been met while others have not. The review indicated that much was accomplished in the areas of domestic deregulation, liberalisation of the current account, and financial sector reforms. By 1994, the foreign exchange allocation system was dismantled; all current account transactions were freed from control; public sector monopoly over the marketing of agricultural commodities was removed; the financial sector was deregulated; price controls were lifted; the deregulation of the labour laws and urban transport was accomplished; and investment licensing was abolished for all but large foreign investments. At the same time, the policy reforms generated many negative consequences, due mainly to their poor sequencing, timing and the lack of consistent implementation mechanisms, which saw legal and regulatory reforms lagging behind deregulation. This allowed powerful individuals and interest groups to capture the state and block the policy reform process for their own benefit (these failures are discussed in what follows).

3.1.1   *Delays in privatisation and civil service reform*

Several implementation failures manifested themselves during the 1991–5 reform period, of which the slow progress registered in the nation's civil service reforms and privatisation initiatives are worthy of note. This should not be surprising because what has been generally observed is that price-based reforms often face minimum resistance during implementation because of the general uniformity of their impact as opposed to project-based reforms, which may be fiercely resisted, or blocked, because of the specificity of their impact on specific interest groups (Hailu, 1997). Needless to say, the downsizing of the civil service without adequate compensation was politically sensitive, so the government, understandably, adopted a gradualist approach in this regard. In any case, by 1995, the civil service was reduced by approximately 23 500 established posts to 169 500, excluding the Ministry of Education and the Ministry of Health and Child Welfare, where downsizing was not permitted.

Some senior civil servants also resisted change. When the performance appraisal system was introduced in early 1994, some of them resisted it. As a tactical manoeuvre, they insisted on appropriate training for their subordinates

Table 7.2: Reform policies implemented in Zimbabwe, 1990–5

Year	Policy reform type
1990	• Movement of selected inputs onto the Open General Import Licence (OGIL) during the second half of 1990. • Government began removing a substantial number of commodities from the price control list, beginning October 1990, except for foodstuffs. • Government further reduced parameters under which collective bargaining could take place and collective bargaining became a permanent feature in wage negotiations. This measure essentially abolished policy on minimum wages which had been put in place in the early 1980s. • Government introduced Statutory Instrument 379 of 1990, which facilitated the hiring and firing of employees; in addition, these regulations introduced labour codes used at plant level to resolve labour disputes. Further, a mechanism for quick retrenchment of excess labour was introduced through Statutory Instrument 404 of 1990.
1991	• Additional inputs were put on the OGIL. • Outputs, which included cement, tyres and light bulbs, were put on the OGIL. • Introduction of import demand management measures as the economy began to experience balance of payments pressures; these included raising tariff rates from about 18 per cent to about 24 per cent on all imported goods between 1990/1 and 1991/2 fiscal years. This was the first reversal of reforms in Zimbabwe. • Price controls on some commodities were reintroduced in September of this year – another sign of reversal.
1992	• Some interest rates were decontrolled. • By July 1992, only five commodities were under government price control. • 15 per cent of imports were now on unrestricted OGIL and 10 per cent were on restricted.
1993	• 20 per cent of imports now on unrestricted OGIL.
1994	• Import licences were removed leading to the replacement of OGIL with an open import system. • Foreign currency accounts (FCAs), which allowed 60 per cent retention, were introduced in January. The retention level was increased to 100 per cent in July 1994. • A two-tier exchange rate was replaced by a market-determined exchange rate. • A policy that required that profits and dividends on pre-1993 investments be invested on 12 and 20 year bonds was abolished.
1995	ESAP officially ends.

and themselves before the introduction of the new performance management systems. They also wanted increased powers over recruitment, firing and financial management. Some progressive social scientists in the country also started to question the appropriateness of some of the reforms. They argued that the requirement that supervisors and subordinates negotiate the subordinate's annual objectives is impossible due to the large power gap between bosses and subordinates. Others pointed out that women and youthful bosses usually have difficulty negotiating objectives with their older counterparts and male subordinates. Thus, in most cases such negotiations were skewed in favour of whatever the culturally senior person wanted as an outcome (Moyo et al., 1998).

3.1.2   *Macroeconomic impact*

Most of the key indicators in Table 7.3 show that the macroeconomic situation at the end of 1995 was quite rosy. At the same time, it is clear that there was a failure to sustain the macroeconomic stability, due to the government's inability to substantially reduce money supply, government expenditure, the level of inflation, the prohibitively high interest rates, and to maintain a competitive exchange rate (*The Herald*, 9 February 1995; Bigsten and Durevall, 2002). These outcomes can be explained by a number of developments, including the two pertinent issues of sequencing and timing of reform. The issues of proper sequencing and timing is important to the political economy debate of reforms. Perhaps the most often asked question is: Which reforms to undertake first, and in what dosage? (Wolff, 1992). Of particular importance are questions revolving around the issue of liberalising the capital account first and the current account last or vice versa; making a choice between gradual or rapid policy reforms; whether trade reform should accompany or succeed macroeconomic reform; and whether or not a country should tackle its fiscal deficit and inflation before embarking on the trade and financial reforms.

According to Villanueva and Mirakhor (1990), for positive outcomes to be generated, an optimal sequencing of the reforms should be adopted. In particular, financial reforms should be preceded by macroeconomic and financial stability, otherwise the potential for a high interest regime, bankruptcy and loss of monetary control becomes higher, the reason being that in most developing countries, fiscal deficits constitute the major source of monetary expansion, hence some concerted efforts should be directed at achieving a substantial reduction of the fiscal deficit prior to the implementation of financial reforms (Chapple, 1990). Liberalisation of trade and capital account controls should be done in that order after the financial reforms. If the capital account is opened before the financial reform, then capital outflows and a balance of payment crisis become more or less imminent. Based on the latter reasoning, sequencing of policy reforms in Zimbabwe shows some inconsistency with what is proposed in the literature where trade and financial reforms are usually preceded by macroeconomic and financial stability before the implementation

Table 7.3: Zimbabwe: key macroeconomic indicators, 1991–2000

	1991	1992	1993	1994	1995	1996	1997	1998	1999	2000
Aggregate Indicators										
Real GDP growth (1990 prices) (%)	5.5	−9.0	1.3	6.8	0.1	7.3	3.2	−0.9	−2.3	−6.4
Manufacturing GDP growth	5.0	−10.4	−8.2	9.5	−13.6	3.6	−0.8	−3.4	−4.4	−11.5
Inflation (%)	23.3	42.1	27.6	22.3	22.6	21.4	16.4	34.5	58.4	55.9
Treasury bill rate (%)	18.5	35.0	26.9	30.0	29.5	24.0	21.1	32.6	49.9	66.6
Deposit rate (%)	16.2	28.8	30.5	27.3	25.0	16.8	23.6	32.1	38.5	49.0
Composition of Expenditure (% of GDP)										
Private consumption	68.1	65.0	64.0	61.6	62.9	59.4	70.2	62.9	68.3	71.5
Government consumption	16.1	24.2	14.9	16.7	16.8	14.7	15.8	15.0	13.4	13.9
Gross fixed capital Formation	20.6	22.4	23.6	21.4	24.6	17.7	17.0	21.2	15.1	13.2
Change in stocks	−1.5	−2.1	−0.8	2.4	−0.7	3.7	–	–	–	–
Exports of goods and services	23.9	27.3	30.7	34.7	35.6	36.1	35.4	42.5	47.8	37.9
Imports of goods and services	27.2	36.6	32.4	36.6	38.1	35.9	42.0	44.2	46.1	38.2
Government finance										
Government deficit/GDP	−1.9	−6.4	−1.8	−7.4	−6.3	−5.8	−3.7	−4.9	−8.5	−17.7
Revenue/GDP	31.6	31.2	32.2	29.4	33.4	31.6	34.3	23.9	27.4	24.9
Expenditure/GDP	33.5	37.7	34.0	36.8	39.7	37.4	38.1	28.8	35.9	42.6
Total domestic debt/GDP	30.1	23.8	22.2	21.4	26.5	46.9	31.8	30.9	–	–
Total foreign debt/GDP	20.0	29.7	35.0	35.5	32.9	32.1	30.1	37.3	–	–

Source: IMF, International Financial Statistics (CD-ROM) and Central Statistical Office (CSO) National Accounts Tables.

of large-scale trade and financial liberalisation. The failure to correctly time and sequence the trade and financial reforms vis-à-vis fiscal rationalisation explains, to a large extent, the many negative outcomes which were recorded by the policy reform.

The rush to liberalise the financial sector before the fiscal position had been consolidated worsened the government's fiscal position. For one thing, interest payments on domestic debt shot up and became a major burden to the whole fiscal process, resulting in unsustainable public domestic debt that was financed mainly through borrowings from the domestic financial market. According to Gunning and Oosterndorp (2002) the resultant fiscal problem led to uncertainty about future economic policies, as agents were unsure how compatibility would eventually be restored. It is further argued that the resulting risk premium contributed to the very high real interest rates experienced in the early years of the reforms and had the negative effect of crowding out private sector investment.

Secondly, the early liberalisation of the financial sector worsened the country's foreign debt position, since large domestic corporate borrowers, including banks, resorted to offshore borrowing, given the fact that in nominal terms the cost of money from abroad was much lower compared to the prevailing domestic interest rates. This, however, was done at a cost, since the central bank had to spend huge resources for protection against currency devaluation on behalf of domestic banks' offshore borrowing. At the same time, deregulation allowed a few powerful elites in the financial sector to consolidate their ownership of the existing financial assets, whilst weakening the capacity of the government to control and adequately supervise the emerging banks. The absence of an effective regulatory and supervisory framework allowed for greater speculative behaviour, non-productive borrowing, influence peddling, inefficiency and related lending practices in which bankers gave preferential and, sometimes, unsecured loans to themselves and their friends.

Thirdly, as the government was implementing its trade liberalisation programme by way of moving items on the Open General Import Licence (OGIL) list, in the absence of adequate external balance of payment support it mismatched the number of items placed on the list and foreign currency availability, leading to the deterioration of the nation's balance of payment situation, as imports were rising much faster than the amount of exports the economy could generate. This is an indication that there were problems in sequencing and implementation of some key policies leading to the first noticeable policy reversals. The government increased trade tariffs contrary to the requirements of trade liberalisation. This observation is quite in line with what some authors (e.g. Collier and Gunning, 1992; van Wijnbergen, 1992) have noted in the past, to the effect that temporary trade liberalisation generates a scope for speculative hoarding of the temporary cheap imports. Such hoarding worsens the current account balance and may indeed make trade liberalisation a temporary event, implying reversal may be imminent. Also the hoarding of imports has an additional negative impact if the accumulation of import stocks crowd out fixed capital formation. Alternatively, this speculative hoarding behaviour can be due to uncertainty arising from policy reform implementation. Economic agents or certain interest groups may doubt the sincerity of the government embarking on credible reforms, based on past experiences with implementation of other policies. They may therefore withhold their consent to the reforms or act in ways that undermine the process altogether. For example, when trade is liberalised, firms and other economic agents may focus on stockpiling imports instead of developing export-oriented activities as expected of them by the government. Such behaviour is usually driven by the perception that the reforms will be short-lived and that the government will reverse the liberalised trade policy regime in the future.[10]

The government's failure to control the abuse of OGIL vis-à-vis the speculative purchasing and stockpiling of raw materials and luxury consumption goods by firms and rich individuals not only worsened the balance of payment situation, but also prejudiced the anticipated capital goods investment drive that gave rise to the oft-cited poor export supply response (Bond, 2002; Hoogeveen and Mumvuma, 2002; Mehlum, 1999).

Fourthly, the macroeconomic instability can also be explained by the late-coming of key complementary institutions on the scene. This meant that the ability of the government to enhance its revenue collection capabilities, establish new revenue sources, ensure fair competition, and gain the support of key interest groups was seriously compromised. The lifting of price controls without a competition watchdog in place, for example, could also explain the high inflation rates experienced after liberalising the economy, given the fact that the economy was, and still is, dominated by many inefficient parastatals and private sector firms, which are oligopolistic and monopolistic in nature. These firms, instead of working towards the improvement of their production techniques to lower costs and thereby enhance their profitability, tended to pass on the resultant high production costs to customers in the form of unwarranted higher prices for them to remain viable.

Fifthly, the sequencing problems were further exacerbated by three fundamental policy mistakes, namely: donors' failure to disburse the funds for financing the programme in a timely manner; the World Bank's second thoughts on the programme's content; and the advice it offered the Grain Marketing Board to sell off 600 000 tonnes of its accumulated maize stock at a loss just prior to the onset of the 1992 drought which contributed to the country's domestic and external debt. These mistakes, coupled with the global recession in 1991/2 which reduced raw material prices and export demand, degenerated Zimbabwe's balance of payment situation and, consequently, destabilised the reforms (Bond, 2002). Furthermore, the failure to adequately support the policy reforms at this crucial phase meant that the initial inequalities, which existed in the economy during the pre-reform period, persisted and deteriorated, thereby posing a serious threat to the reform.

Finally, to make matters worse, the new South African government proceeded to cancel its 1964 preferential trade agreement with Zimbabwe. This led to high tariffs on exports entering the South African market and the entry of cheap subsidised South African imported goods, since Zimbabwe had already reduced its own tariffs under the policy reform programme. With South Africa as Zimbabwe's largest trading partner, the climate of uncertainty that ensued delayed the supply response that contributed to deindustrialisation and further lowering of living standards.

3.1.3   Social impact

The outcomes on the social front were equally negative. Whilst the economy was shrinking at an unprecedented rate, the return to labour was also experiencing an unabatable free fall. Real wages were falling due to inflation after the removal of price controls and rising unemployment.[11] In addition, inflation ravaged workers, with the ZCTU reporting in 1996 that their members found themselves on average 38 per cent poorer than in 1980 and 40 per cent poorer than in 1990. According to the ZCTU, the biggest losers in direct standards of living (average annual earnings, as a percentage of 1980 levels) were civil servants (−65 per cent); domestic workers (−62 per cent); construction workers (−56 per cent); teachers (−50 per cent); farm workers (−48 per cent); miners (−20 per cent); and workers in the manufacturing sector (−19 per cent). This decline is also confirmed by the decrease in the indices of real average earnings in the various sectors indicated in Table 7.4 when compared to the pre-reform period.

Table 7.4:   Zimbabwe: indices of real average earnings by sector, 1980–99 (1980 = 100)

	1980	1982	1984	1986	1988	1990	1992	1994	1996	1997	1999
Agriculture	100	164	143	137	130	130	70	75	85	79	72
Mining	100	130	113	116	113	116	97	90	113	110	106
Manufacturing	100	117	101	103	101	103	83	74	89	80	68
Electricity	100	110	90	93	96	94	79	85	129	133	138
Construction	100	120	107	98	85	78	57	46	66	68	53
Finance	100	103	85	87	89	93	89	78	99	76	73
Distribution	100	115	92	94	88	85	70	58	75	69	61
Transport & Communication	100	108	79	82	80	90	66	61	68	62	63
Public Administration	100	89	66	63	62	61	41	35	60	74	66
Education	100	59	69	73	77	82	64	49	75	82	74
Health	100	102	79	85	81	90	68	56	80	105	87
Domestic	100	115	82	100	92	82	48	31	25	18	8
Other	100	107	85	81	76	80	61	55	70	66	56
Total	100	122	100	102	101	103	78	67	88	88	80

Source: Zimbabwe Human Development Report 2000.

The situation of declining living standards was not helped by the government's cost recovery policies in healthcare, education and many other related social services. Statistics show that relative to the overall Consumer Price Index, the Medicare Price Index rose by a whopping 2106.3 per cent while the Education Price Index rose by 857.2 per cent between 1990 and 2000 as shown in Table 7.5.

The impact of these increases was a rise in school dropout, crude death, and infant mortality rates. For instance, while the crude death rate stood at 15 deaths per 1000 in 1978, it dropped to 10.8 in 1982 and further to 6.1 in 1987, but then rose to 9.49 in 1992 and further to 12.2 in 1997. Infant mortality rate trends tell a similar story, falling from 85 deaths per 1000 in 1978 to 61 deaths in 1988, followed by a worsening of the situation to 66 deaths in 1990 and 80 in 1997. In a similar vein, life expectancy plummeted from an average of 62 years in 1990 to 52 years in 1997 (Dhliwayo, 2001). What these statistics show is that after the policy reforms, all health indicators fell back into the pre-independence brackets, which is a reversal of the impressive achievements of the 1980s in the areas of social service provision. This, together with escalating interest payments on mortgage rates[12] and consumer credit, means that the majority of workers and poor people in Zimbabwe suffered a severe cash squeeze during this period of the policy reforms. A comparison between minimum wages and the poverty line for a family of six in 1996 shows a widening gap, implying increasing poverty. According to Bond (1999: 2), by the end of this phase of the reforms, at least one-third of Zimbabwe's population was unable to afford a basic food basket, shelter, minimal clothing and education.

In one of its 1996 performance audit reports, the World Bank conceded the above negative impact of ESAP on various social groups, particularly the very poor and disadvantaged, when it stated that 'what emerges is a sense that

Table 7.5:   Zimbabwe: consumer, medicare and education indices, 1990–2000

Year	Consumer Price Index	Medicare Price Index	Education Price Index
1990	100.0	100.0	100.0
1991	123.3	116.3	127.6
1992	175.2	144.4	191.6
1993	223.6	169.3	211.4
1994	273.4	419.9	229.1
1995	335.1	496.0	258.5
1996	406.9	632.9	295.7
1997	483.6	734.0	392.3
1998	636.9	818.7	508.3
1999	1009.6	1107.7	678.0
2000	1573.6	2206.3	957.2

Source: Central Statistical Office.

ESAP has, to date, entailed considerable pain but little visible gain'. Thus, the World Bank was admitting that the social costs of the policy reforms have been heavier than originally anticipated.

3.1.4 Sectoral impact

The pain alluded to by the World Bank was not confined only to the ordinary workers and other disadvantaged groups. Some sections of the business community, particularly the nascent Black indigenous entrepreneurial class, also fell victim to it. Despite some assistance provided by the government through different indigenous business organisations, by mid-1995 several thousand Black business persons were facing financial problems and 40 per cent of Indigenous Business Development Centre member companies were facing liquidation. At the same time, a large number of small and large-scale Black farmers could not repay loans they had taken from the Agricultural Finance Corporation.

Even CZI, which was all along seen as the traditional friend of the government, complained bitterly of the tight monetary policies and the continued distorted tariff regime. In an article published in *The Herald* on 29 June 1995, the CZI categorically warned that the country was so deep in recession that delays by government to solve economic problems could lead to deindustrialisation. The CZI painted a gloomy picture of companies struggling to survive under the weight of high interest rates and import duties. Lamenting over the inaction on the part of government, the CZI further pointed out that, 'Promises that action will be taken are no longer enough in a situation where enterprises helplessly watch diminishing profitability margins, while they are caught in a web of punitive interest rates.' Indeed as Figure 7.1 shows, the manufacturing sector, having been the engine of economic growth since the UDI

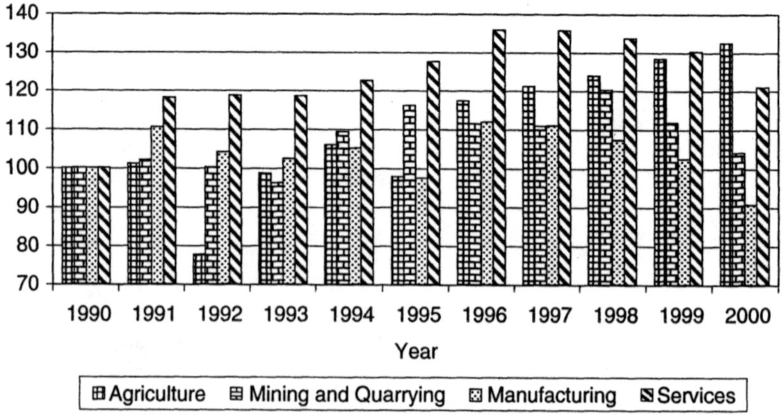

Figure 7.1:   Sectoral performance, 1990–2000 (1990 = 100)

period, was now lagging behind all the other sectors in terms of real growth in constant 1990 prices.

The ZNCC, which represents Zimbabwe's commercial sector, was even more bitter and demanded urgent action by the central bank to reduce the punitive interest rates. Of course this bitterness was justified because company liquidation had become the order of the day as early as 1992 as many companies could not meet the increased interest rate payments on their loans, and this culminated in a lot of lay-offs which swelled the ranks of the unemployed in Zimbabwe.[13]

It ought to be pointed out here that due to the lack of market and export culture that prevailed prior to the introduction of the policy reforms, most domestic firms were insufficiently prepared to compete effectively on the international scene: hence the observed shrinkage of the country's industrial sector. This lack of market culture, combined with poor sequencing and timing of the trade and financial reforms, resulted in untold damage to the local manufacturing and commercial sectors because the big bang type import liberalisation regime was implemented at a time when local manufacturers and traders were faced with severe supply-side constraints characterised by both financial and non-financial resource limitations.

Whilst it is clear that manufacturing was adversely affected by the reforms, the same cannot be said of the service sector,[14] mining and agriculture. Although the drought affected agriculture negatively during the early years of the reforms, the effects were felt mainly by smallholder farmers who lacked irrigation facilities. Large-scale commercial farmers reaped most of the benefits through the production of tobacco, paprika, cut flowers, vegetables, fruit and game meat for export.

3.1.5   A rise in corruption

Another disturbing outcome of the reforms in Zimbabwe was the systematic rise in corruption that was reported by the media. First to hit the headlines was the raiding of a public housing fund, which was diverted to the financing of the VIP housing scheme for top politicians, civil servants and their friends and relatives. This was followed by the looting of the government-sponsored War Veterans Compensation Fund, as well as deals at the National Oil Company of Zimbabwe and Grain Marketing Board, amongst the many other public enterprises, where billions of dollars ended up in the pockets of a corrupt few. There were many other cases of corruption by top government officials, which featured prominently during this period; these included the reported interference with the tender process by government ministers in the cellular telephone business, which resulted in a lawsuit by one of the tenders. Similar corrupt practices were reported in transactions involving the Zimbabwe Electricity Supply Authority and a Malaysian company called YTL, as well as the awarding of a lucrative contract to build the new Harare International Airport. Most of these corrupt activities went unpunished due to the lack of a clear regulatory and institutional framework for addressing such practices at both the political and corporate levels. As a result, the policy reforms, instead of enhancing transparency and accountability in carrying out the day-to-day government and private sector activities, opened a window of opportunity for both new and old rent seekers who captured the state and went on a mission to amass wealth on a grand scale.[15]

3.2   Winners and losers of the policy reforms

Clearly, segments of workers, peasants, industrial and commercial workers constituted the 'losers' of the reforms. But the policy reforms did not give birth solely to losers. There were, quite expectedly, winners as well, although they were in the minority. According to a citation in Bond (2002), leading members of the business community, the ruling and emergent bureaucratic elite, particularly holders of financial assets (huge sums of local and foreign currency), were the greatest beneficiaries of luxury goods imports and the new-found ability to earn and hold hard cash or externalise foreign currency.[16] In addition, many indigenous entrepreneurs did well during the reform period, especially those who were operating in the financial sector. These winners exploited the failure by the Ministry of Finance to control OGIL abuse that gave rise to speculative purchasing and stockpiling of raw materials and luxury consumption goods by firms and wealthy individuals.

Another group of winners is that of large-scale commercial farmers who produced tobacco, paprika, cut flowers, vegetables, fruit and game meat mainly for the export market. The ruling and bureaucratic elite also benefited from political and civil service corruption involving the awarding of tenders to close connections, indulging in conspicuous consumption, and looting of national assets. The collapse of the National Oil Company of Zimbabwe, and the subsequent fuel shortages that followed, is a classic example of such corrupt practices.

It can therefore be concluded that the policy reforms benefited a certain segment of the White population which was historically advantaged, as well as the emergent Black elites from the old system who were in a position to take advantage of the new global market opportunities. The reason for this was that the designers of the policy reforms did not take into account the historically determined skewed ownership structure, and inequalities in wealth and assets distribution, especially with regards to land, which were prevailing in the country before the policy reforms. For example, the 1993 Land Designation Act, which was intended to address the unequal distribution of land, was unceremoniously shelved because it was partly not in line with World Bank and IMF directives and partly not in the interest of the new ruling elites who continued to acquire large commercial farms during the policy reform period. Therefore, as in the 1980s, the interests of the new ruling elites continued to coincide with those of local and international capital. As a consequence, the market-based policy reforms, which continued with the 'willing buyer, willing seller' doctrine failed to integrate land reform, thereby aggravating market failures in land acquisition and further entrenching the skewed ownership structure. In other words, the reforms, like the Lancaster House Constitution, had the effect of reinforcing the highly skewed colonial asset and wealth distribution patterns which – in turn, coupled with cuts in social services expenditure, high levels of corruption and the patronage system – generated more inequalities, poverty, unemployment, contraction of the Black middle class, social exclusion, and resentment of the ruling elites by the peasants, workers, students and some indigenous business interest groups. The World Bank (2004) also concurs with the latter observations when it said that the Zimbabwean experience provided lessons that the Bretton Woods institutions should have given greater attention to reducing the glaring inequalities and poverty that prevailed in Zimbabwe. In fact, the Bank acknowledged, albeit belatedly, that the land question should have been addressed more proactively.

What we can infer from the Zimbabwean experience is that the often talked-about positive correlation between reform implementation and welfare enhancement is not always automatic. The presence of some robust built-in mechanisms to compensate the losers and to ensure the equitable distribution of benefits is an important prerequisite if distributional conflicts are to be minimised. Dixit's (2001) transaction costs politics thesis can shed some light on the negative outcomes of policy reforms in Zimbabwe. Dixit (2001) views economic policy as practised in almost all countries as an equilibrium outcome of a political process, which is influenced by many costs of negotiating and implementing agreements, most notably the costs of coping with asymmetries and costs of making commitments credible. The effect of the former on the success or failure of policy design and implementation is very important to take note of, given the severity of agency problems particularly in most developing countries like Zimbabwe. He also pointed out that the policy reform process is constrained by historically and socially predetermined constitutional rules and frameworks of institutions and organisations. In other words, Dixit (2001) sees economic policy-making as a political process constrained by asymmetric information and limited commitment possibilities, and notes that the often-observed, seemingly inefficient policy reform practices and outcomes, such as the ones which occurred in Zimbabwe, are credible attempts to cope with transaction costs such as opportunism and asymmetric information in the political process of designing and implementing policy reforms.

4   Economic crisis, resistance and policy reversal, 1996–2001

From the analysis above, it is clear that policy reforms of 1991–5 failed to achieve their intended objectives. The situation got even worse in the subsequent years, as we shall see in what follows. In fact it is plausible to assert that the policy reforms resulted in an intensification of the suffering of ordinary people, the shrinkage of the Black middle class, the reduction of manufacturing sector and a political crisis that undermined the legitimacy of the ruling elite to properly govern the country.

These setbacks notwithstanding, the government proceeded to announce what amounted to a second phase of policy reform, starting around 1996, which was meant to complete the unfinished business of the earlier phase. The outcomes of the latter phase were equally disastrous, as the government failed to steer the economy in the desired direction. The failure was caused by a series of political decisions to meet some of the demands that emerged during this period. These new demands triggered a chain reaction that further worsened the underlying economic and social problems. This, in turn, forced the government to come up with ad hoc solutions with even more damaging economic consequences.

4.1   Resistance

After the unpleasant effects of the policy reforms, some serious challenges associated with the progress of Black economic empowerment started to emerge. The economy continued to be characterised by structural dualism, a skewed ownership structure, and exceptionally high levels of race-based income inequality and asset distribution. The government found itself caught in a dilemma. As with the earlier phase of the policy reforms, the risks associated with the implementation of a programme of indigenisation were considerable. It dawned on the government that if, on the one hand, it did not do enough to correct the historical imbalances, political pressures could mount for a reversal of the policy reforms. On the other hand, if the thrust of the affirmative action policies under the indigenisation programme were perceived as unduly punitive, this could discourage the participation of the domestic Whites and foreign investors in the economy. Although it was clear after the experiences of the first phase of the policy reforms that the question of indigenisation would be faced during the second phase, the ruling elites and their counterparts in the private sector were slow to come up with an effective and balanced response to address the concerns of the victims of the policy reforms.

After experiencing accelerating poverty, inequalities, unemployment and the lack of business opportunities during the earlier reform period and the delay by government to adequately compensate the losers, the resultant threats from them started to define a completely different road map from that of the previous years which even generated more punitive economic, political, distributional and social crises that initially stifled, and finally led to the reversal of, the policy reforms.

As early as 1994, the losers of the reforms had started to organise themselves to voice their concern about the adverse impact of the policy reforms on their welfare. Indeed it was around this time that we notice the emergence of radicalised Black middle-class business interest groups such as the Indigenous Business Development Corporation, the Indigenous Business

Woman Organisation, the Indigenous Commercial Farmers Union and the Affirmative Action Group. Also, interest groups representing the war veterans of the 1970s liberation war started to reorganise and resurfaced around this time. As interest groups, which had been hit hard by the reforms, they started lobbying aggressively against the successor programme. They wanted their interests and concerns to be addressed first. Increasingly vociferous demands came from the indigenous business lobby groups which were by this time still shut out of the White-controlled markets and financial institutions. The strong lobbying by these interest groups and by anti-reformers in government was quite effective; for one thing, it led to the delay of the approval of the second phase by two years.

After succumbing to the political pressures which were being exerted on government by the indigenous interest groups and their allies in government and the ZANU PF party, economic empowerment and indigenisation also became key objectives of the reforms. The feeling from the leftists was that in order to successfully restructure the economy, it was necessary not only to 'disturb', but also to completely 'dismantle' the skewed colonial asset ownership and wealth distribution structure as part of the unfinished business of the first phase of the reforms for any meaningful growth to occur and equity to prevail. In other words, from the point of view of these leftists, simply handing over political power was not enough to effectively wash away the historical imbalances of the country's colonial past. By this time, the president was also no longer supportive of the policy reforms. After observing their negative impact and the political harm they were inflicting on the welfare of his Black constituency he openly conceded that certain policy reforms were doing more harm than good to both the growth and development of the country and vowed never again to be dictated to by international financial institutions. Addressing the fourth 'Meet the President' session in Bulawayo in 1995, he had this to say:

> We are wiser than we were some three years ago. Certain reforms are disastrous and we should not listen willy-nilly to what the international institutions bid us to do. Five years was not long enough to undertake all the reforms. So as we talk to the IMF and the World Bank, we tell them openly we cannot do certain things within a short frame. We can do it within an extended frame so that we don't ruin the basis we have established for the development of the country.
>
> (*The Herald*, 2 February 1995)

This statement also reveals the absence of ownership of the policy reform process on the part of the Zimbabwean political leadership, which became even clearer from 1998 onwards.

The real turning point for the worse came in 1997, when the nation's veterans set in motion a chain reaction which completely derailed the reform agenda. The War Veterans Association leadership felt that the reforms and the rampant corruption in government had left its members poorer than before. In July 1997, under the leadership of Chenjerai Hunzvi, the 50 000-strong Zimbabwe National Liberation War Veterans Association marched to the Sheraton Hotel where President Mugabe was hosting a conference for African-American investors and loudly berated the government for squandering resources and looting the pension fund. They threatened to wreak havoc in the streets if their grievances were not addressed before Heroes Day on 11 August 1997. Indeed heavyweight politicians were booed countrywide at the Heroes Day celebrations. President Mugabe's speech at the national shrine was barely audible as the ex-combatants sang revolutionary songs during his address. On 21 August, they demanded and got their meeting with President Mugabe, and the veterans reportedly complained about his ministers, some of whom were described as very corrupt, an allegation which President Mugabe left the meeting convinced of. Given the fact that six months before this mayhem, the government was rocked by revelations that the war veterans' fund had been looted by officials in ZANU PF, the president had little choice but to accede to the demands of the war veterans, by granting them Z$50 000 each, plus a monthly pension of Z$2000.

The war veterans' success in negotiating compensation packages instantly brought into question the government's ability to finance its eighteen-month budget reduction programme. This prompted the World Bank's withdrawal of a US$62.5 million balance of payments support credit in October 1997, mainly because of concerns over financing of a potential Z$4 billion payments package for the war veterans which seemed to have precipitated a broader crisis of confidence in the economic strategy. Of course the result of this political decision to award the unbudgeted gratuities to the war veterans, which amounted to about 3 per cent of GDP, was the immediate ballooning of the budget deficit to unmanageable proportions, which in turn sent the inflation rate skyrocketing as shown in Figure 7.2.

4.2   Economic crisis and policy reversals

The downward trend of inflation which characterised the economy up to 1997 was significantly reversed from 1998 onwards when inflation started to increase sharply – rising from 18.8 per cent in 1997 to 31.7 per cent in 1998, and 58.5 per cent in 1999. This means that although the move to compensate the war veterans was a noble idea, the way the compensation was financed proved disastrous for the economy. The gratuities were in fact financed by printing money. If they were financed by appropriate fiscal[17] and monetary measures then the economic crisis that ensued later on could not have turned out to be as deep as it became. To make matters worse, during this period the economy overheated and the central bank failed to respond with the necessary monetary policy tightening. In fact real interest rates fell too quickly in 1996 with the appointment of Mr Chambati as Minister of Finance in line

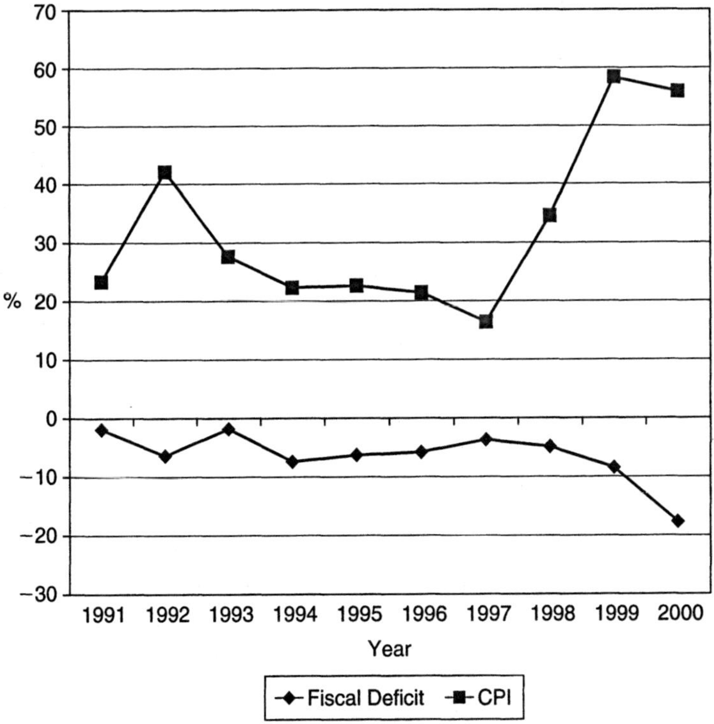

Figure 7.2:   Fiscal deficit and inflation, 1991–2000

with the Millennium Economic Recovery Programme's objectives, resulting in the explosion in the supply of money. This caused the economy to overheat in 1997, which together with other factors such as the collapse of the currency, triggered the crises that the country is still facing.

As if the political decision to award unbudgeted gratuities to the war veterans was not enough, the president, during the same period, went on to make another political announcement to the effect that the government was now going to begin implementing the 1993 Land Designation Act. About 1500 mainly White-owned commercial farms were therefore immediately identified for redistribution. This was not surprising, given the fact that in the first phase of the reforms the rural folk were not spared severe pain and the government was therefore fast losing its largest support base. The only feasible way to compensate and, therefore, appease this restive group in the face of dwindling fiscal resources to subsidise their basic needs was to offer them land. The latter was also viewed as a strategy to address the injustices suffered by the previously marginalised Black majority that would allow them to be economically empowered to actively participate and positively

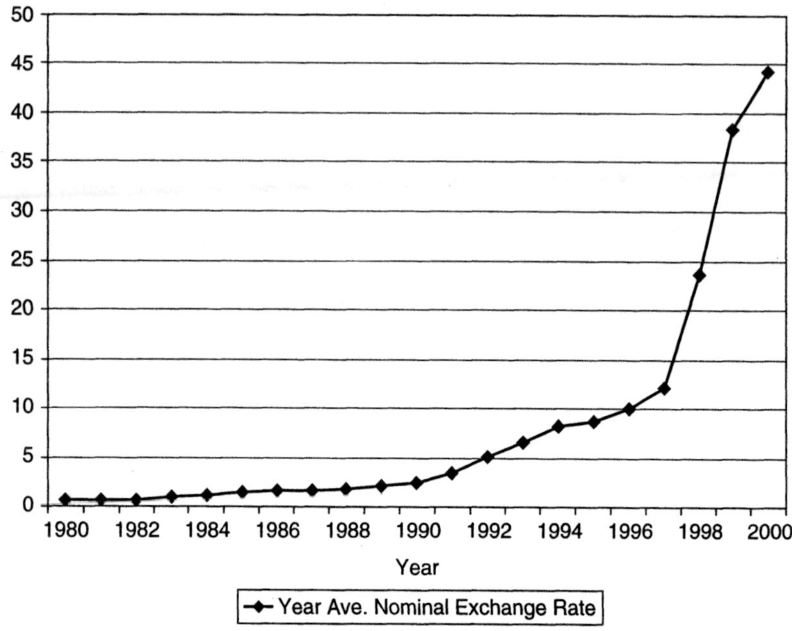

Figure 7.3:   Yearly average nominal exchange rate Z$/US$, 1980–2000

contribute to the development and growth of the economy. However, the ensuing perception of unsustainable fiscal imbalances, a deteriorating external account position, and the uncertainty surrounding the land reform programme led to spontaneous and concerted runs against the currency, flight from the money market and other forms of financial adaptation which in turn led to a crash of the Zimbabwean dollar in the last quarter of 1997. Thereafter, the exchange rate continued to depreciate uncontrollably as Figure 7.3 indicates.

4.3   Mounting economic crisis, riots and threats of mass action

The crash of the Zimbabwe dollar was immediately followed by sharp increases in food prices, which led to food riots later in that year and in early 1998. In January 1998, the ZCTU Secretary General announced his organisation's withdrawal from the National Economic Consultative Forum, an organisation composed of business, labour and government, which the Union had previously assisted in setting up. State–civil society relations deteriorated sharply as the economic situation declined even further. As the policy reforms failed to deliver the expected results and the economic crisis intensified, the anti-reform group within the government, with the backing of indigenous interest groups, managed to strengthen its anti-reform stance. By this time, the CZI and other big businesses and White-dominated interest groups were now increasingly being seen as a grouping of Whites only interested in protecting their interests and therefore whose commitment to the economic emancipation of the Black majority was doubtful. At the same time, the ZCTU was seen as posing a direct political threat to the government, given its popularity amongst students, urban workers and farm workers. Facing increased pressure from a restive populace, the government reintroduced price controls on maize meal in June 1998.

September 1998 saw the birth of another consultative forum, the Tripartite Negotiating Forum, which also comprised representatives from business, labour and the government. The Forum was born out of negotiations by the three parties to avert a threatened mass action by the ZCTU in protest against the continued imposition of a drought levy as well as an increase in sales tax to meet the unbudgeted costs of the war veterans' gratuities. The Forum conceded to the demands of the labour union, and the government resorted to borrowing from the money market, thus averting another mass uprising. The central bank made the problem worse by printing money to finance this borrowing.

It is worth noting that earlier, in August 1998, the country was subjected to an intensive currency speculation and raiding of foreign reserves, which over an eight-week period reduced the Zimbabwean dollar's value by 60 per cent – a situation made worse by the subsequent decisions of the government. In September, Zimbabwe sent its army to the Democratic Republic of Congo (DRC) to defend that country's sovereignty, which was under threat from the Rwandan- and Ugandan-backed rebels. Zimbabwe's involvement in the DRC war, which was estimated to cost US$33 million a month, coupled with the speculative attack on the country's currency, further worsened the government's budget deficit and balance of payments situation.

In a bid to ease the balance of payment problems, the government raised import tariffs on a wide range of products in September 1998. The increases were later partially reversed. With the government getting increasingly desperate in its attempts to address balance of payment problems, it suspended the corporate Foreign Currency Account (FCA) in November 1998. The FCA was later reintroduced with tougher conditions after intense lobbying by the business community. It is important to note that the forced reversal of the policy reforms, and earlier ones, confirms our earlier hypothesis that the political behaviour of interest groups – especially prior to and during the reform process – matters, since it determines to a large extent the ground rules for the reform process.

At the end of the first quarter of 1999, the RBZ effectively pegged the currency at Z$38 to the US dollar. This was a good decision at that particular point in time given that the banks had long been manipulating the currency to their own advantage. Although many of these actions served to stabilise the local currency, the exchange rate did not return to its pre-crisis period, and neither did it lead to any significant improvement in the central bank's

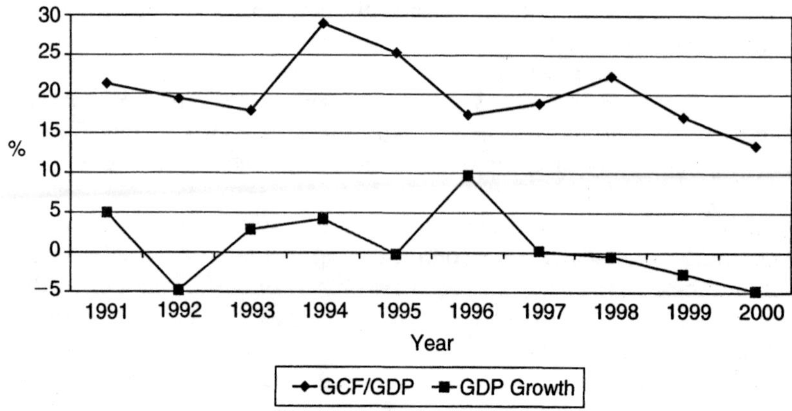

Figure 7.4:   GDP and GCF trends, 1991–2000

foreign exchange holdings, investment flows and output growth. In fact, output growth and investment inflows started their steep downward slide around 1997 as can be seen from Figure 7.4; similarly, foreign exchange shortages started to appear at the end of 1999.

Frustrated by the mounting economic crisis, the ZCTU and forty other civic groups organised a Working People's Convention in February 1999 in which they agreed to form a 'broad-based movement for change', which was later transformed, in September 1999, into a new opposition party called the Movement for Democratic Change. The birth of this labour-backed opposition party did not help the situation, as it put additional pressure on the political leadership to adopt more populist policies, despite their potential long-term adverse consequences. At the beginning of 2000, the government proceeded to increase civil service salaries by a rate of between 69 and 90 per cent just before the referendum on the government's proposed new constitution, which the government lost.[18] Such hefty salary increases were not budgeted for, and the government had to borrow on the domestic financial market to meet the expenditure. This unchecked politically motivated profligacy and other earlier cumulative policy implementation mistakes, as well as the fast-track land reform programme, quickly translated into a hyperinflationary environment, characterised by unprecedented shortages and parallel market activities in virtually every sector of the economy. Additionally, there was an intensification of high-level corruption and the deepening of the patronage system, all of which was meant to ensure the political survival of the ruling elite.[19] So how can these government actions, the sequence of events and their outcomes be explained? A plausible explanation is the one given by Brett (2004). He argues that while the government responded quite effectively to new demands in the early 1980s and possibly the early 1990s, the combination of the economic stress generated by the earlier phase of the reforms and the political stress generated by the threats to the power of the ruling party after 1997 pushed the system beyond its limits and led to the short-term populist political decisions to meet another set of new demands that resulted in the initial reversal, and the final announcement of the termination of the policy reforms by President Mugabe in 2001.

The way the events turned out after 1997, in particular, and how the political leadership reacted to such events is not surprising. When a specific set of economic or political rules of the game produce bad economic and social outcomes by benefiting certain interest groups in society whilst creating huge costs for others, as turned out to be the case in Zimbabwe, it is intuitively appealing to expect political pressure to be generated by the relevant interest groups, as part of the feedback mechanism, that will force the defective or socially harmful rules of the game to be changed. In other words, if the mismatch between what is possible within a given set of rules, at any particular point in time, and what is necessary to cope with pressing problems inhibiting mutually beneficial exchange arrangements becomes wider and wider, the ensuing distributional conflict between various competing interest groups may lead to the abandonment of the existing rules of the game in favour of new ones.

5   Conclusion

Policy reforms which were implemented in Zimbabwe were to a large extent triggered by the economic crisis that gripped the country in the mid to late 1980s. This crisis, aided by the shift in ideas on the part of the key players, temporarily weakened civil society groups and individuals that had the capacity to lobby against policy reforms. This, coupled with the fact that the status quo could also no longer adequately safeguard the economic and political well-being of the major economic and political players, opened a window of opportunity for the government to initiate and implement reforms.

However, very little consultation was carried out before the implementation of the reforms, nor were people educated about the reform programme. It seems there was a perception amongst the political leadership that what was good for them was also good for civil society, and consultation, from their point of view, would only delay or even prevent the implementation of the policy reforms. This proved to be a very costly mistake during the implementation stage, since fierce lobbying by the losers posed serious problems that stifled and eventually caused the demise of the nation's policy reforms.

In addition, adequate attention was not given to the issue of compensating the losers in the face of rising poverty and inequitable income distribution. Instead, pervasive structural dualism continued to prevail in the country, and no proper strategy was built into the reform package to deal with it effectively. This duality, which was further worsened by the reforms themselves, aggravated the nation's economic situation. This, coupled with lack of true ownership of the reforms by the political leadership, forced the government to take a series of political decisions which were meant to garner political support, but in turn put additional stress on the economy. This new economic crisis could also be partly attributed to the reform efforts, which were made without complementary institutional measures to regulate the liberalised business environment. As a result of the non-existence of a credible supervisory and regulatory institutional framework, the policy reforms opened a window of opportunity for both new and old rent-seekers who captured the state and went on a mission to plunder the nation's resources. This exacerbated the inequalities observed after the first phase of the policy reforms, which helps to undermine the much talked-about positive reform–welfare nexus.

One can also conclude from the way the reform policies were implemented that their poor timing and sequencing led to their eventual derailment. It is clear that the designers of the policy reforms forgot to address the major timing and sequencing issues, particularly the sequencing of interest rate liberalisation and fiscal restructuring. Indeed it was not smart to liberalise the interest rates when the parastatals depended on them so much; this obviously fuelled government expenditures that in turn caused the budget deficit to rise. In addition, the liberalisation of trade without a concomitant increase in balance of payment support from key players like the IMF created import pressures, which led to reversals, uncertainty and loss of credibility for the reforms. Also the tightening of the monetary and fiscal policies (e.g. by raising interest rates and reducing social expenditure), created serious problems for ordinary Zimbabweans. It was, therefore, not surprising that as poverty intensified most of the poor and other disadvantaged groups realised that there was not much they could gain from the reforms. This realisation forced the nation's Black population to concentrate more on their empowerment and land problems. What this means is that sometimes good policy reforms implemented at the wrong time or sequenced in a non-optimal fashion can have serious negative consequences and be perceived as a bad policy, especially by those who are adversely affected.

Evidently, Zimbabwe's reform was unsuccessful in the sense that it failed to achieve its intended objectives, particularly the attainment of macroeconomic stability, productive competitiveness, attainment of growth and equity, reduction of poverty, corruption and unemployment, as well as political stability. The implementation process itself was characterised by policy reversals, with the problems of timing, sequencing and severe distributional conflicts being responsible for some of these reversals. There were both errors of commission and omission in the design and implementation of the policy reforms, which also explains their failure. Some of these errors relate to the lack of broader consultation with all relevant stakeholders, while others relate to avoidable delays in the disbursement of funds by the reforms' funding partners.

Notes

1. This discussion of the various aspects of development is based on Fanelli and Popov (2003).
2. It is important to note that according to the World Bank (1985) in 1985, imports of intermediate and capital goods accounted for 70 per cent of total imports, while petroleum made up a further 15 per cent.
3. Price controls caused average prices per unit of output to remain static, whilst average costs per unit of output increased significantly due to rising import costs and minimum wage increases.
4. According to Gunning and Oosterndorp (2002) this shift in thinking on the part of the CZI was a major turning point within the political economy of policy reforms in Zimbabwe because it helped the Minister of Finance to persuade his cabinet colleagues to adopt policy reforms as a desirable policy option.
5. The statement by the minister should not be surprising, for according to Dixit (2001), politicians sometimes manipulate information and hide the truth from citizens in order to minimise political transaction costs and their negative effects on them.
6. This influence of external forces and the reluctance of the ruling party to adopt policy reforms in the first place is further revealed in a rare interview given to *The Herald* on 1 April 2003: 9, by the former Chief Secretary to the President and Cabinet Dr Charles Utete when he admitted that ESAP was a mistake as it was not home-grown, but was a prescription of the World Bank and the IMF, whilst ZIM-PREST was in his own words a 'rehashed ESAP'.
7. As far back as 1985, the Zimbabwean government consulted the CZI, UNIDO and the World Bank on major economic decisions. But the turning point came in 1987 and 1988 at the CZI's annual congress, attended by both government ministers and the major industrialists of the country, which concentrated on liberalisation issues as the economy again slid into recession for the second time since independence. Thereafter, in 1989, the government invited an Australian economist, and representatives of the CZI and University of Zimbabwe to design the ESAP programme to coincide with the collapse of communism.
8. What this means is that economic policy-making should be viewed as the result of political struggles within given institutional settings. This is very relevant in explaining the policy implementation problems often observed in developing countries since there is a tendency for policy-makers to choose rules of the game that reflect the preferences of powerful interest groups or maximise their own or these powerful interest groups' benefits instead of society's total welfare. In other words, rules of the game are created or chosen by those economic and political agents seeking strategic advantage in ways that secure favourable distributional outcomes to them. According to Acemoglu (2003), under such circumstances the resultant equilibrium institutions or rules of the game will not be those that maximise the size of the overall pie, but the slice of the pie taken by the powerful interest groups.
9. This explains why in Zimbabwe policy reforms were not well received. As correctly pointed out by Williamson (1998) it will be in the best interests of policy-makers and other professionals to inform various interest groups about the nature of the benefits that can come out of policy reforms, given that in most cases policy reforms often fail to find a political constituency because the general public will be ignorant of their potential benefits.
10. Sometimes in order to avoid this type of strategic behaviour emerging, it is essential to build institutional arrangements that minimise the risk of policy reversals

and there are a number of ways of building credibility into policy reforms. One way of doing it is to build consultative structures that ensure that all interest groups have a chance to make an input into the desired policy reforms. Another way is to develop institutions that are free from political influence, such as an independent central bank, anti-corruption watchdog and competition commission.

11. The rise in unemployment was due to the failure of the restructuring economy to generate new jobs and the retrenchment exercise. With regard to the latter, ZCTU estimates indicate a shrinkage in non-agriculture employment form 939 800 in 1991 to 844 000 in 1992, whilst the World Bank's own estimates show that out of a total labour force of about 4.1 million, only 1.244 million were formally employed in 1991, and this dropped to 1.217 million in 1993.

12. In 1994 only, mortgage rates went up from 15.5 per cent to 18.5 per cent in the low-density areas and to some 21–22 per cent in high-density areas where the majority of the poor live. It was estimated that as a result of these interest rate increases, some 600 members of the Association of Building Societies were to lose their houses by May 1995.

13. This phenomenon is not unique to the Zimbabwean situation. According to Wolff (1992), in Argentina, Chile, Uruguay and Turkey interest rates were freed in one stroke in the late 1970s and 1980s with the intention of attracting domestic savings and foreign capital transfers. In all these countries, because high inflation and devaluations were expected, real interest rates rose so massively that, on the one hand, investments could no longer be financed, and on the other hand large numbers of borrowers and banks were driven into bankruptcy.

14. The service sector is taken here to include finance and insurance, distribution and hotels as well as transport.

15. It is important to note that most cases of corruption we have highlighted in this section are public sector types. This does not mean that there was no corruption in the private sector, but that the media were not highlighting these cases as much as they were doing with government cases. We are of the opinion that corruption was also rampant within the private sector, particularly in the financial sector where it is now emerging that several indigenous bankers, whose banks have either now collapsed or are under receivership, used their financial institutions for personal gain by abusing depositors' funds.

16. According to Schamis (1998) groups with access to such instruments are cushioned against the vagaries of policy reforms because they assist them to reduce their tax base in an optimal way. They also help in displacing the cost of inflation to groups for which financial adaptation is either not available or too costly. Therefore Zimbabweans owning a lot of local currency benefited from high returns from the money market, trading foreign currency at a high premium on the parallel market and importing luxury goods which they sold on the domestic market at huge profits, generating an instant windfall for them.

17. It is worth noting that the government planned a tax increase to help finance the war veterans' compensation packages but this was reversed after the Zimbabwe Congress of Trade Unions organised street protests against the proposed tax levy.

18. This surprise rejection of the new constitution by the people did not go well with government. As a result, it was followed by a wave of farm invasions, intimidation and attacks on the members of the opposition. The White farmers were targeted because it was by now common knowledge that together with the opposition they campaigned for the no vote. They mobilised their employees to vote no and were the chief financiers of the opposition party. Two contested clauses in the

new constitution were a clause authorising the government to confiscate land without compensation, and another clause which sought to increase the presidential powers and extend the president's period of stay in office.

19. The central bank and the president's anti-corruption crackdown has so far resulted in the closure of more than five key financial institutions and as many as ten prominent business tycoons have fled the country.

References

Acemoglu, D. (2003) Lecture Notes for Political Economy of Institutions and Development, 14.773.

Bates, R. H. and Devarajan, S. (1999) 'Framework Paper on the Political Economy of African Growth', GDN Global Research Project.

Bates, R. and Krueger, A. (1993) 'Generalizations Arising from the Country Studies', in R. Bates and A. Krueger (eds), *Political and Economic Interactions in Economic Policy Reform: Evidence from Eight Countries* (Cambridge, MA and Oxford: Blackwell), pp. 444–72.

Bigsten, A. and Durevall, D. (2002) 'Is Globalization Good for Africa?', *Working Papers in Economics* No. 7, Department of Economics, Goteborg University.

Bond, P. (1999) 'Political Reawakening in Zimbabwe', *Monthly Review*, 50, 11 (April).

Bond, P. (2002) 'Beyond Both the Washington Consensus and the Post Washington Consensus in Zimbabwe and South Africa: the Failure of Structural Adjustment and the Need for a Democratic Approach to Economic Policy', http://globalternatives. nl/voorstudie/studies.html (accessed December 2002).

Brett, E. A. (2004) *Systemic Crises, Conflicting Interests and State Failure in Zimbabwe 1997–2004*, Development Research Centre, London School of Economics.

Central Statistical Office, *Quarterly Digest of Statistics*, various issues.

Chapple, S. (1990) 'A Sequence of Errors? Some Notes on the Sequencing of Liberalization in Developing Countries', UNCTAD Discussion Papers No. 31.

Collier, P. and Gunning, J. W. (1992) 'Aid and Exchange Rate Adjustment in African Trade Liberalizations', *Economic Journal*, 102: 925–39.

Dhliwayo, R. (2001) 'The Impact of Public Expenditure Management under EASP on Basic Social Services: Health and Education', paper presented at the Structural Adjustment Participatory Review Initiative (SAPRI) Poverty Reduction Forum, Harare, Zimbabwe, 9–10 April.

Dixit, A. (2001) 'Some Lessons from Transaction-Cost Politics for Less-Developed Countries', http://www.princeton.edu/~dixitak/home/peldc.pdf (accessed August, 2003).

Drazen, A. and Easterly, W. (2001) 'Do Crises Induce Reform? Simple Empirical Tests of Conventional Wisdom', *Economics and Politics*, 13, 2: 129–57.

Fanelli, J. M. and Popov, V. (2003) 'On Philosophical, Political, and Methodological Underpinnings of Reform', paper prepared for the Fourth Annual Global Development Conference on Globalization and Equity, Workshop on Understanding Reform, organised by the GDN, Cairo, Egypt, 15–21 January.

Gunning J. W. and Oosterndorp, R. (eds) (2002) 'Introduction', in *Industrial Change in Africa: Zimbabwean Firms Under Structural Adjustment* (Basingstoke: Palgrave Macmillan), pp. 1–25.

Hailu, D. (1997) 'What We Don't Know About the Political Economy of Economic Policy Reform', *SOAS Economic Digest*, 1, 1.

Husain, I. (2003) 'Managing Policy Reforms in Pakistan', http://users.erols.com/ ziqbal/ih1.htm (accessed June 2003).

Hoogeveen, H. and Mumvuma, T. (2002) 'Manufacturing Export Performance, Macroeconomic Adjustment and the Role of Networks', in J. W. Gunning and R. H. Oostendorp (eds), *Industrial Change in Africa: Micro Evidence on Zimbabwean Firms Under Structural Adjustment* (Basingstoke: Palgrave Macmillan).

IMF External Evaluation of the ESAF (1998) Report of a Group of Independent Experts, June 1998.

Liew, L., Bruszt, H. L. and He, L. (2003) 'Causes, National Costs, and Timing of Reforms', paper prepared for GDN Workshop, Cairo, Egypt, January.

Martinelli, C. (1993) 'Essays on Political Economy of Economic Reform', a dissertation submitted in partial satisfaction of the requirements for the Doctorate of Philosophy in Economics, University of California, Los Angeles.

Mehlum, H. (1999) 'The Political Economy of Failing Reform', dissertation for Doctorate of Politics, Department of Economics, University of Oslo.

Ministry of Health and Child Welfare (1998) *National Health Strategy for Health 1997–2007, Working for Quality and Equity in Health.*

Moyo, J., Gwarada, T. and Zhakata, C. (1998) 'Civil Service Reform in Southern and Eastern Africa: the Case of Zimbabwe', presentation made at the Eastern and Southern Africa Regional Seminar on Civil Service Reform, Arusha, 4–6 March.

Pierson, P. (2000) 'Not Just What, But When: Timing and Sequence in Political Processes', *Studies in American Political Development,* 14: 72–92.

Rodrik, D. (1996) 'Understanding Economic Policy Reform', *Journal of Economic Literature,* 34, 1: 9–41.

Roland, G. (2001) 'The Political Economy of Transition', CERGE-EI *Working Paper.*

Rushinga, A. (1987) 'New Loans May Ease Forex Shortages', *African Business,* May.

Schamis, H. E. (1998) 'The Politics of Economic Reform: Distributional Coalitions and Policy Change in Latin America', *Working Paper* No. 250, Helen Kellogg Institute for International Studies, University of Notre Dame.

The Herald, Harare, Zimbabwe, various issues.

UNDP (2000), *Zimbabwe Human Development Report, 2000.*

van de Walle, N. (2001) *African Economies and Politics* (Cambridge: Cambridge University Press).

van Wijnbergen, S. (1992) 'Intertemporal Speculation, Shortages and the Political Economy of Price Reform', *Economic Journal,* 102: 1395–1406.

Villanueva, D. and Mirakhor, A. (1990) 'Strategies for Financial Reforms', *IMF Staff Papers,* 24 (Washington, DC: IMF).

Williamson, J (1998) 'Economists, Policy Reform, and Political Economy', keynote address to a conference at the Rajiv Gandhi Foundation, 6 December.

Wolff, P. (1992) 'A Double-Edged Sword: Liberalization May Lead to Instability', *Development and Change,* 2: 12–13.

World Bank (1985) *Zimbabwe: Country Economic Memorandum-Performance, Policies and Prospects* (Harare: World Bank).

World Bank (1996) 'Structural Adjustment and Zimbabwe's Poor', Précis Number 105, Operations and Evaluation Department, Washington DC. http://wbn0018.worldbank.org/oed/

World Bank (2004) *Zimbabwe Country Assistance Evaluation,* Report No. 29058 (Washington, DC: World Bank Evaluation Department).

ZCTU (1996) 'Beyond ESAP: Framework for a Long-Term Development Strategy in Zimbabwe Beyond the Economic Structural Adjustment Programme'.

8
Conclusion: Bringing it All Together

Joseph Mensah

Achille Mbembe opened his critically acclaimed book, *On the Postcolony*, with the observation that 'Speaking rationally about Africa is not something that has ever come naturally.' As he aptly noted, more than any other region of the world, Africa has become the 'supreme receptacle of the West's obsession with . . . the facts of "absence", "lack" and "non-being", of identity and difference, of negativity – in short, of nothingness.' This unflattering, if not prerogative, perception of Africa has, arguably, been fostered by the proliferation of studies on Africa by 'experts' (or outsiders) who have limited knowledge of the local language, culture and world-views of the Africans they study – usually conducting their research from armchairs, with less and less fieldwork. With each of the seven case studies in this book authored by Africans from the respective countries, the spectre of impenetrability, incomprehensibility and 'abnormality' that commonly haunts discourses on Africa is effectively exorcised. Indeed, the accounts of economic reforms presented in the preceding chapters can stand on their own, given their clarity, straightforwardness and, arguably, their 'cultural authenticity', without the need to synthesise them into any grand-narrative, or some super-theory, of what SAPs really are in Africa. However, in the interest of a comparative overview, and by way of bringing the discussion to a close, this chapter refocuses our attention on the three main questions that prompted this book with insights from the experiences of all the seven nations covered: *Why* did the seven nations embark on economic reforms? *What* types of reforms were implemented? And *how well* did the reforms fare?

1   Why reform?

A striking feature of the immediate post-independence economies of nearly all the seven countries discussed in this book is the preponderance of statist, protectionist, inward-looking development ideologies, couched in orthodox socialism or some African versions of it. From the case of Kenya through those of Uganda, Ghana to Morocco, in Part I, and from Burundi and Tanzania to

Zimbabwe in Part II, one finds these ideologies being applied with varying degrees of success. To be fair, many of the countries profiled, including Kenya, Tanzania, Ghana and Uganda, did reasonably well with their statist policies, until the 1970s and the early 1980s, when a number of endogenous and exogenous variables combined quite precariously to wreak havoc on these economies. Kenya, for one, witnessed a GDP growth of nearly 7 per cent per annum, from 1964 to 1973; Uganda did equally well with a GDP growth rate of some 4.8 per cent a year, from 1963 to 1970. The economic growth in Ghana and Tanzania were not much different in the first five years or so following their independence. However, for one reason or another, by the early 1980s the economies of all the early reformers in our sample (i.e. Kenya, Uganda, Ghana and Morocco) had either stagnated or retrogressed discernibly.

As any cursory reading of the preceding case studies would show, the underlying factors for the economic malaise that swept across these countries, and many others in Africa, were strikingly similar. In addition to the OPEC oil shocks of the 1970s and the usual deterioration in their respective terms of trade, one finds the recurrence of war, political instability, corruption, economic mismanagement, tribalism and environmental difficulties behind the pre-SAPs economic woes of several of these nations. With regards to war, for instance, we are reminded of Tanzania's battle with Amin's Uganda, Morocco's war in the western Sahara, Zimbabwe's military adventure in the Democratic Republic of Congo, and, of course, Burundi's numerous, ethnic-laced civil wars, which have claimed some 600000 lives to date. Environmental problems, notably drought, also fed into the economic crises of many of these African countries; notable examples include droughts in Ghana, Zimbabwe and Burundi. And the abuse of power, economic mismanagement and the suppression of business acumen and entrepreneurial spirit perpetrated by the likes of Amin in Uganda, Jerry Rawlings in Ghana, Nyerere in Tanzania and Mugabe in Zimbabwe under their autocracy and one-party rules are too well known to delay us here, suffice it to add, though, that Amin's brutality was in a class of its own, arguably unsurpassed by any leader in the annals of Africa's, if not the world's, political history.

Even though not all nations facing economic crisis embark on IMF- and World Bank-sponsored economic reforms, the narratives provided in the preceding chapters lend support to the hypothesis that 'economic crises tend to foster the initiation of economic reform'. This hypothesis held true for Kenya, Uganda, Ghana and Morocco, in Part I, as well as for Burundi, Tanzania and Zimbabwe in Part II. Given the prevalence of socialism, or versions of it, across nearly all the nations in our study, coupled with their colonial encounter with Western imperialism, it is not surprising that these nations accepted SAPs only grudgingly – with each of them literally kicking and screaming. As they all realised, like personal finances, nations which are in dire need of funding only procure them at a very high cost to their national dignity and their avowed ideological principles. No wonder many of them, most notably Ghana and Tanzania, exhausted all possibilities of procuring loans from their Eastern bloc allies before accepting the IMF and World Bank adjustment packages. These African nations learned to their utter dismay that it is next to impossible to procure any multilateral or even bilateral financial assistance without the blessing of the IMF in particular. In a nutshell there seemed to be very little or no practical, fundable alternatives open to them. Given the inherent dynamism of 'development', regardless of how one defines this illusive concept, and to the extent that nearly all nations the world over are almost always reforming their economies/societies one way or another, perhaps the appropriate question to ask is not *why reform*, but what type of reform or 'how to reform and in whose interest', as Julius Kiiza and his colleagues shrewdly put it in their chapter on Uganda. We address these issues in what follows.

2 What types of reforms were implemented?

It is clear from the preceding chapters that all the seven nations went under virtually the same policy prescriptions, despite discernible differences in their historical, socio-economic and cultural backgrounds. As with SAPs elsewhere in the developing world, the IMF and the World Bank compelled these African nations, by way of loan conditionality, to devalue their currencies; remove subsidies on social provisions, such as healthcare and education; privatise state-owned enterprises; liberalise their trade, banking and financial sectors; promote agricultural exports; and, more recently, democratise their political systems, inter alia. And with their long-standing adherence to inward-looking, protectionist development ideologies it came as no surprise to learn that there was resistance to most of these policy prescriptions from all the countries. While some of the resistance emanated from the respective governments vis-à-vis their dealings with the Bretton Woods institutions, in particular, and the donor community, in general, other forms of resistance were either from segments of the governments or from the citizenry. From the tales of Kenya, Uganda, Ghana and Morocco in Part I, and Burundi, Tanzania and Zimbabwe in Part II, one reads of a tug-of-war between the pro-reformers and anti-reformers in the respective governments, or between the ruling parties and the opposition. Adding to this resistance were the common protests and demonstrations by students, medical doctors, urban workers and many other groups against increases in the prices of food and other provisions as a result of high taxes, currency devaluations, cost-sharing and the removal of subsidies. A few examples will suffice here. Uganda witnessed massive student protests from 1989–92, following the implementation cost-sharing in education; Ghana experienced similar demonstrations in 1988, as did Burundi in 1992 and Zimbabwe in 1998.

For the most part, the governments of these seven nations were caught between the interests of their respective citizens, on the one hand, and those of the donor community, on the other. In their dealings with the citizens, we found a glaring use of ethnic-based favourtism; politically motivated spending,

especially in times of election; secrecy; and general avoidance of public consultation. Arap Moi favoured his own ethnic group in Kenya, as did Jerry Rawlings
in Ghana and many other leaders in their respective countries. But by far the
worst form of such ethnic-based favouritism was recorded in the case of
Burundi, where the Tutsis dominated virtually all spheres of the nation's
political economy, to the detriment of the Hutu population. Indeed economic
reforms in Burundi were woven into a vicious cycle of political patronage in
which distributive policies fed into ethnic-based socio-economic polarisation,
which, in turn, fed into ethno-regional conflicts. Election-induced (over)spend-
ing occurred in several countries, such as Kenya, Ghana, Zimbabwe and Uganda.
In the case of Kenya, we were reminded by Maureen Were and her colleagues of
the political business cycle, in which the ruling party routinely manipulated
policies to maximise its short-term election gains. Such manoeuvres, together
with the several documented cases of improper sequencing, engendered
numerous policy reversals and backsliding in most of the countries covered.

In dealing with the donor community, many of the African governments in
our sample, cognizant of the extent to which SAPs undermined their legitimacy, if not the sovereignty of their respective nations, and with the ghost of
their Marxist-Leninist ideological past still haunting them, sought to implement many of the policy prescriptions in a lackadaisical manner. Perhaps the
best example of this is found in Kenya, where the government responded to
IMF pressure with a stop-go pattern of SAPs implementation. Fairly similar
forms of apathetic commitment to SAPs were documented in the cases of
Zimbabwe, Ghana and Tanzania, with the latter doing most of its foot-dragging
in conjunction with institutional, or second generation, reforms.

3   How well did the reforms perform?

By exploring the political economy of the IMF- and World Bank-sponsored
reforms in the seven nations, we were able to highlight not only the outcomes
of the reforms in their generalities, but, more importantly, to document the
specificities of the 'losers' and 'winners' in each case. In some of the countries
profiled, notably Ghana and Uganda, and to a limited extent, Morocco, there
were remarkable improvements in key macroeconomic indicators. In the case
of Ghana, for instance, we learned of a GDP increase of more than 5 per cent per
annum, between 1985 and 1989, and of 4.3 per cent per annum between 1990
and the year 2000, compared to the pre-SAPs rate of as low as −1.1 per cent for
every year in the decade prior to the nation's SAPs. Also, Ghana witnessed a
slight increase in GNI per capita during the SAPs period, and the rate of inflation, which hovered around a whopping 100 per cent, and over, per annum,
before the SAPs declined to about 10 per cent by 1999. In a similar vein,
Uganda recorded, on average, a growth rate of over 7 per cent between 1987
and 2000, while inflation plummeted from as high as 232.6 per cent in 1987 to
a mere 6 per cent by 2004; Morocco also experienced a drop in inflation from

about 5 per cent in the early 1990s to 2.3 per cent by 2002, and its economic growth rate climbed from −1.01 per cent in 1993 to as high as 6.3 per cent in 2001, before dropping slightly to 4.5 per cent by 2002. Not surprisingly, these countries, especially Ghana and Uganda, have long been touted as SAPs 'stars' or 'success stories' in Africa.

In other countries, such as Burundi and Zimbabwe, SAPs have been close to a disaster, with the latter formally renouncing all of its adjustment programmes in 2001. And in the chapter on Burundi we read that other than some patchy, modest improvements in macroeconomic indicators, the reforms there were generally part of a vicious cycle of violent conflicts, entailing biased distributive government policies that caused repetitive, ethnic-laced wars, which were then used to reshape the nation's political leadership, for yet more rounds of reforms which were invariably skewed in favour of the ruling ethnic group. We thus find Ngaruko and Nkurunziza noting in this volume that 'explaining reform in Burundi essentially requires exploring the reasons for failure more than [for] success'. Zimbabwe's SAPs have been equally bumpy: the Zimbabwe dollar, for one, crashed during the last quarter of 1997, as a result of currency flight associated with the nation's reform failures; GDP in the country stagnated, as the rate of inflation soared. Perhaps of all the seven countries profiled in this book Zimbabwe exhibited the worst forms of consultation, timing, sequencing and supervision, all of which led to spells of policy reversals in the midst of a highly politicised, unequal asset/land distribution among the nation's Blacks and Whites.

Quite expectedly, the 'losers' and 'winners' of the reforms varied not only on the basis of social locations such as race, ethnicity, gender and class, but also from country to country, region to region, programme to programme, and time to time. At the same time, a common thread found in nearly all the countries suggests that the poor, women, the working class, and other socially disadvantaged groups suffered the most from SAPs. In Kenya it was generally the poor who suffered most from the cutbacks in health and educations; and the textile producers who were impacted the most under trade liberalisations, with their industry collapsing under pressure from cheap imported second-hand clothing from outside. Still, it bears noting that it was mostly the small-scale entrepreneurs and the poor who benefited from the importation and sale of this used clothing. The point to stress, therefore, is that the impacts of SAPs are far more convoluted and dialectical than some analysts would have us believe. In Morocco we learned of the large-scale farmers benefiting more from SAPs than their small-scale counterparts. In Zimbabwe, it was the White and upper-class people who benefited more than the Blacks and lower-class people; and in Burundi the main beneficiaries were the Tutsis who dominate the state and its enterprise to the tragic detriment of Hutus. We even learned that social and political stability prevailed in Burundi only when the distribution of SAPs benefits matched the distribution of power among the various ethnic groups, clans, regional and professional cliques, and interest groups. And in Ghana, as in

Uganda, we read of top executives of the public sector and wealthy businessmen and women gaining the most from trade and financial liberalisation. And, finally, in Tanzania, Kenya, Ghana and Morocco we found that rural folk bore a disproportionate burden of the SAPs compared to their urban counterparts.

On the whole the social consequences of the SAPs were generally negative, even among countries such as Ghana and Uganda where there were improvements in macroeconomic variables. One reads of how the poor and other disadvantaged groups suffered under SAPs in nearly all the seven nation studied. It is only fair, though, to acknowledge the IMF and World Bank admitted these 'externalities' and helped initiate a host of poverty-reduction programmes in many of the countries. Notable examples in this regard include: Uganda's Poverty Eradication Action Plan and Vision 2025; Ghana's Programme of Action to Mitigate the Social Cost of Reforms; Tanzania's National Poverty Eradication Strategy, Vision 2025 and, later, the National Strategy for Growth and Reduction of Poverty.

By way of conclusion, let us use the last few paragraphs to draw out the key lessons from this study for future adjustment programmes in Africa. First, without a deep sense of country ownership, foot-dragging, stop-and-go and reactive, as against proactive, patterns of policy implementation become the order of the day. Thus, in as much as the BWIs need to depend on loan conditionality to compel borrowing nations of the South to adhere to their adjustment programmes, we must still note that reform is a human – rather than a mechanistic or economistic – endeavour, with veritable socio-cultural underpinning and ramification, and that conditions that are insensitive to the institutional capacity and the socio-cultural context of the countries involved are bound to fail. As a corollary to this point, we would be better served to conceptualise SAPs, not as an *end* in themselves, but as a *means* towards the enhancement of the human condition in the developing world. Excessive coercion from the BWIs, by way of stringent loan conditionality, may work, but only for a while, for power is never absolute, not even in the hands of the BWIs vis-à-vis their dealings with poor African nations. After all, how else could there be such intense, and sometime ferocious, resistance in the form of riots by citizens and foot-dragging and policy reversal by government with regards to SAPs, if no freedom or power remained in hands of the people and governments of Africa (and elsewhere in the developing world)?

The same argument holds for the African governments in their dealings with their citizens. Unless the well-informed and not-so-well-informed people in these countries are duly consulted on SAPs, resistance is bound to undermine any programme, most likely at the point of implementation, even if not at the point of design. As many governments learned to their dismay, they could use their military, paramilitary and other security apparatuses, and rely on politically motivated spending, ethnic-based manoeuvre, and various divide-and-rule tactics (or the so-called authoritarian advantage) to initiate some programmes, but for them to be sustainable, there need to be grassroots and civil society consultation and support couched in the canons of democracy – i.e. freedoms of the press and of association and a basic sense of social justice. One is at a loss to comprehend, for instance, how the government of Zimbabwe, and the BWIs which backed its SAPs, expected to succeed within the context of the highly dehumanising Black–White socio-economic inequities that prevailed in that country, especially regarding land distribution.

Moreover, the need for proper sequencing of SAPs cannot be overemphasised. In the absence of this, one finds the various governments doing almost everything at the same time, thereby undermining their basic sense of direction and threatening the success of their adjustment programmes. Perhaps nothing threatens the political order and the socio-economic well-being of Africa(ns) more than the debilitating external debt burdens across the continent. The excessive reliance on foreign loans has to be curtailed and, ultimately, replaced by concerted efforts to mobilise domestic resources for development, if Africa is to rid itself of the enduring shackles of neo-liberalism and neo-colonialism.

Heeding all these suggestions would not guarantee the success of SAPs in Africa, or of any development programme, for that matter. Nothing can guarantee success when it comes to an endeavour as complicated and multifaceted as SAPs – a set of complex programmes shrouded in ironies and paradoxes that beat the best of our imaginations. For one thing, we still have a situation where the external debts of African nations continue to mount, notwithstanding the emphasis on cutbacks, removal of subsidies and privatisation enshrined in the neo-liberal Washington Consensus that underpins SAPs. And how do we account for the fact that nearly all African economies are still predominantly agricultural, despite two decades or so of structural adjustment/transformation? It is against the backdrop of such ironies, ambiguities, and the many positive and negative consequences of SAPs, that one finds it apposite to use Dickens's famous expression 'the best of times and the worst of times' as the organising theme for a book like this.

Printed in the United States
81841LV00001B/34-42